W0091391

SAGE was founded in 1965 by Sara Miller McCune to support the dissemination of usable knowledge by publishing innovative and high-quality research and teaching content. Today, we publish over 900 journals, including those of more than 400 learned societies, more than 800 new books per year, and a growing range of library products including archives, data, case studies, reports, and video. SAGE remains majority-owned by our founder, and after Sara's lifetime will become owned by a charitable trust that secures our continued independence.

Los Angeles | London | New Delhi | Singapore | Washington DC | Melbourne

Political Islam and the Arab Uprising

Political Islam and the Arab Uprising

Islamist Politics in Changing Times

Fazzur Rahman Siddiqui

Los Angeles | London | New Delhi
Singapore | Washington DC | Melbourne

First published in 2017 by

 SAGE Publications India Pvt Ltd
B1/I-1 Mohan Cooperative Industrial Area
Mathura Road, New Delhi 110 044, India
www.sagepub.in

SAGE Publications Inc
2455 Teller Road
Thousand Oaks, California 91320, USA

SAGE Publications Ltd
1 Oliver's Yard, 55 City Road
London EC1Y 1SP, United Kingdom

SAGE Publications Asia-Pacific Pte Ltd
3 Church Street
#10-04 Samsung Hub
Singapore 049483

Published by Vivek Mehra for SAGE Publications India Pvt Ltd, typeset in 10.5/12.5 pt Palatino LT by Zaza Eunice, Hosur, Tamil Nadu, India and printed at Sai Print-o-Pack, New Delhi.

Library of Congress Cataloging-in-Publication Data

Name: Siddiqui, Fazzur Rahman, author.
Title: Political Islam and the Arab uprising : Islamist politics in changing times / Fazzur Rahman Siddiqui.
Description: New Delhi, India ; Thousand Oaks, California : SAGE Publications, 2016. | Includes bibliographical references and index.
Identifiers: LCCN 2016034231 | ISBN 9789386042194 (hardback : alk. paper) | ISBN 9789386042187 (epub) | ISBN 9789386042200 (ebook)
Subjects: LCSH: Islam and politics–Arab countries. | Islam and state–Arab countries. | Islamic fundamentalism–Arab countries. | Arab countries–Politics and government–1945- | Arab Spring, 2010- | IS (Organization)
Classification: LCC BP63.A4 A764 2016 | DDC 320.55/7–dc23 LC record available at https://lccn.loc.gov/2016034231

ISBN: 978-93-860-4219-4 (HB)

SAGE Team: Supriya Das, Guneet Kaur Gulati and Syeda Aina Rahat Ali

To all those countless revolutionaries who stood up to change the political trajectory of the Arab world.

Bulk Sales

SAGE India offers special discounts
for purchase of books in bulk.
We also make available special imprints
and excerpts from our books on demand.

For orders and enquiries, write to us at

Marketing Department
SAGE Publications India Pvt Ltd
B1/I-1, Mohan Cooperative Industrial Area
Mathura Road, Post Bag 7
New Delhi 110044, India

E-mail us at **marketing@sagepub.in**

Get to know more about SAGE

Be invited to SAGE events, get on our mailing list.
Write today to **marketing@sagepub.in**

This book is also available as an e-book.

Contents

Preface

Sometimes I wonder how the religion of Islam as a ritual and a faith, confined in the past to the pulpits of mosques and sermons in the seminaries, has become a part of cultural studies, anthropology, sociology, political science, international politics, security studies and policy matters over the decades. What further mystifies the matter for me is the appearance of a large section of academics, strategic thinkers and security experts delivering sermons on Islam through radio and TV shows while the ones trained in Islamic jurisprudence, logic and philosophy are still exploring and interrogating the authenticity of ablutions with honey and whether patting a dog requires a pious bath or not.

No doubt, like every historical entity, the religion of Islam has also passed through several phases, and each phase has been dominated by a theme. The period after the death of the Prophet saw more and more focus on the compilation of the Quran and the later collection of Hadith (statements and acts of the Prophet Mohammad). The era of collection and compilation was followed by an era of Islamic historiography and juridical layout, which culminated in the emergence of four schools of jurisprudence followed by different geographical spreads of Muslim territories.

It was, perhaps, the Abbasid period (750–1258), which saw an intense intellectual churning on different themes of Islam, that consolidation of the Shiite theology and the codification of different juridical codes took place. The Abbasid period saw raging debates on the objectives and purpose of Quranic application in this world, and shariah became the dominant theme for jurists, such as Ibn Taymiyyah, when Quranic phrases were recast in the image of power and a political system.

In modern times, the Iranian Revolution of 1979 introduced a new dimension to the Quranic exegesis, Islamic historiography and jurisprudential commentaries. The Islamic Revolution ushered in a plethora of literature exploring the history of the association of religion and politics and what lies in the future for the proposition, which was called 'political Islam' then. The emergence of political Islam as a new discipline got gradually dragged into the disciplines of social science, international affairs and cultural studies, which made the religion of Islam completely devoid of rituality and spirituality; and today it is treated as a part of an interdisciplinary theme.

The central intent of this book is to highlight the ideologies of the union between politics and Islam. This book presents an ideological narrative about political Islam from the medieval era to the modern day when the Arab world is in an unprecedented turmoil. This book ventures to interrogate the past politics of the Arab world through identification of different streams of Islamic politics. It attempts to trace the historicity of a political ideology informed by Islamic teaching in the modern time, where it takes into account a series of ideologues who shaped and guided the Islamic political trajectory in the 19th and 20th centuries.

The Arab and Islamic world has always been defined as a status quoist by Orientalist perspectives, and the people there have been treated as if they are not a part of the global political process that has influenced the trajectory of an international order. This long-held perception about the region changed when millions of people thronged streets to challenge the status quo and topple a series of dictators with the promise that Arab would never be the same. The Arab uprising of 2011, known as the Arab Spring, which, with the passage of time, changed every aspect of the Arab world, still continues to this day. A major portion of this book is devoted to the study of the Arab uprising, which is likely to redefine the political contours of the entire region in the coming years. An attempt has been made to study the following topics: the linkage of the oppressive political culture supported by dictatorial regimes and the outburst of the masses; how this outburst has been exploited by Islamist politics of the region; and how the engagement of the Islamist with the new evolving politics has impacted the ideological tones of political Islam.

The present uprising has brought the region at the crossroads of political and social transformations. Great uncertainties have enveloped the region and processes of transitions, which are not taking identical routes everywhere, are still unfolding.

This insurrection has pushed the region towards the redefinition of its political landscape, where political Islam has emerged as an inevitable force to negotiate its space in the new emerging sociopolitical order. This has brought a change in the traditional vocabulary and the conduct of political Islam too. In sum, this is a study about tracing the trajectory of Arab's past politics through the Arab uprising.

Political Islam and the Arab Uprising is not only a textbook but also an academic intervention in the political process of the Arab world. This book is an attempt at understanding the present in the light of the past. It merely deals with one of the most fascinating themes of world politics: what the international academia has indiscriminately called political Islam. The current turmoil in the region has raised serious questions about the longevity and the real objectives of the Islamic political system which have not been exercised extensively. The emergence of groups such as the Islamic State in Iraq and Syria and other extremist entities has added a new ingredient to the present discourse on the theme and has raised many questions.

Apart from making a theoretical enquiry into the theme of political Islam, Chapter 1 of the book explicates the ideological underpinning of political Islam in the modern context. This chapter is devoted to the study of the origin and evolution of the phenomenon. It also investigates how the concepts of social science were employed in studying the religious aspect and how a movement that begun with a call for restoring the religious values transformed into a rejectionist philosophy and became a conflicting ideology against the Western sociopolitical and cultural norms.

Chapter 2 is centred on the theme of the Quranic and theological context of political Islam. It deals primarily with the content and accounts of the some of the prominent Quranic commentaries and theological writings highlighting the subject. Chapter 3 highlights the Islamic response to the Arab politics during the colonial and post-colonial phases. This chapter emphasizes the colonial context of the rise of political Islam in addition to focusing extensively on the different contours of responses it provided to the social and economic penetrations by Western culture and politics.

While the issue of the Arab Spring forms the major theme of the narratives in this book, Chapter 4 studies the conjectural points of the event and its subsequent impact on the future of political Islam and regional polity. Chapter 5 presents an account of India's response to the Arab Spring and its short- and long-term implications for India. It also investigates how a political upsurge in the region modifies the balance of power for India globally and regionally. This chapter underlines the impact of the Arab Spring on the Indian foreign policy, and briefly deals with the extent of changes India might require to implement in the aftermath of the unfolding political situations in the region.

Acknowledgments

This book would have been materially impossible without the support of Indian Council of World Affairs (ICWA). It is ICWA which provided an academic environment to write the present volume and it also funded my field trips to Egypt and Tunisia during my research for the book. Therefore, I owe my first and most important thanks to Director General, ICWA, Ambassador Nalin Surie, Deputy Director General, Joint Secretary, all my colleagues here at ICWA, and library staff members.

There is long list of people who wanted me to write a book on the theme which has engaged the global academia from across the disciplines and I must thank them for their untiring academic and moral supports. I am also grateful to my family members who never discouraged me from pursuing a career in academics and even that in international relation and area studies which is not only an alien subject but also very unappealing for a family hailing from a mofussil. I owe a special thanks to my biggest intellectual friend Ghazali, a scholar of high repute and a great human being, who showed all interest in my research works and always encouraged me to continue writing. Likewise, I would like to thank Dr Sohrab who is almost like my teacher and someone who taught me what West Asia is.

I owe a lot to Mr Amin Usmani whose office 'Academy for Jurisprudence' in New Delhi has almost been a library for me and I have benefited a lot from the Arabic resources available in his office. I am also thankful to my publishers and editors at SAGE who posed faith in me and made the book possible. I cannot forget to mention love and care of many like Akif, Tariq, Khalid Lateef, Mirza Beig, Asif, Tasneem, Rumi, Anusha, Sharib, Shamsi Bhai, Tausif, Khalid Khan, Saif and Faizi, and countless others who were always forthcoming whenever I needed them.

Many have encouraged me to write the book but someone who has been all cooperative, accommodative and provided a cordial environment in which I could have worked on it is my wife, Shagufta. Despite having been least interested in my theme of study, she went through a rigorous exercise of proofreading my manuscript at the final stage and she is someone who always shared my happiness and was always the first one to pass on even my smallest story (from appearance on TV to expressing my views on radio to publication of my pieces) to my family members which, no doubt, I never liked. I am really thankful to you for your constant and silent cooperation.

Introduction

This book is not about the Islamic political system, institutions, norms, governance or an explanation about Islamic polity in any historical perspective. Rather, it is about the contents and discourse claiming the religiosity of union between the religion of Islam and politics. The book is about the ideological underpinning of political Islam, one of the most predominant discourses in the last few decades across disciplines. The content touched upon in this volume is about the origin, historicity and evolution, along with different theoretical perspectives of political Islam in the modern era.

There has been substantial contestation among the clergies, social scientists, scholars of international relations and strategic experts over the actual positioning and the centrality of political Islam amongst the existing disciplines of knowledge. Despite the centrality of political Islam as a major discourse in the academia, several crucial dimensions or the core ingredients of the debate remain untouched or misunderstood. Scholars from different disciplines have articulated the subject within the milieu of their respective epistemology, and their accounts sometime complicate the subject.

A great deal or different facets of political Islam have been studied by scholars of different persuasions. Political Islam in the modern context has been well articulated in the writings of Nazih Ayyubi, Mohammad Ayyub, Abu Rabi, Bernard Lewis and Qasim Zaman, and a series of other scholars who have not only drawn attention towards the theme but also examined the contours of political Islam. These studies have been sincere attempts to speculate on the evolution of political Islam in the colonial context. Most of the scholars have problematized political Islam in juxtaposition to the force of modernity.

It has been seldom recognized adequately that the modern notion of political Islam is largely rooted in the historicity of Islam, and classical Islamic teaching has remained the driving force behind the emergence of a proposition called 'political Islam'. Political Islam, as understood in the modern times, has always remained a part of a larger vision of the Muslim world with different phrases and idioms. If one browses through the classical writings of jurists or experts on Islamic jurisprudence, one would come across an abundance of arguments and expositions claiming divinity in the association of Islam and politics.

There are certain Quranic principles which the ideologues of modern-day political Islam have adopted as a catalyst to legitimize the religious context of Islamic revivalism. There are plentiful references related to power, authority and the organization of the state in the Quran. However, these references do not provide a well-defined explanation for the linkage of Islam with politics. Several politically charged terms have been defined in different ways by different jurists in different periods. These terms represent possibility of the political orders and do not prescribe any political principle. Even Sunnah, the second most important and authentic source of Islam, has very little to say on the issue of governance or the state.

The Quranic orientation of politics stems from the claim that the Quran is the primary source of knowledge. The core of the Quranic concept of humanity emanates from a single verse of the Quran that says, 'He created you from single person; created of like nature, his mate, and from both scattered countless men and women'. Unlike Western philosophers like John Locke and others who claim that sovereignty emanates from the ownership, Quran adversely claims that it is not the source from which the political values and sovereignty are derived. Rather, supreme sovereignty and authority of defining the norms are the prerogatives of divine laws.

The real issue of state and its relation with Islamic teachings arose only after the death of the Prophet. It was then that the Muslims needed to innovate and improvise the nature and form of the government. Indeed, the origin of the first disagreement in Islamic community can be traced back to the issue of politics alone. This was the beginning of a shift in the social process from polytheism to monotheism, from rules by customs to rule by law, from natural relationship based on blood and race to moral and spiritual association and from natural monarchy to power delegated by God.

In order to explain and interpret the prophetic tradition, there arose a discursive tradition in Islam and Ulema became its custodians; they were also seen as true heirs of the prophetic charisma, while the discursive tradition was raised to the stature of a sub-tradition. So, the Ulema and their tradition acquired a new power within Islam that later received quasi-sacrosanct status. The guardians of the political theology are the religious scholars and the Ulema. Muslim political theology developed over a period and under different empires. This phase of interpretation and elucidation of Quran and Hadith was coupled with an emergence of a novel philosophical school in Islam.

The philosophical teaching of Islam is further integrated with the exposition of Islamic ethics and political jurisprudence in post-caliphate era, and the political ethics (or the morals of politics) refers to a series of writings from Muslim scholars, who have attempted to advise and guide rulers to a successful and just method of governance. These prescriptions were usually accompanied by stories of previous kings and rulers. These were collections of Islamic teachings, Greek philosophy and some elements from Persian literature. Examples of these include *Siyasatnama* (Book of Government) of *Nizam al-Mulk* (1020–1092) and *Nasihat al-Muluk* (Advice to King) of Ghazali (1058–1111).

The Islam-infested political discourse in the medieval period was of a unilateral nature when theologians were essentially occupied with laying down the rules and norms for the Islamic governance. The classical and medieval eras of Islam exploded and expanded without any external intellectual resistance. The political, territorial and intellectual domains of Islam enjoyed complete internal autonomy and shaped the course of events and developments independently. The growth of unilateral literature on political Islam was reflective of the ascendance of Muslim powers in different parts of the world.

However, the European encroachment, which began in the 18th century and gradually consolidated in the early 19th century in the Arab world, turned upside down and confronted the centuries-old ideas of divine-political governance. The introduction of philosophy of sovereignty of man-made laws ushered in the third stratum of political Islamic discourse which witnessed a departure from the previous contents of the ummah, shariah and jihad and replaced it with the concepts of nation-state, secularism and democracy from the West. The trilogy of caliphate, shariah and jihad vanished completely from the centre of the Islamic discourse with the arrival of Western colonization and the replacement of shariah by the Western legal code.

My purpose here is not merely to document a particular set of writing about political Islam; rather, my main objective is to relate the historical link of the present meaning of political Islam to the past and to ascertain that political Islam of today is rooted in the past and has very flexibly modified its vocabulary and idioms with the changing contours of history and time.

Over the past few decades, the term 'political Islam' with an apocalyptic implication has carved out its own space in both the scholar's lexicon and popular imagination. This concept has become a metaphor of choice in the pursuit of assigning meaning to a range of ideas, actions and behaviours, and it has recently navigated from its narrow religious reference to other domains as well.

Political Islam has become a key feature of the modern-day Arab-Islamic world and has found expression in a number of Islamic revivalist movements that later transformed into a political movement. It itself constitutes the central issue in many Arab-Islamic countries—be its appropriation, its rejection or its transformation.

With the foundation of theocracy after revolution in Iran, Islam became a major site of political and intellectual conflicts throughout the world. The Iranian Revolution threw out five decades of modern, Western and secularist monarchy. Some fifteen years later, absolutists came to power in Afghanistan, stimulating further the discourse on political Islam.

Political Islam is a form of political and religious utopia that acts as an ideological alternative to the invasion of modern doctrines of secularism, communism, socialism and liberalism. It is a form of instrumentalization of Islam by an individual, a group or an organization that pursues political objectives. It provides a political response to today's societal challenges by imagining a future, the foundation for which rests on a re-appropriated, invented concept borrowed from the Islamic tradition.

This is an ideology couched in the language of dissent, opposition and resistance to modern global order, and it seeks to oppose the existing ideology of socialism, Arabism, communism and also the borrowed concept of democracy which have been the dominant force in the Arab world in post-colonial era and acts as a quest for freedom, dignity and sovereignty, and stands against the authoritarian secular modernity of the West. This is a battle between the ideologization of religion and idealization of secularism. Political Islam as a philosophy attempts to synthesize the traditional thoughts to the modern concept of accountability and pluralism and rule of law.

It is more a political ideology than a religion or theology. Its adherents believe that Islam as a body of faith has something important to say about how politics and society should be ordered. Islamists are distinguished from other Muslim fundamentalists by their insistence on engagement with political structure and state apparatus as a means to establishing Islamic society. It is about the rule and primacy of religious authority over directorial authority which believes in different epistemological orders where the West represents different sets of knowledge while the Islamists believe that Muslims are the inheritors of a different set of knowledge and traditions.

Unlike Marxist's overemphasis on the socio-economic aspects of social order, the adherent of political Islam is an ardent believer in moral and cultural transformation. The integration of Islam as a primary agent of identity formation is a major component of the discourse. The colonial entrenchment may have acted as a force behind the ideologization of Islam and confrontationist ideology, but it was also the failure of the Arab regime to deliver wealth, dignity and power to the expectant population which popularized it further. The departure of colonial masters and the advantage of changes never trickled down to the common people in the Arab world. The oppressive nature of the regimes has played a greater role in according the status and legitimacy to this phenomenon.

This is not a universal and translational occurrence, but it has social and political contexts. The quest for political Islam is not driven by religious concern, but it has been more a cry in the crisis. It always arose as an attempt to provide a definitive answer to the existing political and religious predicaments. It has been more of a reaction than an action and stands for an ideological contestation with the far enemy and the near enemy; far enemy being the colonial master and near enemy representing the remnant groups of political and military elites of the Arab world.

All the prominent advocates of political Islam have invoked religiosity of politics in reaction to external domination and internal cultural decadence. Entire discourse of these Islamic advocates speaks of an alternative model to the Western philosophy and modernity.

The revivalist movement in the Arab-Islamic world has arisen as a reaction to the Western cultural onslaught, and this cultural hegemony has provided a context for the text of political Islam. For instance, Muslim Brotherhood (MBH) in Egypt has come into existence in its own imperial context, while the rise of Jamaat-e-Islami in South Asia can be understood in the colonial context. Similarly, the rise of Ennahda in Tunisia and Nahdlatul Ulama in Indonesia has its own contextual specificity. Likewise, Shiite Amal in Lebanon and Sunni Algerian FIS (also called the Islamic Salvation Front) have different histories, backgrounds and philosophies, but both are known as bones of global political Islam.

One can see the external context of political Islam in the form of colonialism and internal context in the form of post-colonial polity based on autocracy and dictatorship. The Islamist forces have found post-colonial regime no better than the old colonial masters who merely acted as an antithesis for the promotion of Islamic values.

The origin of the Arab Spring can be due to the above-mentioned colonial and post-colonial contexts, as it is an outcome of prolonged simmering in the region. This is a rebellion on the part of deprived masses to achieve dignity, freedom, social justice and national sovereignty. This uprising is a response to utter despondence and a call for the rejection of dictatorship and corruption, and reflects a desire for independence. It represents the triumph of Arab streets over the Arab elites and is motivated by the shared vision of responsibility and accountability. Ziauddin Sardar, a renowned scholar of Islam, has aptly called it a post-normal world and a tiger-wounded reaction.

The present uprising has brought the region at the crossroads of political and social transformation. Great uncertainties have enveloped the region, and processes of transitions are still unfolding which are not taking identical routes everywhere. This insurrection has pushed the region towards redefining its political landscape where political Islam has emerged as an inevitable force that wants to negotiate its space in the new emerging sociopolitical order. This uncertainty has brought a change in the traditional vocabulary and conduct of political Islam too, which is already visible. The absence of religious rhetoric in the demonstrations and protests in Egypt and Tunisia is a case in point. The change in the region has triggered a new debate on the future role of Islam, inviting various interpretations of the mode of its operation and politics of accommodation and adaptation in the newly created political vacuum.

The victory of Islamists in Tunisia and Egypt and the subsequent disaster in Egypt itself embody a message that political Islam will be a decisive factor in redefining the politics of the Arab world. Several shades of Islamic voices ranging from moderate to liberal to fundamentalist to conservative to fanatic have emerged which are creating a rift among the Islamic forces. Some of the Islamist parties such as MBH and Ennahda have already started sounding moderate, while others such as Salafists in Egypt are posing as very conservative in their political outlook. Islamists themselves have provided several choices for the Arab masses that might bring about a sharp division among the so-called integrated ideologies of political Islam. It seems that it is not Islamism that will shape politics, but it will be politics that will shape Islamism.

The central theme of my study is to look into the changes taking place in the political ideology of the Islamists and the long-term trajectory of political Islam in the aftermath of the phenomenon called Arab Spring. This research will examine the relationship between Arab Spring and political Islam and explore how political Islam will respond to the unfolding situation in the region. It will also investigate the role of religion in shaping the new Arab world.

Arab Spring is a recent phenomenon and still very much in the process. There has been no comprehensive exposition of the subject. A few expositions in the form of newspaper articles, commentaries and reports of the think tank cover some aspects of the subject. Most of the Arab media have covered the subject in a very ambiguous manner, with a narrow prism, and have not gone into the intricacies of the subject, while Western political commentators have adopted the same conventional tool of looking through the prism of confrontation.

The research intends to study the after effects of Arab Spring on the trajectory of political Islam. Political Islam in the post-Arab Spring contexts has not been examined comprehensively so far because of its transient nature. This study of mine may be one amongst the pioneers of the studies on political Islam in a new phase and form. It will make an important addition to the existing pool of literature on political Islam, treading on a new trajectory altogether. The chief component of my research is political Islam, and the Arab Spring will merely provide a window to look through. This will be in a way an original and innovative study, stimulating further research on the theme.

Apart from making theoretical enquiry on the theme of political Islam, I will introspect the ideological underpinning of political Islam in modern context in the first chapter of the book. This chapter will be devoted to the study of origin and evolution of the phenomenon. It will also investigate how the concept of social science is employed in studying the religious arena and how a movement beginning with a call for restoration of religious values transformed into a rejectionist philosophy and emerged to be a conflicting ideology against the Western sociopolitical and cultural norms.

The next chapter (Chapter 2) will be centred on the theme of the Quranic and theological contexts of political Islam. It will primarily deal with the contents and accounts of some of the prominent Quranic commentaries and theological writings highlighting the subject. This will cover the entire Muslim period, from the four caliphates to the declining phase of the Ottoman era.

Islamic response to the Arab politics during colonial and post-colonial phases will be the theme of the third chapter. This chapter will emphasize the colonial context of the rise of political Islam, in addition to giving an extensive focus to the different contours of responses to the Western cultural and political onslaught and social and economic penetration. The responses to Western imperialism consist of many shades leading to numerous discourses. Various streams of intellectualism emerged where some were of the view that Arab world's future lied in breaking from the past and imitating the West. While some adhered to the cultural past of the Arab world and called for the revival of Arab cultural heritage, there were others who believed in the amalgamation of Western modernism and the Arab past. It was this phase of confrontation in the 19th and first half of the 20th centuries where one could trace the seeds of the present-day Arab Spring.

A major part of the book will deal with the Arab Spring and its subsequent impact on the future of political Islam. Chapter 4 constitutes the central theme of the book, and it will discuss at length the origin and implication of the Arab Spring for the Arab in general and Islamist forces in particular. It will study the responses of Islamic forces to the political uprising in the region and deal with the intricacies of the newly adopted moderation in the tonalities of political Islam. It will make a critical analysis of different shades of Islamic voices in the aftermath of the Arab Spring and why Islamic parties, such as Ennahda in Tunisia, did not shy away from entering into alliance with liberal forces, and on the other hand MBH preferred not only to go alone but showed no sign of accommodative politics.

The fifth and last chapter of the book will be an account of India's response to the Arab Spring and its implications for India. It will also investigate how the political upsurge in that region will modify the balance of power for India. This section will underline the impact of the Arab Spring on Indian foreign policy and briefly deal with the extent of changes India might require to adopt in the aftermath of the unfolding political situations in the region.

1

Political Islam: A Theoretical Framework

It was the Iranian Revolution of 1979 that triggered an unending and still-in-progress debate about political Islam which introduced a new trinity—power, Islam and politics—in the global political discourse. The Iranian Revolution marked an epoch when the phrase *Allah Himself* was replaced by Islam and seen as a discursive tradition—what Michel Foucault later called the first great insurrection against the global system of the West. He further viewed political Islam as a mechanism towards territorialization and governmentalization of Islam.[1]

The term 'political Islam' as an ideology has acquired an apocalyptic implication for both Western academia and Western media. Political Islam as a comprehensive ideology has invaded both the scholar's lexicon and popular imaginations across the world. This concept has recently moved from its narrow religious confines to other domains as well. It has become a key feature of the modern-day Arab-Islamic world and has found an expression in a number of Islamic revivalist movements.

Political Islam as a discipline is being studied in different ways, and different scholars have explored the subject in the theoretical framework of their own disciplines. For some, it is a cultural expression of the Muslims at large against Western modernity and their epistemological hegemony where Islamists

---

[1] Pankaj Mishra, *From the Ruins of Empire: The Revolt against the West and the Remaking of Asia* (London: Penguin Book, 2012), 50.

want to evade the boundary between religion, culture and politics. Others have defined it as the ideologization of Islam, and according to some, it is nothing but summoning of the past to correct the present.

Political Islam is a form of political and religious utopia that promises to act as an ideological alternative to the invasion of modern doctrines of secularism, communism, socialism and liberalism. It is a form of instrumentalization of Islam by an individual, a group or an organization that pursues political objectives. It provides a political response to today's societal challenges by imagining a future, the foundation for which rests on a re-appropriated, reinvented concept borrowed from the Islamic tradition.[2]

Very often, political Islam is treated as an ideology couched in the language of dissent, opposition and resistance to modern global order. It stands to oppose the present sociopolitical ideology; acts as a quest for freedom, dignity and sovereignty; and calls for rebellion against the authoritarian secular modernity of the West. Political Islam can be seen as a philosophical echo to synthesize the traditional Islamic thoughts with the modern concept of accountability, pluralism and the rule of law. This is a battle between the ideologization of religion and the idealization of secularism.

Political Islam, in content, is an interpretation of Islam directed at achieving the political goal.[3] It is not merely an expression of a political project, but it also covers the invocation of a frame with an Islamic reference to social and cultural spheres.[4] The adherents of political Islam believe that Islam as a body of faith has something important to say about how politics and society should be ordered. Islamists are slightly different from other Muslim fundamentalists in their insistence on engagement with political structure and state apparatus in

---

[2] Guilain Denoeux, 'The Forgotten Swamp: Navigating Political Islam', *Middle East Policy* 19, no. 2 (2002): 56–81.

[3] Barry Rubin, ed., *Political Islam* (London: Routledge, 2007), 4.

[4] Salwa Ismail, *Rethinking Islamist Politics: Culture, the State and Islamism* (London: I.B. Tauris, 2003), 2.

order to establish an Islamic society. It is about the primacy of religious authority over other authoritative mechanisms emanating from Western modalities. It believes in different epistemological orders where West represents different sets of knowledge for them and the Muslims are inheritors of a distinct set of knowledge and traditions altogether.

The emergence of the present-day discourse about political Islam can be traced back to the sociopolitical and economic conditions of the 19th- and 20th-century Muslim world. It is a product of engagement with the West in economic, political, social, cultural and intellectual arenas when Muslims had become an object rather than the subject of history. Political Islam, in large measure, is determined by the modern context, and Islamists do not seem to be opposed to modernity but want their own stamp on what Western intellectual discourses define as modern.

Unlike Marxist's overemphasis on materialistic aspects of social order, the adherents of political Islam believe in moral and cultural interpretations of the society and desire its evolution in the light of ethical and moral boundaries defined by the Islamic teachings. The integration of Islam into day-to-day life as a primary agent of identity formation is a major component of this discourse. The colonial entrenchment may have acted as a force behind the ideologization of Islam and confrontationist ideology, but it was the failure of the Arab regimes too to deliver wealth, dignity and power to the expectant population that popularized it further in the second half of the 20th century.

This phenomenon of political Islam can be well understood in social and political contexts. This ideology is not driven by religious concern alone but has been a cry in a crisis. It has always arisen as an attempt to provide a definitive answer for the existing political and economic predicaments in society. It has been more of a reaction than an action, and stands for an ideological contestation with the far and the near enemies—the far enemy being the colonial masters and the near enemy representing the remaining political and military elites of the Arab world.

All political Islamic movements in the Arab world have arisen as a reaction to the Western sociopolitical and cultural

4 POLITICAL ISLAM AND THE ARAB UPRISING

assault that provided a context for the text of political Islam. The early and mid-20th century witnessed the emergence of a number of Islamic political groups in Asia and Africa carrying their indigenous attributes but not devoid of the commonalities among themselves.

For instance, MBH in Egypt came into existence in its own imperial context, while the rise of Jamaat-e-Islami in South Asia can be interpreted in the colonial, religious and nationalistic contexts of its own era. Similarly, the rise of Ennahda in Tunisia and Nahdlatul Ulama in Indonesia have their own indigenous specificity. Likewise, Shiite Amal in Lebanon and the Sunni FIS in Algeria carry altogether different historical and cultural burden, but both are known to be the bone of global political Islam.

In the late 20th and the early 21st centuries, political Islam with its different connotations has emerged as one of the most dominant political and ideological discourses across the world. The study of political Islam as an ideology, sociopolitical movement, cultural assertion, anthropological evolution, ethnographic union and religious activism has acquired the most prominent place amongst the world academics, global think tanks as well as national and international policy research institutes. Over the last three decades in particular, political Islam and the rise of the Islamist movements across the continents have captured the centre stage not only in the scholarly analysis but in media analysis too focusing on the socio-economic background of the Islamic actors and the contextual emergence of the these movements.

Political Islam, very often called 'Islamism', as a subject has come to receive extensive attention in the aftermath of the Iranian Revolution of 1979, and its success has further stimulated the scholarship and acquired the pivotal feature in the study of this new ideology along with other political undercurrents. The theorists and the advocates of political Islam have been around since and were followed by an extraordinary explosion of Islamic activism in the Muslim world afterwards. These four decades have witnessed the true ascendency of the force 'political Islam' in action, confronting physically and ideologically all the ideas not resonating with their vision of Islam.

The romanticized leader of the Iranian Revolution Ayatollah Khomeini is credited with the creation of the first theological state in the modern world and with transforming a theory into action as he became a practical force in global politics. He was a prototype of a charismatic leader, predominantly for Iran, shown through world media for the whole of the Muslim world (much like Mao, Castro or Guevara who played such a role for the international Left in a previous moment). It was the Iranian Revolution that laid the foundation for the novel meaning of political Islam in terms of opposition to the West and its modern authenticity where the West sees itself in realm of enlightenment and measures Muslims in realms of religion, tradition and customs alone.[5]

Of course, it was the revolution in Iran that brought Islam on the ascendancy and aroused much interest, and later grew in conjunction with a series of events such as the assassination of President Sadat of Egypt, Iraqi invasion of Iran, Pakistan's material support to Afghan fighters against Russian red perils, Hamas uprising in Syria in 1982, Israeli attack on Lebanon, Trade Centre bombing of 1993, 9/11 attack on the World Trade Centre in 2001, Hamas victory in the election of 2006 in Palestine and, last but not the least, the creation of several Islamist groups in and around the Middle East.

This unending chain of events in the Arab world, together with the loss of credibility of the Arab rulers, helped the appearance of a new Islam that was devoid of any ritualistic or spiritual elements from inside and acquired more the shape of a political document. Islamic movements came to the fore in many countries and the entire Arab political domain was swamped by Islamic tide. This was the phase when Islam had become the dreaded medium of subversion and revolt for many governments and for the world powers intent on maintaining their past hegemony. Leaders at home rushed to adopt Islamic posturing and the vocabularies along with the tones to pacify and weaken the rising Islamic tide and to compete with the breeding ideology of the time. To quote Professor Samir Zubaida

---

[5] Anne Norton, *On the Muslim Question* (Princeton, NJ: Princeton University Press, 2013), 15.

here, 'Indeed this was a charismatic period of the political or revolutionary Islam.'[6]

Those who believe Islam to be an indissoluble part of politics disregard the spiritual elements of Islam, and in its mature phase, they tend to divorce Islam completely from its ritual and spiritual contents, which not only constituted an enduring component of traditionalist and orthodox Islam but also were the hallmarks of this universal religion. Given the ascending significance of Islam, which was studied earlier under the rubric of theology, religious and mystic studies, it has entered into the realm of social science and international affairs, and has subsequently achieved the status of an independent academic discipline. The magnitude of the attention that political Islam has received over the decades questioned the present scope and prospect of religious studies itself disputing the traditional role of Ulema and Islamic heritage and confronting the centuries-old religious authority of Ulema too.

Political Islam is also an extension of rebellious provocation against orthodox Islam that relied much upon the theory of speculation and consensus while the new forces of Islam-driven political ideology sought to spread out the theological content for a liberal adaptation and individual interpretation. This takes into account the contents, history and a host of diverse interpretations instead of adhering to or being subjugated by the literalist views of an individual or a particular school. The proponents of political Islam endeavour to revisit the entire gamut of Islam in terms of authenticity and inauthenticity, and do not harbour a very optimistic and sanguine view of Islamic past, customary religious views, modern political culture, Western modern ideas and subalternality of Islam. Here, Islam acts like a referential point to express all the sociopolitical ideas that seek to evade boundaries between culture, religion and politics.

Political Islam has always maintained apprehensive views about the modern cultural values of Islam, its association with the modern world and its identification with the secular West.

---

[6] Samir Zubaida, 'Trajectories of Political Islam: Egypt, Iran and Turkey', *The Political Quarterly* 71, Issue Supplements, August (2000): 60–78.

The faith of political Islam lies in the dictum that there is a difference between traditional and modern Islam. Political Islam raises the question about the Islamic identity and digs the genealogy of clashes between Orientalism and Occidentalism, colonizers and colonized, old and new, East and West, and internal and external, what subsequently transforms into 'us' versus 'them'. This emanates more from the Western dictum manifested in Derrida's words that claim, 'Muslims are alien to democracy which belongs to Greco-Christian and globalizing tradition—concept of democracy and secularisation even of the right to literature are not merely European but Greco-Christian and Greco-Roman.'[7]

In the sphere of political Islam, religion tends to capture a key position in day-to-day behaviour of Muslims. One comes across a reborn Islam that brings itself in public sphere and gradually becomes an actor in the global arena. The politicization of Islam or Islamization of the existing politics has forced a kind of dissolution between Islam and its ritual and spiritual contents.

Certainly, some classical Islamic jurists and Quranic exegetes have treated Islam as more than a collection of moral, spiritual and ethical teachings, but the modern-day debate on Islam has reduced this revealed religion to a mere political document and a principal source of identity. Political Islam or Islamism has reduced the religiosity of Islam to a conventional term and enhanced its scope by proliferating it in various disciplines of Islamic sociology, polity, culture, anthropology and epistemology. It is a critical prelude towards the possibility of rethinking of Islam itself and is directed towards problematizing of the politics itself.

Numerous scholars, intellectuals, culturalists and policy experts have looked at the subject in different ways and studied it in the light of their own exclusive disciplinary paradigm and methodology. Mainstream scholars define political Islam in terms of a fundamentalist and revivalist movement. The origin of this fundamentalist and revivalist movement can be traced back to the 19th-century Arab world that was wrapped

---

[7] Norton, *On the Muslim Question*, 124.

in a battle between Western modernity and the core of Islamic values that treat Islam not only as a part of common sense alone but in its totality reflecting a way of life.

Before I move further and decipher the broad meaning of political Islam, I would like to discuss the nuances involved and the ambiguities of other similar phrases, idioms and concepts used interchangeably and generously with political Islam such as Islamic fundamentalism, radical Islam, Salafism, Wahabism, neo-fundamentalism, jihadism and Islamism. These concepts seem to convey a similar genealogy and echo the same connotation, but if they are examined empirically, one finds that these terms neither imply political Islam in terms of meaning nor come under the realm of political Islam itself.

Fundamentalism

Borrowed from the Christian Protestants, this term has been used to describe the anti-modern sentiments of a particular group of Christians opposed to the Darwinist theory of man's origin and has been in practice for almost a hundred years.[8] However, for the last three or four decades, it has gained currency in the countries witnessing the rise of the Islamic fundamentalist movement accompanied by the rise of similar fundamentalist movements in other religions such as Hinduism, Judaism, Christianity and Buddhism. It is a very broad term, used almost synonymously with medieval, militant, reactionary and oppressors of women. Fundamentalism can be distinctively defined as an easy approach to get into some more compelling and discrete reality, unlike conservatism of Ulema, pirs and mullahs who seek to return to the laws of Islam but reject militant and political instances.[9] Political Islam is distinguished from other 'fundamentalisms' in the sense that it insists on

---

[8] Fred Halliday, 'The Politics of Islam—A Second Look', *The British Journal of Political Science* 25, no. 3 (July 1995): 399–417.

[9] Humeira Iqtidar, *Secularizing Islamist: Jamat-e-Islami and Jamaat-ud-dawa in Urban Pakistan* (Chicago, IL: Permanent Black, 2011), 100.

engagement with the political structure and state apparatus as a means of establishing a Muslim order and society.[10] In contrast to fundamentalism, political Islam can be referred to as the activities of the organizations and the movements that mobilize and agitate in the political sphere while deploying sign and symbol from the Islamic tradition. It is also used to refer to political activism involving informal groupings that reconstruct repertoires and frames of reference from Islamic tradition.[11]

Fundamentalism, on the other hand, can be seen as a reactive movement driven by individuals who have come to feel that their faith was subjected to a deadly threat to its survival and that it can only be saved through a return to its original principles and values. If one sees in this light, the demands of Islamic fundamentalists echo a similar rhetoric emanating from many Christians, Hindus, Sikhs and Jews.[12] One prominent scholar discussing the scope of fundamentalism writes that the concept of fundamentalism applies to the 'beleaguered believers' who, when confronted with 'the encroachment of outsiders who threaten to draw [them] into a syncretistic, a religious, or irreligious cultural milieu', go back to their faith's basic doctrines and practices in an effort to 'preserve their distinctive identity' as a people or group.[13]

The Islamic fundamentalists are worried by the fact that the 'Islamic countries' are not Islamic for the simple reason that their legal structure, social norms, educational system and moreover popular culture do not reflect the true Islamic teaching and hence the project of Islamization comes to transform a Muslim nation into an Islamic one.[14] Moreover, fundamentalists do not claim to have a comprehensive political programme for the future.[15]

---

[10] Iqtidar, *Secularizing Islamist*, 2.

[11] Ismail, *Rethinking Islamist Politics*, 2.

[12] Denoeux, 'The Forgotten Swamp', 57.

[13] James Piscatoria, ed., *Islamic Fundamentalists and the Gulf Crisis* (Chicago: The American Academy of Arts and Sciences, 1991), xii.

[14] Aijaz Ahmad, 'Islam, Islamism and the West', *Socialist Register* 44, no. 2 (2008), 44–55.

[15] Denoeux, 'The Forgotten Swamp', 61.

In the words of Emmanuel Siwan, '[F]undamentalism is nothing but harking back to the essential varieties of the faith—thus it seems to be restricted to the militant alone: it permeates conservative circles too.'[16] Political Islam refers to a wide variety of political activities undertaken in the name of Islam, while extremism, for instance, seeks to impose changes from above through holy war, and others pursue the bottom-up approach what Gilles Kepal calls 'Islamization from below'. Sometime, fundamentalism is taken as a return to a religious text or combining religion with a political goal. Some see fundamentalism as a variant of Islamism, while Islamism denotes religious-infested trend. The fundamentalist movements are not common to Islam alone but are very active in Israel, the United States, India and other places craving for power. Fundamentalists proclaim originality and authenticity vis-à-vis other political movements seeking their derivation from a timeless perennial source of legitimation.

Seeking or resorting to the fundamental teaching or edicts of the religion is nothing new and not linked to a collective political action or any political project. The similarity between Islamic, Jewish or Christian fundamentalists can be contested on the ground that fundamentalist thought within the Jewish and Christian communities had arisen when they were imbibed with all democratic structure and enjoyed all sorts of political freedom unlike Islamic fundamentalism which had witnessed its rise amidst the complete lack of power alternative and in a complete absence of genuine social and political transparency.

Salafism

Similarly, there is another ideology coloured with the brush of political Islam containing political ingredients known as 'Salafism'. Salafism is brushed with political Islam without any second thoughts, which does not resonate even remotely with

---

[16] Ismail, *Rethinking Islamist Politics*, 30.

political Islam. Salafism is a current of thought that emerged in the second half of the 19th century in the Arabian Peninsula. The word emanates from *Salaf,* meaning companions of the Prophet, and more comprehensively referred to as *Al-Salaf-al-Salih* echoing the meaning of the virtuous companions of the Prophet.[17] For Mr S.N. Eisenstadt, fundamentalism constitutes a distinctive form of modern political movement and, arguing further, he claims that Salafism is a variant of Jacobean tendencies that are intrinsic to the modern political movement. It arises in part because of inherent contradictions between totalizing and more pluralistic conceptions between reflexivity and active construction of nature and the society, between autonomy and control.[18]

Salafism calls upon the believers to return to the puritanical Islam and completely rejects all kinds of innovation like Sufism, new rituals or beliefs in sainthood and other heterodox actions in the name of Islam. Instead of a customary way of following the classical interpretation of the Quran and Hadith and following the jurists or one particular school, Salafi believes in the individual interpretation of the Quran and Hadith, and not necessarily imitating blindly the edicts and decrees of the theologians or the classical Jurists of the past. Meanwhile, they insist on the individual believer's right to interpret the Quran and Hadith according to his or her own rational mind through the practice of *Ijtihad* (scientific and rational interpretation of the Quran and Hadith).[19]

Salafism as a contour of Islam did not develop as a monolithic ideology, but one can witness its local variants reflecting its own context of evolution. It expresses itself in a multiplicity of the movements around the world mirroring the specific local circumstances and local historical conditions. At large, Salafism has been intellectual–cultural exercise eschewing the political arena, but, in the last two decades, it has entered into the political arena too, again replicating or focussing on the indigenous

---

[17] Denoeux, 'The Forgotten Swamp', 59.

[18] S.N. Eisnensadt, *Fundamentalism, Sectarianism, and Revolution: The Jacobean Dimension of Modernity* (Cambridge: Cambridge University Press, 1999), 62.

[19] Oliver Roy, *Failure of Political Islam*, trans. Carol Volk (London: I.B. Tauris, 1994), 33.

condition and the context. It resembles Protestantism in many ways and may also be compared to counter-reformation of Roman Catholic against Protestantism.[20]

Wahabism

In order to achieve political articulation, Salafists have heavily drawn upon Wahabism, another brand of Islamic activism echoing the radical and puritanical Islam. The term Wahabism comes from the name of an 18th-century religious reformer, Muhammad Ibn-Abd al Wahab (1703–91 AD) of central Arabia. On the constitutional issues of the Imamate, the attributes of God and other metaphysical foundations of the religion of Islam, Wahab strictly followed the propositions of Ashab Al-hadith (believers in Hadith), and on everyday jurisprudence, he practised the Hanbali school of law. In his arguments on the fundamentalist belief of Islam, he was more swayed by the ideas and opinions of Asharite.[21] He stood against the laxity and the moral corruption dominant in the erstwhile culture of the region. To combat the existing heresies, social ills and innovative and deviated habits of Islam, he preached to resort to the puritanical teachings of Islam and vehemently called for eradicating anything that was not in concurrence with the literal and strict interpretation of the Quran.

Abd al Wahab resorted to etymological and linguistic explanations of the Quran and believed that there was only one way of interpreting it.[22] One can gauge the rigidity in the thought of Wahabism that in today's pictorial world, portraits of people in general are contentious issues in the Wahabi's conservative doctrine of Islam. They allude to the Hadith, 'Angel will not enter in a house containing a dog or a picture'.[23] Wahabism in central Arabia remains characterized by its intolerance towards

---

[20]   Roel Meijer, 'Towards a Political Islam' (CLINGENDAEL diplomacy paper no. 22, Netherland Institute of International Relations, Netherland, 2009).

[21]   Tamin Al-Barghouti, *The Umma and the Dawala: The Nation State and the Arab Middle East* (London: Pluto Press, 2004), 27–28.

[22]   Al-Barghouti, *The Umma and the Dawala*, 28–29.

[23]   Erich Kolig, *Conservative Islam: A Cultural Anthropology* (Maryland: Lexington Book, 2012), 237.

any perceived innovation or deviation from the dogmatic interpretation or the teaching of the Quran. Wahabism in itself cannot be equated with the political Islamic movement or a version of political Islam. For instance, Saudi Arabia, the cradle of Wahabism, has established a system of separate religious and state authority quite contrary to the ideal notion of Islamism. Islamists in the Kingdom of Saudi Arabia are not happy with the present political model and it can be witnessed in both the strange and strained relationship between the Saudi regime and the Islamic political movements of the Middle East. What emerges of it is that Wahabism is a very orthodox and restrictive interpretation of the Quran and Islam. The clergy class of Saudi Arabia envisions Wahabism as a conservative and politically quietist concept. Today, Wahabism believes in political status quo, works with the existing institutions and its core area of operation and exercise is morality.

Unlike Salafism, Islamic fundamentalism and Wahabism and other similar concepts discussed earlier, political Islam is a relatively recent phenomenon and the term itself was coined during the 1970s to connote the rise of movements and ideologies drawing on Islamic referents—terms, symbols and events taken from the Islamic tradition—in order to articulate a distinctly political agenda (hence, the expression 'political Islam', which is usually seen as synonymous with Islamism).

Political Islam: Definitions, Theories and Explanations

A large number of theoretical formulations have been offered by a host of scholars from various disciplines to define political Islam. A vast amount of academic work has been dedicated to study and explain the subject that has been further scrutinized in multiple ways. Political Islam has been articulated through the language of culture, orientalism, modernity, colonial and post-colonial politics, religion, theology, authenticity and inauthenticity, and hegemony.

There are no inherent meanings or persistent ideas generating the unity of a totality called Islam.[24] There are certain essentialist attributes of political Islam, but these suffer from a certain level of constraints. For example, the essentialist perspective of the culturalist framework not only constrains the boundary of explanatory or interpretative power but also obscures the multiplicity and diversity defining Islamism or political Islam. Insertion of Islamism into socio-historical and political context helps us to understand the subject in its entirety.

Political Islam must be seen, first and foremost, as a contextual reaction to the events. Fundamentals of these actions are embodied in the 18th-century Islamic revivalism. Elucidating on the nature of interactions with the Western world and the resultant rise of revivalism, Mr John O. Voll categorizes the response and interaction in four ways: adaptation, conservatism, fundamentalism and individualistic reaction.[25] Political Islam involves a process in which various domains of social life are invested with symbols and signs associated with the Islamic culture and tradition.[26]

Political Islam can be defined as a revolutionary movement seeking to transform the existing political and social order.[27] Professor Mohammed Ayoob traces its origin in the womb of the Islamist belief that sees Islam as a body of faith and has something important to say about how politics and society should be ordered in the contemporary Muslim world.[28]

Professor Salwa defined political Islam as a set of activities of an organization and the movement that agitates and mobilizes the public sphere deploying the sign and symbol of Islamic tradition. Islamism is a process where various domains of social life are invested with the signs and symbols associated with Islamic

---

[24] Ismail, *Rethinking Islamist Politics*, 26.

[25] John O. Voll, *Makers of Contemporary Islam* (New York City: Oxford University Press, 2001), 30.

[26] Salwa Ismail, 'Being Muslim: Islam, Islamism and Muslim Identity Politics', *Government and Opposition* 39, no. 4 (August 2004): 614–31.

[27] Rubin, ed., *Political Islam*, 1.

[28] Mohammed Ayoob, *Political Islam: Image and Reality* (Chennai: Centre for Security Analysis, 2008), Available at http://www.csa-chennai.org/Files/Pol%20 Islam.pdf (Accessed on 28 November 2013).

culture and tradition.[29] It is this belief in the authority of Islam that drives the Islamist thinking and creates such varying groups in different contexts that come under the umbrella of 'political Islam'. Political Islam is similar to several previous movements, including nationalism, communism, socialism and liberalism, in the history of the Middle East and other parts of the world.

Typically, this project, called political Islam, provides a comprehensive critique of the existing political architecture, and not only intends to challenge it but also wants to change it. It addresses the social, political, economic and cultural challenges faced by the contemporary Muslim societies and claims to provide solutions to all sorts of problems. It makes more or less a sustained and persuasive effort to reflect upon what an 'Islamic economy' or 'Islamic society' might look like. The political activities of political Islam draws upon Islamic precepts, Islamic history, Islamic vocabulary and presumably the Islamic models of governance.[30]

In the words of Hrair Dekmejla, '[P]olitical Islam or Islamism is an expression of revivalist tradition in Islam and a response to internal decay.'[31] The term political Islam itself broadly refers to the politicization of the religion of Islam by individuals or organizations in order to achieve political goals. The current pace of urbanisation and after-effect of globalization impacting all aspects of human life has substantially shaped the phenomena called Political Islam.

In contrast to the other variants of political Islam in exercise across the globe, a true political Islamic thought is rooted in the context of the political and intellectual turmoil of the colonial period and post-colonial time. It contains all political elements of modern day ranging from engagement with electoral politics to mass mobilization on ideological basis and other remnants that constitute the ingredient of today's politics.

[29] Ismail, *Rethinking Islamist Politics*, 2.
[30] Mohammed Ayoob, 'The United States and Political Islam: The Dialectic of Hegemony and Resistance', *Middle East Insight*, No. 3, Middle East Institute, National University of Singapore. Available at https://mei.nus.edu.sg/wp-content/uploads/2011/04/MEI-Insights-003.pdf (Accessed on 25 March 2015).
[31] Ismail, *Rethinking Islamist Politics*, 32.

A series of narratives, approaches and tools propounded by scholars belonging to different disciplines and following divergent methodological schools have been used to study the phenomenon. Apart from sociological, political and economic models, other combinations of narratives have also been applied to explore the subject. Some of the narratives have remained very central to the subject, like colonial narrative in the form of 'other' and 'predestined' superiority of Islam. There are other sets of discourses and narratives applied to study the contentious subject and it is being defined and redefined uninterruptedly in terms of power, culture, religion, history, politics, orientalism, colonialism, modernity, hegemony, authenticity versus inauthenticity and the narrative of shariah versus the modern legal reform extensively applied or sought after to explain the subject in a comprehensive way. The objective of this section is to survey these different narratives and perspectives to reflect upon political Islam that itself has been defined in varying manners and through diverse theoretical prisms.

While tracing the origin and emergence of political Islam in terms of its association with the power, the whole phenomenon can be defined as a process of acquiring the power and subjectivization. It talks of linking Islam most poignantly, romantically and metaphysically to the absolute necessity of state power.[32] For those who subscribe to the philosophy of great 20th-century French scholar Michel Foucault, political Islam is nothing but an urge and an attempt to capture the state power where Islam acts as a dense transfer point for the transfer of power.[33] Through the prism of power discourse, political Islam can be further understood as the governmentalization of Islam where Islam acts like a counter engine for the modernity, a unified homogeneous plot against the Western modernity. It is a desire for political space, geopolitical security and preserving Muslim identity and further for the adherents of Political Islam, Islam needs to be dwelled

---

[32] Najeeb A. Jan, *The Metacolonial State: Pakistan, The Deoband 'Ulema and the Biopolitics of Islam* (PhD dissertation, Michigan University, 2010), 120, http://deepblue.lib.umich.edu/bitstream/handle/2027.42/75807/janna_1.pdf (Accessed on 23 June 2012). p. 110.

[33] Jan, *The Metacolonial State*, p. 112.

in the abode of political space as well instead of confining it to ritual and ceremony.

More comprehensively, the term political Islam connotes the process of fusion between authority and power, and this very fusion leads to other sets of complications while explaining the subject. Political Islam calls to uphold the authority through the promotion of tradition and, subsequently, it is a desire for power through the promotion of political activism. Political Islam applies symbolical and sentimental weight of Islam to advance its class of political leadership and power above and over both the civil society and the sovereign authority of the state. It never believes in a fixed and essentialized notion of space of modernity and Western others. The main thrust of political Islam or Islamist in power is an endeavour to gain power and implement its own version and vision of Islam.

The imperative of political Islam lies in its will to reorder the existing political system furthering the role of Islam beyond policing and moralling of the life alone. It is not Islam but politics that is decisive. Islam is merely incorporation into the space of politics where it is enforced without Allah. It has arisen in a political setting that has witnessed the lack of real prospect for a genuine, peaceful alteration of the power.

The rise of political Islam in terms of power stands for absolute power to shape the personal and the collective worldview of the Muslim community. This perspective on political Islam displaces all other dynamics and perspectives and brings into focus the politics of identity and the power relation at the global level.[34]

This power-infested dynamic of political Islam takes into account an expansive view of power of the state; the state must not merely let people live an Islamic life but should actively uphold and implement the Islamic laws. It must enable people to live according to such laws and must allow nothing that contravenes it.[35] The power of modern nations to intrude into and regulate all aspects of the life of its citizens means that religion

[34] Ismail, *Rethinking Islamist Politics*, 4.
[35] Muhammad Qasim Zaman, *The Ulema in Contemporary Islam: Custodians of Change* (Princeton, NJ: Princeton University Press, 2007), 100.

occupies an uneasy place in any modern state. In terms of power, political Islam can be defined as a struggle for power and hegemony. In other words, it is the deployment of religious symbols, signs and the frame of reference derived from religious tradition that belongs to a power-laden field of action and practices.[36]

There are intellectuals and experts on international relations who, while tracing and exposing the intricacies and complexities involved in political Islam, do not move beyond the confines of colonialism. They ascribe the rise of political Islam to the exploitative character of colonial power of the last centuries. They locate its origin in the historical marginalization and subalternality of Muslims against the backdrop of colonialism. Reactionary forces within Islam suffered from the sense of deprivation and firmly believed that pure Islam was corrupted by political intervention and ensuing events in the Arab world. The adherents of political Islam resort to the preaching for Islamizing not only the modern political order but also the entire Islamic vocabulary itself.

For them, political Islam is an extended and unfinished battle of Muslims around the world against their past colonial masters and according to them who have never been the part of past for them. Islamists take Islam as a major political force for freedom, revolution and sociopolitical changes, and anti-colonialism and the present Islamic model as a viable alternative for fresh and renewed political arrangement and new Islamic history.[37] Islam too has a full spectrum of potential symbols and concepts of absolutism and hierarchy and foundation for liberty and equality. Political Islam can be phrased as nostalgia for the past, an act of hatred towards occidental hater and an act of apologia for the Islam.

The centrality of politics in Islamic thoughts is not of any theological compulsion within Islam but is the context in which it was founded. The formation of political Islam is part of a multifaceted response generated as a consequence of a colonial encounter.[38] At the heart of the Islamist's endeavour was to make use of modern arguments to support Islamic conclusion

---

[36] Ismail. *Rethinking Islamist Politics*, 17.

[37] Oliver Roy, *Globalised Islam: The Search for a New Ummah* (New York: Columbia University Press, 2004), 2.

[38] Iqtidar, *Secularizing Islamist*, 52.

to present it as a rational religion that was not outdated as the naturalist claim. The outside influences over the Arab world created a deeper longing for an identity or faith that was imagined to be the authentic Islam for people. The longing for Islam, or the nostalgia for how the Cairene communities had been before the changes that took place under the influences of colonialism and technological advances, resurrected the desire to renew Arab identity through the Islamization of culture and politics. Echoing the same intent and feeling of modern Islamic activism, Wilfred Cantwell Smith asserts that

> Islamic society is endangered not only from without but from within, and not only its existence but essence…. One may blame the British or Americans for their injustice. One may inveigh against the ideas that they impose. But how come it that they can wreak such injustice, can get away with their ideas? How comes it that the Islamic world is impotent, and backward.[39]

Similarly, a well-known Arab novelist, Mahfouz, portrays the religious and politically ideological questions in terms of a struggle against alien powers, rather than in terms of their own merits and how they look for meaning behind the dominance of colonialism in all the facets of their lives.[40] Most of the academics inhabiting the territory of political Islam see this wave of Islamism across the spectrum of global politics as an Islamic resistance to the intangible colonial and Western presence on the Arab territory and dictating the politics of the Arab nations.

In the words of Talmiz Ahmad:

> Arab world failed to experience the democratic order witnesses in other parts of the world after the liberation of most of the Asian and African territories. Throughout the 20th century Western domination over the politics in the WANA remained in place,

---

[39] Cantwell Smith, *Islam in Modern History* (Princeton, NJ: Princeton University Press, 1957), 110.

[40] Mehnaz Mona Afridi, *Naguib Mahfouz and Modern Islamic Identity* (PhD thesis, University of South Africa, 2008), 30, http://uir.unisa.ac.za/bitstream/handle/10500/2745/dissertation_afridi_%20m.pdf;jsessionid=3FFB4530F5047485B9E5E9F12FD0F2A8?sequence=1 (Accessed on 23 April 2012).

although the Anglo-French Alliance was after the Second World War and the lead-role players for promoting Western interest. [41]

This resistance movement of the Islamists not merely intend to oust the external powers and lessen its influence but also pushed to undo the past and re-establish an Islamic universal order and execute the commandments set down by the Prophet Mohammed. One of the pioneers of Islamic reform of Egypt, Muhammad Abduh, rallied for an indigenous Islamic enlightenment through offering an Islamic alternative to Western secular notions of democracy. [42]

Mr Francois is of the same view and he blames the Western colonial policy in the Middle East for the radicalization and Islamization of politics. He argues that West labels everything Muslim as political Islam and fails to understand its role in the present scenario. The history of colonization of the Middle East, Burgat argues, is a significant factor in today's politics. During the colonial period, the West viewed its culture and values as universal notions, imposing its worldview on others. Muslims were forced into the category of 'others' and denied the right to consider their values universal. [43] While for some Islamists, disdain for the West emanates from hatred and hostility towards Western and European enlightenment. One of the pioneers of political Islam in South Asia, Maudoodi, himself says in his booklet, *The Sick Nation of the Modern Age*, 'In short this [unfettered freedom] was the pernicious seed that was sown by the European renaissance which has grown over the centuries into a massive and deadly tree. Its fruits are sweets, but are poisonous'. [44] It is not Western imperialism that offends the Islamist but the unfettered freedom and individual liberty that is the cause for concern.

---

[41] Talmiz Ahmad, 'Arab Spring and its Implications for India', *Strategic Analysis* 37, no. 1 (2013), http://www.tandfonline.com/doi/full/10.1080/09700161.2013.73760 7#.UndkfXByDcM (Accessed on 10 September 2013).

[42] Afridi, *Naguib Mahfouz and Modern Islamic Identity*, 48.

[43] 'Fletcher Features: Francois Burgat Discusses the Western and the Islamist Role in the Middle Ease Political Strategy', http://fletcher.tufts.edu/News-and-Media/2008/11/27/Francois-Burgat-Discusses (Accessed on 25 December 2014).

[44] Tarak Fateh, *Chasing a Mirage: The Tragic Illusion of an Islamic State* (Ontario: John Wiley and Sons Canada Ltd, 2008), 18, http://lubpak.com/wp-content/uploads/2010/04/Fatah-2008-Chasing-a-Mirage-The-book.pdf (Accessed on 13 April 2013).

Of late, political Islam has been treated in terms of its contestation with modernity. A new trend has emerged among the present orientalists to measure and gauge the extent and scope of liberal and democratic elements within Islam in the light of Western modernity, and Islam has been subjected to the canvass of modernity, enlightenment and rationality.

A great deal of literature on political Islam has ventured in juxtaposition to the modernity intending to create a dialectical frame of thoughts between Islam and modernity. Islamism is seen as incompatible with modernity and, in turn, Islamism too rejects modernity, branding it a Western plot. The antithesis of Islam to modernity is taken on the edifice that modernity and secularization go together. It can be best explained in the terms of renowned Iranian Revolutionary ideologue Al-e-Ahamd's philosophy of *Garabzadegi* (Westoxification or Occidentosis of Pahlavis), who spoke of danger to Iranian culture under the impact of Western consumerism that had every chance of being overrun and destroyed. He yearned for alternative modernity and that would be authentic Islam blended with indigenous culture of Iran.[45]

Amongst all other discourses and narratives about political Islam, the issue of locating Islam in terms of modernity has remained the thorniest one. In terms of modernity, political Islam is a manifestation of civilizational disparity between Islam and the West, and this disparity has been invoked repeatedly by invoking the cultural superiority of the West. The authenticity and legitimacy of political Islam are always determined by their attitude towards the Western concept of modernity.

This orientalist notion of disparity is rooted in certain stereotyping not only about the 'Islamic East' but also about its discursive opposite, 'the West'. The more sophisticated among the civilization-obsessed theorists hold certain views about the enlightenment, rationalist secularization of Christianity, sufficient capitalism in the West, the inherently egalitarian and rationalist core of Christianity and the thoroughgoing secularization of Christian societies. All these Western distinctions

---

[45] Adam Shatz, 'A Little Feu de Joie', *London Review of Books* 35, no. 8 (25 April 2013): 15–18.

are then contrasted with the lack of these distinctive elements within Muslim societies. Those who compare modernity with Islam believe in the unbridgeable gulf between the two which is said to separate Islamic East from the secular West.

Islam and the West have disputed the European map and beyond for more than 1,300 years. Islamists call for restoration of the 7th-century originality of Islam. Mohammad was an answer from the east to Alexander of the West.[46] Political Islam is about Europeanized Islam or Islamized Europe on the one hand and European Islam or Islam of shariah on the other hand. The Islamist of the modern era discards the entire philosophy emanating from modernity because of its promotion of apostasy. It puts all blames on modernity for cultural and religious decadence, and calls modernity the religion of irreligious and calls for its replacement with shariah.

Political Islam is a political movement because it aims to seek the mentality of power, to govern mentality and to shape, control, discipline, protect and liberate society. It can be said to be a sociopolitical expression of contradictions and shortcoming of modernization; meanwhile, it is a quest to restore the past and insulate them from society. Political Islam is the product of modernity and at the same time reaction to it. It is also an attempt to resuscitate traditional Islamic teachings—that all should live and think more Islamically—rather than emulate the Western models.

The furious reaction of Muslims and the gradual transformation into a wide range of political Islam may be owed to the relentless flow of alien imported ideas and detested competitive culture of the West. The core of Western political modernity offers a combined creation of pluralistic political structure, rule of universal law and advancement of market economy which stand in sharp contrast to the Islamic teaching of shariah, a feudal–political structure and a split-level economy.[47] Islamism's romanticized imagination is based on worldwide felt notion of ummah within the patchwork of the administrative unit

---

[46]   Peter D. Beaulieu, *Beyond Secularism and Jihad: A Triangular Inquiry into Mosque, the Manager and Modernity* (Maryland: University Press of America, 2012), 304.

[47]   Beaulieu, *Beyond Secularism and Jihad*, 314–15.

engrafted from a nation-state. Islamism sees Western individualism to reintroduce the pre-modern Islamic culture, and in turn, political Islam is an attempt to search for imaginative past and to return to the past glories.[48]

Modernity deals with religion as a creed and a remnant of medieval superstition based on ignorance and supernatural thinking with a firm belief that there is inevitability of the decline of religion in public sphere in favour of extensive rationality that is based on maturity and free choice. This work has been the mainstay of the Western secularism in the last 400 years, whereas Islamists bring God to every sphere—constitution, legal, political, economic, cultural, economic and even into the realm of science. The challenge of modernity presented by the West caused many Islamic societies, especially in the post-colonial period, to regress towards original mythology, in a hope that it will resolve all the moral sufferings and social inequalities in miraculous fashion.[49]

Arabs could not replicate the Western cultural transformation in order to be modern and democratic because of a different past and diverse socio-historical context. Although a host of Muslim clerics in the mid-19th century preached Islamic reform to make it compatible with the requirement of modernity, but an equal number of Muslims remained content with adherence to their religious tradition and venerating official Islam.[50] The growing habit of grappling among the Muslim with their heritage and the subsequent intense multi-level interaction between the West and Islam have caused a fresh spurt in political activism of Islam. The most pertinent question posed today is whether Islam is compatible with democracy or modernity, whose entire objective is to separate religion from politics.

Islamism is always posited in relation to Western material progress and values where Western modernity is taken as a master narrative whose linearity and teleology presumed to

---

[48] Beaulieu, *Beyond Secularism and Jihad*, 316.

[49] Hilal Khashan, 'The Arab Spring and Democratisation in the Middle East', *World Affairs* 16, no. 4 (2012): 132–47.

[50] Khashan, 'The Arab Spring and Democratisation in the Middle East', 132–47.

capture the spirit of the progress.[51] Civilized self as a model of the West was a source of cultural subjugation for Muslims at large. Meanwhile, the process of objectification of Muslims under Western modernity as a driving force reshaping the Muslim identity is seen as a threat. Those who trace the genealogy of political Islam in the confines of modernity rebuff any argument seeking the explanation of political Islam in the history or religion or its language itself.

Much of modern Islamist thought have developed in the traditions of counter-posing Islam to the echoes of modernity. It stands for the rejection of cosmopolitanism, internationalism and universal application of Western democratic values. The philosophy of the Iranian Revolution of 1979 can be taken as a true reflective of Islamic polity. It comes with new vocabulary of Islamism replacing the idiom and phrase couched in the ideas of modernity. The advent of Islam in an ideological form can be viewed in terms of redefining the relationship of Islam with the Western modern political and cultural discourses.

The novel face of politics-dominated Islam hinges upon the assumption that modernity not only acts as antithesis to Islam but also represents its complete negation, and here, Islam emerged as a source of normative clash with modernity.[52] In the words of Tarek Haggy, 'The hard truth is that the clash between values system of political Islam and modernity is so total as to make them incompatible.'[53] Political Islam is the rejection of meta-narrative of Western modernity which not only harbours the hegemonic design inside but also sustains this modernity. This has been put in a context and argued in a very articulate manner by S. Boby Sayyid in the following words:

> It is not essentially an anti-modern movement but an effort at dislodging the west from the position of the centrality that it claims.

---

[51] Salwa Ismail, 'Islamism, Re-Islamisation and the Fashioning of the Muslim Selves: Refiguring the Muslim Sphere', *Muslim World Journal of Human Rights,* 4, no. 1 (2007), http://eprints.soas.ac.uk/5328/1/IslamismReIslamization.pdf (Accessed on 30 December 2010).

[52] Ismail, *Rethinking Islamist Politics*, 3.

[53] Tarek Haggy, 2012, 'Political Islam versus Modernity', *Ahram Weekly*, http://weekly.ahram.org.eg/2012/1113/op4.htm (Accessed on 12 September 2012).

Islamism is located in the space that is freed through the deconstruction of the relationship between the west and modernity.[54]

The stretched canvass of liberty within modernity reduces the faith of religion in the subjective opinions and narration. Overdrawn secularist projects offer no resilient quarter for freedom. There seems to be no convergence between pragmatic ideology of Islamic leaders and ideological pragmatic of the West. Western civic rationalism removes God from public square, while political Islam removes public square from God.[55] Residual human denies the existence of natural laws, but Islam absorbs parts of natural laws into shariah in a way that disclaims common origin. The reduction of man as a means rather than an end is a part of Western modernity that finds no resonance within Islam, and moreover, Islam claims to have no need of philosophy because the Islamic political ideology is fully vindicated by direction–action of Allah.[56]

Political Islam seeks to venture itself in binary to the ethos of modernity, what it calls to be devoid of religious ethics and divine morality, and discards it for its cultural counterfeit and unreal. Modernity or post-modernity, according to the Islamists, leads to uncertainty and self-reflexivity unlike absolutism and eternity of Islamic faith. The yearning of Islamist for absolute introduces a concept of absolute human knowledge that, for them, cannot be derived from Western modernity.[57]

In the words of a liberal Egyptian author, Tarek Haggy, 'For an Islamist who believes his ideology is the absolute truth; any dissent is an abomination that runs counter to the words of God Himself. Indeed Islamists bring to every sphere—constitutional, legal, political, economic, cultural, educational, even scientific.'[58]

---

[54] Boby S. Sayyid, *A Fundamental Fear: Euro Centrism and the Emergence of Islamism* (London: Zed Books, 1997), 120.

[55] Beaulieu, *Beyond Secularism and Jihad*, 321.

[56] Beaulieu, *Beyond Secularism and Jihad*, 332.

[57] Jan, *The Metacolonial State*, 67–68.

[58] Tarek Haggy, 2012, *Islamists and Modernity*, http://www.ahewar.org/eng/show. art.asp?aid=1664 (Accessed on 15 June 2012).

The process associated with modernity and post-modernity is objectification, standardization, individualization and relativization, where men are defined through objectified consumerism providing ground for self-reflexivity, inquiry into self-identity and remaking that identity. All these teachings of modernity go against the basic core of Islamic identity. Relativization is a mainstay of present-day modernity and is born from the womb of faith in pluralism and acceptance of otherness which claims that all judgements, explanations and opinions are relative, but for an Islamist it echoes as an antithesis to Islamic creed.

To quote Tarek Haggy once again, 'Islamists are unable to comprehend and accept (let alone admire) modern state system which is a product of centuries of social, political, cultural and economic struggle for the advancement of human kind.'[59] Islamism is also a creation of the post-modernity because it is threatened by post-modernist icons like Madonna.

Akbar S. Ahmad maintains the same views while arguing Islam and modernity. Jihad is unleashed to fence against the McWorld.[60] Islamism is a reaction against the failure of modernism and defence against post-modernity.[61] Islamism is particularly a modernist take on defining the relationship between faith and the politics. Islamists' focus on politics is generally understood to be the result of an internal compulsion within Islam, but the centrality of the politics in the Islamic thought is a result not of theological compulsion within Islam but of the context in which Islam was founded.[62]

Politics and political history present the view of the clash between modernity and tradition within Muslim society. Dr Iqtidar puts it very succinctly, 'Islamism is often taken as a traditional reaction against modernity. The rationality and secularism of the western modernity has always been contrasted with the

[59] Haggy, *Islamists and Modernity*.

[60] Benjamin R. Barber, *Jihad versus McWorld* (New York: Ballantine Books, 1995), 67.

[61] Salawa Ismail, 'Being Muslim: Islam, Islamism and Identity Politics', *Government and Opposition* 39, no. 4 (2004), http://www.scribd.com/doc/91512952/Being-Muslim-Islam-Islamism-and-Identity-Politics (Accessed on 23 March 2011).

[62] Iqtidar, *Secularizing Islamist*, 52.

irrationality and backwardness of religions.'[63] We should recognize modernity as a historical period and as a project where Islamism is a distinctive modern phenomenon rather than a traditional response to it.

One will find this argument of locating Islamism in contrast to modernity more substantial and significant when one notices the response and the attitude of Muslims towards globalization, another trait of Western modernity for them. One of the strong anti-globalization impulses emanates from the dictum that the West is intent upon destroying the Islam culturally and ideologically. Through an Islamic perspective, globalization is usually perceived as a form of Westernization, an instrument to impose Western culture and to lead a future world that is essentially 'Western'. It is also taken as an incarnation of European colonialism and is labelled as westoxification. The entire design of globalization is subsumed under the rubric of evil influences bringing with it all the amoral, anti-religious impulses of Western civilization.[64]

In terms of religious assertion in Islamism, it acts against the generic philosophy based on the decline of religion in public sphere in favour of the extension of rational thinking that is based on maturity and free choice of mankind.

There are preponderant groups who do not preferably extricate from this scholarly perception of modernity as a counterfeit to Islam, but rather they see political Islam as an extension of modernity in a different semblance. If one notices the trajectory of the Islamic ideological contestation against modernity, one will find that Islamists have gradually retreated from their overblown reactions towards the contestation and what they want is the recognition of their authentic share in today's world of modernity. Political Islam is well rooted in modernism because its intellectual position is formulated in terms heavily indebted to the discourse of the present enlightened age.

Bruce Lawrence argues that Islamists not only use the modern way of organizing and communicating but the very

---

[63] Iqtidar, *Secularizing Islamist*, 159.
[64] Kolig, *Conservative Islam*, 33.

categories, notion and laws that they hope to defy or modify are also modern constructs.[65] According to him, this is not because Islamists rail against the Western epistemological assumption of enlightenment, rationalism and the overarching power of nation-state but political Islam was on march because of Western inability to control the mass mobilization.[66] In its own, political Islam is also modern because its intellectual positions are formulated in terms heavily indebted to the discourse of the modern age. Islamists are distinguished from other type of revivalists by their background in modern educational institutions. For instance, Maududi's own career is a useful illustration of this very trend as he moved from Hyderabad to Jabalpur to Delhi for employment. Similarly, Sayyid Qutb, in his conception of social justice, is far more indebted to modern Western ideas than he is to Quran.[67]

Qutb's views of social justice probably emanated from notions of distributive justice of Western provenance. It did not mean that Qutb directly drew his views from Western writings on social justice but the social discourse of late-1940s Egypt, influenced by Fabian and other European currents of socialist thought, resonated with ideas of welfare, public good and collective responsibility—in the word—'social justice'.

Modernists and Islamists differ very significantly within their rank in their attitude to the Islamic tradition. Some like Mohammad Shahoor of Syria are sharply critical of the pre-modern reading of Islamic laws and call for the radical re-reading of the Quran, while others like Fazlur Rahman, another modernist from Pakistan, call for a sustained engagement with the historic formulation of Islam—juristic, theological and spiritual—in the course of reinterpreting Islam in the modern world.

Along with the treatment of political Islam in the light of modernity, secularism too emerged as another yardstick to study this phenomenon, and like modernity, imposition of

[65] Iqtidar, *Secularizing Islamist*, 41.
[66] Voll, *Makers of Contemporary Islam*, 159.
[67] Shahrough Akhavi, 'The Dialectic in Contemporary Egyptian Social Thought: The Scripturalist and Modernist Discourses of Sayyid Qutb and Hasan Hanafi', *International Journal of Middle East Studies* 29, no. 3 (1997): 377–401.

Western secularism (nothing more than an anti-region for today's Islamists) too was alleged to be responsible for the rise of a political Islamic movement across the Arab world.

To offer a traditional understanding of secularism in the words of Assad Talal:

> Western secularism is not that one-time phenomena that separates church and state but it is constant refashioning and remodelling of religious practices by the state giving rise to new version and from of religion. Traditions put to service of legitimising to seek the competing claims of authenticity, whether by Islamist or other, may be of very recent origin.[68]

The secularism that emerged in the pre-modern Christian West was a matter of bitter conflict between different segments of the society over many centuries and not just an intellectual exercise rooted in Christian theology and practice. In recent years, a kind of polemical contrast is made between Islam and secularism. Most of the Western intellectuals like Bernard and Myron Weiner have suggested that Islam rejects secularism and is intrinsically hostile to it. Other scholars, like Huntington, claim that the totalizing worldview of Islam could not accommodate liberal values, particularly those of personal freedom and secularism. On the contrary, Earnest Gellenr claims that no secularization has taken place in the Muslim world of Islam— that the hold of Islam over its believers is as strong and, in some ways, stronger now than it was hundred years ago.[69]

The post-colonial imposition of Western secularism in most of the Arab world caused the spur of the Islamic movement calling to reorder the political and social systems in the light of Islamic teaching. Secularism emerged as the flashpoint of battle between the adherents to political Islam and the West-inspired modernity, of which secularism was an indissoluble component. It was not later than the first half of the 19th century when the echoes of secularism were being resonated in the Arab world after the expansion of Western colonialism. To quote Bernard Lewis:

---

[68] Iqtidar, *Secularizing Islamist*, 38.

[69] Ernest Gellener, 'Islam and Marxism: Some Comparisons', *International Affairs* 67, no. 2 (1991): 1–6.

French revolution was first great upheaval in Europe to find intellectual expression in non-religious term. The early attraction of western ideas amongst the Arab is to be found in secularism.[70]

The wave of secularism in the Arab world ranging from Nasser's Egypt to Saddam's Iraq to Hafiz Assad's Syria to Gaddafi's Libya prepared a fertile ground for those who believed that secularism was a notion based on the antithesis of Islam and a narrative which calls for the abolition of a centuries-old practice of shariah on the part of Muslims and that resorts to the laws based on modern constitutionalism.

Mr Richard Martin argues the point very precisely when he says:

> Within the Islamic world, the colonial rulers established 'secular' systems of education patterned after their own. As a result, the traditional Muslim educational systems came to be labelled religious.... With the eventual achievement of political independence, Muslim countries entered a transitional stage of working toward a political, economic and social identity that would conform once again to their religious and cultural heritage.[71]

It has always remained a part of Muslim imagination that secular state or life is purely Western and thus Christian and immoral.[72] According to Taqi Uthmani, a renowned Pak Islamic scholar and well-known jurist:

> Secularism is a sort of unbelief that goes to the extreme of maintaining that religion is limited only to certain rituals and to one's private life, and that it has nothing to say on matter of material life which is recognized to have its own Gods.[73]

---

[70] Ismail Bin Mat, 'The Impact of Western Colonization and Secularism on the Application of the Shariah Laws on the Muslim World' (Paper presented in a conference on Muslim and the Islam in a Modern World, Temple University, Philadelphia, 2005), http://www.amss.org/pdfs/34/finalpapers/IsmailbinMat.pdf (Accessed on 2 March 2012).

[71] Richard C. Martin, *Approaches to Islam in Religious Studies* (Tucson, AZ: University of Arizona Press, 1985), 182.

[72] S.N. Yared, *Secularism and the Arab World* (London: Saqi Books, 2002), 92.

[73] Zaman, *The Ulema in Contemporary Islam*, 100–01.

The tension between modernity and Islam is the result of the binary construct imposed by the Western understanding of the secular state, one that is not included in the affairs of God. Moreover, Western secularism has introduced scepticism towards an overtly religious leadership of Muslims what claims revelatory experiences and prophetic vision.[74]

In the words of William Graham:

> [T]raditionalism ought to be seen as a defining feature of Islamic thoughts. This traditionalism consists not in some imagined atavism, regressivism, fatalism or rejection of change and challenge but rather in conviction that a personally guaranteed connection with a model past, especially with the model person, offers the only sound basis... for forming one's society in any age.[75]

The most troubling feature of proponent political Islam is the idea of secularism seen as a constitutive element of modernity that is most of the time treated similar to atheism or at most the irreligious acts on the part of the practitioner or what the Islamist call it, the first step towards the atheism.[76] The Western secular movement is a rejection of the religious principle and an outcome of the Judeo-Christian religious experience itself.[77] Secularism is something that moves man away from a transcendental religious belief and makes him or her adopt a belief in human mind that denied the unseen and transcendental world where belief in unseen is part of Islamic faith.[78]

Muslims could not have understood secularism in isolation from Christianity (Western colonial) supremacy. The history of a particular type of secularization in Europe has meant that religion has been removed from the domain of rational discussion. The secularity of modernity calls for containing faith and ritual in a protected private sphere and rational argument is said to exhaust public life, suppress complex register of persuasions,

---

[74] Kolig, *Conservative Islam*, 12.
[75] Zaman, *The Ulema in Contemporary Islam*, 3.
[76] Iqtidar, *Secularizing Islamist*, 7.
[77] Eltigani Abdelgadir Hamid, *The Qur'an and Politics* (London: IIIT, 2004), 140.
[78] Hamid. *The Qur'an and Politics*, 156.

judgement and discourse operative in public life, whereas the ideology of political Islam is primarily based on omitting the lines between the profane and the pure.

Islamist argumentation is articulated in a way that declares secularism alien to the island of Islam and is treated purely on historical experiences and the contextual outcome of historical development.[79] Islamists are of the firm belief that secularism as a principle of social organization can be applied to the European territory alone and not to the Arab world. Secularization is presented as an object of Westernization that aims at removing the power of Islam from the centre of influence in social and political spheres.

The relationship between Islam and the West is traditionally predicated on the ideology of secularism, and this has remained a yardstick for the Western secular forces to gauge the level of cultural advancement inside the Arab world. It is the Western origin and the rise of secularism as an ideology that vindicates the Islamic instance of treating secularism as an ideology and as a threat to the future of Islam.[80] Islam is a totality that does not involve an opposition to either the material or spiritual world, and it is all-encompassing in terms of the spiritual and material worlds.

Unlike the claims of many traditional scholars of the rigidity of Islamic tradition, Qasim Zaman, Michel Cook, Wael Hallaq and L. Carl Brown have highlighted the adaptive creativity, dissent and the rethinking process of the traditional Islamic legal and theological processes. In pre-colonial time, shariah was practised on the basis of diversified, subjectivities and localized interpretation. However, with the onslaught of colonialism on the cultural and religious domains of the Muslims, a new process of codification set in motion. This new imposition of colonialism and the introduction of a particular mode of the state that is called modern led to much rethinking and revaluation within the non-Western and not just Muslim societies. Islamism

---

[79] Ismail, *Rethinking Islamist Politics*, 42.

[80] Masud Muhammad, 'The Construction and Deconstruction of Secularism as an Ideology in Contemporary Muslim Thought', *Asian Journal of Social Science* 33, no. 3 (2005): 263–83.

is primarily opposed to the colonial secularism that defines its limits, its focus and contentions.[81] This engagement led to the emergence of new schools of thoughts in the form of Islamism under the rubric of MBH of Arab and Jamaat-e-Islami in South Asia. The relationship between tradition and the modernity led to a combined outcome of engagement and antagonism.

Most of the adherents and faithful to the idea of modern secularism harbour a romantic vision that religion will cease to exist once the man is able to engage rationally with human needs without recourse to the religious dogma. While political Islam rebuffs the idea of relegating religion to the background, the core edicts of modernity derive from the basic principle of insulation between religion and power.

The proponents of political Islam are of the view that philosophy could have emerged only in modern age as proved by the modern context of rejection of the Western ideas. Elucidating the modern Islamic views about secularism and how it has antagonized the Islamic discourse of the 20th century, one of the outstanding experts on Islamic history, Bruce Lawrence, says, 'Islamism is inconceivable in any but modern age.'[82]

Secularism which claims to have universal values has been reduced to a European geographical connotation. Western secularism was a response to the religious state specific to the West, and Islam distrusts the identity of secularism because of Christian origination. In the words of Ammar Ali Jindah, 'Fact cannot be transcended as the world is two cultures—Islamic and non-Islamic cannot meet in a single frame.'[83] Islamism's views believe in the dictum that one cannot take moral self from the political self as the project of self is tied to Muslim politics. Self-reform is tied with social reform and does not necessarily operate in the narrow political sphere alone.

Further I will explore some of the cultural thrusts of Islamism that resort to the religion of Islam for its protect-culture project in order to draw cultural and moral boundaries between the Islamic East and the secular West. If one sees the rise of political

[81] Iqtidar, *Secularizing Islamist*, 39–40.
[82] Zaman, *The Ulema in Contemporary Islam*, 8.
[83] Ismail, *Rethinking Islamist Politics*, 45.

Islam in terms of cultural protection, one will find that cultural discourse has remained the sizeable component of Islamism. A series of the cultural theorists allude to cultural antagonism between the world of Islam and the liberal West.

In cultural terms, political Islam can be defined as a project to be at the guard against the onslaught to Western cultural immorality. It is a move to defend oneself against the 'cultural other' where Western cultural domination is taken to be a prelude to threat of cultural attack on Islam.[84] Different shades of Islamism find themselves under cultural siege and Islamicists pay a great deal of attention to what their enemies or imagined enemies are saying about them, about themselves, about the animosity and the difference between us and them.[85] Culturalists offer a cultural explanation for the rise of political Islam and the cultural conceptualists place their argumentation in a continuum of self–others relations produced through a sequence of historical encounters between the discursive space of the East and the West.

The core of the culturalists' discourse moved around the dichotomy between the essentialist and the reductionist concepts of democracy and Islam. Culturalists base their views on the claim of incompatibility of Islam and the West. In cultural term, cultural and social aphorism of Islamism stems from the belief in the superiority of the self (Islam) and degradation of the others (West). The superiority of Islam is presented in the contemporary Islamist discourse as a given or as an element of the religious truth that bestows on the faith the higher duty of leading humanity since the collapse of the fragmented and decadent other is inevitable.[86]

The cultural assertion of ummah finds Western culture as unauthentic, counterfeit and impure, not derived from indigenous heritage. Islamism, thus, stands to defend against the Christian proselytization, intellectual invasion and subjugation

---

[84] Ismail, *Rethinking Islamist Politics*, 34.
[85] Ahmad, 'Islam, Islamism and the West'.
[86] Salwa Ismail, 'Confronting the Other: Identity, Culture, Politics and Conservative Islamism in Egypt', *International Journal of Middle East Studies* 30, no. 2 (1998): 199–225.

of Islamic creed to the Western rationality and enlightenment. Islamism believes in a cultural system that encompasses all aspects of Muslim identity. The assault by the 'others' is cast in an attempt to encircle and destroy the make-up of the Muslims and denigrate their thoughts.[87] In the present era of identity politics, culture has emerged as the central instance of existence and one of the determinant factors of social behaviours where religion and politics inflame each other and religion becomes synonymous with the culture.

To quote Huntington:

> In the post-Cold War world, the most important distinctions among peoples are not ideological, political, or economic. They are cultural.... We know who we are only when we know who we are not and often only when we know who we are against.[88]

The cultural authenticity finds an important place in the political discourse of the Islamists, and all sorts of ideological or intellectual dominance of the West are assumed to be a cultural penetration polluting the historicity of Islam. The core of modern social and political philosophies in the form of Marxism, Freud, Darwin, and Durkheim is complete negation of Islamic underpinning.

The ardent believers of political Islam have strong faith in the intimacy of historical culture and politics and lay stress that historicity of the culture should enjoy all sorts of liberty and legitimacy in the formation of the politics of a particular sociocultural group. It is a contestation between contesting identities where political Islam acts as an idea restoring the basic elements and practice in an effort to preserve distinctive identity as people and group.[89] Political Islam is a mission working towards political, economic and social identities that would conform once again to their religious and cultural heritage. Theology of customary does not

---

[87] Ismail, *Rethinking Islamist Politics*, 34.
[88] Huntington, Samuel P. *Clash of Civilization and Remaking of World Order* (New York: Simons and Schuster, 1996), pp. 20–21.
[89] Denoeux,' The Forgotten Swamp', 56–81.

allow importing the culture. Political Islam believes that Islam should be the central and fundamental of Muslim identity.[90] The Islamic organization draws upon a long history of political theory and practices based on the pre-colonial sense of identity. These organizations are 'dwala', non-territorial temporary political arrangement whose allegiance lies with the whole of 'ummah'.[91] Culturally, political Islam is an invocation of frame with an Islamic reference in social and cultural spheres. In the culturalists' term, political Islam reflects the conservative face of Islam which is confined to morality and religiosity and proposes Islamization to the cultural level. Islamism produced an identity totalized in religious and moral terms.

Threat of attack is always present in the 'others' and its penetration in the institution is a source of major worry for the culturally inspired Muslims. The cultural explanation of political Islam can be understood by referring to the ideas of Durkheim, Freud, Darwin and Marx who are treated as others aborting the cultural core of Islam. There are few instances of the treatment of the others—infiltration, misrepresentation and distortion of Islam—which are cultural assaults.

The presence of the others is represented by multifaceted characters, such as crusaders, communism, secularism, Marxism and atheism, who are associated with the West and the meaning of other is confined to the boundary of the West. The rise of Islamism has been attributed to the presence of internal others too, such as the Arab nationalist, Marxist and the secularists. For instance, it is claimed amongst the Islamists that prisoners of secularism are those who are immersed in Western culture.[92] Culturalist interpreters of Islamism find Islam complete, comprehensive and unitary, while the West for them is fragmented, divided and the other.

Political Islam can be articulated or problematized under the rubric of representation or fashioning of the self. This is an effort to bring in Muslim-self in public domain as the presentation

[90] Zaman, *The Ulema in Contemporary Islam*, 88.
[91] Al-Barghouti, *The Umma and the Dawala*, 2.
[92] Ismail, *Rethinking Islamist Politics*, 38.

of any self contributes to the refiguring of the public sphere.[93] Essentialists see political Islam in the context of Islam itself and the language it generates. For them, the Islamic world is dominated by a set of revolutionary's relatively enduring and unchanging processes and its meaning to be understood through text of Islam alone. The modernist talks of relativity, while Islam is more concerned with absolutism in public sphere and the otherness is the mainstay of political Islam. Essentialist explanation posits Islamism as a determining factor embodying some unchanged essential beliefs that instigate believers to act. They are moved by an early belief of unity of religion and politics where it serves as an attempt to redeem forgotten identity and escape from post-modernity identity.

In a historical perspective, one will come across altogether different understanding of this phenomenon. One of the renowned Arab thinkers, Azmi Bishare, traces the evolution of political thinking in Islam in relation to politics and social changes occurring in Muslim countries over the past few centuries. There is specificity to socio-historical context in the gradual evolution of political Islam. There are a number of scholars who have applied a historical–anthropological perspective to understand the political role of Islam. The Islamist movement constituted a political force shaped by the socioeconomic and political contexts in which they operate. In this condition, Islam is taken as a discursive tradition where meaning and actions are related to material condition such as institutional relation and actor's position of power. All phenomena of political Islam are related to the historical situation of the actors, the discourse and the frame of reference. Political Islam is the process of Islamization of the social arena and the appropriation of the public sphere. The Islamic movement here should be placed in a socio-historical conjecture and understood by examining how it has reshaped by sociopolitical resetting in the recent past.

In the case of Islamism, history is used to establish the truth, and most of the symbols of the past are presented as analogues

---

[93] Ismail. 'Islamism, Re-Islamisation and Fashioning of Muslim Selves'.

of the previous symbols. Islamic history is shown to be an epoch full of constant strain and tension. The dominant sense of the continuity of the history and the tradition plays an important role in shaping the ideological content of political Islam. Colonial rupture or interruption is taken to be a short phase intervention in the incessant Islamic history where colonial raid was a short-lived experience. Historical continuity constructs as seminal space for authenticity and truth of Islam.[94]

The continuity is a dynamic process of power and resistance involved in the production of practices and ideas labelled as Islamic. Furthermore, the claims to orthodoxy embody the power to authorize practices and ideas as Islamic under discursive tradition. Political Islam is about historical situatedness of Islam and the Muslims and Islamism are geared to a political field and developed within the infrastructure of actions.

Meanwhile, the horizontal dominance of the ideology of Islamism has been seen by many as the continuity of the history where religion and belief have not been taken as trans-historical entities but as entities grounded in historical and material terms. The belief in God in the 7th century and the 20th century has to be understood in material context that is well impacted by other fields of social life. What John Esposito has observed is that present political Islam reflects nothing but the pattern set in the earlier historical period. The continuity of Islamic history provides a basic framework for understanding the Islamist movement where Islamism involves the creation of new and affective forms of continuing the vitality of the message.

In the light of the above narration and its context, the materialization of political Islam can be remotely attributed to the nature of historical relationship between the West and Islam. The designation of the West as 'other' can be found in the act of crusades, the proselytizing mission of the Christian West, the orientalist, the Westernizers, secularist, communist and zionist, too. All these actors are seen in alliance with the crusaders and proselytizers, if not in virtual synonymy with the West. Political Islam can be referred to as a wave against the intrusion and

---

[94] Ismail, *Rethinking Islamist Politics*, 42.

reaction against Christianity brought in at some critical historical juncture in the name of political reforms and secularism.

There are other theoretical frameworks too that have been offered by the experts of international relations and Islamic political thinkers to revisit the pedigree and ancestry of Islamism. The binary position of authenticity and inauthenticity between the East and the West is held by many to be one of the philosophical underpinnings of Islamism. While scrutinizing the issue of authenticity and inauthenticity, one will observe that the generic of political Islam emanates from both claimed and acclaimed truths that Islam enjoys a distinctive identity of its own. The identity of its own is completely divorced from the other religious tradition. The generic Islam is constructed in a relationship of anonymity with the tradition of Christianity and Judaism. Islam is presented as a complete message while the religion of the West is taken to be only a belief system. Historical continuity constructs a seminal space for authenticity and truth. This exclusive paradigm for Muslim identity originates from the belief that it is through Islam that one can attain the key to soteriological success. This popularization of exclusive parading has spurred this belief in cultural and religious superiority of the Muslims.[95]

The authentic historical meaning of Islam can be unveiled only through phenomenological hermeneutics. This phenomenological hermeneutics differentiates the authentic from the unauthentic highlighting the difference between the authenticity of al-Turath (Islamic heritage) and inauthenticity of present decadent and inertia.[96] The concept of authenticity is predicated on the notion of a historical subject which is self-sufficient and self-evident. Arab, Muslims and other *Assalah* become a central notion in a romantic conception of history. Believers in political Islam romanticize the Islamic past and that past must be understood as the real and final truth. This actualized experience of Islamic intellectual heritage must form the bedrock of Muslim selfhood.

---

[95] Mohammad Hassan Khalil, *Islam and the Fate of Others: The Salvation Question* (New York: Oxford University Press, 2012), 134.

[96] Discourse, Modernity and al-Turath. Between Context and Contextualization, 24.

Explaining the question of Islamic authenticity, Binder Leonard claims that authenticity is the life choice that the preferred element of tradition demands under the present circumstances in order to be affirmed as real and appropriated as an aspect of being Muslims.[97] The reluctance of the Muslims to accept the in authenticity of present has been an obstacle in the integration of Western modernity into Eastern authenticity based on intellectual heritage. There is an urge to re-read history, polity and culture in the Arab world, and there is a demand for synthesis between Islamic philosophy and political ideology of modern times in order to construct a rational and authentic method to define the Islamic heritage. Past gives a sense of identity and guidance in the present and the future.

Arab is reluctant to accept the inauthentic present and to allude to the teaching of the Turath, which is authentic and Islamic. A dichotomy seems to exist between modernity and the Turath. The Turath has been regarded as a shield against the invasion.[98] It is a cluster of cultural, social, literary and people's practices.[99] Turath and authenticity can be seen in a close relationship, protection of which is a desire for national autonomy and cultural dignity. What political Islam believes is that Western modernity cannot scrutinize the Arab reality due to different historical conditions of both Europe and Islamic past.

To enforce its belief in the Islamic authenticity, Islamism stands for the rejection of all Western and modern thoughts as inauthentic and completely divorced from Islamic epistemology. For instance, Iqbal, one of the greatest Asian poet–philosopher of the 20th century, saw the West as the centre and divided the East and the West under two contending camps where the East is the world of *mann* (heart) and the West is the world *of tan* (body). The main driving force of the West is the intellect. Iqbal finds an inherent brutality in the Western power based on

---

[97] Binder Leonard, *Islamic Liberalism: A Critique of Development Ideologies* (Chicago, IL: University of Chicago Press, 1988), 294–95.

[98] Discourse, Modernity and al-Turath Between Context and Contextualization, 28.

[99] Ibrahim Abu Rubi, *Intellectual Origin of Islamic Resurgence in the Modern Arab World* (Albany: State University of New York Press), 41.

the culture of subjugation and annihilation and its knowledge paradigm too was full of perversion and misrepresentation. He finds no truth and authenticity in the Western claim of civilizing mission in the East but, for him, it is not more than a physical implementation orientalist design.[100] His criticism of Western democracy, its associated philosophies and the Marxism can be well understood under the rubric of contestation between authenticity and inauthenticity when he deciphers the dark aspects of Western democracy in the garb of capitalism and the lack of religious spirit. Iqbal is completely ambivalent of Western democracy because it has failed to eliminate class and has normalized the elite privilege in the name of the people; tossing God out of history, for Iqbal, is completely inconsistent with Islamic philosophy.[101]

Philosopher Iqbal, a product of the colonial system, observed the West very differently from his earlier predecessors. He did not critique the West merely in terms of the geographical position, but his critique of the West hails from within the Western philosophies of self-representation and Western liberal democracy's promotion of class hierarchies and lopsided wealth distribution is exposed. Iqbal viewed that a modern system must offer the best of all other systems and to him Islam is a true system. The natives are not just fighting for or appealing for inclusion in the colonial system but offering their own philosophical and political system as a solution to the problems of the colonial masters.[102]

The question of cultural and traditional authenticity was always vital for the colonized Muslim. The question of authentic native under the layer of Western influence formed an instrumental entity for the promotion of Islamism. It was the question of authenticity that struck the most when the Arab identity shifted under the external influence, and in counter, Arab was being defined in terms of nationalism and Islamism. The

---

[100] Masood A. Raja, 'Muhammad Iqbal: Islam, the West, and the Quest for a Modern Muslim Identity', International *Journal of the Asian Philosophical Association* 1, no. 1 (2008), 37–47.

[101] Raja, 'Muhammad Iqbal'.

[102] Raja, 'Muhammad Iqbal'.

question of authenticity and inauthenticity further deepened the question of identity when colonized Muslims were grappling with the set of political and cultural identical questions amongst the Arabs, what Robinson has summarized as follows: 'The increasing ease with which Muslims were able to travel to be with Muslims in other lands; they need to find a sense of identity as they grapple with the meaning of modern state in colonial form.'[103]

Islamists assess authenticity on the basis of originality of knowledge derived from the Quran and the Hadith, and the question of originality of knowledge directly leads to the question of epistemology. In the debate on authenticity and inauthenticity, Ulema are the decisive component and have their own interior say. Here, religion is taken as a universal category and an agent of historical formation. It looks towards history in a dialectical framework and its evolution is between us and them.[104] The believers in the concept of authenticity call for the Islamization of culture and identity and the purification of Islamic text as a whole. Political Islam stood against the colonial project of eradicating the internal and embracing the external.

Traditional character of Islam is rooted in style of authenticating the statement attributed to the Prophet or his conduct. In terms of cultural authenticity and the religious authority, cultural authenticity of the West in the form of socialism, liberalism and nationalism seems to be a failing one and there seems to be no concordance between Islam and the West. The Islamists are typically a product of modern and secular education and are committed to alter the contour of their societies and the states through the public implementation of norms they take as truly Islamic and authentic. For them, the canonical Islamic text is the only authentic source, and as an extension, Middle East roots the modern understanding of the state, nation and politics in

---

[103] Francis Robinson, 'Technology and Religious Change: Islam and the Impact of Print', *Modern Asian Studies* 27, no. 1 (1993), 229–51.
[104] Jan, *The Metacolonial State.*

those ancient texts and considers them only authentic, essential and eternal.[105]

Islamic resurgence is an expression of desire for authentic modernization as opposed to Westernization.[106] A famous Arab sociologist, Aziz Al-Azmeh, sees the rise of political Islam as an expression of self-explanatory, self-sufficient and utterly sui generis nature and reality whose vicissitudes are internally propelled by the community in its successive generation responding to their vision under different external circumstances.[107] The linking of secularism with democracy excludes the discursive space of Islam from the discursive realm of democracy which may be defined as inauthentic.

There are scholars who discover Islamism to be an outcome of binary dynamics between shariah and the Western penal code. Shariah has remained the most catalytic issue for the adherent of Islamism and it constitutes a common strand binding the Islamic forces across the spectrum. Restoration and reintroduction of shariah in day-to-day's domain of Muslim is the long-standing goal of Islamic movements. It has been a common missionary zeal of variant Islamic groups operating in different political and geographical entities. Shariah has remained the core essence of Islamic civilization, hallmark of social and moral lives and a key component in the fabric of Islamic thoughts. The entire social and behavioural code of Muslim emanates from the edict of shariah, and to quote Nathan Brown and others who argue that in much of the Islamic history, shariah is better understood not as a code in the modern sense of the term but as an ongoing discursive tradition articulated in and through practices associated with the educational and judicial institutions.[108]

Most of the Muslims believe that shariah is God's law and it is taken as a reflection of God's will for humankind and therefore must be in its purest sense, perfect and unchanging.[109] The modernists, traditionalists and fundamentalists all hold different

---

[105] Al-Barghouti, *The Umma and the Dawala*, 7.

[106] Voll, *Makers of Contemporary Islam*, 332.

[107] Aziz Al-Azmeh, 'The Articulation of Orientalism', *The Arab studies Quarterly* 39, no. 4 (1981): 384–402.

[108] Zaman, *The Ulema in Contemporary Islam*, 97.

[109] Quran. 48–23.

views of shariah as do the adherents of different schools of Islam. For instance, Salafists take the saying and action of the first three generations of Muslims as part of shariah in contrast to the established meaning of shariah which merely confined it to the deed and statements of Prophet.[110]

The political and cultural hub of the Muslim power in the 19th century was the Ottoman Empire, the seat of the caliphates where the royal laws could not contradict basic principles of shariah. Ulema were designated to see the Sultan's legislation, administration and justice agreed with shariah. Legal and administrative reforms in the second and third quarters of the 19th century marked the retreat on legal, institutional and constitutional fronts, and this was the arrival of the first West-inspired legal norms in the Middle East. The Muslim world had a novel experience of being dealt with the French-inspired commercial laws, penal laws and codified version of Islamic laws.

Furthermore, within the Ottoman Empire, an Italy-inspired *Majallah* system was introduced which was a collection of civic codes. Tanzimat created a binary legal system: one derived from shariah and the other inspired by Western legal norms. Egypt witnessed the same things, where most of its Islamic laws were put on the path of secularization and Islam as an institutional and political force succumbed to the Western colonial force. The incursion of European imperialist forces paved the way for the unseating of Islamic shariah and the imposition of a new and bizarre set of Western laws.

Before colonization and encounter with the Western world, Muslims at large were characterized by the predominant role of Islam and local systems. Muslims were always of the firm belief that the real ruler and the lawgiver was Allah and that shariah was the laws of the land. Several schools of jurisprudence regarded Islamic laws as immutable and at most can be amended but no new legislation can be introduced.[111] Islam by asserting its Islamic identity, heritage and its religious legal past

---

[110] John L. Esposito, *The Future of Islam* (New York City: Oxford University Press, 2010), 74–77.

[111] Mat, 'The Impact of Western Colonization and Secularism'.

intend to rescue that edict of shariatic rules that always regulates a man's life which has an ontological span from the very private to the very public. The Islamists prescribe everything implicitly or explicitly from conducting personal hygiene and sexual activity to risking one's life in service of God to political leadership, conducting business, polygamy and gender relationship.[112]

However, the infringement of modern regulatory and disciplinary systems was introduced in the Muslim world in the backdrop of colonialism that forced a comprehensive alteration in the existing law system paving the way for Western-type codification in many areas of the law. The introduction of foreign laws in the Muslim world occurred at different stages and in different circumstances, and its reception varied from colonial imposition to voluntary adoption of a foreign civil code. European ideas and institutions posed intellectual challenges to the Muslim world notwithstanding the dominant religious underpinning in Islamic societies that brought gradual and substantial changes in the politico language of Muslim societies.

Western legal reform was introduced in an otherwise different cultural and religious environment and the process was somewhat disillusioning. Colonization and its impact on the existing shariah undermined the Islamicity of Muslims leading to a legal pluralism in which different forms of legal models emerged. The colonial gradual incursion had reduced the scope of application of Islamic shariah where it has remained confined to personal issues and the rest is governed under Western laws. Colonial models of laws caused a constant clash between state ideology and law on the one hand and Islamic ethics and religious norms on the other hand. Now, the people were the real source of the authority, and external reference to the authority was no more required. Governance had shifted from enforcing God's laws to developing public interest.[113] Islamist's notion of justice, freedom and the individual differs significantly from the dominant in the contemporary liberal discourse.[114]

---

[112] Kolig, *Conservative Islam*, 50.
[113] Mat, 'The Impact of Western Colonization and Secularism'.
[114] Iqtidar, *Secularizing Islamist*, 161.

With the emergence of a new Western code, Islamic laws or shariah put to test the name of democracy, women rights, human rights, relations with the minority, homosexuality, women freedom, freedom of speech and emancipation of slavery.

Gradually, shariah lost its authority in the governance of the state and its role retreated to the personal laws of the Muslims. This upside down in the Islamic code led to the rise of reformist, secularist, traditionalist and fundamentalist, and these strands of fundamentalists are at the forefront of preaching the restoration of shariah.

The basic difference in shariah and the modern system of laws is the yardstick according to which unlawful or immoral character of certain acts is measured based on public interest and the morals of the community, while in shariah, the yardstick is the revealed words of God and where religion, law and ethics all are one.[115] Political life under shariah contrasts with political life in the West; with its heritage of universal laws embedded within human person, natural laws are directly written on human heart.[116] A universal natural law tells who we are and alters the boundary of what not to do, while shariah tells what to do.

As we understand, modernity as opposed to medievalism is based on the assumption of primacy of reason. Modernity in relation to shariah aims at adopting shariah to modern condition by renovating its parts that are seen as being out of touch with modernity.[117] But here Islam and shariah should not be taken as passive recipients of modernity and one should also not overrate the impact of modernity on shariah as observed by Fazlur Rahman.[118]

Here, political Islam is seen as a cultural cornerstone to reclaim something of past glories for the world of Islam and is also an attempt to fill the moral vacuum by the reintroduction of shariah.[119] In the West, sovereignty resides only in the

---

[115] Mat, 'The Impact of Western Colonization and Secularism'.

[116] Beaulieu, *Beyond Secularism and Jihad*, 163.

[117] Mohammad Hashim Kamali, 'Shariah and the Challenge of Modernity', *Journal IKIM* 2, no. 1 (January–June 1994), 1–27.

[118] Fazlur Rahman, 'The Impact of Modernity on Islam', *Islamic Studies* 5, no. 2 (1966): 112–28.

[119] Beaulieu, *Beyond Secularism and Jihad*, 173.

body politics and ultimately in the free and responsible human person of which state is an instrument, but under Islam, God is the only sovereign.

In the light of the above-mentioned brief juridical history of Muslim land, political Islam can be defined as a movement to restore the primacy of shariah. Every political Islamic movement craves to re-enforce the role of Quranic laws as shariah occupies the central place in its discourse. Shariah drives Muslims towards reuniting the religion and politics, and according to Esposito, on the issue of shariah, there is no question of the context as for him all contexts elicit some type of responses.[120]

The campaign for the primacy of shariah must be seen as an instrument of use of values to confer authority and power to those in possession of shariah Hence the power is enabled by another set of power to issue fatwa and eventually Political Islam becomes an instrument to Islamize the state through judicial reform.

The whole act of juridical reform and reduction in the application of shariah after colonial encounter with the Muslim world is linked to a great degree to the notion of separation of law between private and public. This separation does not correspond to the ideological underpinning of Islamism. Islamists have always insisted on the internal cohesion of religious practices and its appropriateness to tackle the challenges of modern times and further have expressed their dislike for binary attitude in the application of shariah. To them, public and private cannot be separated as easily as it has been suggested.[121] In the words of Safran:

> As long as power had actually confined itself to its own sphere, its legitimation regardless of how it was achieved was plausible, since it still permitted society to live according to the Shariah. But as power began to shift... it became clear that to legitimize such power would be to turn the Shariah into an instrument of the state... a new interpretation of the principles of legitimation of power was urgently needed.[122]

---

[120] Ismail, *Rethinking Islamist Politics*, 7.

[121] Iqtidar, *Secularizing Islamist*, 157.

[122] Navad Safran, *Egypt in Search of Political Community: An Analysis of the Intellectual and Political Evolution of Egypt, 1804–1952* (Boston: Harvard University Press, 1981), 40–41.

It is further stressed by Smith that shariah, however important it may have been, in fact, was not basic or central or emphasized as a concept in Islamic thought in the early centuries.[123]

Thus, political Islam can be seen as an indicative of Islamic resilience to the imposition and assertion of its own values.[124] Shariah has always shown a remarkable resistance to the Western modernity not only during the colonial period but ever since. According to Mahmassani, there has been a series of legal reforms in the Arab world, and there has been partial or complete borrowing from the Western legal too, but only in cases when there was no contradiction with Islamic shariah.[125]

While the believer in political Islam considers shariah as a total discourse, it is a set of institutions and practices that pervaded and shaped the varied aspects of people's life in pre-modern Muslim society.[126] Islam regards law (shariah) as a tool and instrument for the establishment of justice in society, a means for man's intellectual and moral reform and his purification.[127] According to Esposito, it is this commitment to shariah and the model of an early community that motivates Muslims in a variety of contexts, to engage in a restorative or corrective active through political Islam.[128] It is assumed that shariah contained all answers to contemporary problems and its following would eliminate necessity of the politics.[129]

The fact of rising Islamism can also be defined and explained by alluding to the religious proximity between Islam and Islamism. In the religious term, political Islam is the political reading of the Quran and the reduction of divine revelation to

---

[123] W.C. Smith, *An Understanding Islam: Selected Studies* (New York: Mouton Publishers, 1981), 95.

[124] Kamali, 'Shariah and the Challenge of Modernity', pp. 1–27.

[125] Subhi Mahmasssani, *Muqaddimag Filhaya Uloom al Shariah* [An Introduction to Revivalism of Knowledge and the Islamic Law] (Beirut: Daral Ilm Lil Malayin, 1962), 142.

[126] Zaman, *The Ulema in Contemporary Islam*, 6.

[127] Hamid Algar, ed. and trans, *Islam and Revolution*, Writings and Declarations of Imam Khomeini (Berkeley, CA: Mizan Press, 1981), 80.

[128] John L. Esposito, *Islam and Politics* (New York: Syracuse University Press, 1987), 31.

[129] Meijer, 'Towards Political Islam'.

a political document. Religiosity and devoutness of political Islam emanate from a literal belief in the political underpinning of the Quran exhorting to put the religious text to their social and political lives where it is claimed a handbook of political conduct and social life. John L. Esposito, a renowned Islamic scholar, not denying the sociopolitical context of political Islam emphasizes the ideas of a totality called Islam and its conviction in the unity of religion and politics and what he calls it — an Islamic imperative.[130]

Centring the religion at the forefront of political Islam and tracing the rise of political Islam to the generic of Islam, Esposito observes that a totality called Islam explains the basic core of Islamism. Belief in the unit of religion and politics that is the Islamic imperative functions as the basic belief that motivates Muslims with regard to state and government and guides their assessment of whether or not their government is monitored by God.[131] Islamism favours the politicized reading of the religion that distinguishes them from the traditionalists. Islamist engagement with the politics serves as the primary means of defining their relationship to Allah. Islamists' exclusive focus on the politics combined with the emphasis on the unmediated and individualized reading of the Quran and the Hadith text is in contrast to the traditionalist emphasis on personal piety through the act of prescribed worship and mediated access through Ulema.[132]

This obsession of Islamists with the politicization of religion gives enough scope to Taqi Uthmani of Pakistan for critiquing the instance of making politics instead a part of religion; they have made the religion itself a political entity. He further argued that in their zeal to refute secularism, some writers and the thinkers of the present age have gone so far as to characterize politic and the government as the true objective of Islam.[133] Islamists have focused on the political domain as the key areas

---

[130] Esposito, *Islam and Politics*, 4.
[131] Esposito, *Islam and Politics*, 4.
[132] Iqtidar, *Secularizing Islamist*, 111.
[133] Iqtidar, *Secularizing Islamist*, 111.

of worship, but they have also subjected religious practices to a certain rationalizing.

Modern Islamists' belief is that 'Islam as a body of faith has something important to say about how politics and society should be ordered in the contemporary Muslim world'.[134] Politically, Islamism can be defined as an instrumentalization of Islam by individuals, groups and organizations that pursue political objectives. The manifestation of political Islam today is to comprehend that it is a political and religious ideology. Its goal is primarily not theological but a revolutionary change compelled by the vision of an ideal society.[135]

It provides political response to today's societal challenges by imagining a future, the foundation of which rests on reappropriated, reinvented concepts borrowed from the Islamic tradition.[136] Politics lies at the heart of Islamism, which ultimately has far more to do with power than with religion. To Islamists, Islam is more a political blueprint than a faith, and the Islamist discourse is to a large extent a political discourse in religious garb.[137] They believe, in particular, that political action is essential to the transformation of society into a truly Islamic one. The purpose of political Islam has been to maintain Islamic principles and to implement them in the history. According to Albert Hourani, the Arab attitude to every aspect of Western civilization will be largely determined by the political treatment they receive from the Western power.[138]

Here, the sociology of knowledge, in Durkheim's term, would be relevant to show how religions mirror the way society should be structured. Durkheim has suggested in one of his theories of religions how individuals and groups resurrect the past in understanding the present religious life or lack thereof. In other words of Durkheim:

---

[134] Mohammed Ayoob, 'Political Islam: Image and Reality', *World Policy Journal* 21, no. 3 (2004): 11.

[135] Rubin, *Political Islam*, 2.

[136] Denoeux, 'The forgotten Swamp', 56–81.

[137] Denoeux, 'The Forgotten Swamp'.

[138] Jermy Salt, *The Unmaking of the Middle East: A History of Western Disorder in Arab World* (London: University of California Press, 2008), 134.

There is something eternal in religion which is destined to survive all the particular symbols in which religious thought has successively enveloped itself. There can be no society which does not feel the need of upholding and reaffirming at regular intervals the collective sentiments and the collective ideas which make its unity and its personality.... In a word, the old gods are growing old or already dead, and others are not yet born.[139]

What Mr Barghouti argues is that the monotheistic message of Islam has for itself a political content and that belief in only one God entails oneself to one law; therefore, subjecting the whole people and several tribes to one worldly authority that represents law and the very testimony itself leads to the acceptance of the political authority of Islam.[140]

What Mohammad Abduh says to stress the same is, 'If the spirit of the religion is not strengthen[ed] among Egyptians and if religion is weakened[,] these moral qualities will also collapse. Religion is the basis on which moral conduct has been built. Moral conduct will disappear when religion collapses'.[141]

The idea of political Islam emanates from the belief that religion provides a world view for both individual and corporate lives and this shared view translated into a public commitment to sharia being shared in the primary principle. In a pure religious term, Muslims at large by opting for political Islam are abiding by Islamic religious imperative of uniting religion and politics. Further, it is an expression of mood of discontent towards the condition of religious and moral decay. This is a question of idealism, and as long as the full religiosity is established, Muslims will continue to agitate and engage in reform actions.

The same observation was made by J.O. Voll when he saw the current resurgence as a continuation of the basic theme, even though these themes expressed in a different way. For him,

---

[139] E. Durkheim, *On Morality and Society* (Heritage of Sociology Series, Chicago: University of Chicago Press, 1973), 201.

[140] Al-Barghouti, *The Umma and the Dawala*, 12–13.

[141] M. Abduh, 'Theology of Unity', in *Intellectual Traditions of Islam*, ed. F. Daftary (London: I.B. Tauris in association with The Institute of Ismaili Studies, 2000), 67.

religion plays the guiding role and past guides the present.[142] The exercise of political Islam involves the instrumentalization of the language of religion in the public space where religiosity feels incorporated into political engagement. Unlike modernity, the Islamic norm needs no rational justification in terms of Western liberal thoughts; the sole rationale for their implementation is that they express the will of God.[143]

In recent years, the spurt of Islamism in the Arab world is being also viewed as an outcome of constant hegemonic policy of Western powers vis-à-vis the Arab nations. There are multiple factors that help explain why political Islam is especially prone to taking anti-West position in modern-day. There are abundant signs of Western cultural, intellectual, financial, military and economic hegemony. It cannot be denied that the hegemonic design hides a plethora of Western influences in the Arab world and acts as a force for the adoption of Western ways, values and cognition.[144] One may see that the primary target of the 1970s generation of Islamists was the 'infidel ruler' who was condemned and denounced for having sold out completely to the West and for toeing the Western dictate in both internal and external affairs. The complex interplay among these variables tends to strengthen the anti-hegemonic strand in Islamist political activities as well as adds to its standing and popularity among diverse Muslim populations.

The extent of American hegemonic instance towards the Muslim world in general and the Middle East in particular can be gauged from the pronouncement of former US Secretary of State Condoleezza Rice when she justified the Israeli attack on Lebanon terming it as the teething problem for the creation of a new Middle East.[145] The United States deployment of half a million American soldiers to Saudi Arabia—the home of Islam's two holiest sites—following the Iraqi invasion of Kuwait in 1990

---

[142] Voll, *Makers of Contemporary Islam*, 4.
[143] Zaman, *The Ulema in Contemporary Islam*, 8.
[144] Kolig, *Conservative Islam*, 34.
[145] Ahmad, 'Islam, Islamism and the West'.

presented Al-Qaeda with an opportunity to rally Arabs and Muslims against the new crusaders and their regional clients.[146]
Smith aptly described it saying:

'The British army in the Canal Zone was resented by the Egyptians not only as a remnant of foreign domination (though we must never get too far away from the realization of that crushing power), not only because it reminded them of their own decline. It was rejected also because it symbolized the dilemma of their souls.[147]

Political Islam can be taken as a reaction to hegemonic discourse imposed by Western modern epistemology echoing complete negation of Islamic source of knowledge. Here, this is an intellectual contestation against other intellectual traditions.

There are several acts that explain anti-hegemonic position of political Islam, like historical antecedents of Islamists which Smith described as follows:

The nature of regimes in the region and its past and present alliance with western power further enhance and deepens the anti-hegemonic instances of political Islam. Anti-hegemonic is not merely reflective of historical memories of past European domination but also current distribution of power in international system in form of constant US support for Israel and its invasion of Iraq in the name of WMD.[148]

The current distribution of power is a unipolar concert and is heavily skewed in favour of the industrialized West led by the United States leading to the emergence of a dialectical relationship between hegemony and resistance. Political Islam of today embodies the ideas of resistance to hegemony for more than any other ideology in the Muslim world and even beyond. It is an expression of anger against joint muscle power of the concert

---

[146] Marwan Bishara, *The Invisible Arab: The Promise and the Peril of Arab Revolution* (New York: Nation Book, 2012), 200.

[147] Smith, *Islam in Modern History*, 111.

[148] Smith, *Islam in Modern History*, 115.

consisting of America and Europe.[149] Europe and the Arab world are from Venice and America is from Mars and no amount of concentration of the Europe–United States divide can distract them from acting hegemonic vis-à-vis the Arab world.

The unabated support of the United States to the government of Israel is another factor chanting the anti-hegemonic trend of political Islam and adds to the popularity of Islamist forces. This act on the part of the United States demonstrates to politically conscious Muslims that the United States is committed to treating the Muslims and Arabs not only with insensitivity but with utter contempt. The American policy of vetoing or threatening to veto UN Security Council resolutions condemning Israeli policies provides proof beyond doubt to most Muslims of American–Israeli collusion to dominate the Muslim Middle East politically and militarily.

The singling out of Americans and Israelis for special attentions demonstrates that political Islam is less anchored in absolutism of pure faith than in the geopolitics of hatred.[150] The demise of Russia gave free reign to unipolar concert in terms of ideological supremacy and subsequently Islamism emerged as a forceful ideology to mobilize resistance in South.

Remarkably, a large number of Islamists hail from the Western education system, and they have also borne the brunt of European domination in their respective nations. The Islamists are well acquainted with day-to-day behaviour of interventionist powers and experience a complete disjuncture between words and deeds. The existing power structure is so asymmetrical that it forces one hegemon to be more hegemonic as the images of many countless civilians getting killed by the Americans and the Israelis on screens makes them jittery.

The Western media along with the establishments do not deem their own killing of civilians as terrorism, or even remotely comparable to what their own people had suffered in the past.

---

[149] Mohammad Ayoob, *The United States and Political Islam: The Dialectic of Hegemony and Resistance*, National University of Singapore, Insight, 3 July 2009. http://theamericanmuslim.org/tam.php/features/articles/the_united_states_and_political_islam_the_dialectic_of_hegemony_and_resista (Accessed on 25 June 2013).

[150] Shashi Tharoor, *Pax Indica* (New Delhi: Penguin, 2012), 30.

To defy this lopsided behaviour, they resort to several responses and Islamism appears to be one of the choices for them. Islamism provides a sense of emancipation and empowerment in the face of continuous historical submission to the Western hegemony.[151] The hegemony of the Western discourse and their fixation and promotion of two-facedness democracy has been contested but remains unchallenged on the part of the Arab regimes in order to provide explanation and make an excuse for its state of political backwardness.[152]

Renowned French sociologist Burgat pointed out that 'good culture' usually refers to people who agree with the West and for him it is symbolic of cultural hegemony and this is the worst thing that can happen to all. He calls the Westerners to give up the notion that the West only owns the universal belief. The West should abandon the notion that Western culture is the norm and there is open space for others to share their perspectives.[153]

The phenomenon of physical hegemony cannot be attributed alone to augmenting space for Islamism but equally potent is hegemonic intellectual campaign of the Christian priests and popes in line with orientalists' conventional behaviours which brushed the Muslim history and their religious icons in a very odious manner. Pope Benedict XVI raised the question of violence in Islam. He referred to the Byzantine Empire collapsing under the onslaught of Ottoman Turks. He placed violence near the core of Islam, insinuating that it was an integral belief of this system.[154]

Given the augmenting complexities of Islamism, the adoption of an alternative interdisciplinary approach to the study of Islam and its Islamic ingredients has become the norms among the academia. There are sociological approaches and analyses towards political Islam which stand in contrast to the essentialist views of John Obert Voll with regard to Islamism. This approach

---

[151] Sarah Rendtorff Smith, 'Democracy as the Conceptual Battlefield of East–West Encounters: A Destruction of the Incompatibility Claim and Islamist Discourse of Democracy', *Journal of Political Enquiry*, no. 2 (Spring, 2009), 1–12.

[152] Smith, 'Democracy as the Conceptual Battlefield'.

[153] 'Fletcher Features'.

[154] Kolig, *Conservative Islam*, 319.

is inspired by Durkheim's views of social changes which offer a political explanation of Islamism. The social reality of the Islamist action involves interrogation of the background and socio-psychological profile of the group in terms of age, education, social transformation, industrialization and urbanization.[155] To interrogate the sociological aspect of political Islamism, the tools of frustrated aspirations, uprootedness, disenchantment and disintegration, impersonal relation in urban setting, weakness of adjustment and absence of integrative mechanism are deployed. Under this analysis, Islamists seek refuge under Islam to sooth the alienation emanating from the deprivation.[156] In the same way, it can be seen as a counter-ideology appealing to the disadvantaged social group and in reaction to the bankruptcy of secular ideology.[157] Sociological explanation of political Islam can be found in the new International Monetary Fund (IMF)-dictated economic policies of the Third-world states. States' retreatment from welfare scheme and the new fiscal policy of the West Asia and North Africa (WANA) region have provided ample space with its better social and other humanitarian services to carve a political base for itself. One lacuna in aspect of sociological explanation of Islamism is that it ignores the cultural facet of Islam, merely focuses on structural and institutional conditions, and accords no primacy to culture in interpreting political Islam.

There is a political economic approach to the study of political Islam too. The proponent of these views envisages the nature of the social strata where the Islamist ideology tends to fascinate more to those believers who reject other ideologies as false notions. Islamists seek refuge under Islam to sooth the aberrations emanating from deprivation.

The political and economic condition as represented by the environment causes a major spurt in the rise of Islamic activism. Islamism developed as a counter-ideology appealing to the disadvantaged social groups and arose in reaction to the bankruptcy of the social justice system. According to Anderson,

---

[155] Islam, *Rethinking Islamist Politics*, 11.
[156] Islam, *Rethinking Islamist Politics*, 2.
[157] Islam, *Rethinking Islamist Politics*, 13.

'Political Islam is the product of environment created by the government and is a part of wider setting where political Islam operates.'[158] While theorizing the modern phenomena of political Islam, one needs to distinguish the general socio-economic process and the specific historical condition. Islamism is conditioned by a particular micro setting and a specific process tied up with the changing local conditions. In most of the Arab countries, national economy articulated with the international economy.

There are other set of scholars like Ernest Gellner who look into the present phenomenon through a complete different perspective. Gellner sees Islamism as a product of higher Islam of urban and metropolitan setting that resembles protestant ethics and morality. For him, Islamists are the rational fundamentalists whose zeal is unattenuated by modernization. It is the victory of higher Islam over lower Islam of rural area that causes the rise of Islamism or political Islam.

Apart from the above-mentioned approach to study Islamism, there are other metaphysical claims on the part of Islamists who preach mutability for the sake of stability in antagonism to the West which is in the process of constant change and progress. The notion of change seems to be a major point of contestation between Western and Islamic metaphysics causing a rift between these two.

Western progress is laden with moral and ethical negativism, and their change is absolute transgressing norms and order of the universe. Change in the West is defining the character of values and ethics. However, the change within Islam is always inwardly and remains limited to the confines of fundamental teachings of Islam. Mohammad Abduh was always apprehensive of growing peril in strands of Western metaphysical doctrine undermining certain levels of faith necessary for the moralist foundation of the society.[159]

---

[158] Lisa Anderson, 'Fulfilling Prophesies: State Policy and Islamic Radicalism', in *Political Islam: Revolution, Radicalism or Reform*, ed. John L. Esposito (Boulder, CO: Lynne Reinner, 1997), 17–31.

[159] Albert Hourani, *Arab Thought in the Liberal Age 1798–1939* (London: Cambridge University Press, 1976), 138–44.

Genealogy of Political Islam

Islamic activism in the form we know today is a not-so-old modern phenomenon. Political Islamism attempts to classify other Western ideologies as a machination to oppress and subjugate the Muslim world. Islamism is as much a creation of modernity as it is a reaction and extension of it. In the thousand years of Muslim history before the advent of European colonial power, it was a rarity that Islam was used as a political tool to challenge temporal authority when Muslims ruled over Muslims.[160] In the words of Smith himself, 'Shariah, however important it may have been in fact, was not a basic or central emphasised as a concept in Islamic thought in the early centuries.'[161]

The defence of the political order was based on an unwritten compact between the state and Ulema where the political quietism of the latter acted as a quid pro quo for minimal interference in the religious sphere by the former.[162]

The growing intensity and enhancing extent of the interface between the West and the Muslim world led to a significant reconfiguration of the power dynamics. Since then, multifaceted dialogues have shaped the important trajectories in the present contexts. Historically, mainstream Islam has remained at least for the last 500 years in case of Iran and 1,000 years in case of the Arab relatively apolitical. Traditionalist Islam might have governed the social behaviour and given legitimacy to the erstwhile government in many cases, but essentially, it was far removed from political governance.[163]

Ulema were generally politically quietist as long as temporal rulers met the minimum standards of successfully defending the lands of Islam and non-interference in the practice of religion

---

[160] L.C. Brown, *Religion and State: The Muslim Approach to Politics* (New York: Columbia University Press, 2001), 5.

[161] W.C. Smith. *An Understanding of Islam: Selected Studies* (New York: Mouton Publishers, 1981), 95.

[162] Mohammad Ayoob, *The Many Faces of Political Islam* (Singapore: Institute of Defence and Strategic Studies, series no. 119, 29 December 2006), http://www.rsis.edu.sg/publications/WorkingPapers/WP119.pdf (Accessed on 28 July 2010).

[163] Rubin, *Political* Islam, 2.

by their subjects. The state was minimalist in character and largely left civil society alone as long as subjects paid their taxes and did not threaten rebellion. There was basically a policy of 'live and let live' between temporal and religious authorities. Political mobilization at the popular level, which was inherent in the message that the Prophet preached during his lifetime, became very much the exception under the dynastic rule.

European colonialism drastically changed the nature of political authority in the Muslim world by putting the non-Muslims in control of Muslim lands either directly or indirectly. Simultaneously, increasing mass literacy and the introduction of the printing press provided scholars and activists with instruments challenging the religious authority of Ulema. This led to a proto-reformation that introduced scriptural literalism and the priesthood of the individual—essential components of the Reformation in Europe—into the Islamic world.

Marshall Hodgson claims that no rupture is greater in the history of Islam than the one brought about by the impact of Western modernity. Modern Western societies managed to retain a much deeper, more coherent and more integral relationship with their tradition than Muslim societies had.[164] It does not mean that there is no rupture in the Western thought but their thought is less severe in comparison to that of Muslims. The West now may reside and inform imaginaries around the world but draws its strength from a particular kind of universalism.

The 'ideal' image of Islam began to be transformed with the advent of colonialism and the subsequent political, social and cultural changes in the Arab world. Islam was the oldest and the most consistent entity within the region and it was itself under assault. Now, an Islam that had served as an ideal and was a carefully selected memory of how things were based and how things were completely transformed.

In the words of Hodgson, 'The most significant element in the region is religion and religious consciousness.'[165] The new theological movement was almost rebellious against orthodox

---

[164] Zaman, *The Ulema in Contemporary Islam*, 7.
[165] Marshall G.S. Hodgson, *The Venture of Islam*, 3 vols. (Chicago: University of Chicago Press, 1977), 166–67.

displaying compatibility with 19th-century enlightenment. This was about the question of deriving knowledge from sources external to Quran and Islam. Islamic identity was not unadulterated but influenced by its encounter with Western modernity. Cross had always accompanied the orientalist project and was a part of the Project of European domination over non-European lands.[166]

Calls for proto-nationalist resistance against colonialism were often couched in Islamic terminology. The faithfuls were called to resist colonial encroachment and to overthrow European domination as part of their individual and collective Islamic duty in order to prevent Islamic lands and Muslims from falling under the rule of the infidel. Consequently, the anti-colonial resistance movement became the quintessential jihad in modern times. This notion of jihad has been carried over into the 21st century. It is now being redefined as resistance to the hegemony and domination of non-Muslim great powers—the 'Taghut' (arrogant ones rebelling against God), to use the terminology of the Iranian Revolution.

Even the militantly secular Ataturk led a 'jihad' against the carving up of Anatolia by European powers at the end of the First World War. At Mustafa Kemal's behest, the mufti of Ankara issued a fatwa, endorsed by other muftis, sanctifying Kemal's decision to resist the vivisection of Anatolia in defiance of the wishes of the Caliph (who had signed the treaty with the Allies ceding large parts of what later became Turkey to Greeks, Armenians, Italians and French). In 1921, the Grand National Assembly honoured Mustafa Kemal with the title of 'ghazi' (victorious warrior in the way of God) years before he was proclaimed Ataturk (father of the Turks).

The Western intrusion produced reaction not only against Christianity but against classical religious tradition, externally stimulated but the upheaval was internal.[167] All Arab ideologues tried to negotiate the tension between secularization and the

---

[166] Ayoob, *The Many Faces of Political Islam*.
[167] Clifford Geertz C., *Islam Observed: Religious Developments in Morocco and Indonesia* (Chicago: A Phoenix Book University of Chicago, 1971), 65.

modernization within an Islamic context. Political Islam, thus, is the product of two to three centuries of Muslim interaction with the West militarily, economically, politically, intellectually and culturally which had made Muslims the object rather than the subject of history.

Edward Said's orientalism has sensitized one to the construction of irrational others in the oriental to offset the rational West that was as much a justification of colonization as it was a product. The colonized was lesser than the colonizers in the imaginations but critically this imaginary is backed by something imbricated with the structure of power.[168]

Islam emerged as a valuable force for post-colonial Muslims and therefore they visited the past to determine the purity of Islam of the modern-day. The very invention of the term 'Islamic state' is the outcome of political Islam reconciling the romanticized version of Islamic polity with the idea of modern sovereignty that were product of the twin process of colonization and decolonization and modelled after the modern European state.

Navad Safran argues that irresistible encroachment of Europe on Muslim territories drove home more forcefully the realization of the overwhelming supremacy of the Western power. It breathed the notion that all power came from Allah, snubbing the absolute divine determinism of traditional doctrine of Islam which had become extremely difficult now to maintain.[169] The formation of the Islamic identity went into the process of being shaped and reshaped by external forces and gradually the image of Arabs became a reflection of amalgamations of old, new, corrupt, religious and modern.

According to Yvonne Yazbeck Haddad:

Colonial experience appears to have left a mark on the consciousness of those who were colonized.... The bureaucrats and missionaries struggled to cast doubt about Islam by propagating the superiority of western culture through such colonial institutions

---

[168] Iqtidar, *Secularizing Islamist,* 9.

[169] Navad Safran, *Egypt in Search of Political Community: An Analysis of the Intellectual and Political Evolution of Egypt, 1804–1952* (Boston: Harvard University Press, 1981), 41.

as schools, hospitals and publishing firms, whose goal was to separate Muslim from Islam.[170]

Deconstruction of political Islam originated from the contemporary situation and arises from the crisis of the present which claims in such a way that is solicit to respond. This response on the part of Muslims is not a reaction but a constant practice of thoughts. Islam as a historical religion had always stated that all things happened by the will of Allah as long as the government power legitimizes the basic Islamic values. Now this had become impossible after the European rule over so many people who were not ambivalent to the fact that the Islamic empire was no longer the force in the government.

With the deepening influence of the Western economic and cultural model in the Arab world, the Islamic world lost its ability to respond effectively and a process of oscillation experienced between the traditional and modern ways of life, belief in traditional culture and the desire to modernize. The secularity emerged as a cogent force in many Arab countries, and this phenomenon can be well testified in the following excerpts depicted in one of the novels of Nguib Mahfouz:

> I have marvellous ideas, I will adopt British nationality. In England everyone is equal. A Pasha and a garbage collector's son are equal. In England coffee owner's son can become Prime Minister.[171]

The colonization, the foreign presence, nationalism and the revival of Islam in the region changed the traditional image of Islam as a pure monolithic. Arab is struggling between new ideas, ideal norms, values and traditional Islamic conception. Some rulers, like of Egypt, tried to turn Cairo in Paris that was cultural clash and a deep desire for the imitation.

The intense exchange of ideas with the West and the subsequent disintegration of social and political communities

---

[170] Y. John Haddad, John O. Voll, and John L. Esposito, *The Contemporary Islamic Revival* (Westport, CT: Greenwood Press, 1991), 61.

[171] Naguib Mahfouz, *Midaq Alley* (Cairo: The American University of Cairo Press, 1992), 253.

left no optional space for the social and political development of Muslims barring internal polarities. Of late, this polarity has been metamorphosed into a clash of civilizations: the tug between tradition and modernity, the past and the future, the madrasa (religious college or seminary) and the university, the veil (or *chador*) and Western dresses and values. It was not earlier than the last quarter of the 19th century when the discrepancy between the traditional ideology and the implications of the new reality began to provoke intellectual discomfort and elicit some attempts to reconcile it.

All this led to the creation of a new group of Muslim activists who now interpret the Islamic scriptures and use Quranic vocabulary to mobilize populations for the political ends. These simultaneous transformations within Islam along with the proto-nationalist resistance to colonial domination were often couched in Islamic terminology. Bassam Tibi, a renowned Syrian scholar, argues that throughout the modern era, the world of Islam has been confronted with two compelling concepts: secular nationalism as a legitimation of the nation-state and the rival calling for universal order for the entire Islamic ummah as a community of all faithful Muslims.

The Triple Temporalities of Islamism

Different phases of political Islam are marked by different style of behaviour, and each behaviour is marked by its own exclusive context. One can see the scant antecedent to political Islam and modern-day political Islam has reached to us through different phases. The foundation of this entire movement what we know as political Islam or Islamism was laid down during the 19th century when for the first time the Arab world came into contact directly with the colonial world. The first sequence was that of the emergence of Islamic mobilization as a mean to challenge the colonial presence. It was the reformist preamble of the 19th-century Islam that gave impetus to the subsequent phases.

The term itself refers to 'the rise of movements and ideologies, drawing on Islamic [doctrine]… in order to articulate a distinctly political agenda'.[172] Further to this, the manifestation of political Islamist groups rests on an interpretation of Islam as a religion for providing a response to localized concerns.

There are three broad contexts and hence three successive overarching sequences in the deployment of the Islamic mobilization. It is true that identity problematique applies more or less to the sum total of factors, but it does not immunize them from history; under these historical phases that I would divide Islamism in three main temporalities.

The first temporality may be characterized in the form of emergence of Islamic intellectual mobilization to thwart the colonial design in the region. This phase is characterized by the mobilization of the endogenous religious culture to instigate the political resistance. The intellectual mobilization of the 19th century had become bedrock and a reformist preamble to the succeeding generations of political and intellectual Islamism. The 19th-century Muslims' response to the Western imperialism was couched in the language of Islamic ethics, morality and culture, which later metamorphosed into a representation of Islam as an alternative political system. The creation of MBH in 1928 (10 years after carving out of the Ottoman Empire, four years after the abolition of caliphate and eight years before the signing of treaty with London) is the best reflective of later mutation of Islamic intellectualism into political Islamism, and it was a mirror image of the manifestation of the Islamist reaction.[173]

The first phase was well represented by thinkers such as Afghani (1838–97), Abduh, (1849–1905) and Rashid Ridha (1865–1935). Later, MBH prolonged the intellectual effort by altering its political and religious ideas into the political field to strengthen the notion that there was no rupture between contemporary Islamism and the ancestral legacy of thinkers. Islamism of the modern times, as an ideology of popular mobilization, is the heir to these proto-nationalist resistance movements preached

---

[172] Denoeux, 'The Forgotten Swamp'.
[173] Francois Burgat, trans., *Islamism in the Shadow of al-Qaida* (Austin: University of Texas Press, 2008), 33.

by Jamal al-din al-Afghani, the most prominent amongst them. Al-Afghani was a pioneer in terms of using the vocabulary of Islam in order to mobilize Muslims against colonial domination. He found no contradiction between the twin forces of nationalism and pan-Islamism in Muslim countries colonized by European powers. He found them as two sides of the same coin that could be employed simultaneously as a tool of resistance and as a means to promote pan-Islamism.

The other successors of Afghani, Abduh and Ridha offered a pivotal argument for the cause of the decline of the Arab, and this has been acknowledged by several contemporary Islamists like Algerian-born Malek Bennabi who himself claims that two books *Moral Bankruptcy of Western Policy in the Orient* and *Rissalat al-Tawheed* by Ridha and Abduh, respectively, made a generational impression.[174] Similarly, Imam Yehya of Yemen acknowledges the fact that the modernizing movement of free Yemen was never politically distinguished from the influence of Banna and that of his predecessor.

The first-generation preachers of Islamism contributed to the usage and reaffirmation of religious-inspired lexicon amidst the pro-independence struggle in both intellectual and political terms. No doubt, they drew heavily on the conceptual arsenal of the colonial power and particularly that of Russian sloganeering such as anti-imperialism and socialism. However, many future members of Islamist generation passed through this universe of the socialist and secularist rhetoric and experienced an identical need to restore the religious reference in the expression of the pro-independence project.

The second Islamist temporality can be classified between the periods stretching from the post-independence phase and the early 1990s. The second temporality was represented by the voices of descent against the authoritarian politicization of the first generation of nationalist elites who had taken the reign of power and were acting like political agents of the departed Western imperial force. It was an era when the legitimacy of new political elites was itself questioned. One can imagine

---

[174] Burgat, *Islamism in the Shadow of al-Qaida*, 34.

the growing hostility between the Islamic forces and the pro-independence Nasserite generation in Egypt for not having estranged themselves clearly from the colonial past; the contestation itself may be attributed to the cultural deficit observable in the realization of independence. Islamists are vehemently opposed to any kind of ideological subjugation of Islam and dream of a new freedom where Islam will reign the supreme.

The real target of both Islamists and the activists has been the modernizing elites who are constantly being condemned for, if not romanticizing, not resisting the cultural and symbolic universe of the colonizer. These elites are targeted for their incapability to perfect the distancing of foreign masters by restoring the primacy of endogenous Islam.

For instance, in Morocco, the present tension among different forces is directly linked to the persistent use of the French language and the state's policy of marginalization of the religious institutions and the Arabic language.[175] The elites in power are being identified as belonging to the French party. Mr Ghannoushi, Ennahdha leader, has observed very rightly when he remarked, 'Much more than a victory over the French occupier constituted instead a victory over the Arabo-Islamic civilization of Tunisia.'[176] These rulers were taken to be the agents of external power, and it is considered as an extended rule of the imperialist forces. The rulers act to secure the colonial interest and fail to gain the legitimacy and acceptance from their population. Arab nation-states are constrained by economic dependency, military vulnerability and international law which altogether could not achieve the demand of their population.[177]

The ideological battle between the MBH leadership and the Nasserite regime in the 1950s and the 1960s, and the subsequent oppression brought by the Nasserites regime and the emergence of reverence for Qutb and his ideas and subsequent trial of many radical leaders of MBH were the manifestation of second temporality. After a phase of nationalist exuberance,

---

[175] Burgat, *Islamism in the Shadow of al-Qaida*, 37.
[176] Burgat, *Islamism in the Shadow of al-Qaida*, 32 and 38.
[177] Al-Barghouti, *The Umma and the Dawala*, 5.

an inversion in that oil price and global economic integration led pro-independence elites to make more concession to the Western environment as their popular underpinning weakened. In Saudi Arabia alone, Ulema were reduced to the position of power accessories acting like a silent opposition. Similarly, the political price of dependency on the West was revealed to be proportional to the European and American appetite for oil.[178]

Over the course of the early to the mid-20th century, the attraction to political Islam increased as 'governing elites failed to deliver on the promises of economic progress, political participation and personal dignity to expectant populations recently emerged from colonial bondage'.[179] It is in this era, that is, from the 1950s to the 1970s, that political Islam, as we know it today, came of age. In particular, during the Cold War, the heirs to the British and French colonies in the Middle East, the United States and the Soviet Union allowed those nation-states to act with more freedom and assert the legitimacy of their nationalism vis-à-vis the native Islamic culture as a form of natural progress and modernity.[180] Moreover, the catastrophe of Arab nationalism to defeat the challenge of Zionism dealt a considerable blow to this fragile state paving way for non-state actors to exercise the authority over the lives of their subjects much more than the formal nation-state in which subjects were citizens.[181]

The third and the last Islamist temporality appeared in the early years of 1990 following the collapse of the USSR and stretched to the occurrence of the Arab Spring in 2010. The demise of the USSR had coupled with the birth of the so-called world order which revealed itself to be ordered on the confines of interest of global US order.[182] The third timeline is represented and reflected by a combined design of Western forces and the national elites of the region to ruin the oppositional struggle aimed to end the rampant re-colonization.

---

[178] 'Fletcher Features'.
[179] Denoeux, 'The Forgotten Swamp.
[180] Al-Barghouti, *The Umma and the Dawala,* 4.
[181] Al-Barghouti, *The Umma and the Dawala,* 4.
[182] Burgat, *Islamism in the Shadow of al-Qaida,* 32.

Iraq after Saddam provides a glaring example of such a configuration: even more than the new elites elevated to the office of governance by the American military occupier. It is the later who have become the main target for the resisting groups who did not accept the political order perceived as imposed by the United States. Pointing out the dynamic of present-day Islamism, Osama himself noted, 'None of the reason has anything to do with our freedom, liberty and democracy but everything has to do with the US policies and actions in the Middle East.'[183]

He further argued, 'Did you ever wonder why it was not Sweden that was attacked.'[184]

What has induced the emergence of Islamism as the natural counterpart to the authoritarian regime in the Arab world is the latter's failure to cope with the wilting forces of globalization. Islamism spread in the Arab world when the Arab was shifting from state-led development to the market-led development, and this phenomenon was dominant in the 1980s which led to the causal connection. It was the failure of Washington Consensus policies in achieving rapid and sustained economic growth and protecting those marginalized by market forces.

Liberalization and privatization have given rise to crony capitalism with the local entrepreneurs busy in cultivating good relation with the entrenched state elites and bourgeois for subsidies, financing and contract. Crony capitalism alienated the weaker sections of the society who bore the brunt of incompatible liberalism and turned to radical ideas of Islamism.[185] This phase underwrote a sort of shift or a return of the oppositional struggle to the international scene where the United States reverted to the status of the main adversary. A new strategy, to quote Egyptian Ayman al-Zawahiri, to fight the distant enemy instead of the close enemy in the form of the United States was carved out by the extremist elements of Islamism.[186]

---

[183] Burgat, *Islamism in the Shadow of al-Qaida*, 2.

[184] Francois Burgat, *Islamism in the Shadow of al-Qaida*, 39.

[185] Aswini Mahapatra, 'Arab and Turkish Response to Globalization', *India Quarterly* 63, no. 3 (July–September 2007), 25–50.

[186] 'Fletcher Features'.

The occurrence of the Arab Spring can be conceived to be the most important extension in the present temporality of political Islam that represents a pragmatic spurt in Islamism touching the shore of Arabian Sea and Mediterranean Africa to Asia to the borders of the European landscape. This Arab Spring reflects the inclusive voices of the masses and represents the Islamic voices of the people who were present in the heritage of Islam.

The Arab Spring demonstrates that modern political values are not alien to Islam but rather they are derived by Islam itself. Arab nationalism that began as a de-Islamized religion is now reappearing as an Islamic nationalism or simply Islamism. The commotion in the Arab world appears to be one of the greatest events in modern Arab history. A genuine popular revolution, spontaneous and apparently leaderless, yet sustained and remarkably determined, overthrew a system that by all accounts had been most entrenched and secure in the whole region. Just as in the case of the Iranian Revolution more than three decades ago, what is now happening in the region is watched by all in the Arab world—either as a likely model of the transformation to come in their respective countries or at least as a badly needed source of revolutionary inspirations.

So far, one has merely experienced the abstract of political Islam in the form of theory and deliberation, but in the post-Arab Spring phase, one may perhaps see the practical part of political Islam in the form of law application, formation of political institution, coordination between different centres of power, election and the governance reflecting the trial and error. The current political site will open new vistas for theoretical discussion on the compatibility of democracy and Islam. A series of normative statements are already in the offing by the leaders and ideologues of different political Islamic movements exhibiting the changes in their instance, introducing new orientation and shapes to the meaning and contour of the phenomenon called political Islam.

2

Quranic–Theological Context of Political Islam

The purpose of political authority in Islam is to establish the religion of God in its entirety and make His words supreme.[1]

Judah ho Din Siyasat se-tau Rah jatee ha Changazi (If governmental rule becomes devoid of religious righteousness, then that which remains Changazi).[2]

Before moving ahead to discuss the political ideas of Islam as elaborated in the Quran and subsequent writings of prominent theologians, it seems prudent to interrogate briefly the subject of human society in the light of the holy book which has shaped the theological trajectory vis-à-vis political Islam during the era of truly guided caliphates.

There are basic differences between Quranic views of humankind and the views propounded in the philosophical and political writings of others over the centuries. Islam,

---

[1] Muhammad Abdul-Haq Ansari. (ed. and trans). *Ibn Taymiyyah Expounds on Islam: Selected Writing of Shaykh al-Islam Taqi ad-Din Ibn Taymiyyah on Islamic Faith, life and Society* (Kingdom of Saudi Arabia: Imam Muhammad Ibn Saud University, 2000), p. 500.

[2] Zofshan Taj. 'The Political Thought of Tahir-ul-Qadri in Its Islamic Context: Understanding the Concept of Khilafat and Its Relevance in Modern Society in Light of Medieval Islamic Teaching'. *IMW Journal of Religious Studies*, Vol. 3, no. 1 (2011), pp. 1–21. http://digitalcommons.usu.edu/cgi/viewcontent.cgi?article=1014 &context=imwjournal (Accessed on 30 September 2014).

like the other schools of political thoughts and philosophies, emphasizes social life, but it does not end here rather takes it as its high moral duty to attend to social problems and to strive for the benefit of all human beings. This concern for social reform and promotion of social idealism constitutes the core of Islamic religion which necessitates the formation of an Islamic polity.

The formation and execution of law for social life is equally important in Islamic teaching. In Islam, the goal of law is not only to bring about social order and discipline but beyond this to maintain social justice. In the absence of justice, the social order would not be durable and would lose the opportunity for desired growth and development, and hence, the goal of man's creation and social life would not be realized.

Social laws in Islam are meant to be moulded in such a way as to prepare the ground and context for the spiritual growth and eternal felicity of the mankind. These should not be inconsistent with spiritual development for, in the view of Islam, the life of this world has a fundamental role in human destiny despite its short duration.

The issue of legislation in Islam is completely adverse to the dominant manner we see in the modern democratic world. The accepted theory in the most current societies is that the laws should be legislated and approved by the people themselves or their representatives. However, from the Islamic perspective, the core principles of the laws should emanate from the Quranic and prophetic teachings.

In the light of Islam, all human beings have been created equal; no individual enjoys any inherent right of sovereignty and guardianship (imam/caliph/wilayah) over others. No race, nationality, geographical location, class and other discriminatory factors confer any right of sovereignty on any individual or group. God, the Almighty, is the master of the universe, and it is He who is the sovereign over all creatures. All are equal before Him, and none enjoys any preferential right of sovereignty over others. This idea finds a recurring echo in several Quranic verses like the Almighty says:

> Say: 'People of the Book! Come now to a word common between us and you, that we serve none but God, and that we associate not aught with Him, and that none of us shall take others as Lords apart from the God'.[3]

Another Quranic verse claims, 'They (the Jews and the Christians) have taken their rabbis and their monks as lords apart from God.'[4] It further claims: 'Verily, His are the creation and the command (amr)'.[5]

To reinforce it further, the Quran reads:

> Submission to the will of laws of Allah is the source of all freedom. It liberates the mind; soul and behavior form the evil influence of the world. Allah himself says that 'And We have not sent you but as a mercy to the world'.[6]

The question of freedom is equally important in the teaching of Islam. The Ulema and the jurists have struggled with the question of freedom and pointed out that if man is deprived of freedom, he or she will fail to reconcile its relationship with Him because the Almighty has granted man the freedom which allows him to choose his course in life, man is answerable to Allah for his actions: 'Surely We have shown him the way: he may be thankful or unthankful.'[7]

Political freedom in Islam is a means of leading mankind to justice, goodness and peace. It guarantees and protects the political rights of all. Freedom does not mean to satisfy all his instincts nor does it mean to give into the pressure of lusts and desires. Behaviour should be guided always by our insane sense of what is right and should not be motivated by our desire for pleasure or immediate gratification.

For explanatory purpose and periodical division of Islamic political discourse (political Islam), we can draw a divisionary line between different parts or segments while debating the

---

[3] Quran, 3:64.
[4] Quran, 9:31.
[5] Quran, 7:54.
[6] Quran, 21:107.
[7] Quran, 76:3.

content of political Islam. The first segment begins with an era of revelation and the Hadith, and the second is the era of the interpretation and elucidation of the Quranic text and the Hadith at the hand of theologians and jurists. The third and the last part is the complete overturn through the writing of modern scholars on the subject. The first two segments will be dealt with in this chapter, while the last phase will be the subject of the next chapter when I will discuss the issue of encounter between the Muslim world and the Western imperialism triggering the debate of political Islam in the modern era of the 19th and 20th centuries.

With these preliminary remarks, now I will turn to the Quranic and theological context of present-day political Islam what can be termed as the political theology of Islam. The political theology of the Quran is expounded by those who believe in puritanism of Islam and supremacist philosophy. It seeks statehood, political power and mastery. Islamists of today present this sordid past as their manifestation of the future unlike those who are the followers of Quranic dictum: One section believes in the Quran of 'To you your religion and to me mine'.

The ensuing section will reflect upon the ideas of political Islam as derived in the light of the Quran and the Hadith and will also put forward the views of the prominent exegetes and commentators of the Hadith regarding the role of Islam in political spheres. If one sees the origin and journey of modern political Islam painstakingly, he or she will find that the protagonist of political Islam draws upon the Quran as much as it draws upon its colonial context.

Quran, Exegesis and Political Ideologization of Islam

There are certain Quranic principles that the ideologues of modern-day political Islam have taken as a catalyst to legitimize the religious context of Islamic revivalism. There are plentiful references related to power, authority and organization of the state in the Quran. However, these references do not provide a well-defined explanation for the linkage of Islam with the politics. There are several politically charged terms defined in different ways by different jurists in different historical periods. These terms represent the possibility of the political orders and do not prescribe any political principle. Even Sunnah, the second most important and authentic source of Islam, has very little to say on the issue of governance and the state.

However, before deliberating further on the subject, I would like to highlight some fundamental teachings of the Quran about the relation of mankind with the God and from where the basic essence of political teaching of the Quran emanates.

The core of the relationship between Islam and politics emanates primarily from the dictum that 'sovereignty is for God' alone and people on earth are vice-regent of God alone, as men rule themselves in the name of God. There are scholars and jurists who view the impossibility of the fulfilment of the Quranic injunction without the command of political power. There are numerous scholars who view political Islam of today as an extension of the Quranic teaching and an effort in the direction of realization of divine objectives.

One of the renowned scholars of Islam, Ahmad Schalabi, says that the Prophet was both ruling and teaching his people in his era.[8] He further argues that foundational principle of Islamic teaching of commanding rights and forbidding wrongs could not be fulfilled without acquiring power and establishing a state, and to achieve a just society, an agency like state is very much required.[9] The welfare of man lies in a community, and the community needs a ruler to command them, and the worldly inspired ruler cannot help mankind to achieve the revealed objective as enshrined in the Quran.[10]

The Prophet had come with such a religion that was meant to put the things right in order. In Mecca, the Prophet was constrained by the pagan power of Quraysh, but in Medina,

---

[8] Ahmad Schalabi. *As-Siyasah-Fil-Fikr-el-Islami* [Politics in Islamic Thought] (Cairo: Maktabat-el-Nahza-al-Misriyah, 1992), p. 28.

[9] Ahmad Schalabi. *As-Siyasah-Fil-Fikr-el-Islami*, p. 30.

[10] Ahmad Schalabi. *As-Siyasah-Fil-Fikr-el-Islami*, p. 31.

he had acquired the power to execute the rulings of God. In the words of the 10th-century Islamic jurist Thslibi, 'God had allowed Mohammad to unite prophethood and kingship so that he could accomplish his mission in the form of execution of laws and overcoming the infidels.'[11]

The Quranic orientation of politics stems from a fact that claims Quran to be the primary source of knowledge. The core of the Quranic concept of humanity emanates from the single verse of the Quran that underlies: 'He created you from single person; created of like nature, his mate, and from both scattered countless men and women.'[12] The concept of resurrection is a major part of the Islamic creed from which emerges the origin of political thought of Islam and all other Islamic values.[13] Islam as a religious phenomenon is a result of various causes and some of them are related to the assumption that Islam is a universal moral system. Others are related to the assumption that Islam is mainly the legal and ideological system that has evolved step by step.[14]

The Quran says that man is created from a single sound soul, so no one among children can claim sovereignty over others and that unity of human origin is shared by both messages and the Prophet. The supreme source of authority is the creator himself.[15] The core of Islamic polity in the light of the Quran and the Hadith is centred on the belief that religious laws are not inherited in the nature of the things nor deduced from the nature of a social relationship.[16]

Unlike the modern notion of power, in classical injunction of Islam, God alone possesses absolute attributes and absolute power, and unquestioned sovereignty belongs to him alone where legislation is his only prerogative. Islamic belief is a system of normative values which act as a criterion for identifying the major social objectives that evaluate social institution and

---

[11] Patrica Crone. *Medieval Islamic Political Thoughts*, p. 11.

[12] Quran, 4:1.

[13] Eltigani Abdelgadir Hamid. *The Quran and Politics* (London: International Institute of Islamic Thought, 2004), p. 5.

[14] Eltigani Abdelgadir Hamid. *The Quran and Politics*, p. 6.

[15] Quran, 2:22.

[16] Eltigani Abdelgadir Hamid. *The Quran and Politics*, p. 16.

then justify the claims of legitimacy. This faith justifies political powers and use of force in obedience.

Unlike Western philosophers like John Locke and others who claim that sovereignty emanates from the ownership, the Quran says that it is not the source from which the values and sovereignty are derived. Rather, the supreme sovereignty and authority of defining the norms are the prerogative of divine laws only.[17] There are plenty of references in the Quran about the sovereignty of God, 'To Allah belongs the dominion of heavens and the earth and Allah is all powerful.'[18]

There are plenty of references in the Quran highlighting the claims: 'To Allah belongs the dominion of heavens and the earth and all that is in them and He has the full power over everything.'[19] 'Are you not aware that the dominion of the heavens and the earth belongs to Allah.'[20] 'O Allah Lord of all dominion! You bestow dominion on whomever You please and take away dominion from whomever You please and You exalt whom You please and abase whom You please. In Your hand is all good.'[21] 'Allah's is the kingdom of the heavens and the earth.'[22]

The Quran presents a different view of the origin of human society, namely, of sovereignty and political legitimacy. Adam's prophethood established the principle of human submission to the divine sovereign.[23] There are frequent references to power, authority and the organization of the political community in the Quran. There are numbers of politically infested terms in the Quran that represent possibility of the political orders and do not prescribe any political principle itself. There are abundant references in the Quran that highlight the political injunction of Islam. The Quran says:

---

[17] Eltigani Abdelgadir Hamid. *The Quran and Politics*, p. 173.
[18] Quran, 3:189.
[19] Quran, 5:120.
[20] Quran, 2:107.
[21] Quran, 3:26.
[22] Quran, 45:27.
[23] Eltigani Abdelgadir Hamid. *The Quran and Politics*, p. 45.

Believers! Obey Allah and obey the Messenger, and those invested authority among you; and if you were to dispute among yourselves about anything refer it to Allah and the Messenger if you really believe in Allah and the Last Day; that is better and more commendable in the end.[24]

In the true political model of the Quran, sovereignty and legislation are the domains of Allah, and even messengers had no legislative powers or command of obedience. The sovereignty of God is exercised by Imam, whose legitimacy itself is derived from his obedience to the Quran and Sunnah and his appeal to Muslims. The legitimacy of any other ruler with a territorial jurisdiction is derived from his following of the Quran as well as his following of the imam through which such a ruler would symbolize his appeal to the whole of ummah.[25]

In Islam, there is a catalytic difference between legitimacy and legality. Legitimacy can be measured only in terms of satisfaction and contentment that the subjects feel.[26] This is the legality that creates a sort of bond between the ruler and the ruled, and the biggest source of lack of legitimacy is the absence of justice.

Necessitating the power and politics for the supremacy of religion of Islam, the Quran claims:

Allah has promised those of you who believe and do righteous deeds that He will surely bestow power on them in the land as He bestowed power on those that preceded them, and that He will firmly establish their religion which he has been pleased to choose for them.[27]

Highlighting the linkage between authority and religion, the Quran further asserts, 'Allah will certainly help those who,

---

[24] Quran, 4:59.

[25] Tamin Al-Barghouti. *The Umma and the Dawala: The Nation-State and the Arab Middle East* (London: Pluto Press, 2004), p. 56.

[26] Ahmad Bahauddin. *Al-Shariah-wal-Sultah Fil-Alam-el-Arabi* [Islamic Shariah and Authority in the Arab World] (Beirut: Darul-Shorooque, n.d.), p. 9.

[27] Quran, 24:55.

were to bestow authority on Him in the land, establish Prayer, render alms, enjoin good and forbid evil.'[28]

In Islamic politics, the main thrust is to establish the religion of God, and with the intent of executing the divinely edicts, there is a necessity of establishing a state as an entity is the long-drawn political culmination. The Quran is very categorical in laying down that He has sent the Prophet to establish justice on the earth: 'Indeed We sent our messenger with a clear signs and sent down with them the Book and the Balance that people may uphold justice.'[29] The Prophet had already begun this mission of spreading the words of God only in Mecca, but he succeeded after he landed in Medina and established a state there.

Another Quranic principle conducting the principle of political Islam is derived from the fact that the Quran necessitates the establishment of power for the welfare of *din* (religion) and there can be no din in the absence of a state and no state in the absence of the imam.[30] One may resort to the statement of Joseph to the Pharaoh where the Quran mentions the story of Joseph and Pharaoh explaining the relation between justice and politics in Islam. Joseph said: 'Place me in charge of the treasure of the land. I am a good keeper and know my task well.'[31]

Allegiance is the other core of political principle of the Quran where the Prophet was reported to have said, 'Who dies without allegiance to someone, he dies like an ignorant.' And in another Hadith, he says that there has to be one ruler or master if there are three or more than that.[32] The second caliphate is reported to have once said that there would be no Islam without group, no group without state and no state without obedience.[33]

Sovereignty and power are neither divine delegations nor inheritance but depend on the contract between two parties

---

[28] Quran, 22:41.
[29] Quran, 57:25.
[30] Hakem Al-Mutairi. 'Al-Hurriyah Ao Al-Tufan'. [Freedom or Storm] (PhD Thesis, Tunis University, Tunisia, 2003), p. 10.
[31] Quran, 12:55.
[32] Ahmad Schalabi. *As-Siyasah-Fil-Fikr-el-Islami*, p. 29.
[33] Ahmad Schalabi. *As-Siyasah-Fil-Fikr-el-Islami*, p. 29.

and here one can see that Islam predates the principle of social contract as expounded by John Lock (d. 1704) and Rousseau (d. 1778). Under this social contract, community surrenders some of the freedom to the authority in exchange of good governance and collective welfare. The Quranic origin of social contract is not derived from some philosophical underpinning but is simply based on real practical experiences. The Aqaba agreement was the first of its kind when the Prophet entered into an agreement with the people of Medina, and it was truly suggestive of the first contract between two consenting sides.[34]

The Prophet sought a series of allegiances from his companions at the eve of the treaty of Hudaibiyah to strengthen the principle and the core objective. The principle of allegiance is the compliance and obedience. Allegiance is not confined to the Prophet alone, but God himself promises this allegiance to those who are noble and has said that those who do noble tasks will be made caliphate.[35]

Even the first caliphate, Abu Baker, did not become the ruler until he had sought the allegiance from the people. The same was the case with Omar and Othman, who had not become the caliphates merely after their nomination by the respective predecessor or collegiate, but they had also to seek the allegiance of the companions of the Prophet and the wise and mature people.

Explaining the enthronement of Abu Baker or Omar, Ibn Taymiyyah says that merely with the support of their respective tribes and without the aid of companions and people of wisdom and knowledge, they would not have become the sovereigns in Medina.[36]

In this regard, Imam Ahmad Ibn Hanbal is very candid in his judgement when he says that the nomination of imam is not the prerogative of his predecessor, but he should enjoy the allegiance of the subject and there should be an open agreement between the two sides. Another 10th-century jurist Al-Mawardi goes on to the extent of saying that if a person possesses all the

---

[34] Hakem Al-Mutairi. 'Al-Hurriyah Ao Al-Tufan', p. 17.
[35] Quran, 24:55.
[36] Hakem Al-Mutairi. 'Al-Hurriyah Ao Al-Tufan', p. 19.

noble qualities to become an imam but yet if he fails to secure the allegiance of people, he cannot be selected as an imam. On a similar note, Imam Ahmad Ibn Hanbal claims that it is for the people to pose their trust in the imam, without which he cannot be elected. So, people are the real and true arbitrators.[37]

The Prophet is reported to have told one of his companions, Abu Zar, that you do not ask for imamate because you are weak and the imamate is a trust and faith, and because on the day of judgement, one will have to face ignominy except those who have fulfilled the duty.[38] Unlike today's situation, the imamate in Islam is not to accord majesty, solemnity and dignity but to bring justice and order and, of course, it is a cumbersome task.

The Quran not merely talks of allegiances or contract but exhorts that there should be fearless contract between the master and the subject. The allegiance should not contain any coercive element and should be devoid of any intimidation. The Quran commands, 'Let there be trading by mutual consent.'[39] The greatest jurist of his time Al-Mawardi opines that there could be no allegiance without the consent of 'Ahlul Hal Wal Aqd' and the approval of people of rational and wisdom was must.

Echoing the subject of the authenticity of allegiance, 13th-century Hanbalite Baghdadi exegesis and jurist Ibn al-Jawzi says that revolt of Hussein against Yazid was right because the allegiance he had achieved was full of mockery of the principle of allegiance.[40] Ali is reported to have told his inmates that his allegiance would not be fulfilled unless it is received from all the Muslims.[41]

Similarly, the Quran is quite candid in its injunction that the people are the real source of authority, as God says in the Quran, 'And the People were told: Will you join the assembly.'[42] Consultation is an equally important part of the political principle of the Quran. Caliphate Omar says that Emirate is all about

---

[37] Hakem Al-Mutairi. 'Al-Hurriyah Ao Al-Tufan', pp. 20–21.

[38] Hakem Al-Mutairi. 'Al-Hurriyah Ao Al-Tufan', p. 13.

[39] Quran, 4:29.

[40] Hakem Al-Mutairi. 'Al-Hurriyah Ao Al-Tufan', p. 25.

[41] Hakem Al-Mutairi. 'Al-Hurriyah Ao Al-Tufan', p. 33.

[42] Quran, 26:39.

consultation as claimed in the Quran too further adding: '[T]ake consent from them in matter of importance. And when you are resolved on a course of action put your trust in Allah.'[43]

Consultation in the Quran is the basis of governance and it is an obligatory act. There is another reference in Quran about the consultation: 'Most of the secret conferring is devoid of good, unless one secretly enjoins charity, good deed, and setting the affairs of the men right. We shall grant whoever does that seeking to please Allah a great reward.'[44] The Quran also quotes: 'Who obey their Lord and establish prayer; who conduct their affairs by consultation, and spend out of what We have bestowed upon them.'[45]

Jurists of Spain (Islamic Undlus) were very particular about this feature of Islamic politics, and Ibn Atiyyah has called consultation as one of the pillars of shariah and one who does not seek the opinion of Ulema is worth being removed from the power.[46] From the principle of consultation emanates the Quranic principle of freedom, and political freedom was one of the principles of political discourse in the phase of the revelation. If God cannot force on to surrender to his will, how can a ruler make his subject to obey his dictates.[47] The Prophet is reported to have once said that highest Jihad is to speak truth in the presence of an oppressor. One of the pioneers of Egyptian nationalism, Saad Zaghlool, claimed that right is above power and the nation is above the government.[48] It is a belief that man's mind and rationality do not move without freedom and conviction.[49]

Given the growing application of religion in the modern-day identity politics of Muslims, Mr Ali Dashti, an Iranian scholar, in his book *The Twenty-three Year*, argues that the further the Prophet's death receded into the past, the greater became the

---

[43] Hakem Al-Mutairi. 'Al-Hurriyah Ao Al-Tufan', p. 26.

[44] Quran, 4:114.

[45] Quran, 24:38.

[46] Hakem Al-Mutairi. 'Al-Hurriyah Ao Al-Tufan', p. 27.

[47] Hakem Al-Mutairi. 'Al-Hurriyah Ao Al-Tufan', p. 46.

[48] Ahmad Bahauddin. *Al-Shariah-wal-Sultah Fil-Alam-el-Arabi*, p. 19.

[49] Ahmad Bahauddin. *Al-Shariah-wal-Sultah Fil-Alam-el-Arabi*, p. 50.

tendency to treat the religion as a means rather than as an end.[50] It has, thus, been shown how the Quran claims the authority to rule and lays down the Islamic principle of governance. The Quran philosophy of governance and social organization emanates from its exclusive epistemology of knowledge of the human being, its own vision of the cosmology and its own mechanism of worldly affairs. The Quranic vision of the human being stands in sharp contrast to the modern-day rational and scientific approach to human being and a set of issues concerning politics and society.

Theological Elucidation, Classical Islamic Philosophy and Roots of Modern-day Political Islam

The real issue of state and its relations with Islamic teachings arose only after the death of the Prophet. It was then that Muslims needed to innovate and improvise about the nature and form of the government. Indeed, the origin of first disagreement among Islamic community can be traced back to the issue of politics alone.

The transformation of the post-Prophet phase has been explained by Hasan Askari in the following words:

> This was a beginning of shift in the social process from polytheism to monotheism, from rules by customs to rule by law, from natural relationship based on blood and race to moral and spiritual association and from natural monarchy to power delegated by God. In Arabic terminology, it means a movement away from *shirks* to *tawheed*, from *Jahiliyyah* to *Shariah*, from *asabiyya* to *taqwa* and from *mulk* to *wilayah*.[51]

---

[50] Tarek Fatah. *Chasing a Mirage: The Tragic Illusion of an Islamic State* (Ontario: John Wiley and Sons Canada Ltd, 2008), pp. 91–92.

[51] Hasan Askari. *Society and State in Islam: An Introduction* (New Delhi: Islam and Modern Age Society, 1978), p. 92.

With the end of the prophecy of the Prophet, the role of guiding the community passed on to his pious political successors or to the members of Prophet's household. This was the phase of the process of political theorization at the hands of a series of Jurists who framed the political ideology of Islam in the light of the Quran, and those formulations were not devoid of local, regional, political, ethnic, tribal and racial considerations. The political doctrine of Islam developed by jurists was derived from the cultural norms too dating back to the antiquity era. Political theologies—theories crafted during the period of Muslim empires—were aimed at salvation.

In order to explain and interpret the prophetic tradition, there arose a discursive tradition in Islam: Ulema became its custodians, they were also seen as true heir of the prophetic charisma and discursive tradition were raised to the stature of a sub-tradition. So Ulema and their tradition acquired a new power within Islam that later received a status of quasi-sacrosanct too. The guardians of the political theology were the religious scholars and Ulema. The political theology, according to Jan Assmann, is the 'ever-changing relationship between political community and the religious order or between power of authority and the salvation'.[52] The requirement of reverence and respect for religious figures, especially the persons of the Prophet, became a part of substantive theological values, commitment and spiritual practices for Muslims' Ulema and the theologians became the gatekeepers of the Prophet's legacy.

The Quranic template of political Islam is followed by the second segment of the discourse that was introduced with the transformation of caliphate from consultation to an era of monarchical rule. The era of Umayyad saw the grave retreat from the true Quranic teachings when the wrong interpretation of the text started replacing the real text of the Quran. This era of propagandist interpretation stretches from last days of Umayyad to the declining days of the Ottoman Empire. This

---

[52] Ebrahim Moosa. 'Muslim Political Theology: Defamation, Apostasy and Anathema Muslim Political Theology—Conflict and International Politics, http://www.lb.boell.org/downloads/Ebrahim-Moosa.pdf (Accessed on 20 March 2013).

interpretative or theological phase of Islamic political discourse was laden with nepotism, lobbying, treachery and political manipulation. Hereditary rule had become the order of the day thereby completely depriving the free choice of election and people making false claim about prophetic preference in favour of a single person. The Umayyad, Abbasids and Alawite came along with different interpretations of the Quran, prophetic gradation and the Hadith.

This second phase of interpretation and elucidation of the Quran and the Hadith was coupled with an emergence of a novel philosophical school in Islam. Political philosophy refers to a set of political consequences that are inferred from fundamental metaphysical–moral issues. The political writings of Al-Farabi are a typical example of Islamic achievements in this field. By definition, political philosophy should remain independent of any particular religious system or set of beliefs, as it is based upon metaphysical and rational foundations. However, Islamic political philosophers formed deeply rational grounds for many Islamic doctrines before applying these as religious–philosophical premises in their political formulations.

To deny the validity of Islamic political philosophy is to ignore the philosophical and ideological aspects of political issues. Many philosophical problems in politics have a close relationship with religion. In addition, there are many Islamic teachings that offer, either directly or indirectly, suitable answers to some essential questions in political philosophy.

The philosophical teaching of Islam is further combined with the exposition of Islamic ethics and political jurisprudence in the post-caliphate era, and the political ethics (morals of politics) refers to a series of writings from Muslim scholars who have attempted to advise and guide rulers to a successful and just method of government. These prescriptions were usually accompanied by stories of previous kings and rulers. These were collections of Islamic teachings, Greek philosophy and some elements of Persian literature. Examples of these include *Siyasat Nameh* (*Book of Government*) by Nidham al-Mulk (1020–1092) and *Nasihat al-Mulk* (*Advice to King*) of Ghazali (1058–1111) and others.

Muslim jurists (*fuqaha*) adopted the method of political jurisprudence (or *fiqh ul-siyasi*) to explicate and define the Islamic political system and juridical aspects of political affairs. They discussed the duties of rulers over their subjects, the means for appointing and the grounds for dismissing of political leaders, the personal qualities that an imam or deputy (caliph) should possess and the relationship between different elements of the government to one another. Political jurisprudence overlaps political theology in several areas, such as the discussion concerning leadership. However, political jurisprudence is distinguished by its methodology and the large scope of its subject matters.

For the theologians and the jurists of the post-caliphate era, it was the issue of imamate or caliphate instead of governance, shura instead of modern-day legislative assembly, ummah instead of modern nation-state and allegiance instead of modern-day electoral practice; shariah rather than modern-day penal code was close to their hearts. Their entire political model was based on these themes and they drew the legitimacy for their views from its scant reference in the divine revelation.

The linguistic origin of the word 'caliphate' may be traced back to the institution of the deputyship of the Prophet.[53] In Muslim usage, the term 'caliphate', for which the term imamate is loosely referred to as synonyms, refers to an overall leadership of the community in spiritual as well as temporal affairs.[54] The name 'imam' is derived from the comparison of the caliphate with the imam of prayer, since the caliphate is followed and taken as a model just like the prayer leader. Therefore, the caliphate is called the greater imam. Since the primary duty of the imam or caliphate is to ensure the strict observance of the religious principles and to implement the legal provision contained in the Islamic shariah, so the imam is a political ruler with the objective of preaching and consolidating the Islamic edicts and ethics on the land. Caliph does not share the authority with anyone else as he represents the Prophet and his book of

---

[53] Ali Abdel Razek. *Al-Islam Wa-Usoolul-Hukm* (Tunis: Darul-Maarif-Littabah-Wal-Nashr, 2011), p. 25.

[54] Ali Abdel Razek. *Al-Islam Wa-Usoolul-Hukm*, pp. 25–26.

the Quran, and so he is directly or indirectly implementing the word of God on the earth.[55] Abu Jaafar al-Mansur went so far as to presume that he was God's power on the earth.

It was perhaps Abu Hassan al-Mawardi (991–1058) who, for the first time in the Islamic history, theorized the notion of imamah or imamate and laid down a comprehensive view on the issue of the political authority in Islam. He lived in an era when Islamic political doctrine had completely come under the influence of Greek rationality and philosophy. His commentaries on Islamic polity were confined into one of his famous books, *Al-Ahkam-al-Sultaniyyah-wa-al-Wilayatud-Diniyyah*. He strongly pleaded for the establishment of the institution of imamah. He regards caliphate is being derived from the divine laws rather than reason. According to him: 'Imamate is a succession to Prophet to protect the religion and run the worldly affairs.'[56]

He also asserted that the reason cannot be the source of guidance in every sphere and all walks of life as leadership cannot be deduced from reason alone.[57] He argued that the obligation to commanding right and forbidding wrong is well rooted in revelation and reason as well.[58] His caliphate is the replacement of the Prophet, and for him, the former is necessary to maintain religion and administer worldly affairs.[59] Al-Mawardi, the pioneer of the political Islamic thought also stipulates that the establishment of imamate is must and that its creation is mandatory because its absence might lead to anarchy.[60]

For Mawardi, caliphate is the keystone of the political system: 'Establishment of *Caliphate* is an obligation and

---

[55] Ali Abdel Razek. *Al-Islam Wa-Usoolul-Hukm*, p. 31.

[56] Abu Hassan al-Mawardi. *Al-Ahkam-al-Sultaniyyah-wa-al-Wilayatud-Diniyyah* [The ordinance of the Government] (Beirut: Darul-Kitab-al-Arabi, 1991), p. 29.

[57] Abu Hassan al-Mawardi. *Al-Ahkam-al-Sultaniyyah-wa-al-Wilayatud-Diniyyah*, p. 30.

[58] Michael Cook. *Commanding Right and Forbidding Wrongs in Islamic Thought* (London: Cambridge University Press, 2000), p. 344.

[59] Hasan Askari. *Society and State in Islam: An Introduction* (New Delhi: Har Anand Publication, 1994), p. 94.

[60] Abul Hassan Ali Bin Mohammad Bin Habib-al-Basri-al-Mawardi. *Al-Ahkam-al-Sultaniyyah-wa-al-Wilayatud-Diniyyah* (Beirut: Darul-Kitab-al Arabi, 199), p. 3.

common duty on the part of Islamic community and it is as important as seeking knowledge and waging jihad.'[61]

In his words, there is conjunction between the religious order and the political order. Muslim political theology was directly related to the idea of prophecy, which in turn was a pathway to salvation. He also envisaged that the imam must be selected from the tribe of the Prophet, the Quraysh and must possess physical, moral and spiritual qualities.[62] People who choose the imam must be the men of justice, wisdom and wise. They must know the priority of the common people and should enjoy the confidence of the masses.[63] He does not explicitly deny the right of the subject to refuse the obedience to an impious imam.[64] The imam can be chosen either by elders or by the outgoing caliph himself.[65] *Bayah* (the oath of allegiance) to the imam on the part of people is must to accord him the legitimacy, but according to Mawardi, no one can be forced to express his allegiance.

Highlighting the significance of the institution of imamate itself, the 13th-century renowned sociologist and philosopher Ibn Khaldoon exhorts that the establishment of an imamate is a necessity as enshrined in the legal system of the Quran, and he finds it more a religious requirement than the rational requirement.[66] He further elaborates that the establishment of the caliphate is necessary to govern this world judiciously and is equally required for the welfare of this world and afterwards. In the eyes of Khaldoon, caliphate is bound by certain Islamic norms and values, and he acts as a successor to the Prophet, and a caliphate does not take away the right from others as he is bound by shariah.[67]

---

[61] Al-Mawardi. *Al-Ahkam-al-Sultaniyyah-wa-al-Wilayatud-Diniyyah*, p. 30.

[62] Hassan Askari. *Society and State in Islam: An Introduction*, p. 94.

[63] Al-Mawardi. *Al-Ahkam-al-Sultaniyyah-wa-al-Wilayatud-Diniyyah*, p. 31.

[64] H.A.R. Gibb. 'Al-Mawardi's Theory of the Khilafah'. *Islamic Culture*, Vol. XI, no. 2 (1987), pp. 291–302.

[65] Al-Mawardi. *Al-Ahkam-al-Sultaniyyah-wa-al-Wilayatud-Diniyyah*, p. 33.

[66] Ibn Khaldoon. *Al-Muqaddemah* [The Introduction] (Karachi: Nafees Academy, 1986, pp. 134–35.

[67] Ahmad Schalabi. *As-Siyasah-Fil-Fikr-el-Islami* [Politics in Islamic Thought] (Cairo: Maktabat-el-Nahza-al-Misriyah, 1992), p. 38.

Caliphate, as defined by Tahir-ul-Qadri, denotes Islamic rules or government and in the literal sense of the term, Khilafat may be defined as *Niyabah* or *Amanah* (Trusteeship and Sovereignty).[68]

Political vicegerent has been discussed in the section Nour of the Quran, where it says that He will surely bestow upon them the right of trust to rule as He granted rule to those before them.[69] Khilafat in relation to government would indicate the rule of man on earth as God's vicegerent.

There are a host of scholars and Islamic thinkers who have maintained the view that it was God himself who appointed the caliphate and bequeathed his authority to him as illustrated in the following verse which was well cited in the classical period.

He became the Caliph
Or rather the Caliphate
Was destined for him—
Like Moses
Who was destined
To approach God.
Hisham, the God's chosen one
For the people,
For whom darkness withdraws
From all over the earth
The sky to which they look,
Praying for rain.[70]

One can also understand the high-esteemed stature of the caliphate in the classical phase of Islam by studying these lines of a jurist, Abd al-Hakim al-Sialakuti, when he says:

I have made this work a gift to the one chosen by God for eternal sovereignty, favoured by the supreme super ... the propagator of the true faith, the founder of the principle of the Holy Law, the shadow of God in the two lands, the saviour of Islam and

---

[68] Zofshan Taj. 'The Political Thought of Tahir-ul-Qadri in Its Islamic Context'. http://digitalcommons.usu.edu/cgi/viewcontent.cgi?article=1014&context=imwjournal
[69] Quran, 24:55.
[70] Ali Abdel Razek. *Al-Islam Wa-Usoolul-Hukm*, p. 31.

of Muslims, the builder of God's nation, the successor to the Prophet, graced with the divine support and victory.[71]

This theory is quite similar to the idea propounded by Thomas Hobbes when he says that the power of the king is sacred and divinely ordained.

There are other set of scholars who expound the view that a caliphate derives his authority from the Muslim community (ummah) which designates and confers sovereignty on him. Al-Hutay'a seems to hold this view claiming, 'You are the Imam to whom, after his companion, Men entrusted the rein of authority. In choosing you it not you they favours, it was for their own sake that they did so.'[72]

Here one needs to be careful about the distinction between kingship and the institution of the caliphate. In the case of kingship, natural authority means to cause the subjects act as required by the rational and intellectual desires of the ruler, being oblivious to the facts of the divine teaching or edicts of shariah. However, the main thrust and objective of the institution of the caliphate is to make the masses act as required by the religious ethics and Quranic morality. The central characteristic of the caliphate remains the preference of Islam and its ways, and adherence to the path of truth.

According to one Hadith attributed to Abu Hurayra that claims disobedience to imam is equivalent to disobedience to God,[73] while Quran says, 'I shall appoint a deputy on earth.'[74] There is another verse claiming, 'It is he who made you the inheritor of the earth.'[75] Ahmad Schalabi has categorized three kinds of government: Islamic, political and natural. By Islamic he means where shariah is the overwhelming force, by political he means where democratic that is based on human rationality and

---

[71] Ali Abdel Razik. *Al-Islam Wa-Usoolul-Hukm*, p. 33.
[72] Ali Abdel Razik. *Al-Islam Wa-Usoolul-Hukm*, p. 33.
[73] Ali Abdel Razik. *Al-Islam Wa-Usoolul-Hukm*, p. 27.
[74] Quran, 2:30.
[75] Quran, 6:165.

acts in the interest of the world alone and by natural government he means oppressive and where self-pleasure is the law.[76] One of the renowned legal experts of classical era, Qartabi, finds that there was no diversity of opinions among the group of Imam over the establishment of the caliphate or imamate. Had the institution of imamate not been important, the post-Prophet era would not have witnessed a series of intense discussions and the dialogues over the issue of the succession of the Prophet.[77] Ibn e Hazam, a great 11th-century Andalusian scholar of Islamic jurisprudence of Zahiri school, goes on to the extent of propounding that in the absence of imamate or the Islamic authority, the religion of Islam cannot survive.[78]

Another Islamic jurist and great expert of Quranic exegesis Imam Ghazali holds the view that establishment of an Islamic kingship is highly required for the welfare of the world and world after. Islamic governance is essential for the happiness in the life after death, and this has been the true objective of our prophets and existence of imamate is a religious obligation and, in no way can it be neglected.[79]

He also propounded the case of the application of religious teaching in the political mobilization and the structure of the nation. For instance, Imam Ghazali claims that the world cannot be ruled without an authority and that the authority must be based on the teaching of the Quran.[80] This contextual underpinning of political Islam was contested by scholars like Abdel Razek who linked the issue of governance to the subject of rationality. Meanwhile, he conceded the fact that organization of Muslim political community is prescribed in the religion and, of course, the Prophet presented a model but there was no religious sanctity of it.

Similarly, the 14th Islamic political jurist Ibn Taymiyyah claims that political governance of people in the light of Islam is one of the greatest obligations of the religion of Islam as there can

---

[76] Ahmad Schalabi. *As-Siyasah-Fil-Fikr-el-Islami*, p. 38.
[77] Hakem Al-Mutairi. 'Al-Hurriyah Ao Al-Tufan', p. 10.
[78] Hakem Al-Mutairi. 'Al-Hurriyah Ao Al-Tufan', p. 12.
[79] Hakem Al-Mutairi. 'Al-Hurriyah Ao Al-Tufan', p. 11.
[80] Ahmad Schalabi. *As-Siyasah-Fil-Fikr-el-Islami*, p. 32.

be no religion without the imamate, and God himself entrusted the mission to the community of commanding the rights and forbidding the wrongs. He laid down that the question of imamate or Emirate should be taken as a religious obligation and this is the thing which brings one closer to the God.[81] Ibn Taymiyyah pointed out that there can be no religion without the state and he further argued that men's interest can be served only in community, and the community could survive only on the behest of the ruler. Similar views were held by the disciple of Taymiyyah, Ibn Kaseer, who put that the discussion over the succession of the Prophet immediately after his death, and the appointment of collegiate by Umar underlines the importance of imamate in Islam and how Islam and the politics are interlined.[82]

Al-Izz Ibn Absdus-Salam, a 14th-century expert of Islamic shariah in the Ayyubite era of Egypt, maintained that all the Ulema of his time had reached the consensus that Islamic sovereignty is one of the most valuable manifestations of obedience and that a just governance is the most rewardable task.[83] These arguments are evident of the facts of the level of political consciousness among the companions and subsequent generation of the jurist for whom the politics were an act of obedience to God.

The question of imamate was directly linked to the ummah, and imamate was meant to lead the ummah in order to preserve the supremacy of Islam and Islamic heritage. Medieval scholars and theologians were very much concerned with preserving the unity of the ummah, and the classical ummah stands in sharp contrast to the modern-day notion of nation-state.

The ummah (community) was a community linked by bond of faith, belief, feeling, thoughts, aims, purpose and loyalty to Allah and arbitration according to shariah. This term *ummah* has different shades of meaning and covers a journey from a religious group to a people to a nation to an association of

---

[81] Hakem Al-Mutairi. 'Al-Hurriyah Ao Al-Tufan', p. 11.

[82] Hakem Al-Mutairi. 'Al-Hurriyah Ao Al-Tufan', p. 13.

[83] Hakem Al-Mutairi. 'Al-Hurriyah Ao Al-Tufan', p. 12.

believers (the Muslim community in Mecca) to a complete and organized social, economic and political system (in Medina).[84]

When the term ummah used to mean people, it refered to the socio-religious association of individuals gathered around a common leader. This meaning of ummah was broad, and the emphasis was directed at the religious, moral and ethical aspects of life. At the early stage of Medina, this term assumed another meaning when for the first time the term referred to a sizeable group of people united by common bonds of religion, shared experience and common aspiration as well as it became part of geographical and institutional arrangements that transcended ummah into a nation.

Like imamate or caliphate, shariah remained the core essence of medieval Islamic civilization, hallmark of social and moral life and a key component in the fabric of Islamic thoughts. The entire social and behavioural code of Muslims emanates from the edict of shariah. Nathan Brown and others who argue that in much of the Islamic history shariah is better understood not as a code in the modern sense of the term but as an ongoing discursive tradition articulated in and through practices associated with educational and judicial institutions.[85]

Most of the Muslims believe that shariah is God's law and is taken as a reflection of God's will for humankind, and therefore, must be in its purest sense, perfect and unchanging.[86] Traditionalists and fundamentalists differ on the subject like Salafists take the saying and action of the first three generations of Muslims as part of shariah in contrast to the established meaning of shariah which merely confined it to the deed and statements of the Prophet.[87] There is a muddled assumption that scholarly interpretations are as sacred as the Quran and the Hadith.

---

[84] Quran, 2:134, 20:16, 36:21, 3:103, 22.
[85] Muhammad Qasim Zaman. *The Ulema in Contemporary Islam*, p. 97.
[86] Quran, 48:23.
[87] John L. Esposito. *The Future of Islam* (UK: Oxford University Press, 2010), pp. 74–77.

Shariah is derived from 10 sources such as local customs, Quran, Sunnah, independent opinion, public interest, reasoning, consensus, presumption of continuity and old law of culture and scripture.[88] Shariah was the core object of theological exposition for the jurists of the medieval era. Even today, it has remained the most important tool of reference for those aspiring for political Islam. Shariah is a legal framework within which the most private aspects of life are regulated in a Muslim-majority society.[89] Shariah has become the governing tool of political Islam, and its followers believe that God's divine global command is to apply shariah. It is an informal institution of political Islam defined by one of the founding fathers of political Islam in the 20th century in the following words: 'Islam wishes to destroy all states and governments anywhere on the face of the earth which are opposed to the ideology and programme of Islam.'[90]

Allegiance and Shurah are the two components of classical writing that are very often cited by the modern-day political Islamists to accord a comprehensive nature to the Islamic political system. The case of Shurah constitutes the core of Islamic governance and acts as a replica of modern-day democracy. Prophet was very much fond of seeking opinion on all matters of political and social importance except in the case where revelation was very categorical and obvious.[91]

If Mawardi is credited with laying down the intellectual foundation of political Islamic discourse, there are others such as Ibn Sina (d. 1037), Imam Ghazali (1058–1111), Ibn Taymiyyah (1263–1328) and others who further enriched the Islamic discourse on politics, and their writings have become a catalyst for the present generation of Islamic revivalism.

The notion of philosopher king of Al-Farabi matured further with Ibn Sina who was more attracted to neo-Platonism of

---

[88] Tarek Fatah. *Chasing a Mirage: The Tragic Illusion of an Islamic State* (Ontario: John Wiley and Sons Canada Ltd, 2008), p. 250.

[89] Tarek Fatah. *Chasing a Mirage*, p. 249.

[90] Tarek Fatah. *Chasing a Mirage*, p. 252.

[91] Mohammad Shauqi Fanjari. *Kaifa Nahkumu Bil-Islam Fi-Dawlah-al-Asriyah* [How to Rule Islamically in the Modern State] (Alexendria: Al-Haiatul-Ammah Lil-Maktab-al-Iskindriyah, 1990), p. 56.

philosophy. He based his theory of state on the empirical generalization that it was in the nature of human being to complement one another.[92] He was of the view that a lawgiver or ruler must possess the combination of theoretical wisdom, justice and prophecy which make him an earthly king or God's deputy on the earth.

He saw the reality of human life not only in the presence of human government but also for Islamic religious polity. Ibn Sina proposed that the Prophet was superior to any philosopher because he was not dependent upon human reason.[93] For him, the religion was more concerned with the social affairs and, thus, to be a successful ruler; a lawgiver must possess all the qualities of the Prophet. In his proposition, Muhammad is presented as a combination of a philosopher and Prophet who combines theoretical wisdom, justice and prophecy.[94] For Ibn Sina, the ruler, to ensure obedience to him, must act exceptionally well that would make him earthly king and God's deputy on the earth.[95] According to him, imam should be capable of exercising independent judgement in legal matters (*ijtihad*) that is the feature of higher caliph.

In Ibn Sina, we can see the Greek rationality synthesizing with Arabo-Islamic political thoughts. Their political writings mainly emerged under the intense influence of the syncretism—synthesis of Greco-Arabic ideas. He was more influenced by the Platonic and the Aristotle philosophy of rationalism and logic. He analysed the issue of state and kingship through the prism of philosophical and rational eyes of Greek rather than through the puritan Islamic doctrine.

It was Imam al-Ghazali, the greatest theologian of the Seljuk period and a crucial and emblematic figure in the religious philosophy, who provided a new orientation to the philosophy of political Islam. He was a genius of the *Shafi* School of Islamic jurisprudence and penned his masterpiece *Ihyaul-Ulumu-Ddin*

---

[92] Antony Black. *The History of Islamic Political Thoughts: From the Prophet to the Present* (Pakistan: OUP, 2004), p. 74.

[93] Karen Armstrong. *A History of God* (London: Vintage Press, 1993), p. 211.

[94] Antony Black. *The History of Islamic Political Thoughts*, p. 74.

[95] Antony Black. *The History of Islamic Political Thoughts*, p. 74.

(*Revival of the Knowledge of Religious Science*) covering all aspects of social and religious life. The acquisition of knowledge is central to his political philosophy and superior to worship and legal observance.

He insisted that knowledge was the substitute for the charismatic authority of the Prophet in the post-prophetic community era, and thus, he exhorted that knowledge is equal to prophecy.[96] Knowledge stimulates prophetic authority since it is the only trace left after the departure of Mohammad and there is a close relation between prophecy and knowledge as has been mentioned in the Hadith: 'The learned are heir to Prophet.'[97]

He categorizes politics into four different compartments: prophetic, deputies, learned and preachers.[98] Ghazali asserted that even a single person, rather than being appointed by his predecessor, should elect the imam. His election must be followed by *Bayah* on the part of *Ahlal-hal waal-Aqd*. The imam must distinguish himself by observance of the laws and ought to have knowledge of ijtihad.

For him, the legitimate power emanates from the ruler only, and in his absence, all public office would be illegal and invalid.[99] Imam Ghazali called for the development of new political jurisprudence to meet the demand of a new social and political situation.[100] For Ghazali, the obedience to the ruler was more important than questioning the legitimacy of his authority. Any ruler is better than anarchy and chaos.[101] Commanding right and to forbid wrong is obligatory on the part of ruler in the light of

---

[96] Ebrahim Musa. *Ghazali and Poetics of Imagination* (Karachi: OUP, 2005), p. 197.

[97] Ebrahim Musa. *Ghazali and Poetics of Imagination*, p. 197.

[98] Antony Black. *The History of Islamic Political Thoughts: From the Prophet to the Present* (Pakistan: OUP, 2004), p. 103.

[99] Patricia Crone. *Medieval Islamic Political Thought*, p. 238.

[100] Dr. Ahmad Al-Mousalli. *Jadliyat-al-Shura wa-al-Dimmuqeratiyyah: Al-Dimmuqeratiyyah wa Huququl Insaan Fil-Fikril-Islami* [The Contestation between Islamic Shura and Democracy: Democracy and Human Rights in Islamic Thought] (Beirut: Markazi-Dirasat-Al-Wahadatul-Arabiyyah, 2007), p. 55.

[101] Hassan Askari. *Society and State in Islam: An Introduction*, p. 95.

the Quran and, in this regard, consensus and common sense are also very important.[102]

Taqi al-Din Abu al-'Abbas Ahmad ibn 'Abd al-Halim ibn 'Abd al-Salam al-Harrani al-Dimashqi, who is better known as Ibn Taymiyyah, was a jurist consult, a theologian and the most influential scholar of the late Hanbali School. He had grown up in an environment that was plagued by a series of intellectual and political crises, where Mutazilites were at forefront to have recourse to Greek philosophy buttressing the position of Islam.

Like all political reformers, he also referred to the Quran and the Hadith for his ideological formulation, and his political ideas were inspired mainly by the vision of shariah. He pleaded for rediscovering the original teachings of Islam and called for individual judgement in the interpretation of religious doctrines. His religious mission was based on presenting the correct meaning of the Quran and the religious laws, and he himself puts these in the following words: 'I have examined all the philosophical and theological methods and found them incapable of curing ill or quenching any thirst. For me the best method is the Quran.'[103]

His most important political treaty is *Al-Kitab al-Siyasa al-Sharaiyyah* (*The Book on the Government of Religious Laws*) written in 1311–15. He argued in favour of moulding the politics in colour of all embracing and adaptable shariah and for him the application of shariah in matters of governance was an Islamic project that must be taken with all seriousness.

Unlike his contemporary Islamic thinkers and modern-day Islamists, Ibn Taymiyyah's idea of Islamic state was not inspired by the Prophet's rule in Medina. He argues that the Prophet did not establish any Islamic state and, according to him, Medina state was a prophetic state rather than an Islamic state since the institution of prophecy was a divine arrangement.[104] Ibn Taymiyyah did not believe in the assumption, unlike Shiite the thinkers of his time, that the institution of imamates was the first

---

[102] Michael Cook. *Commanding Right and Forbidding Wrongs in Islamic Thought*, p. 428.

[103] Karan Armstrong. *A History of God* (London: Vintage Press, 1993), p. 298.

[104] Qamruddin Khan. *The Political Thought of Ibn Taymiyah* (Pakistan: Islamic Research Institute, 1983), p. 60.

faith of article but rather he claimed in *Minhajul-Sunnah* that faith and not the state was the foremost consideration in religion. For him, state was a necessary culmination of acceptance of faith and not the vice versa.

However, despite all these reservations and limitations, Ibn Taymiyyah did not ignore or belittle the importance of a political agency but regarded it as an instrument of the highest necessity for the fullest realization of the aims and objectives of religion. The existence of public authority is inbuilt in the social structure of human life. Reason and religion both necessitate the establishment of a moral authority with the sole intention of establishing the rule of God on the earth.

He believed in the dire necessity of an Islamic state but refuted the claims of others that creation of a state is the principal aim of prophecy. He argued that the creation of a state was a part of Islamic teachings and the propagation of Islam could not be subordinated to the creation of the state. He insisted that the religion of Islam must be taken in totality where it encompasses politics, governance, authority and the state itself. To put the argument in his own words: 'Purpose of authority in Islam is meant to enforce the words of God on earth, to achieve happiness and prosperity, establish justice and accept his superiority in the governance of his subject.'[105]

For Ibn Taymiyyah, the purpose and mission of an Islamic state is rooted in the subordination to the sovereignty of God where the ultimate judgement belongs to His will only. In the schema of Ibn Taymiyyah, state is the part of the divine system of justice and ordained for affecting it on the earth. On the issue of caliphate, he differs from his predecessors and is said to never treat this entity as an Islamic institution; this could never become the part of his model of Islamic polity. Instead of using the term imamah or caliphate, he designated this political body as imarah (government), and while discussing the qualification of ruler, he focused on *wilayah* instead of caliph or imam.

---

[105] Henry Laoust. *Nazariyyat Sheikh-al-Islam Ibn Taymiyyah fi-assiyasah wal Ijtama* [The Social and Political Thought of Ibn Taymiyyah]. trans. Abdul Azim Ali. (Cairo: Dar-al-Manar, 1979), p. 224.

Thus far we have seen how the ideas and concepts of political authority in the medieval period crystallized with the passage of time. A good deal of literature on the subject evolved and grew under the shade of different sectarian schools that had its own sociopolitical and historical contexts. In the next section, I would deal with the subject in the modern context when secularized humanities and social science had made their way into the heritage of Muslim civilization. Modern theoretical tools of social science were applied comprehensibly, and new conceptual tool were too put to test to study the Islamic repository of politics and culture.

When the Muslims encountered the colonial power of the West, social and human science were mature enough which was the outcome of gradual and long-term evolution of Western Christianity. Religious dogma, belief and perception were for the Westerners not more than a subject of study and distinctly not an object of any privileged status. Religion was put to test under the light of rational investigation and an alternative of Muslim religious beliefs, religion and new religious attitude was carved out at the hand of new enlightened thinkers of the West. It was European ideas that had started controlling the nations of the Arab region. Arab faced the question of who controlled the power and nation and the issue of intellectual and spiritual realm.

It was the phase when the Arabs were struggling between new ideas, ideals, norms, values and traditional Islamic conception. It was the phase of oscillation between modern and traditional ways of life. It was an era of belief in traditional culture but with a desire to modernize.

3

Islamic Response to the Arab Politics During Colonial and Post-colonial Phases

Religion is essential but reform is equally necessary.[1]

—Sayyed Jamal al-Din al-Afghani

The Islam-infested political discourse in the medieval period was of a unilateral nature when theologians were essentially occupied with laying down the rules and norms for Islamic governance. The growing literature on Islamism in the Abbasid period was combined with the consolidation of the supremacy of Islam as a religion over the vast tract of lands.

The classical/medieval era of Islam exploded and expanded without any external resistance. The political, territorial and intellectual domains of Islam enjoyed complete internal autonomy and shaped the course of events and developments independently. The growth of unilateral literature on political Islam was reflective of the ascent of Muslim powers in different parts of the world. The explanatory and interpretative phase of Quranic teachings, during the Abbasid era in particular, centred on preserving the fundamental Quranic principles of ummah, shariah, jihad and the caliphate. The Quran and deeds of the Prophet were the fountain head of political discourse where men's liberation and God's worship were considered the primary objective of the human existence. The Quran and

---

[1] Armstrong, *A History of God*, 416.

the shariah were sought primarily to establish justice and to achieve a just society.[2] State and the ummah were supposed to be in the service of Islam.

But the European encroachment beginning in the 18th century and its gradual consolidation in the later part of the 19th century in the Arab world turned the nature of political Islamic discourse upside down and confronted the centuries-old ideas of divine political governance. The introduction of the philosophy of sovereignty of man-made laws were ushered into the third stratum of political Islamic discourse. It witnessed a departure from the previous contents of the ummah, shariah and jihad, which were later replaced with nation-state, secularism and democracy of the West. The trilogy of caliphate, shariah and jihad vanished completely from the centrality of the Islamic discourse after the arrival of Western colonization when the shariah was replaced by the Western legal code.[3]

The 19th century saw a retreat from all these principles of the past, and an era of unilateral discourse or recitation was replaced by an epoch of ideological contestation and political confrontation against the West in terms of culture, history, religion, philosophy and state of religion itself in man's life. It was an era of spread of new 'ism' in the form of communism, socialism and liberalism which called for the end of the role of the Ulema. Interest and necessity became dominant over welfare and the Quranic and theological text. The impact of expansionist Europe on the Arab land was pivotal in shaping both the political Islamic and modernist thoughts of Muslims as these thoughts were driven by the European experiences of military, technological and intellectual superiority.

The Arab world, in reaction to the Western penetration at all levels, witnessed two streams of reactions: the first called for complete integration with the European model of moral behavioural norms; the second was plagued more by uncertainty whether to reject the influences of the West altogether or to recreate an Islamic state according to shariah and the Quran. The modern era was accompanied by constant internal contestations:

---

[2] Quran, Hadid: 25 (Fifty-seventh chapter of Quran).
[3] Al-Mutairi, 'Al-Hurriyah Ao Al-Tufan', 268.

either the West should be the model of progress or development or it should be treated as 'other' enemy, as the Europeans have been treating the Arabs. According to Mandeville: 'The Christian West had much strong notion of the Muslims as "other" than the Muslims did of Christians.'[4]

The adherents of the former were believers in an evolutionary view of history with the West being at the pinnacle of world civilization and they had all praise for Western culture and civilization. For instance, one Moroccan scholar Muhammad Al-Saffar was baffled by cleanliness of France in the 19th century and says:

> So it was until all had passed, leaving our heart consumed with fire from what we had seen of their overwhelming power and mastery. In comparison with the weakness of Islam, the dissipation of its strength, disrupted conditions of its people, how confident they are, how completely they are master of state, how firm their laws, how capable in wars and successful in vanishing their enemies.[5]

Another 19th-century Egyptian liberal thinker Rifaa Tahtavi had great admiration for Western culture and owed his intellectual formation to his stay in Paris alone. He puts his impression of the French society, which deserves attention here, as follows: 'How civilized the French are and how their state is bound to justice who treated even the representative of toppled regime so well.'[6]

Those who believed in the Western technological and cultural supremacy called for reformulating the Islamic methodology in a manner congruent with the standards of the 19th-century social theory of democracy and constitutionalism and rejected the polygamy and male domination. Karen Armstrong has seen its effect in the context of the Arab Muslim society as follows: 'Muslim world were engaging in a struggle to catch up with

---

[4] Peter Mandeville, *Transnational Muslim Politics* (London: Rutledge, 2001), 74.

[5] Ibrahim M. Abu Rabi, *Intellectual Origin of Islamic Resurgence in the Arab World* (Albany: State University of New York Press, 1996), 7.

[6] Bassam Tibbi, *The Challenge of Fundamentalism: The Political Islam and the New World Disorder* (Los Angles: University of California Press, 1998), 184.

the West and some saw secularism as an answer where religion would be relegated to a minor rule.'[7]

In contrast, there were others who completely rejected the notion of social evolution and portrayed the West as having an aggressive political system, exploitative and materialistic economic institutions, and decadent culture. Rather than attempting to reform and modernize Islam, they aimed at virtually Islamizing all social institutions and rejected any level of dissociation between religion and politics. During this so-called political reform period in the Arab world, one can notice the different and divergent reactions to the European political philosophy and culture. Ali Pasha of Egypt, reacting to Machiavelli's Prince, said: 'The Europe couldn't claim to teach us much about the art of ruling and I have nothing to learn from Machiavelli.'[8]

The intellectuals confronting the Western onslaughts reacted to the West either by borrowing some of the Western elements, and accrediting them the true expressions of Islamic idealism and values, or by resorting to the Islamic revivalism going back to the basic source of revelation.[9] Mainly two different waves emerged among the intellectuals in the wake of the growing presence of the West and both had the claim over Islamic heritage. The thoughts of one were very much confined to the promotion of political Islam that was well couched in Islamic idioms and frameworks. The second wave was not oriented towards an Islamic idealism and, instead, it was more concerned with the worldly affairs alone. The two emerging tendencies at the dawn of the 19th century were at odds with each other. The former was an ideology of contestation and the latter can be described as an apologetic ideology of acceptance.[10] The 19th-century Islamic political thoughts can be best understood as a reflection of an enduring conflict between two antagonistic ideologies. I will broadly confine myself to elucidate upon the ideology of contestation, which subscribes to the idea of political Islam.

---

[7] Armstrong, *A History of God*, 414.
[8] Black, *The History of Islamic Political Thoughts*, 281.
[9] Black, *The History of Islamic Political Thoughts*, 279.
[10] Charles E. Butterworth and I. William Zartman, eds., *Between the State and Islam* (New York: Cambridge University Press, 2001), 90.

The nature of political, cultural and economic contact with the West instigated a feeling of deep resentment and revolt among the Arabs. The Arab followers of Islam started questioning its own role and status in the existing circumstances. They also questioned the very legitimacy of the presence of the West in the Islamic domain. Thus, the very presence of the West became the root cause of the revivalism in the Muslim world, which was qualitatively different from the earlier phase of the awakening movements. The appearance of the West on the cultural and political horizons of the Arab world played the role of a prince whose kiss awakened a king who had been sleeping for long and later disrupted the society, causing much of the power disequilibrium.[11]

The French Revolution had already pioneered the idea of modern nationalism, new ideas of freedom and equality, and European intellectuals along with the orientalists, and the colonial and imperialist hawks exploited these new political notions to pin down the Arab-Islamic intellectuals in order to degrade the Arab polity, culture and religious values. It was a time when the Christendom was expanding culturally, economically, militarily and, of course, politically in the form of colonialism.

Over a period of time, the Islamic world became weak and more vulnerable to the external pressure and demand. It was for the first time that the new ideas and practices, imported from the European philosophical and political lexicon, were applied to define Arabs' political identity. The territorial nation was conceived for the first time by Saidik Rifaa Pasha, who composed the edict of 1839. This era is also considered to be the beginning of political nationalism in the Arab world.[12] An institutional reform was also introduced under this programme to redress the political and economic pressure of Europe. A Europe-inspired federal and bureaucratic model was adopted to resolve the myriad grievances of different communities. Western powers had become so arrogant of their political system and governance that after the occupation of Egypt in 1798, Napoleon had remarked:

---

[11] L. Carl Brown, *Religion and State: Muslim Approach to Politics* (New York: Columbia University Press, 2000), 87.

[12] Black, *The History of Islamic Political Thoughts*, 283.

'I found no Arab officials to take over as an administrator and so I had to ask Albanians and others to look after this job.'[13]

For the first time, the Muslim world lost its political and cultural sovereignty and autonomy in the sphere of its foreign policy. A greater part of the Muslim world had become a closed book. Its nature and impact can be described in the language of Ernest Renan: 'Iron circle enclosing the head of the faithful in orient and Africa making them impervious to fresh ideas and incapable of anything new.'[14]

G.W.F. Hegel narrated the drama of the vanishing role of the Islamdom in the following words: 'Islam had long vanished from stages of history and had retarded into orient ease and reposes.'[15]

To quote M. Arkaun here: 'The encounter between Arab and West created a new condition to which Arab and Muslim thoughts responded by creating a new expression.'[16]

The Arab political and intellectual response to this new development can only be understood in the backdrop of *Nahdah* (the Arab Renaissance) of the 19th century. This Nahdah stood against perpetual erosion of Islamic culture and belief as a force under the colonial impact. It was the doctrinal, philosophical and historical discourse that emerged as the bedrock or mainstay of Nahdah. It was the doctrinal aspect that was more prominently discussed by the erstwhile thinkers and intellectuals. For them, doctrinal reform was a true source of political and social reform in the 19th century and all those who talked of doctrinal reform were great proponents of going back to original sources for affecting a realistic reform.

While the main thrust of philosophical doctrine was to prove the authenticity of the traditional Islamic discourse and its significance to the present Muslim generation, the discourse of Nahdah was more involved with the subject of religion–state relation; these discourses underwent several transformative phases since the Arab Renaissance. Initially, Islam assumed the

---

[13] Benjamin Walker, *Foundation of Islam: The Making of World Faith* (Delhi: Rupa, 2002), 345.
[14] Walker, *Foundation of Islam*, 346.
[15] Walker, *Foundation of Islam*, 345.
[16] Rabi, *Intellectual Origin of Islamic Resurgence in the Arab World*, 8.

nationalist meaning in order to build a strong state that would be able to compete with the West, while later the phase shifted towards pan-Islamism which was pioneered by philosopher–thinkers like Afghani, Abduh and Rashid Rida. It was only in the midst of this transformation of the reform process that the notion of political Islam emerged, which could be put more aptly in the words of Bilqazir: 'It was in the womb of Islamic reformist movement that notion of puritan Islamic state was conceived.'[17] It was the last phase of the historical and political discourse of Nahdah that was marked by the emergence of several Islamist movements that had completely abandoned the two previous components of Nahdah: doctrinal and philosophical.

Sayyed Jamal al-Din al-Afghani (1837–97)

Sayyed Jamal al-Din al-Afghani was one of the most dramatic figures of the 19th-century Arab world who tried to restate the Muslim tradition in a way that might meet the agonizing problems brought by the growing encroachment of the West. He is regarded as a path-breaker anti-imperialist thinker and leader. There was scarcely a social and political tendency in Muslim lands—modernism, nationalism, pan-Islamism—that Al-Afghani's catholic and vital sensibilities did not touch. Abduh, one of his enlightened disciples, praises him in the following words: 'He was the one who lit the lamp of knowledge and enlightened the intellect and removed all oddness from the mind of the people.'[18]

He was a neo-traditionalist and ideologue rejecting both pure traditionalism and pure Westernism. His mode of reinterpreting the past in modern and nationalist terms displayed his disposition that was to become popular in the Arab world.[19]

---

[17] Abdullah Balqazir, *Ad-Daulah fil-Fikril islami al-muasir* [The State in Modern Islamic Thought] (Beirut: Center for Arab Unity Studies, 2002), 19.

[18] Al-Mutairi, 'Al-Hurriyah Ao Al-Tufan', 284.

[19] Nikki R. Keddie, *An Islamic Response to Imperialism: Political and Religious Writings of Sayyid Jamal ad-Din al-Afghani* (Berkeley, CA: California Press, 1964), 3.

Sayyed Jamal al-Din al-Afghani, whose national origin is disputed, was a journalist, an activist and a travelling theorist. He himself composed a prose evoking the misunderstanding about him in different parts of the region. He says:

> The English people believe me a Russian
> The Muslims think me a Zoroastrian
> The Sunni think me a Shiite
> And Shiite thinks me an enemy of Ali
> Some of the friends of the four companions have believed me a Wahabbi.[20]

He spent his good span of time in Calcutta, Cairo, Istanbul, Russia, England and Paris during his active pursuit. He remained actively engaged in debating culture and politics with leading intellectuals of his time, such as Ernest Renan of France and Sir Syed Ahmad Khan of India. For most of his life, he kept on travelling around the world and, wherever he went, left deep impact on the Muslim intellectuals and Islamic and political movements of the country. One of his disciples and his contemporary, Sheikh Mohammad Abduh, who also founded with him the tribune of pan-Islamism, al-Urwa al-Wuthqa (Indissoluble Link), published in the year 1884, called him a master thinker who was burning with zeal to speak for religion and was faithful.[21]

A well-known authority on Islamic history, Karen Armstrong, has described Sayyed Jamal al-Din al-Afghani's personality in the following words:

> He attempted to be all things to all men. He was capable of presenting himself as Sunni to Sunni and a Shiite martyr to Shiites, a revolutionary, a religious philosopher and a parliamentarian.[22]

He called for a new dawn of Islam, and an Algerian scholar Malik Bin Nabi describes him as the one who asked Muslims to strive for success and the one who woke up all slumbering

---

[20] Nikki R. Keddie, 'The Pan Islamic Appeal: Afghani and Abdulhamid', *Middle Eastern Studies* 3, no. 1 (1966), 54.

[21] Butterworth and Zartman, *Between the State and Islam*, 95.

[22] Armstrong, *A History of God*, 416.

Muslims.[23] He was a man of Islamic culture and maintained a unique identity of his own; he found the reason behind spiritual and materialistic poverty in the Muslim world. He called a war against the rotten thoughts and redundant ideas of Islam. His first objective was to establish a political system based on Islamic brotherhood which had been torn by the intervention of the imperialist powers.

Al-Afghani was pained by the suppression of Muslims in India and of Tatars in Russia in the last quarter of the 19th century. He did not believe in the imitation and insisted that the Quran itself contained several of the Western values like freedom, dignity, justice, reason and patriotism.[24] He was an ardent believer in tracing the origin of Western modernity in the Islamic tradition and teaching.[25] The desire to Westernize and the need to avoid identification with the West was one of the major contradictions of his life.

He wrote in 1897, exhorting the Muslims, 'O, son of the east do not you know that power of the western and their domination over you came about through advance in learning and education and your decline in those domain.'[26]

In 1877, James Sanua established a satirical journal with Afghani's help—*Abu naddara Zarqa* (The Man with Blue Spectacles). The conversations contained in the journal condemned the Ottoman-Egyptians as well as European infidels looting the Muslim countries.[27]

He wrote the *Refutation of the Materialists* (the most famous work in Persian known in the West) and *The Benefits of Philosophy*. The letter was translated in Arabic too by Abduh, in which he was assisted by a Persian servant of Afghani Abu Tuirah who, despite being an illiterate, furnished Abduh with knowledge about Al-Afghani's Persian works.[28]

---

23 Al-Mutairi, 'Al-Hurriyah Ao Al-Tufan', 280.

24 Mishra, *From the Ruins of Empire*, 68.

25 Keddie, *An Islamic Response to Imperialism*, 42.

26 Mishra, *From the Ruins of Empire*, 55.

27 Mishra, *From the Ruins of Empire*, 81–82.

28 Keddie, *An Islamic Response to Imperialism*, 8–9.

Afghani was an ardent supporter of Muslim unity and in a letter to Ottoman Sultan Abdulhamid in 1892, he had articulated the following:

> All have only one desire that of making our land disappear up to our last trace. And in this there is no distinction to make between Russia, England, Germany or France, especially if they perceive our weakness and our impotence to resist the design. If on the contrary we are united, if the Muslims are a single man, we can be of harm and of use and our voice will be heard.[29]

The Ottoman ruler Abdulhamid invited Al-Afghani in the year 1892 to discuss some of his important political plans. Availing the opportunity, Al-Afghani openly called for political unionism. He called upon political leaders to take every possible action to dislodge the Europeans from their respective countries. He took the ideas of return to the principle of Islam first from India, demand for charismatic leadership from Shiites and holding common and positive views of Western science from Sayyed Ahmad Khan and Khair-al Din Tunisi.[30] It was the same Tunisian Khayr al-Din al-Tunisi who had become a devoted admirer of Voltaire, Condillac, Rousseau and Montesquieu, regretting only the philosopher's bitter attack on the religion.[31]

For Al-Afghani, the adoption of the culture of materialism by Muslims was a source of apprehension, and the central focus of *Risala Fi radd ala al-Dahriyin* [Rebuttal to Atheism] was the harmful aspects of the materialistic culture. He held the belief that the history of pagan Greek to capitalism and communism had proved that how materialism with numerous manifestations had corrupted the religion and its basis. Analyzing the degeneration of the Muslim mind, he wrote:

> The beginning of weaknesses of Muslim goes back to the day when belief and faith in materialism appeared like religion. In the land of Islam, each period of doubts and decline had a

---

[29] Keddie, 'The Pan Islamic Appeal', 46–67.
[30] Black, *The History of Islamic Political Thoughts*, 302–03.
[31] Mishra, *From the Ruins of Empire*, 51.

correspondence with the appearance of materialism in one form or another.[32]

His Islam included an idealized picture of the age of the Prophet and the first four caliphates, and according to him, if scriptures contradict reason or science, scriptures must be reinterpreted. A reopening of the door of *ijtihad* combined with a return to emphasize on the Quran which could lead to a Protestant type of reform of Islam.[33]

He believed that Muslims could repel the West not by rejecting their reason and science but by re-appropriating reason, science and technology, which according to him was integral to the religion of Islam. He had all appreciation for Western intellectualism, science and technology and called for resistance as well as its adoption in the light of Islam.[34]

Al-Afghani was inspired by the idealism of going back to the origin to recover Muslims' glorious past, to achieve the Muslim unity by bringing a separate Muslim state under the single caliphate so as to restore Islam to its past glory and finally to fight against those imperialist countries that sought to seize the Islamic land, subjugate their people and enslave them politically and culturally. The only solution to the present crisis lay, according to him, in the following true Islamic principles of politics and philosophy.[35]

Few Arab historians consider Afghani to be 'the first Arab intellectual to look into the global political world through the prism of the East and the West by considering the East and the West as two historical antagonistic blocks'.[36]

One of the greatest Islamic thinkers of the 20th century, Iqbal, holds the same views about him:

---

[32] Keddie, 'The Pan Islamic Appeal', 46–67.

[33] Keddie, *An Islamic Response to Imperialism*, 37.

[34] W.C. Smith, *Islam in Modern History* (Princeton: Princeton University Press), 56.

[35] Black, *The History of Islamic Political Thoughts*, 303.

[36] Ahmad Bilqazir, *Ad-Daulah fil-Fikril Islami al-muasir* (Beirut: Center for Arab Unity Studies, 2002), 44.

The man, however, who fully realized the importance and the immensity of the task and whose deep insight into the inner meaning of Muslim engendered by his wide experience of men and manners, would have made him a living link between the past and the future was Jamal-ud-Din Afghani. If his infatigable but divided energy could have devoted itself entirely to Islam as a system of human belief and conduct, the world of Islam, intellectually speaking, would have been much more on solid ground.[37]

He described Islam as a faith that is distinguished by its rootless cult of reason. He perceived Islam not as a religion but as an entire civilization divested of its particular political division and which should unite in a single pan-Islamic movement against the West.

Al-Afghani was proposing nothing short of Prophet's shariah and compared the Prophet with the philosopher king. He called for the strengthening of the parliamentary system of government and praised republicanism and constitutionalism and condemned the Ottoman rule to impose backward interpretation of Islam.[38] Afghani initiated the partial transformation of Islam from generally held religious faith to an ideology of political use in uniting Muslims against the West. In the words of Sylvia Haim, 'What Afghani did was to make Islam into the mainspring of solidarity, and thus he placed it on the same footing as other solidarity producing before....'[39] Al-Afghani tried to unify the Islamic philosophy and mystical traditions with the call to restore Islam to the political ascendancy.

He completely rejected the Western secular tendency and pleaded for demonstrating Islamic activism in this world only. For him, Islam was a comprehensive religion that encompasses ritual practices, civil laws, government and society. According to him, a true Muslim should struggle to carry out the words of God in history and, thus, seek success in this life and the thereafter. To quote him here:

---

[37] Muhammad Iqbal, *The Reconstruction of Religious Thoughts in Islam* (New Delhi: Kitab Bhavan, 1990), 97.

[38] Mishra, *From the Ruins of Empire*, 82.

[39] Keddie, *An Islamic Response to Imperialism*, 35.

The principle of Islamic religion cannot be restricted to calling man to truth or considering the soul only in spiritual context. There are more besides: Islamic principle is concerned with relationship among believers, they explain the laws in general and in detail, they define the executive powers, which administer the laws. Thus in truth, the ruler of the Muslims will be their religious, holy and divine laws. Unlike the other religion, Islam is not only concerned with the life to come but is also associated with the believers' interest in this world.[40]

Afghani stressed the practical political side of Islam rather than its speculative or theological side. When the religious ideals conflicted with the practical goals, it was the former that gave the way.[41] It is hard to escape the impression that in early Islam and in the modern West what he valued most was power and political strength. He attempted to prove that the Quran enjoined the acquisition of the most modern and effective armaments. When there was a conflict between justice and equality on the one hand and building a strong Islamic state capable of withstanding the Western encroachment on the other, he consistently opted for the latter.[42] He was well convinced that people could be ruled well by men of their own community, tradition and belief.[43] He explained the ideas of unity among the independent Muslim states in the following words:

I do not mean to plea for the rule of any particular person as it may be considered to be difficult. However I do wish the command that Quran should prevail over them and the religion of Islam should be as means of their unity.[44]

He was also of the view that jurisprudence among the Muslims includes all domestic, municipal and state laws. Thus, a person who has studied jurisprudence is profoundly worthy

---

[40] John L. Esposito, *Islam: The Straight Path* (New York: OUP, 1998), 128.

[41] Keddie, *An Islamic Response to Imperialism*, 41.

[42] Keddie, *An Islamic Response to Imperialism*, 41.

[43] Keddie, *An Islamic Response to Imperialism*, 42.

[44] Sayyed Jamal al-Din al-Afghani, *Al-Urwa al-Wuthqa* [The Deepest Bond] (Cairo: Dar-al-Arab, 1957), 221–22.

of being the prime minister of the realm or the chief ambassador of the state.[45] He envisaged that mosques and educational institutions should play both political and cultural roles.[46] Afghani stressed for alliance and coordination among the Ulema of different nations and propounded the view that Ulema should have an organization in every respective country and a central office in Mecca. This organization would extend all kinds of religious and political cooperation at the time of crisis.

His socio-religious and cultural programme was mainly a political project to revive the Islamic community (*Millah*) and re-establish a political power. His revival of Islam in the political and religious sphere depended mainly upon the adoption of constitutional and republican government with an active civic spirit. To quote him in the following words:

> We need a patriotic zeal who knows that their honour is only in their race, their power is in their community (*Ummah*) and their glory is in their fatherland and we need parliamentary rule.[47]

He further says, 'My brother, arise from the sleep of neglect. Know that Islamic people were one the strongest in rank, the most valuable in the worth ... only laziness, stupidity, and ignorance are obstacle to [our] advance.'[48]

Al-Afghani claimed that religion is the mainstay of any nation and their prosperity comes through it. It is the religious dogma that provides a solid base on which the foundation of any civilization is built.[49] He makes an equivalence expression between patriotism and religious faith and both are seen leading to the same virtue, and it is reflected in his equal zeal to protect local nationalism, pan-Islam and the defence of the Islamic religion.[50]

Perhaps he was the first one to cite the Quranic passage as an admonition to modern changes and progress. His imagination

---

[45] Keddie, *An Islamic Response to Imperialism*, 106.
[46] Al-Afghani, *Al-Urwa al-Wuthqa*, 119–20.
[47] Black, *The History of Islamic Political Thoughts*, 302.
[48] Nikki R. Keddie, *Sayyed Jamal al-Din al-Afghani: A Political Biography* (Berkeley, CA: University of California Press, 1972), 64.
[49] Butterworth and Zartman, *Between the State and Islam*, 96.
[50] Keddie, *An Islamic Response to Imperialism*, 67.

of Muslim emanates from their glorious past and he claims that the world has been witness to the excellence achieved by Muslims in the past.[51]

He had more psychological role to play than political and was not a thinker exploring the reason and the cause but was an activist. He was more concerned with reorganizing the Muslim polity of the Arab world and organization for him was reorganizing the Islamic laws. He knew what had plagued the ummah, and instead of seeking a solution, he preferably called to change the system and the laws itself.

Disintegration of Ottoman Empire and Islamism as a Response

The collapse of the Ottoman Empire in 1924 further deepened the political, moral and religious crises of Muslims. For the first time since 632, Muslim global community became caliphate-less and the Muslim world had no political legal authority. The caliphate authority had been on the wane since the rise of Europe, but the abolition came as a jolt for the Muslim world.

The question of caliphate galvanized globally, inciting the question of religiosity of the caliphate. This question regained significance and people went back to the Quran to affirm the legitimacy of the caliphate as an institution, and this question of legitimacy laid the foundation of the context for the search of political and novel sorts of debates and arguments that dominated the academic discourse about the organization of the political community and political authenticity.

The Western concept of nation and nationalism as the sole legitimate framework for political action was imposed on most parts of the Arab-Muslim world. Demise of the Ottoman Empire inaugurated a new era in the history of Islamic thought and awakening that generated new discourses and narratives for coping with the new situation and demands.

---

[51] Keddie, *An Islamic Response to Imperialism*, 83.

After the abolition of the Ottoman Empire, there appeared a different set of writings and a new political Islamic discourse. One set of thinkers envisaged the solution of the erstwhile peril of the Muslim world in resorting back to the political mobilization in the name of Islam. The other school led by Ali Abdul Razzaq and Sheikh Muhammad Mustafa al-Muraghi, Azhar's rector, baffled the Islamic world by their innovative ideas calling to abolish the caliphate and the Islamic Court. Ali Abdul Razzaq also claimed that Islam did not subscribe to specific political principle or ideology and called for the abolition of the caliphate system and Islamic state.[52]

It takes back one to the era of Ibn Taymiyyah of the 14th century, where he had drawn attention to the presence of a group in the city of Kufa, which had discarded and disapproved the political elements of Islam and created a cleavage between shariah and the politics.[53]

Qazi Mansoor Al-Sharai in his writings justified the politics of Kamal Ataturk of forced secularization and referred to the rule of Abu Baker which, according to him, was not religious or Islamic governance.[54] Ali Abdul Aziz Fahmi Pasha, a great Egyptian legal expert of the first half of the 20th century, claimed that religion is for God and politics is for mankind.[55]

While browsing the pages of history, one comes across another set of writing propounded by a host of Islamic ideologues who were overwhelmingly romanticizing the Islamic heritage and were desirous of replicating it in the modern era when Western ideas and thoughts were reigning in the intellectual landscape of the time.

These groups were represented by Mustafa Sabri, a great philosopher and theologian of the 20th century, who saw the separation of religion and politics as the exit from the house of Islam and pointed out that a state must be governed under the laws of Islam.

---

[52] Al-Mutairi, 'Al-Hurriyah Ao Al-Tufan', 268.
[53] Al-Mutairi, 'Al-Hurriyah Ao Al-Tufan', 269.
[54] Al-Mutairi, 'Al-Hurriyah Ao Al-Tufan', 302.
[55] Al-Mutairi, 'Al-Hurriyah Ao Al-Tufan', 325.

For Muhammad Ahmad Shakir, the Quran and Sunnah should be the sources of law in Egypt and went so far as to claim that the origin of decline of Muslims could be traced to the imitation of Western laws by the Muslim community instead of Quranic laws.[56] He also argued that Muslims were forced to adopt the Western code of laws merely after translating them, which had no root in the indigenous society in terms of religion, culture and values. Another 19th-century prominent Syrian scholar, Abdurrahman Kawakebi, referring to Western cultural onslaught, observed that if one goes today with the wind, tomorrow certainly he would lose his tent.[57]

In the following pages, I would present and argue about the views of those set of ideologues and thinkers who had borne the brunt of demise of the Ottoman Empire and vehemently supported the ideas of integration of religion and politics. These scholars were at pains to see the replacement of the Islamic political model with the modern Western system at variance with the traditional Islamic teaching. They pleaded for the revival of political teaching of Islam, and men like Hassan Al-Banna (1906–49), Sayyed Qutb (1912–66), Sayyed Abu al-Ala Mawdudi (1903–79), and Imam Rohollah Ayatollah Khomeini (1902–89) left a long-lasting influence on the ensuing generations of proponents of Islamic activism or Islamism itself.

Hassan Al-Banna was one of those thinkers who stands out for having exerted lasting influences on the theoretical foundation of Islamic resurgence in the modern Arab world. After Al-Afghani, he was the first Arab thinker who had captured the imagination of Arab streets and, in some respect, his popularity was more widespread than Al-Afghani who had transcended the intellectual circles. He played a pivotal role in shaping the ideology of *Ikhwan* (MBH), founded by him in 1928.

According to Mohammad A. Khalafallah, 'His charisma stem from his being the founder of biggest socio-religious movement in the modern Arab world who defined the parameters of its

---

[56] Al-Mutairi, 'Al-Hurriyah Ao Al-Tufan', 324–25.
[57] Al-Mutairi, 'Al-Hurriyah Ao Al-Tufan', 329.

mission, purpose and method.'[58] His ideological foundation had taken place in the backdrop of a number of alarming developments at home, like the establishment of several secular universities in Egypt in the late 1920s, which for him was nothing but a prelude to Turkish style of the gradual abandonment of Islam. The secularist and rationalist outlook of Western modernity was venturing in the common masses. Not only secularist ideas were being propagated by writers such as Salam Musa, Taha Hussain and others but some scholars from Azhar even seemed to have adopted the Western tools in interpreting the Islamic issues.[59]

He narrated the erstwhile situation in the following words:

> After the last war (World War 1st) and during the period I spent in Cairo, there was increase in spiritual and intellectual disintegration in the name of intellectual freedom. There was also a deterioration of moral behaviour and deeds in the name of individual freedom. I saw that social life of beloved Egyptian nation was oscillating between her dear and precious Islamism which she had inherited and defended, live with and became accustomed to ... and this severe Western invasion which is armed and equipped with all the destructive and degenerative influences of money, wealth, prestige, ostentation, material enjoyment, powers and means of propaganda.[60]

He had developed his own Islamic political ideas and later became a great political theorist. The basic thrust of the MBH was to fulfil the objective of Islam by reorganizing the society in the light of Islamic teaching and the formation of true Muslim community by injecting moral values and self-righteousness. He said at the time of the inauguration of the MBH: 'Only those people who can sacrifice their life can be workable for this organization.'[61]

---

[58] Rabi, *Intellectual Origin of Islamic Resurgence in the Arab World*, 64.
[59] Nazih N. Ayubi, *Political Islam: Religion and Politics in the Arab World* (London: Routledge, 1991), 130.
[60] Rabi, *Intellectual Origin of Islamic Resurgence in the Arab World*, 65.
[61] Mohammad Shauqi Zaki, *Tahrik-i- Al-Ikhwan al-Muslimeen:Mazi aur Hal* (Karachi: Majlisi-Nashriyatu-al-Islam, 1999), 100.

It was under his ideological and organizational leadership that the MBH became a powerful political and social movement. He, through this organization, called for the establishment of Islamic order in the country. Banna was calling for return to the religion in its true sense and spirit, and to abide by the true vision of Islam. He envisaged that secularism as propagated by both the Western modernist and the Islamic modernist was anathema to the true Islam.

His Islamic orientation and approach was based on a particular worldview that was not confined merely to religion. Islam, for Banna, was simultaneously a civilization, a way of life, ideology and finally a state in itself.[62] To put his thought more properly in his own words:

> Islam dominates every aspect of life. Islamic teaching provides leadership and those who associate Islam with spiritualism is on the wrong track. Islamic faith is a worship, nationalism and patriotism, religion and state.[63]

Banna wrote *Nizam-al-Usrah* (Family System), which serves as a blueprint for spiritual training. In this manifesto, he addressed a group of Mujahideen: 'God should be objective, Prophet should be leader and Quran should serve as a constitution.'[64] He took the Quran as an ideological text and an all-encompassing document. According to him, the Quran provides a standard for social reform and political unity. For Hassan Banna, the Quran serves as the foundation of Islam, which takes it beyond a reformist movement and allows it to take the character of radical movement.

In the formative phase of Banna's ideological foundation, mosques played a very important role. Mosque for him was a place of Islamic revolution, radical transformation and renewal, and a symbol of Islamic rule. Mosque is such a place where secular domain and space cease to exist. By this proposition, Banna wanted to instil the feeling in the mind and heart of people

---

[62] Rabi, *Intellectual Origin of Islamic Resurgence in the Arab World*, 65.

[63] Zaki, *Tahrik-i- Al-Ikhwan al-Muslimeen*, 99.

[64] Zaki, *Tahrik-i- Al-Ikhwan al-Muslimeen*, 95.

that sovereignty finally belongs to none other than God and secular rulers are helpless at the final analysis.[65] For Al-Banna, MBH was an inheritor of the Salafiyyah-Sunni traditionalist and reformist thinking. It was a Sunni way, Sufi truth, political organization, athletic group, economic enterprise, scientific culture and social idea.[66]

His Islamic thoughts and state ideology are a version of moderate thinkers who adhere to the idea that man must be ruled by Islamic shariah and these must be adaptable to the modern needs. Islam in the eyes of Banna is a religion, society and a state while shariah is a social model, which must be permitted to operate in this real and pragmatic world.[67] For him, government and politics were an integral part of Islam and so governance is obligatory for mankind. According to him: 'All Muslims are guilty if Islamic state is not installed. This amounts to betrayal not to one Muslim alone but to entire humanity.'[68] He did not see any contradiction between the Islamic model of *shura* and the Western constitutional model. He considered both the models as the basic principle of governance and the practice of authority.[69]

For him, the religion of God cannot be established without a state power. To appropriate it more suitably, he said, 'Existence of faith is subject to the existence of Islamic government.'[70] One of the basic credos of the MBH was to take Islam as a universal entity, working to establish God's religion on earth and an Islamic order with the intention of executing the words of God. Banna, who was also influenced by his predecessor Rashid Rida, called for comprehensive and activist Islam. Richard Mitchell argues that the ultimate goal of MBH was to create an Islamic order (*Nizam-i-Islami*) rather than an Islamic state.[71] According

---

[65] Rabi, *Intellectual Origin of Islamic Resurgence in the Arab World*, 77.
[66] Enayat Hamid, *Modern Islamic Political Thought* (London: I.B. Tauris, 2005), 85.
[67] Ahmad, *Jadliyat-al-Shura wa-al-Dimmuqeratiyyah*, 69.
[68] Hamid, *Modern Islamic Political Thought*, 85.
[69] Ahmad, *Jadliyat-al-Shura wa-al-Dimmuqeratiyyah*, 69.
[70] Zaki, *Tahrik-i-Al-Ikhwan al-Muslimeen*, 138.
[71] Ayubi, *Political Islam*, 131.

to Richard Mitchell, 'Islamic' had a broad meaning and his Islam was inclusive, involving all affairs of life.[72]

He favoured the ultimate restoration of caliphate, but as a principle of pragmatism, he approved the existence of separate Islamic states too.[73]

Banna completely rejected any school of *fiqh* or Islamic system where religious minority has no right to practise their religion. However, on the contrary, he envisaged such a system where every section of society, irrespective of its religion or sect, should extend full cooperation for the establishment of a free and prosperous society.[74]

Al-Banna represented the moderate face of the 20th-century Islamist ideologues who never believed in the principle of ideo-logical contestation either with the state or with any political group. So long as the MBH was under his leadership, it never entered into any kind of confrontation with the state for the sake of the implementation of its political ideology. The MBH under his guidance was more interested in social and educational work rather than achieving political power. He was more interested in creating a condition where a smooth transfer of power could take place from secular people into an Islamist hand.

It was under the impact of Sayyed Qutb's radical ideology that the MBH turned against the state. It was only after the departure of Banna in 1949 when Qutb took over its ideologi-cal leadership and gave different orientation to this movement. Qutb's radical Islamic thoughts and his ideological substances placed Qutb and Ikhwan on a different horizon altogether.

Sayyed Bin al-Haaj Qutb Ibrahim Husayn Shadhili, better known as Sayyed Qutb, was one of the leading Islamist politi-cal thinkers of the 20th century in the Muslim world.[75] He had developed a systematic political, economic, moral, intellectual and social reading of Islam and Islamic traditions. He began his carrier as a literary critic and journalist, but later on transformed

---

[72] Ayubi, *Political Islam,* 132.
[73] Brown, *Religion and State,* 147.
[74] Ahmad, *Jadliyat-al-Shura wa-al-Dimmuqeratiyyah,* 163.
[75] The term 'Muslim world' refers to both Muslim-minority and Muslim-majority population living under any juridical-political dispensation.

himself as one of the greatest Islamic ideologues of the 20th century. His ultimate goal was to establish Islamic social, cultural and political order represented by an Islamic state, supervised and guided by the concept of sovereignty of God (*Hakimiyya*) and exemplified by the application of the shariah laws (Islamic code).

Sayyed Qutb was a prominent figure in the Egyptian MBH. His works were considered the manual of the Islamic groups in Egypt and other parts of the Muslim world. His importance stems from the fact that he influenced the succeeding generations of Egyptian and Arab intelligentsias striving to understand and apply Islam as a political ideology.[76]

According to E. Sivan, Qutb's influence, though started in Egypt, went beyond Egypt and the traditional Arab world and reached the Muslim world.

He writes:

> Qutb's thoughts of 1950s, 60s left a clear mark on Turkey, a country that is not Arabic speaking but with Sunni majority. In Pakistan, his important works have been translated into Urdu and have reached to the wider masses. Several of his writings have been published in Malaysia. He occupies the central place in the scholarly and intellectual works on the Islamic revivalism.[77]

Gradually, he transformed himself as an independent political and literary thinker whose political thought was influenced to a greater extent by the existing socio-economic and political situation of Egypt, the geo-political situation on the regional level and the nature of the cold war politics at the global level. He was of the views that the colonial masters, in reality, did not introduce the universal-rational core of the philosophy of modernity but the colonial projects, in fact introduced the Westernization framework of transformation by 'imposing' their cultural, political and economic hegemony in the name of modernization.[78]

---

[76] Ibrahim Abu Rabi, 'Sayyed Qutb: From Religious Realism to Radical Social Criticisms', *Islamic Quarterly* 28, no. 1 (1984), 103–13.

[77] E. Sivan, 'Sunni Radicalism in the Middle East and the Iranian revolution', *International Journal of Middle Eastern Studies* 21, no. 1 (February 1989): 10.

[78] Armstrong, *A History of God*, 412.

Qutb played a very instrumental role in the 1952 Free Officers revolt in Egypt, and he said that real revolution had begun now and the people should not sit idly as the real aim of revolution was not merely to oust the monarchy but to mould the Egyptian society into Islamic colouration and to restore the faith of people in Islam. He said:

> We want to bring about the movement which is beyond knowledge; we want the knowledge of Islamic concept to lead people towards the realization of its content in the real world.[79]

It was in the year 1953 when he joined the Ikhwan (MBH) and became its full-fledged member and gradually started withdrawing himself from the closeness of the Free Officers. He openly acknowledged it, 'I was born only in 1953 and my joining the MBH was the result of existing socio-economic and political situation in the country.'[80]

After joining the MBH, Qutb took recourse to the Quran for seeking Islamic solution of the problems confronting the Arab Egyptian society. For him the Quran was the source for political, social, cultural and economic reforms and not merely a literary piece of art. He was profoundly influenced by the missionary zeal of the Quran and strictly adhered to this, which can be aptly described in his words: 'We must make it clear that we do not desire to seek the truth of Islamic concept merely for the sake of academic knowledge. Rather, we want to bring about the movement which is beyond knowledge.'[81]

During the rise of Nasserism in Arab politics in the 1960s and 1970s, he turned into an arch enemy of his socialist ideology and said, 'The people want to turn to religion and I am with them.'[82]

Qutb offered an Islamic alternative in the face of Nasserite socialism and said:

---

[79] Salah Abdul Fattah Khalidi, *Sayyed Qutb: Min-al-milaad-ilal-Istishhad* (Syria: Dar-al-Qalam, 1991), 304.

[80] Khalidi, *Sayyed Qutb*, 323.

[81] Rabi, *Intellectual Origin of Islamic Resurgence in the Arab World*, 138.

[82] Ashmawi Mohammad Saeed, 'July Revolution Nationalized the Religion', *Sabah-e-Khair*, no. 1789 (1990), 123–43.

The sole banner that binds us in our struggle against imperialism is Islam but some of us prefer the banner of Arab nationalism [to that of Islam]. There is no serious contradiction between Arab nationalism and Islam as long as we perceive the former as a step on the road to establishing the Islamic state.[83]

Qutb's Islamic ideological construction was not shaped only in the background of the Nasserite state but was also the outcome of the emerging global scenario. His previous critique of Christianity and the West was narrowed down to a mere critique of Americanization, its symbols and its intellectual allies in Muslim worlds. In very provocative essays entitled 'Islam-Americani', he accused America of patronizing Islam for its perceived needs to combat communism. According to Qutb, America does not oppose Islam per se but it does not want Islam which would oppose the colonialism and imperialism. To put Qutb's understanding of American view of Islam:

They (Americans) do not want Islam to rule as they know it very well that when it will rule, it will mould the people and the masses will be able to identify the enemy. Both communism and colonialism is the real enemy of Islam and American and its allies want American brand of Islam in the Middle East.[84]

Most of his political and social writings during his confinement (1954–66) focused on and applied to Nasser's regime, and were completely couched in the Islamic idioms. He argued that the primary task of the Islamic faith is to preserve the religious belief in time of crisis and reckless and directionless change and transformation. Qutb was of the opinion that men strongly needed faith, which could help mankind to consolidate the power, and a unified ideology, which would evolve out of this faith, to confront the life and its problems and an ideology that would solidify the strength against foreign and domestic enemies.[85]

---

[83] Rabi, *Intellectual Origin of Islamic Resurgence in the Arab World*, 134.
[84] Sayyed Qutb, *Dirasatun Islamiyyah* [The Studies in Islam] (Beirut: Dar Al Shorouk, 1973), 119–20.
[85] Rabi, *Intellectual Origin of Islamic Resurgence in the Arab World*, 127.

Arguing about faith, he says, 'Religion of Islam is purely based on the faith and faith of individual must be reflected in his or her social interaction and it must be represented in laws of the society and laws must be the explanation of this faith.'[86] For Qutb, submission to power other than God's in itself is an act of unbelief. The Muslim community can come into existence only when individuals and groups of people reject servitude to anyone except God.

He writes, 'Worship in Islam does not merely mean to follow the rituals but to pose complete belief in Him and surrender completely to the will of Allah.'[87] The belief and action were the core principles of Qutb's political theme in the later stage of his life; in one of his writing on jihad, he claims: 'Action is the reality of religion of Islam and this action and movement combats the wrong faith in the societies and carries along certain principles also.'[88]

He outlined the new strategy and the vocabulary of the discourse known as *Jahiliyyah* and Hakimiyya. Defining the society of Jahiliyyah, he says: 'Any society that is un-Islamic is *Jahiliyyah* or more precisely any society that accepts the sovereignty of any other entity than God is a *Jahiliyyah* one. Any society lacking the basic belief in Islam is *Jahiliyyah*.'[89] For him, Jahiliyyah is one-man lordship over another and, in this respect, it is against the system of universe and brings the involuntary aspects of human life into conflict with its voluntary aspect. He maintained that Jahiliyyah of the modern world is based on the separation of religion and the state. Qutb portrayed Jahiliyyah as an antithesis to the original Islamic community that, in turn, itself had once served as antithesis to pre-Islamic Jahiliyyah, which has resurrected itself everywhere in the world today.

He derived his concept of *Hakimiyya* from Quranic word *hukm* (to govern and rule). It, according to him, is the highest

---

[86] Sayyed Qutb, *Marakatul Islam wa-Rasmaliyyah* [Battle between Islam and Capitalism] (Beirut: Dar Al Shorouk, 1966), 57.

[87] Sayyed Qutb, *Al-Adalah Ijtimaiyah fil-Islam* [Social Justice in Islam] (Beirut: Dar Al Shorouk, 1967), 11.

[88] Sayyed Qutb, *Al-Jihad Fi-Sabililllah* [Struggle in the Path of Allah] (Riyadh: Al-Ittihadul-Islami Lil-Munazzamt-attulabiyah, 1970), 100.

[89] Balqazir. *Ad- Daulah fil-Fikril Islami al-muasir*, 197.

government and legal authority; so, Allah is the highest government and legal authority. To put it in his own words: 'Hakimiyya means the *Shariah* of *Allah* is the foundation of legislation and *Allah* himself did not descend himself to rule but sent this *Shariah* to govern.'[90] Elaborating further the concept of Hakimiyya, he says, 'Islam is a belief system and it is also a legal system which has laid down the principle of *Hakimiyya* of God contrary to *Hakimiyya* of men as prevalent in the *Jahiliyyah*.'[91]

Sovereignty of God for Qutb is a shield against abusive government and a platform for promoting individual freedom. Sovereignty was the preserve of God and no entity, including government, could assume it. 'Islam does not allow differentiating between here and hereafter, worship and treatment and faith and laws.'[92]

The most stunning example of the success of political Islam in the late 20th century was the Islamic Revolution of Iran (1979). The sole architect and chief ideologue of this revolution was Imam Rohollah Ayatollah Khomeini. The Islamic Revolution in Iran under Khomeini's organizational stewardship and the ideological banner witnessed the most successful experiment of the application of the philosophy of political Islam as the guiding principle for national reconstruction and transformation.

It emerged as the role model and the greatest source of inspiration for all the Islamic movements across the world. To put it in the words of Hamid Algar:

> Islamic revolution of Iran differs from other events of the present century. It has been firmly rooted in the history unlike other events so far. Despite being a radical departure from the past, it is, on the contrary, is being considered as the continuation and fruition of long year of political, spiritual and intellectual development'.[93]

Ayatollah Khomeini was born in Iran in 1902 and his ideas on Islamic state and political thoughts passed through several

---

[90] Sayyed Qutb, *Fi-Zilalil Quran*, 19th ed. (Beirut: Dar Al Shorouk), vol. 1, p. 297; vol. 2, 889–91, 893, 897.
[91] Balqazir, *Ad-Daulah fil-Fikril Islami al-muasir*, 207.
[92] Qutb, *Al-Adalah Ijtimaiyah fil-Islam*, 26.
[93] Ayubi, *Political Islam*, 146.

phases, like those of his other contemporary ideologues. Imam Khomeini's political views were expressed in an eventful era under various political and social conditions.

Khomeini's firm commitment to his thought regarding Islam and politics can be vividly read in his address of 1943 where he called upon the 'Ulema' to initiate uprising against the tyrannical and oppressive rule of the Pahlavi regime in Iran. His most striking contribution to the modern debate on the association between religion of Islam and politics is his idea that the core quality of the Islamic state is reflected neither by its constitution nor by the commitment of rulers to the shariah. It is characterized chiefly by the special quality of its leadership. Khomeini very categorically exhorted that the Fuqaha will provide this special quality of the leadership. He viewed that all responsibilities except receiving the revelation had been put on the Ulema after the death of the Prophet of Islam and the disappearance of the Twelfth Imam.[94] Khomeini's political ideas were not evolving in a vacuum. The context under which Khomeini's political philosophy metamorphosed was provided by the gradual invasion and domination of the West over Iran and over other parts of the region.

He defined his own self and the self of the Islamic nation by contextualizing the 'others'—the cultural and political domination of the West over Iran through the invasion of modernity. Here, a close similarity between Khomeini, Qutb and Mawdudi can be drawn in their definitional approach for reconstructing their self and the self of the Islamic nation by negating everything the West stood for. He envisaged Islam as an ideology providing a sense of meaning and direction to the life as well as to the government. According to him:

> Islamic government has greater responsibility. It should protect Islam, including the unity of Islam. Islam cannot be like Christianity relegating religion to the realm of personal matter between individual and God. Islam is a program for life and for the government.[95]

---

[94] Ayubi, *Political Islam,* 147.

[95] Vanessa Martin, *Creating an Islamic State: Khomeini and the Making of a New Iran* (London: I.B. Tauris, 2000), 113.

According to Khomeini, God is the only valid legislator and has provided indispensable legislations for leading a proper life on this planet. Absolute sovereignty belongs exclusively to Him. He talked of sovereignty in the following words: 'Any sovereignty other than God is against the well-being of the people and is tyranny and except for the laws of God all the laws are void and useless.'[96]

His initial political philosophy seemed to be very close and similar to the Sunni political doctrine. It was very much in conformity and harmony with the Sunni political ideologues of the 20th century, such as Mawdudi and Qutb. Khomeini outlined his political principles publicly in lectures delivered at Najaf in 1970. These lecturers were published in the form of a book entitled *Hukumat-i-Islami* (Islamic government). He was of the firm views that religion requires political authority and that the intention of the religion of Islam cannot be achieved without holding of the political space. Muslims cannot accomplish the mission of Islam without capturing political domain.[97]

Amongst his contemporary, Khomeini is credited with offering a new theoretical political formulation known as *Wilayat al-Faqih* (rule of Jurist). It forms the central axis of Khomeini political thought and advocates a guardianship-based political system and relies upon a just and capable jurist (*faqih*) to assume the mantle leadership of the government in the absence of an infallible imam. Khomeini negated the traditional school of Shias who saw no legal justification in establishing an Islamic state in the absence of imam by popularizing the idea of the Wilayat al-Faqih. Khomeini held the view and propagated that the vacuum in political power was not because of the absence of imam but because of his occultation.

The entire concept of Wilayat al-Faqih, which was evolved by Khomeini during his exile before the revolution, represents a comprehensive political model. He calls upon the jurist to perform all the tasks that an imam would have performed in his presence. Khomeini drew upon the old Shiite tradition, which suggested that a jurist might rule as an agent of imam in the

---

[96] Martin, *Creating an Islamic State*, 106.
[97] Black, *The History of Islamic Political Thoughts*, 333.

absence of the Twelfth Imam. According to Khomeini, there is no difference between imam, the Prophet and jurist as far as his rule and legitimacy is concerned.

The principle of Wilayat al-Faqih was based on the notion of a theocratic state at two levels. It was divine government where jurists were at the helm of the affairs and they rule in their capacity as the agents of the Prophet and imam. The jurist rulers do not derive their legitimacy from the people but rather their legitimacy and authenticity were equal to the legitimacy and authenticity of the Prophet as they rule on the basis of being an official representative of the shariah.

Indian Subcontinent and the Islamic Political Renaissance

It is generally assumed that the advocacy or ideology of political Islam merely surfaced in the land of West Asia and North Africa, and it is completely an Arab phenomenon. It has been seen that scholars on international relation and related disciplines have remained hostage to the Arab region alone when it comes to mapping of political Islam. However, the story is completely contrary to what the general audience or Arab-centric scholars expound.

In the predeceasing section of this chapter, my narrative of the ideological navigation among the Islamist ideologues were confined to those parts of the world in the Arab which produced the pioneers in the field of political Islam. I also threw some light on the colonial, political, historical and sociological milieu which offered a favourable environment for the propping up of these Islamic ideological thoughts which are still shaping the political discourse in the Arab world.

In the following section, I will briefly shift to the other territorial location of political Islam which was not less forceful in term of ideology or theme and it was equally reflective of political, colonial, and sociological context existing in the territory of South Asia. In a merely scant glance of South Asian history, one will find out a large degree of similarity between the rise of Islam-centred political surge in South Asia and the

Arab world when it comes to contextualization of the themes in the backdrop of the colonial onslaught. Like the evolution of political Islam in West Asia, the rise of Islamic polity centred on jihadism, Wahabism and other Islamic renaissance is marked by a set of templates affecting and shaping one after other.

The origin and the evolution of Islamic political renaissance like that in the Arab world can be traced back to the cultural and political penetration of an alien ideology in the form of Western imperialist forces which was not merely different to the test and experience of traditional and cultural accumulation of the erstwhile Indian subcontinent which was itself very much in the downward phase: the Mughal Empire.

By the 17th century, the Muslims of India were confronted with a series of internal and external challenges paving the way for not an alternative discourse alone but also for a major deviation from the past, and offered a new course and template. It was a template where Islam was conceived to be incomplete without political application, and politics was deemed to be spiritless without the Islamic coating. Mughal court in its dwindling years had turned into a sapped intellectual and religious controversy which had stained the Muslim body politics. The custodians of religious tradition (clergy and spiritual leaders) were more than content that their seminaries and shrines were well protected and served.[98]

The late Mughal period was represented by a series of the weakest rulers from 1707 to 1857 when the nominal political Mughal rule came to an end. It was the declining phase of Mughal rule that enunciated an intellectual, political and religious churning among the Indian political and religious elites, and the foremost pioneer among them was Shah Wali Allah of Delhi who was followed by Ahmad Shaheed and later by the foundation of seminary of Deoband not only to perpetuate the idea of Islamic renaissance but also to confront the Western imperialist cultural and political onslaught.

---

[98] Mahmood Ahmad Ghazi, *Islamic Renaissance in South Asia (1707–1867): The Role of Shah Wali Allah and His Successors* (New Delhi: Adam Publishers and Distributors, 2004), xx.

In complete concurrence with the jihadist discourse embodied in today's discourse of political Islam in the Arab world, the narratives, ideologies and religious political movements propounding and flourishing in the 18th and 19th centuries were well informed by the content of radical ideas, call for jihadism, resistance to the Western hermeneutics of life and politics, purity of Islam and political coating of Islamic theology and binary division of the West and the East. Any articulation or enunciation on the Islamic renaissance in the Indian subcontinent in the modern period has to be embarked on with the pioneer of Islamic intellectual resurgence: Shah Wali Allah of Delhi.

Shah Wali Allah of Delhi

Shah Wali Allah was a figure whose political, intellectual, philosophical, spiritual and religious legacy not only finds resonance within religious sphere and intellectual inquiry of the immediate succeeding generation of Ulema, but also, even today, no seminary or Islamicly-informed intellectual sphere in South Asia can claim to be devoid of his influences.

Shah Wali Allah's family belonged to the Muslim elite of Delhi and the family is marked by the privilege of producing a series of great scholars and intellectuals who played an invaluable role in enriching the intellectual and social reformers of the succeeding generation; the most valuable contribution of the descendants of Wali Allah is in the field of Hadith and spread of the seminaries throughout the Indian subcontinent. His lineage and descendants both were known for the pursuit of Islamic knowledge and spiritual learning.

Shah Wali Allah was born in 1703, four years before the death of the last Mughal ruler Aurangzeb. His father Abd al-Rahim was a reputed Islamic scholar and well known among the contemporary scholars. In concurrence with the tradition of learning, he memorized the Quran, studied grammar, logic, philosophy, Persian and Arab languages and all the education he received in the seminary established by his father, Madrasa Rahimiyya.

Wali Allah was largely inspired by his father in the pursuit of enlightenment, mysticism and wisdom, and on one occasion he wrote:

> The attention and care he gave me during my boyhood and my student life is never given by any father to his son. I have yet to come across a father, a teacher, or a spiritual guide who has so meticulously and compassionately taken care of his son or disciple as my late father took care of me.[99]

Shah Wali Allah sought learning from a series of known scholars of his time in addition to his father, and foremost among them were the host of Hanafi jurists and experts on Hadith. It was pedagogy of Hadith which later became the hallmarks of his intellectualism.

His stay in Hejaz for one and a half years made a tremendous impact upon is thinking and helped him crystallizing and combing his religious, political and social thoughts into a well-defined ideology. Shah Wali Allah was an idealist who could shun his eyes or remain oblivious to the political and social milieu of his time. He opened his eyes in a declining political and cultural environment in South Asia, and the declining Islamic ethos and values and weakening Muslim powers had a direct and shrilling influence on the evolution of political thoughts of Shah Wali Allah.

Though his thoughts were mainly devoted to intellectual and educational revival, but he was of the views that intellectual and educational advancement would naturally bring a political resurgence. He also said that no reform could be effective without armed struggle. His thought and concerns about political decline of the Muslim power are well articulated in two letters he wrote to Afghan King Ahmad Shah Abdali and Prime Minister and the Emperor of the Mughal Empire, respectively. In his first letter to Abdali, he identified the forces and players acting against the integrity of the Muslim community. He stated to the monarch that he is writing to him because prestige and dignity

---

[99] Shah Wali Allah, *Anfas al Arifin* [Saints and Saviors of Islam] (New Delhi, 1887), 405–06.

of Islam are at stake and could be protected by a powerful ruler whose presence is blessing of the Almighty.[100] His letter to the king was reflective of the existing political scenario in the continent when the regional powers were raising their heads and challenging the central leadership, and Islamic values, norms and customs were under threat.

Encouraging the Afghan ruler, he wrote that it would not be difficult to defeat the enemy of Islam (*Maratha*) if the *Ghazi of Islam* takes it as a responsibility to rescue the land of Islam. His memorandum to the king of Afghan is also a concern about rising of other powers like Jats near Delhi and, according to him, all these forces were wakening and challenging the dominance of Islam in the continent. No other document is more reflective or suggestive of his appeal or urge for an Islamic/Muslim resurgence than his letter to the Afghan Emperor. Through this letter, he was not only exhorting the ruler to intervene in the country but also his appeal was more couched in the expression of sorrow and grief over the declining supremacy of religion of Islam which is indicated in the erosion of power of the Mughal dynasty. One can notice the inference of ummah in his appeal to the king of Afghan and employment of a political etymology couched in the terminology and phrase of Islam. Wali Allah addressed Abdali in the name of Allah and asks him to wage jihad against the infidels so that beautiful reward is written in the record of Majesty for him.[101] He also reminded Abdali of transgressions of Nadir who had plundered the Muslims and made the Jats and other infidels more prosperous and weakened the Muslims in their own country. He also wanted Abdali to act for the protection and ascendency of Islam and suggested this in his writings that special care should be taken to promote the interest of the Muslim community and particular attention should be paid to strengthen the weaker Muslims. These appeals and exhortation were indicative of his appeal for resurgent Muslims and the restoration of Islam and consolidation of the Muslims in the subcontinent.

---

[100] Ghazi, *Islamic Renaissance in South Asia (1707–1867)*, 97.

[101] Ghazi, *Islamic Renaissance in South Asia (1707–1867)*, 103–04.

While addressing his letter to the Mughal Emperor, Shah Wali Allah wrote that the first step to restore the rule of Muslims should be to wage jihad, which would yield desirable result here and hereafter.[102] Though Shah Wali Allah was known to be a philosopher–intellectual, his ideas were not confined to advocating religious or spiritual ideas alone, and he counselled about the politics and economics of the time with equal passion. He talked about land reforms and advocated about the management of lands to reduce inequality and the gap between the rich and the poor. To retard the social, political and moral decline in South Asia was the long-term aim of Shah, and he did not have the ideal views of Mughal rule but wanted to last it until some alternative was found.[103]

Shah Wali Allah was one of the greatest thinkers in the history of Muslims in South Asia and a bridge between the medieval and modern periods in the religio-intellectual history of the region. He adopted a metaphysical approach to political problems and was able to establish relationship between all major aspects of Islamic thoughts—religious, social, political, economic and ethical. His political thoughts emanated from his detailed expounding of God, creation and the universe, where he considered that men are bestowed with distinctive quality and that must be manifested in all behavioural fields of mankind.

Shah wrote extensively on the issue of politics and series of treaties such as *Hujjat Allah al-Balighah* and *Al-Budur al Bazighah*, which contain his views on politics. Like his predecessors of past centuries, for him the institution of caliphate was a hallmark of the Islamic political system. His reason for the establishment of caliphate is twofold: first, for dispensing the justice and another is for *Millat* (community of Muslims) and for the exaltation of the religion of Islam, which according to him would not be possible without the caliphate.[104] He argued in favour of the necessity of caliphate and, according to him, collective reasons

---

[102] Ghazi, *Islamic Renaissance in South Asia (1707–1867)*, 107.

[103] See Foreword by Shikh Abd Al Rashid in Khaliq Ahmad Nizami, ed., *Shah Wali Allah Dehalvi Ke Siyasi Maktuibat* [The Political Writing of Shah Wali Allah] (Aligarh: AMU, 1969), 3–4.

[104] Shah Wali Allah, *Hujjat Allah al-Balighah* [The Conclusive Argument from God], vol. 1 (Cairo: Darul-Tabaah, 1322 AH), 34.

require caliphate to safeguard the interest of the mankind. He opined that caliphate is appointed to accomplish the goal for which the Prophet was sent, and obedience to imam amounts to obedience to the Prophet and God. He also exhorts that in the absence of caliphate, the humanity will sink into anarchy what Sayyed Qutb argued 250 years later.

For him, politics was the means through which one preserves the relationship among different groups of citizens, and state is a closed community of people who have mutual transactions and relationships.[105] He also categorizes a state into perfect and imperfect states and according to him, a perfect state is one in which the imam ruler is perfect and is capable enough to mobilize the army from across all the sections to confront the enemy.

Wali Allah was aware of the nuances involved in the running affairs of the state, and moreover of the difficulties in creating unanimity and consensus over legal issues. Therefore, he called upon an individual to be the ruler of the states, who is endowed with power and has a team of brilliant and enlightened lieutenants along with the people of *Ahl al-hall wa al-aqd* who are obedient to the individual, and he calls such an individual an imam.[106] Shah not only inferred from the theological teaching of Islam when he laid down his theory of state, but he was also equally influenced by erstwhile political situations of the continent and he always advocated for a strong state because he had seen the declining rule of Mughal and how it had weakened the Muslims and Islam as a whole.

He underlined few of the basic qualities for a ruler, most prominent among them being bravery, because in the absence of bravery, the ruler will have difficulties in execution of power. His theory of imamates is not much different from that of the Mawardi of the Abbasid period, who first expounded the imamate in the light of Hadith and the Quran. He not only talked about the imam, but he also focused equally on its team and what should be the basic characteristics of the lieutenant as he was an advocate of a strong state with a strong imam in terms of military strength.

---

[105] Ghazi, *Islamic Renaissance in South Asia (1707–1867)*, 139.
[106] Wali Allah, *Hujjat Allah al-Balighah*, 34.

Sayyed Ahmad Shaheed and Foundation of Jihadism in the Subcontinent

The intellectual and philosophical tradition representing different streams did not die away with the departure of Shah Wali Allah, but he left a comprehensive legacy as well as a school of followers who did not only advocate his ideas but also tried to accomplish the mission imagined by their mentor. He left behind a host of Ulema who imitated his tradition in Sufism and politics and, moreover, forwarded his mission of jihadism for the establishment of an Islamic system. One of the close disciples of Wali Allah was Sayyed Ahmad Shaheed, who not only emerged as a real torchbearer of the thoughts and ideas of Wali Allah but also earned a separate name for himself in the history of South Asia when it comes to the history of Islamic resurgence.

Today's entire proposition about political Islam is marked by the negation of Western values, reflected in its secularist ideas and the application of shariah in the mode of governance, and some Islamists of radical shade go far away to call for jihad against whatever they conceive to be the part of heretic ideas. If one explores and deciphers the legacy or the thoughts and ideas of the descendants of Wali Allah, he or she will come across these elements of modern-day political Islam in the advocacy and illustrations of these medieval-cum-modern-day proponents which we today call Islamism.

Sayyed Ahmad Shaheed was one such disciple of Wali Allah's school and can be said to be the first political Islamic leader of South Asia.[107] He was born in a town in central Uttar Pradesh in 1786 to a family reputed for scholarship and missionary work. The forefathers of Ahmad Shaheed were closely knit with the intellectual mission of Wali Allah. He himself was one of the nearest disciples of one of the sons of Wali Allah, Shah Abdul Aziz. By mid-18th century, the families of Shah and Ahmad Shaheed were cooperating with each other in the pursuit of

---

[107] Mahmood Hussain, *A History of the Freedom Movement*, vol. 1 (Karachi: Pakistan Historical Society, 1957), 380.

knowledge, and the two families were personifications of resistance to Western ideas and moreover political opponents of regional rulers poised to destroy the supremacy of the Mughals in India. His initial education took place under the guidance of Shah Abdul Aziz. Since inception, he was a radical in his ideas and never hesitated in raising voice against wrong.

He was the one who did not approve of all the traits prevalent in many Sufi schools at a time when Sufism was the most prevalent feature of the learning. He also served in the army of Nawab Amir Khan of Tonk, where he learned the art of warfare and diplomacy in addition to instigating the ruler launch the organized jihad against the English rulers, and perhaps it was the beginning of jihadism in the political culture of South Asia. Disappointed with the apathy of the ruler to the idea of jihad, Ahmad Shaheed left Tonk and rejoined the seminary of Abdul Aziz in Delhi. From here, he prepared himself for a longer war against the usurpers of power and the heretics who had become the biggest enemy of Islam as assumed by him. During 1818–19, he travelled extensively in the Doab region, preaching jihad and mobilizing anti-English and anti-Hindu forces to wage jihad. It was the movement to sow the seed of the first ever jihad in the minds of people in South Asia.[108]

He enunciated the practice of learning of martial art within the Sufi camps, which was not only novel but a departure from the past teaching of the peaceful Sufi order. Wherever the opposition was raised to his ideas of martial art or his aggressive campaign for Islam, he explained the relevance of jihad in present circumstances. He left no stone unturned for the propagation of jihad, and while he was going to Mecca for hajj, he chose the longer route so that he could interact with more people to advocate it. The level of his political awareness, political engagement of the day and concern can be judged by the fact that he had special meeting with the sons of Tipu Sultan in Calcutta on his way to hajj who told him that their father (Tipu Sultan) had close ties with the successors of Wali Allah. Few days later, they swore allegiance to Sayyed Shaheed and requested him to initiate them in his Sufi tradition. During

---

[108] Ghazi, *Islamic Renaissance in South Asia (1707–1867)*, 193.

his stay in Arabia, he came into contact with a large number of Muslim figures of different cultural, religious and political lineages from across the world, which left a deep impact on the evolution of his thoughts.

After his return from hajj, Ahmad Shaheed stayed in his hometown for two years (1824–26). Meanwhile, his mentor Shah Abdul Aziz, son of the pioneer of the Islamic renaissance in South Asia, Shah Wali Allah, passed away and the entire responsibility to confront the political situations of the time came on the shoulders of Ahmad Shaheed himself. To advocate his jihad movement further, he soon wrote letters to erstwhile Muslim political elites expressing his intention of declaring an open jihad against the political system and called upon other members of the Shah Wali Allah family to join his mission.[109] Two prominent members of Shah's family had already joined the group of Ahmad Shaheed—Maulana Abdul Hayat and Maulana Mohammad Ismail Shaheed—after they had tested the spiritual stature of Ahmad Shaheed. Their contemporaries addressed those two with so many ornamented titles such as 'Honour of Hadith, Master of Islam, Crown of Hadith, Master's scholars and eternal scholars'. Even poet Iqbal, a 20th-century Islamic philosopher, had all love for Ismail Shaheed, and he once said that even if a single religious scholar of Ismail Shaheed's stature had been born after him, Muslims of India would not be living in such a miserable and pitiable condition as they do today.[110]

One could notice some shade of similarities between today and the era of Ahmad Shaheed as the real jihad's call was against the introduction of a new legal system introduced by the English, which for them was the violation of the spirit of shariah, which even today is the attribute of Islamist movements in most parts of the Arab world. Ahmad Shaheed was not the first one to advocate jihad, but he in person moved on the ground and led the battle against the English and the Sikhs in the fulfilment of his mission and religious duty which he termed jihad.

---

[109] Abul Hasan Ali Nadvi, *Sirati-iSayyed Ahmad Shaheed,* vol. 1 (Karachi: Pakistan Historical Society, 1975), 121–25.

[110] Ghazi, *Islamic Renaissance in South Asia (1707–1867),* 196.

Before him, it was Shah Abdul Aziz, his mentor, who had also issued a fatwa against the English and the Sikh for their anti-Islamic posturing and the implementation of the laws that did not concur with the spirit of Islam. The scope of the fatwa was further widened by the disciple of Shah Abdul Aziz, Abdul Hayat, who declared that entire South Asia from Calcutta to Delhi needs to be declared 'the abode of war' because the laws of the shariah tend to be disregarded, and moreover because the region was dominated by the Christians, and infidelity and poly-theism had become rooted in the continent.[111] Throughout the years of Shah Wali Allah and Shah Abdul Aziz, Jats, Marathas and Sikhs were the targets of the newly emerging ideology. After the attack of Abdali, Jats and Marathas were subdued, and the only existing threats were the Sikhs. Ahmad Shaheed, before embarking on jihad and *Hijrah* [Migration], prepared a blueprint and sent one of his deputies, Ismail, to assess the situ-ations on the spot. North West Frontier Province, inhabited by the martial Pathans, was chosen as the venue of jihad and the centre of the movement, while the venue of the movement was a zone adjacent to central Asia and Afghanistan.

Sayyed Ahmad Shaheed formulated the military strategy and created several divisions of the battalions to wage the war against the Sikhs. He appointed his deputies and representatives throughout India, assigned the tasks of furthering their mission in addition to fund and volunteers after the Hijrah, which serves today as one of the pillars of proselytizing mission of Islam in north India.[112] After making all the preliminary arrangements, Sayyed Ahmad Shaheed, in January 1826, along with 500 ghazis moved towards the destined land crossing over a large difficult geographical terrain and lanes and reached in December of the same year. He received allegiance from some local notables and sent a message to the Sikh rulers of Lahore.

The note of the message had all three traditional and historical elements of alternatives which had remained the hallmark of

---

[111] Ghazi, *Islamic Renaissance in South Asia (1707–1867)*, 197.

[112] Ghulam Rasul Mihr, *Jamaat-i-Mujahidin* [The Group of Islamic Fighters] (Lahore, n.d.), 21.

any jihadist Islamic mission in the past: conversion to Islam, the payment of *jizyah* (a religious tax imposed on n non-Muslims in medieval times), or death.[113] The Sikh ruler took some time to respond and they moved in February 1827 to confront the army of Ahmad Shaheed. After scoring a series of victories, the victorious army moved into Peshawar triumphantly. Meanwhile, a nominal Islamic state was established and Ahmad Shaheed was elected its amir. In accordance with the past practice of Islam, judges and accountants were also appointed. Friday sermons were read in his name, which was recited as *Amir al-muminin* commander of the faithful, and shariah was promulgated.[114] When things were still amidst the planning and procedure, Ahmad Shaheed dispatched his trustees to the nearby region announcing the proclamation of Ahmad Shaheed as amir. Revolt by different notables of Peshawar started and horrendous massacres of the army of Ahmad took place, making his Islamic state a short-lived one. Later, he decided to move to Kashmir but was prevented by a huge army of Sikhs at Balakot, and in May 1831, an elite army of Ahmad Shaheed, including himself and his most faithful commander, Muhammad Ismail, were slain. This incident brought to an end the first wave of jihadist politics or an Islamic revivalist movement in South Asia, but it left deep imprints on the successive Islamic political intellectual discourse.

The thoughts and ideas of Shah Wali Allah left a deep impact on Ahmad Shaheed, and some scholars view the action of Ahmad Shaheed merely an extension and implementation of the thoughts of Wali Allah. Even Sayyed Abu al-Ala Mawdudi, one of the greatest Islamic revivalists of the 20th century, holds that the jihadist movement was another facet of Wali Allah's movement.[115] The legacy of jihad did not end with Shah Wali Allah, but it was kept alive by his descendants and their successive disciples. Apart from the descendants of Wali Allah and his close allies, there were a large number of graduates from

---

[113] *Ghazi, Islamic Renaissance in South Asia (1707–1867)*, 199.
[114] Nadvi, *Sirati-iSayyed Ahmad Shaheed*, 396–97.
[115] Sayyed Abu al-Ala Mawdudi, *A Short History of Revivalist Movements in Islam* (Lahore, 1963), 100.

the school and tradition of Shah Wali who were working in the jihad movement at that time.

The spirit of jihad did not die among the disciples of Shah and Ahmad Shaheed, and throughout the 19th century it was visible in different parts of the country. Several disciples travelled to different places carrying the messages and traditions of their masters in order to keep the mission alive. There were scholars who earned the term 'scholars of jihad', and there was a mission on the part of the graduates of Rahimiyya seminary (opened by father of Shah Wali Allah) to defend the teaching of jihad. The scholars associated with the jihad movement produced literature on the relevance of Sunnah and launched the campaign to revive the Sunnah (practice of the Prophet). The opposition to the newly creeping non-Islamic ideas in the backdrop of colonial consolidation was at both polemical and intellectual levels by the clergies of Shah Wali Allah's traditions.

The most visible impact of Shah Wali Allah and his disciples' thoughts and ideas is visible in the spread of Islamic seminaries throughout the subcontinent. Almost each and every seminary of the 19th century in North India had some association with the tradition of Shah Wali Allah. Several old seminaries were either revived or new ones were opened by the descendants of Shah and Ahmad Shaheed. Mufti Sadr Al-Din Azurdah (d. 1868) revived a seminary of Shah Jahan's era, Dar al-Baqa, which was later destroyed in the revolt of 1857.[116] Today's Zakir Hussian Delhi College (first known as Madrasah Ghazi al-Din and later known as Delhi College) was joined by a disciple of Shah Abdul Aziz as the senior professor of Arabic and Islamic studies. An association was also opened by the contemporaries for the publication of religious books.

The impact of Shah Wali Allah, his descendants and his disciples also found its resonance in the revolt of 1857. The believers in Shah Wali Allah's thoughts took it as jihad, particularly in Delhi and nearby towns, and a series of Ulema signed a fatwa exhorting people to join the revolt against the non-believers in the form of Christians. In Delhi, only immediately after the

---

[116] Ghazi, *Islamic Renaissance in South Asia (1707–1867)*, 205.

revolt, Ulema jointly issued a fatwa calling all Muslims to join the war against the British as a religious obligation. Most prominent among those who signed the edict were either direct disciples of Shah Abdul Aziz, or son of Shah Wali Allah or his lieutenants.[117]

The Ulema of Wali Allah's school played a very crucial role in calling people for jihad in the town of Aligarh, areas of Rohilkhand and Kanpur. Nasim Allah, a disciple of Mufti Azurdah, chased the English out of Aligarh and took the administration in his own hands for three months, and an announcement was made in typical Islamic style, 'The people belonged to God, the country belongs to Mughal and authority belongs to Nasim Allah'.[118] In the areas of Muzaffarnagar (western Uttar Pradesh), the jihad was completely organized and on the pattern of the classical Islamic system, a shura (consultative body) was convened to discuss the prospect of jihad against the Christians.[119] There were a series of similar revolts in different parts of northern India which were inspired by either Shah Wali Allah or his son or his long series of disciples who were scattered across the region of fertile lands of North India.

One such figure was in Kanpur, Maulana Salamt Allah Kashfi Badayuni, who issued a fatwa and was a noted *alim* (scholar) and belonged to the disciple group of Shah Abd-al Aziz and his brother Shah Rafi al-Din. Similar gallantry and bravery were shown by Inayat Ahmad Kakorvi in Aligarh during the revolt of 1857, and he is also credited with establishing the first *tabligh* (missionary work) of Islam along modern lines. He was deported to the Andamans for life imprisonment where he wrote the first major treaty on the life of the Prophet in Urdu. He opened the seminary called Faiz-i-Aam in the city of Kanpur, which is said to be the precursor to the famous seminary for the Arabic literature Dar al-Ulum Nadwat al-Ulama, in the capital city of Lucknow in the state of Uttar Pradesh in northern India.[120]

---

[117] Ghazi, *Islamic Renaissance in South Asia (1707–1867)*, 210–11.
[118] Mohammad Ayyun Qadiri, *Jang—Azadi 1857* [Freedom Struggle] (Karachi: Pakistan Historical Society, 1976), 195.
[119] Ghazi, *Islamic Renaissance in South Asia (1707–1867)*, 213.
[120] Qadiri, *Jang—Azadi 1857*, 447–48.

Near the town of Muzaffarnagar, a jihad was organized under the shura, and after deep consultations, it was decided that jihad should be launched against the infidels and enemies of Islam. To give a proper shape to the jihad, a council was created to provide a precursor to the governance ordained by Islam. Haji Imdadullah was elected the amir (head) of the council. Maulana Muhammad Munir Nanautavi became the military secretary and Maulana Rashid Ahmad was appointed a Qazi. All three were associated in one way or other with the traditions of Shah Wali Allah.

By the time the revolt against British forces collapsed and the last Mughal emperor was taken a prisoner, a series of Ulema felt it obligatory to establish the Islamic rule after the departed central authority of Mughal to fulfil the verdict of the Islamic shariah.

After much pondering and contemplation, a central authority was established where Maulana Ahmad Allah Shah was elected King, Nana sahib, the Maratha Pesheva, the Diwan (Finance secretary), General Bakht Khan, the Defense Minister, and Maulana Sarfaraz Ali, the Chief Justice, and other prominent members were appointed ministers.[121]

We have seen how the tradition of Shah Wali Allah was kept alive by a series of his disciples; numerous seminaries sprang up in the vicinity of Delhi that kept the intellectual, philosophical, Quranic and jihad's tradition of the great Islamic revivalist of the 18th-century South Asia alive. The traditions of Wali Allah continue to shape and orient even today the political and religious ideas of successive Ulema and array of religious and Islam-laden political mission with a higher objective of islamization of culture and society as a whole.

The suppression of revolt of 1857 was something that not only created a power vacuum but also left the Ulema and clergies without social, economic and political base in the Indian subcontinent. They were not merely deprived of pecuniary support, but were also left with no receptive audience around. They saw in the departure of the Mughal role a sign of intellectual, political and moral decline of Islam, which must be contained accordingly. Different sets of political, social, intellectual and religious groups

---

[121] Ghazi, *Islamic Renaissance in South Asia (1707–1867)*, 218.

reacted to the circumstances differently, and each had its own explanation for the cause of the decline of Muslim power in the continent. A group of Ulema saw the decline of Muslim power in the constant decline of religious and moral values amongst a large number of the Muslims in the subcontinent. These Ulema were adherents to the principles that collapse of power merely lay in the gradual abandonment of religious values and disregard for shariah, and they embarked upon the renaissance for reviving the lost Islamic values and cultivating and nurturing these across the sections of the Muslim society. These efforts were reflected in the establishment of one of the oldest religious seminaries in South Asia in the second part of the 19th century called Deoband, which today stands as synonymous to the religious education, revival of learning of Hadith and the Quran, and reinforcement of the prophetic pattern of day-to-day life. In the next section, I will deal with the seminary of Deoband.

Seminary of Deoband and the Islamic Renaissance

It was the beginning of the decline of the Mughal Empire in the early 18th century and the subsequent onslaught of colonial powers and rise of numerous regional players in northern and southern parts of India as an aggressive counter-force that affected a chain of alterations in the inward and outward polity along with Islam.

Islam as a cultural and social force was always seen as a hostile entity before the growing Western ascendency, particularly after the revolt of 1857. The entire blame for the revolt of 1857 was laid on the door of Muslim elites, middle-class intelligentsia and the Ulema as a whole. Gradually, this newly acquired notion on the part of British officials assumed a form of ideological clash between the West and the Islam, though the former happened to be a geographical entity and the latter a religious entity.

British colonial officials invoked their own category, peculiar to the traditional religion of Islam, while the religious elite (read Muslims) had a clear and coherent view of the way the world was and the way one ought to choose.

Moreover, after the defeat in the mutiny of 1857, Ulema had no option but to shift towards religious and intellectual revivalism. The founders of Deoband were well convinced that the future of beleaguered Indian Muslims did not lie in full-hearted embrace of the Western system of education but rather by the way of Islamic learning in legal tradition.

In this long-drawn background to political, religious and social subjugation, the seminary of Deoband came into existence. Darul Uloom Deoband was founded in 1868 in a small town of Uttar Pradesh in northern India. The establishment of the seminary came as a response to the declining religious and social influence of Ulema who had once enjoyed all sort of reputation, fame, appreciation and an economic status for themselves. The Ulema associated with Deoband represented only one of the many streams of Islam that emerged after the revolt of 1857.

Historically, Indian soil has been known for its religious, social and cultural integration of alien religions, ideas and philosophies. One of the renowned 18th-century Arabic-Persian Scholar, Ali Azad Bilgrami (1704–86), who travelled widely in the Middle East and wrote a comprehensive Arabic treaty called *The Coral Rosary of Indian Tradition*, had described that Arabia was the ritual centre, but the network of religious scholarship and humanistic cultures is firmly based in India.[122]

When the revolution was suppressed by the British, reign of terror was established in the country and Ulema were convinced that the British were invincible, they set and drew a strategy. They decided to transform the field of their activities from the battlefield to the field of education. The real goal of Ulema was now to create a community both observant of spiritual life and follower of religious laws, and to do so was to turn to the tradition 'the tongue and the pen' espoused by Shah Abdul Aziz.[123]

---

[122] Carl W. Ernst, 'Reconfiguring the South Asian Islam: From the 18th Century to the 19th Century', *Comparative Islamic Studies* 5, no. 2 (December 2009): 247–72.

[123] Barbara D. Metcalf, *Islamic Revivalism in British India: Deoband, 1869–1900* (New Delhi: OUP, 1982), 87.

During the mutiny, one group of participants along with Hajji Imdadullah had gone to Mecca while the other along with Nanotvi and Gangohi stayed back and established a religious seminary at Deoband (Saharanpur). On 30 May 1866, a group of concerned persons assembled in Deoband (an old centre of Muslim culture and religion) and decided to establish a madrasa which was inaugurated under the shade of a pomegranate tree on the uncarpeted floor of old Chattah Wali Masjid, the most celebrated mosque where the great Sufi Fariduddin Ganj-i-Shakar was reported to have mediated once.[124] It was the town about which Sirhindi and Ahmad Barelvi both had reported to have said that odour of learning came from the very ground of Deoband.[125] It can be claimed without any dispute that Deobandi orientation is among the most influential facets of Islam in modern South Asia.[126]

Darul Uloom was distinctive in the terms of its support, organization, goal and objective. Funds were raised and the first teacher to contribute was Mulla Mahmood (1851–1920). The first student to get enrolled there was Mahmood, who rose to be the most popular teacher in the same institute and later became a figure of an international fame and became known as Shikh al-Hind.[127] In the first year, 16 students enrolled, which swelled to a figure of 78 the next year.

Haji Abid Ali was the first to seek contribution, but the real man behind the scheme was Maulana Qasim Nanotvi who was the first rector of the institute. It was Maulana Qasim who had headed the small government under Imdadullah in the small town of Thane during the mutiny and showed a patriotic and religious zeal. He had fled to Mecca along with Imdadullah to evade the arrest and came back after general amnesty was granted by the Queen.[128] Qasim became the director of Deoband and Maulana Mazhar became the first principal. Qasim used to

---

[124] Metcalf, *Islamic Revivalism in British India*, 88.
[125] Metcalf, *Islamic Revivalism in British India*, 92.
[126] Muhammad Qasim Zaman, *Modern Islamic Thought in Radical Age* (New Delhi: Cambridge Press, 2012), 40.
[127] Ghazi, *Islamic Renaissance in South Asia (1707–1867)*, 233.
[128] S. Abid Husain, National Culture of India (New Delhi: National Book Trust, 2007), 68.

teach the higher classes, and the burden of last pilgrimage got him ill and he died in 1880. After his death, Ahmad Rashid became the rector of the seminary. The patriotism of Deoband can be gauged from the fact that a group of Ulema issued a fatwa prohibiting joining the group 'Patriotic Association' created by Sir Sayyed and called them to join the Indian National Congress.[129]

The respect Qasim commanded among the intellectuals of the time could be judged from the obituary Sir Sayyed wrote about Qasim despite all his differences with him and expressed his grief at the departure of his close associate and intellectual and ideological rival. 'He was a man of angelic qualities. The seminary of Deoband is a worthy memorial to his greatness'.[130]

A renowned Islamic scholar of Pakistan, Taqui Uthmani, claims that when the Ulema perceived British colonialism as intent upon destroying their religion, they had no option but to conserve their intellectual resources by rejecting any further change in the existing curriculum.[131]

A consultative body of seven at Darul Uloom was created, and all members belonged to Wali Allah tradition. The cerebral chain of all these was linked to the school of Shah Wali Allah as all of them were disciples of the descendant of Shah Wali Allah and greatly influenced by his thoughts and ideas. The seminary of Deoband received inspiration from Shah Wali Allah for social and religious reforms and became a centre for British opposition. The founders of Aligarh Muslim University and Qasim Nanotvi were the disciples of the same masters, but there was a yawning difference between the approaches and the orientations of the two.[132] Sir Sayyed had inherited the aristocracy while Qasim Nanotvi represented best of the religious traditions.

Deoband comes closer to the stature of Azhar and sometimes the Deoband clergy calls it Azhar of Asia, and Deoband represents only one of the several streams of Islam in South Asia. Many of the founders of the seminary in Pakistan were educated at the Deoband of India. Deoband emerged as the

---

[129] Husain, 70.
[130] Husain, 69.
[131] Zaman, *Modern Islamic Thought in Radical Age*, 82.
[132] Husain, 68.

biggest centre of religious Puritanism, political freedom and patriotism. Deoband stood for religious nationalism. Historically, the religious seminaries within South Asia had been an informal space for the dissemination of various forms of Islamic knowledge but with the emergence of the Deoband, they have become a more formal disciplinary space for the production of 'pious' bodies.

Deoband was set up as a part of religious movement to offer resistance to religious and political supremacy of the colonial power. Deoband has influenced the life of Muslims for hundred years and continues to do so even today. The Deoband movement was different from Wahabi and was not inspired by the religious ideas of Abdullah Wahab of the Arabian Peninsula, as many assume, but it is more impacted by the ideas of Shah Wali Allah. Deoband School believed in both shariah and Sufism, unlike Wahabis of Arabia who had discarded all orders of Sufism, and so there was no commonality between the two.[133]

Their order was influenced by Wali Allah, and political learning was inspired by Ahmad Shahid. As any casual observation of the sociological makeup of the vast majority of *talibs* within the Deoband religious seminary network will reveal, they belonged very clearly to a subaltern class. The majority of the 'Ulema were themselves indeed subaltern'. The effective historical marginalization and subalternality of the 'Ulema were undoubtedly key factors in understanding the violent turn of the Ulema.

Dar al-Ulum of Deoband had since its inception in 1866 spawned one of the most influential global 'traditionalist' (orthodox) institutions within the wider Muslim world. According to Barbara Metcalf, one of the Western world's foremost scholars of the Indian Deoband, the Deoband is one of the several groups that sought to 'reproduce Islamic culture in a colonial period characterized by considerable challenges to the preservation of traditional learning…. They became known not only as a school but as a school of thought'.[134]

---

[133] Husain, 66.
[134] Barbara D. Metcalf, *Islamic Contestation* (Cambridge: Cambridge University Press, 2004), xx.

Gradually, a number of seminaries were established on the pattern of Deoband, and some were affiliated while other preferred to work independently. Thousands of seminaries share the same doctrinal and sectarian orientation inspired by parent Deoband seminary studying law and the tradition attributed to the Prophet. The Ulema of Deoband preached self-conscious reformist ideology, defined in opposition to the existing popular belief about Islam. Religious education was an important means of safeguarding the Muslim identity. Unity of God and condemnation of *Shirk* (integrating other divine figure with the almighty) ran through the basic vein of the Deoband movement like all the movements of the past. It also opposed the Hindu practices and Sufism that crept into Islamic tradition. The major concern of Deoband was to modify the past heritage of knowledge to make it relevant for the present.

Under the influence of the Western bureaucratic system, Deoband too had a set of curricula, separate rooms for the students of different classes, well-defined academic year and annual examination.[135]

The goal of the Darul Uloom was to train the well-educated Ulema who would be dedicated to reform Islam; they would become writers, preachers and teachers. They would disseminate their learning. It was also decided that students would be taught three basic specialties—Hadith, the Quaran and rational science—of North India in terms of knowledge and wisdom. Delhi is known for Hadith and Quran. The rational science (law, logic and philosophy) is the distinction of Lucknow and Khairabad.[136] The seminary followed the Dars-i-Nizami, a curriculum prepared in Firangi Mahal of Lucknow in the 18th century, but they reversed the emphasis on rational science and shifted their focus to Hadith.

Their next emphasis was given to fiqh (jurisprudence) because it was more important for the followers of Shah Wali Allah that youth must learn correct performance of ritual and ceremonial duties and their focus was bit deviated from the jurisprudence.[137]

---

[135] Zaman, *Modern Islamic Thought in Radical Age*, 68.
[136] Metcalf, *Islamic Revivalism in British India*, 100.
[137] Metcalf, *Islamic Revivalism in British India*, 101.

One major thrust was to evade the habit of innovative practices in Islam, and Shah Wali Allah and his son Aziz were the main proponents of these new practices having crept into Muslims from Hindus and later from the Shiites. Deoband defined itself in opposition to the rational science or any ideas or acts resembling those of Hinduism. Gangohi opposed visit to the shrines because it resembled the Hindu practices despite the fact that it was an old practice amongst the Muslims.[138]

No doubt, Deoband offered a forum to the Ulema who, under British rule, were almost invisible and very rarely had any opportunity to serve in the bureaucracy. It was an opportunity for them to seek and preach both the path of shariah or Sufi—two main streams of Islam at the time. The arrival of Ulema on the intellectual horizon triggered the debate about the supremacy of Sufi or shariah, enriching the understanding of Islam and diversifying the discourse in public spheres.[139] Some Ulema and teachers advocated the combined following of both while few chose to stride the path of Sufi tariqa alone. Deoband, like Sunnis, had full belief in all four schools of Islamic jurisprudence and in that way they were conformists, unlike Ahl-i-Hadith.[140] There was a new trend of debate and discourse among the Islamists on fiqh and shariah, and one such debate took place between Qasim and Sir Sayyed, one traditionalist and the other a modernist. Qasim accused Sayyed for not adhering to the four schools of jurisprudence before inferring any final judgement.[141]

Immediately after the beginning of the seminary at Deoband, the major objective of the Ulema was to make the Quran and Hadith relevant to the present circumstances. There were new efforts to make the revelation relevant and dynamic for the present needs. There was new emphasis on human will, and it was realized that through will, one can alone create the Islamic society; it also ushered in transformation and rationalization of Islam by ideologizing and by the reification of Islam itself.[142]

---

[138] Ernst, 'Reconfiguring the South Asian Islam', 247–72.
[139] Metcalf. *Islamic Revivalism in British India*, 139.
[140] Metcalf. *Islamic Revivalism in British India*, 141.
[141] Metcalf. *Islamic Revivalism in British India*, 144.
[142] Francis Robinson, 'Islamic Reform and Modernities in South Asia', *Modern Asian Studies* 2/3, no. 42 (2007): 259–81.

Metcalf has drawn attention to the study of Hadith amongst the Ahl-e-Hadith, too, who relentlessly advocates that one ought to base his or her perception and vision only on the basis of the Quran. However, the Ulema of Darul Uloom Deoband were adverse to it as they had shaped their Islamic jurisprudence on the basis of the teachings of the six medieval schools of jurisprudence and had accorded a new salience and dynamics to the teaching of Hadith. It was the Darul Uloom that invigorated the teaching of these jurists in South Asia.[143]

Maulana Mahmud-ul-Hasan (1851–1920) was among the first batch of Muslims educated at Deoband and was one of the brilliant students of Qasim. When, in 1905, Gangohi passed away, he took over the headship of the seminary. He was very liberal and patriotic, and formed a group comprising his sincere students under the name of Jamiat-ul-Ansar and trained them in the freedom movement. For this purpose, he had hired Ubaidullah Sindhi, a non-Muslim, who had converted to Islam. Ubaidullah went to Delhi to interact with modern educated Muslims and later he was sent to Kabul to sow the seeds of freedom. Their plan was to liberate Indians with the help of Turkey and Afghanistan.

The success of the school could be measured by the far and wide spread of similar institutions and, by 1967, Deoband claimed to have founded more than 8,000 seminaries in its image.[144] From these institutions had come the teachers and scholars who disseminated knowledge to the common masses. One major development that took place after the creation of Deoband was opening of Dar ul-Ifta ready to receive questions and issue a fatwa.

Post-1857 era and the subsequent establishment of Deoband ushered in an era of oral debate where scholars from different schools of thought assembled and preached their points of view. Who can forget the interesting debate between a European Christian and Shah Abdul Aziz about the rescuing of grandson of the Prophet?

---

[143] Zaman, *Modern Islamic Thought in Radical Age*, 39.
[144] Robinson, 'Islamic Reform and Modernities in South Asia', 259–81.

Nineteenth-century Islamic renaissance inspired and pioneered by Deoband and other affiliated scholars introduced many changes in the philosophical understanding of Islam itself. The growing sense of individual responsibility towards God was a new experience and it was more an outcome of the plight of the Muslims who had suffered. For instance, Sir Sayyed claims:

> I regard it as my duty to do all I can, right or wrong, to defend my religion and to show the people the true, shining countenance of Islam. This is what my conscience dictates and unless I do its bidding, I am sinner before the God.[145]

The sense of personal responsibility was further enhanced in the writing of Maulana Ilyas, founder of Tabligh-i-Jamaat, and other activists of Tabligh-i-Jamaat and in the work of Iqbal. Iqbal exhorts:

> It is not an intellectual act but a vital act which deepens the whole being of the ego and sharpens his will in creative assurance that the world is not just something to be seen and known through concept, but to be made and remade by continuous action.[146]

The school of Deoband not only resorted to past, but it also opened a new vista to engage with the modernity after demolishing the past authority. New reformist forces focused on the human will, making the way for the modern understanding of the undiluted human instrumentality in the world. In the reformist phase, the reification and rationalization of Islam enabled the Muslims to engage with broad-based political identity.

Deoband has emerged as one of the most highly organized and yet remarkably polycentric institutions that claim orthodox religious authority. One must harbour, no doubt, that knowledge imparted at Deoband had nothing to do with the Wahabi sect of the Arabian Peninsula. No doubt, there was close nexus between the ancestors of Deoband and the Wahabi group of

---

[145] Speech of Sir Səyyed Khan quotes in Altaf Hussain Hali, *Hayat-i-Jawid*, trans. K.H. Qadiri and David. J Matthews (Delhi: Idarah-i-Adabiyat-i-Delli, 1979), 172.
[146] Iqbal, *Reconstruction of Religious Thought in Islam*, 154.

Arabia, but there was little exchange on the religious issues. The British called those Ulema associated with Wali Allah School Wahabi because they were struggling against the new forces of Islam in India.

Of late, the seminary of Deoband has taken a 'sectarian' dimension and an ardent proponent of Hanafi school of laws, closing all the windows of ijtihad (scientific interpretation of religious text). Today, Afghan- and Pakistan-based Deoband variants have attained global notoriety, principally because of the nexus between the Deoband and the Taliban.

Sayyed Abu al-Ala Mawdudi and His Jamaat-i-Islami

The seeds of Islamic revivalism in South Asia were first sown by none other than Shah Wali Allah, which were later consolidated by his disciples in different forms and shapes. There were several other movements in the early 20th century, like the Aligarh movement and demand for Pakistan, which drew largely upon the thoughts and ideas of the early period embodied in the work of numerous Islamist ideologues that altered the conception about the objective and meaning of religion of Islam. However, it was ideas and thoughts of Mawdudi that first emerged in a codified form that we know today as political Islam. He was one of the first and foremost modern Islamic political thinkers who not only articulated and highlighted the political ideas enshrined in the Quran and Hadith but also presented it as the most important component of Islamic canon. He is credited with the codification of the writing of the pioneers who laid the foundation of an Islamic revivalist movement in the Indian subcontinent.

Sayyed Abu al-Ala Mawdudi is one of the most important ideological voices of political Islam in South Asia in modern times. Mawdudi was born in 1903 and migrated to Pakistan after the partition of the subcontinent. His ideas were not monolithic throughout his life, and in the earlier phase of his public life, he was tilted towards the evolving Indian nationalistic vision. He wrote many essays in support of the Indian National Congress party. He also praised Gandhi's role and worked for a pro-Congress party paper before taking over the editorship of the mouthpiece of the Jamiat-i-Ulama-i-Hind. He was closely associated with the Khilafat movement.[147] However, with the passage of time, his relationship with the Congress party and the nationalistic discourse soured beyond redemption. He withdrew himself completely from the national movement and evolved himself to be an architect of the Islamic renaissance and social reconstruction in South Asia.

Mawdudi embarked on the path of Islamic reconstruction, which continued until his death in 1979. He expounded his Islamic vision through numerous lectures, articles and books. He propagated his ideas through his journal *Tarjumanu'l-Qur'an*.

He argued that one has to get hold of political power in order to build an Islamic order as revealed and sanctified by the holy Quran and Prophet Mohammad. For him, it is the political power that influences the human civilization and morality in the strongest way.[148] He chided Muslims for having separated politics from religious life and considered this development an outcome of gradual withdrawal and deviation from Islam's true teachings. He advocated a complete obedience to shariah law.

For him, politics was an integral and inseparable component of the Islamic faith, and the 'Islamic state' which Muslim political action sought to restore was viewed as the panacea to all problems being faced by the Muslims. He devoted much of his writings against the ideas of secularism and democracy and stood for total rejection of nationalism that would unite Hindus and Muslims. He regretted the rise of nationalism and its imitation by Muslims in the following words:

> What is regrettable is that all Muslim countries are following the same doctrine of nationalism that they had imbibed from their Western masters. They are not fully conscious of the evolutionary

---

[147] This was a movement launched in India under the leadership of Gandhi in the second decade of the 20th century to protest against the abolition of caliphate in Turkey. The basic intention of this movement was to propagate Hindu–Muslim unity.

[148] Black. *The History of Islamic Political Thoughts*, 320.

character and role of Islam which has potential and enough resilience to fully link them with each other which would finally culminate into the re-emergence of the Muslim Ummah. [149]

He expounded the idea of an Islamic state by saying that an Islamic state '[i]s an ideological state that would be run only by those who believe in this ideology and would be exclusively based on the Quran and Sunnah and the divine laws which is assigned to administer'.[150]

Mawdudi founded Jamaat-i-Islami in 1941, and in its very first convention, he opposed and challenged the most celebrated All India Muslim League Lahore resolution calling for a separate Muslim state. He appealed to the Indian Muslims that they must establish their own separate state which should not be a nation-state on the European model but rather an Islamic state with a religious rather than ethnic, geographical or linguistic identity and based on Islamic rather than European political principles.[151]

Like Qutb, Mawdudi systematically mixed religion with politics, and faith with social action. He streamlined the Islamic faith so that it could accommodate his new-found aims. He reinterpreted the Islamic concepts and symbols, giving them new meanings and connotations. This allowed him to comprehend a political reading of Islam, in which religious piety was transformed into a structure of authority. Faith became ideology and religious work assumed the form of social action. Mawdudi's vision was the product of a discourse with the 'other' — the West. His perspective was also developed in response to greater Hindu ascendancy in Indian politics during the interwar period. He had also sought the establishment of an international union of Muslim states in order to rejuvenate Islam's efficacy in world politics.[152]

Like Qutb's Islamic vanguard, he pleaded for the creation of Salih Jama'at (noble group), to be followed by a truly Islamic state. He always insisted on the indispensability and imperative

---

[149] Mandeville, *Transnational Muslim Politics*, 78.
[150] Ayubi, *Political Islam*, 128.
[151] Black, *The History of Islamic Political Thoughts*, 320.
[152] Mandeville, *Transnational Muslim Politics*, 78.

of Islamization of Pakistan first. Unlike many Islamic modernists, Mawdudi never attempted to reinterpret the literalist readings of the scriptures that would be most jarring to modern sensitivities. He was the first key Islamic thinker to reject explicitly and wholeheartedly the modernist programme of Al-Afghani and others in adapting the shariah laws to the modern world through the renewal of ijtihad.[153]

To elaborate the concept of sovereignty of God, Mawdudi popularized the notion of Hakimiyya, which later on reached its intellectual climax in the writings of Sayyed Qutb. His principle of Hakimiyya contained four major obligations: one must believe in the unity of God, that is oneness of God; must follow wholeheartedly God's guidelines; must obey God's will by fulfilling his revealed laws; and that worship should be confined exclusively to him.[154]

Mawdudi firmly believed that Islam required a setting up of a state on the basis of its own ideology and programme. For Mawdudi, the existence of an Islamic state was absolute necessity for the achievement of social justice and, therefore, he believed that Islamic reform had to come from the top to down.[155]

Sayyed Qutb and Mawdudi propounded several similar concepts and notions of Islamic state. Qutb was also greatly influenced by some of the political ideas of Mawdudi. Mawdudi's influence on Sayyed Qutb's thought is perhaps most evident in Sayyed Qutb's appropriation of Mawdudi's ideas of Hakimiyya.

We have seen that these Islamic ideologues of the 20th century envisaged a comprehensive social reform and the Islamization process for establishing the ideal Islamic social and political order, whereas Khomeini was more concerned with the execution of the political project visualized by him. Like Qutb and Mawdudi, Khomeini's idea also evolved in the background of Western political and cultural onslaught and his primary target was to confront the Western political model.

---

[153] Black, *The History of Islamic Political Thoughts*, 320.
[154] David Zeidan, 'Typical Elements of Fundamentalist in Islamic and Christian Theocratic Worldview', *Islam and Christian–Muslim Relations* 13, no. 2 (2002), 207–28.
[155] Mandeville, *Transnational Muslim Politics*, 78.

4

Arab Spring and the Future of Political Islam

All praise be to Allah, today I can see those faces in Parliament whose presence and utterance in past were a legal crime.[1]

—Former Egyptian Prime Minister, Kamal Ganzouri, in his address to the National Assembly

Another world is possible for all of us.[2]

—A young Egyptian activist, Asma Mahfouz

A great wave of anger, frustration, defiance and democratic demands swept across the Arab world in the last days of 2010. This was the single biggest uprising in modern Arab history, what was termed by Western media as the 'Arab Spring' and by Professor Aijaz Ahmad, a renowned literary critic and expert on international affairs, as an 'autumn of the patriarchs'.[3] The same feeling was expressed by Ms Goufran Mansour in a column in the daily *Guardian* where she wrote: 'It feels good to be Arab these days.'[4] Similarly, another Arab scholar Rashid Khalidi wrote: 'Suddenly to be an Arab is a good thing.'

---

[1] *Al-Ahram Newspaper*, Cairo, 31 January 2012.

[2] Marwan Bishara, *The Invisible Arab: The Promise and the Peril of Arab Revolution* (New York: Nation Book, 2012), 229.

[3] Aijaz Ahmad, 'Autumn of Patriarchy', *Frontline*, February 2011.

[4] Goufran Mansour, 'It Feels Good to be Arab these Days', *Guardian Newspaper*, 3 February 2011.

The Arab Spring (Al-rabyi' al-arabi) is a metaphoric name for the protest movement against the social and political status quo in the region. This Arab Spring was termed as 'awakening of under-privileged classes', 'Arab Revolution', 'Arab uprising' (*intifada*) and 'Arab renaissance', and Marwan al-Muasher, a Jordanian intellectual, called it 'the second Arab awakening'.[5] Some called it a post-normal world, a tiger-wounded reaction and a movement of 'creative destruction'. Enormity, simultaneity, commonality and trans-nationality were the most surprising aspect of upheaval for everyone.

The region is still clouded with a lot of uncertainties, but with one certainty that the Arab world would never be the same. The Arab Spring is a prism to the pain through which Arab made the sense of their political condition. It is the reflection of an Arab endeavour to fly from the culture of authoritarianism, an urge for democratic participation and a cry for transformation of political self-power of the Arab. This rebellion is nothing but a refusal of the obedience to the autocratic and foreign-dictated regime.

In the last month of 2010, the self-immolation of an unemployed graduate, Mohamed Bouazizi, from a small town, Sidi Bouzid, in central Tunisia, detonated the revolution. The protest of millions presented a call for creation of an Arab world of its own preference and not an imposition of the external power. It was a yearning for a political system where social justice, equality and national sovereignty and dignity would be the central component and primary ingredients. It predominantly reflected people's flight from culture of authoritarianism and a call for shift from policy of surrender to politics of assertion.

The self-immolation sent a powerful statement of despair about achieving happiness on the earth and begged for hope of redemption in the afterlife.[6] This individual act was a collective expression of the grievances against the prevailing socio-economic and political system that also created a reverberation in other parts of the world. The four Arab leaders who were

---

[5] Marwan Muasher, *The Second Arab Awakening and the Battle for Pluralism* (London: Yale University Press, 2014), 25.

[6] Hilal Khashan, 'The Arab Spring and Democratization in the Middle East', *World Affairs* 16, no. 4 (2012): 132–47.

forced out of power since the Arab uprising (Egyptian President Mubarak, Tunisian President Bin Ali, the Libyan President Qaddafi and the Yemeni President) spent a total of 130 years in power and average of more than thirty-two years each.

Arab uprising unsettled many assumptions and notions about the Arab landscape. It debunked several culturalist assumptions on the sociology of the Arab region highlighting inherent incompatibility between Islam and democracy. It challenged the predominant perception about the 'Arab Street' as violent, chaotic, unmanageable, undemocratic and fundamentally patriarchal. It was not only assumed but also firmly believed that Arab women were condemned to lead a secluded life and the Arab social structure was not receptive to new ideas. The uprising already laid to rest the 'Westocentric' myth that Muslim masses could only be mobilized through religious exhortation, and it also rebuffed the claim of American-sponsored dictators that they were the great bulwark against a rising tide of 'Islamo-fascism' and moreover Muslims could not represent themselves but should be represented.

The protests spread from villages to towns, towns to cities, region to region, from one country to another, and eventually became an overall pan-Arab uprising bearing all the hallmarks of the information age. The great weapon of this uprising had been the Internet and the electronic media. Much had happened because of the immediacy with which visual images of the latest events could be circulated around the world through 24×7 news channels, YouTube, Al-Jazeera and even cell phones. Similarly, there was a breathtaking rapidity with which millions could be brought into overlapping networks of communication through e-mail, SMS, Facebook, Twitter and so on.

Video clips and images of the revolutionary drama had passed from one camera and cell phone to laptop and satellites television networks, making the Arab uprising perhaps the most filmed and communicated revolution in world history. The image of young revolutionaries overcoming brutal force perhaps seduced the entire Arab nation, arguably people around the world. The Arab Spring proved that the world is more dominated by multimedia culture, where images are more effective, than rhetoric, and human stories are more real than the analysis.

Images of young revolutionaries drowned in their own blood in the green revolution in Iran and a naked man being dragged in Iraq sent horrible images.[7] The sloganeering of God willing had been overtaken by God willed. Invisible Arabs suddenly became citizen journalists and the images became indispensable to 24/7 TV coverage.

A plethora of multiple and variant interpretations are being offered in order to explain the Arab Spring. Some theoreticians are looking at it as a culmination of class struggle through the prism of Marxism, while others submit it as a reflection of failed state, an urge for democracy and long-drawn outcome of changing global order and politics of globalization. There are Quranic interpretations too being offered by those who see it as the divine fulfilment in the light of the Quranic verses, which claim, 'There are guardians over everyone, both before him and behind him who guard him by Allah's command. Verily Allah does not change a people's condition unless they change their inner selves.'[8] A renowned Egyptian Scholar, Jaseer Auda, argues that once the people broke their own barriers, God removed the fear from their life.[9]

Genesis of the Arab Spring

The origin of the Arab Spring can be traced back to the womb of the autocratic character of the regimes in the post-colonial Arab world. The autocracy in the Arab world was embedded at every level and was a multilayered phenomenon where no social institution was untouched from the reach of the clasp of the rulers.[10] One can decipher its genealogy in colonial and post-colonial background, and it is an outcome of a prolonged turbulence

---

[7] Bishara, *The Invisible Arab*, 214.

[8] Quran, 13:11.

[9] Jasser Auda, *Baynal-Shariahwa-l-Siyasah: Aselah Ma badas-Sauraat* [Between Islamic Law and Politics: What in the Post-Revolution Phase] (Beirut: Arab Network for Research and Publishing, 2012), 56–57.

[10] Auda, *Baynal-Shariahwa-l-Siyasah*, 57.

and turmoil in the region. This was an expression of collective anger on the part of the masses against the deprivation of dignity, freedom, social justice and national sovereignty. This was a response to utter despondence against the dictatorship and a passionate desire for independence of oneself and the nation too.

All forms of political opposition and mobilization known to modern societies—political parties, trades unions, the independent press and liberal liberties of various sorts—were thoroughly and successfully suppressed, or at least compromised, by all the dictatorial regimes of the Arab world. There were mainly two pillars of state apparatus; one dealt with the politics of the country and the other was associated with the intelligence. In the Transparency International Corruption Perception Index of 2011, of the ranked 182 countries worldwide, 13 Arab countries were ranked 8th or higher, including Syria, Egypt, Yemen and Libya.[11]

In Egypt alone, one can find the immediate cause of the rebellion in the emergency laws in existence for last thirty years, rising level of poverty, unemployment, rampant bureaucratic–army corruption and presence of a surveillance police state where 1.5 million security personnel are employed only to watch the common people's activities. The insular political elites have often hardened into tightly linked cronyism, monopolizing the wide sector of the economy. One of the former Egyptian ministers did not hesitate in accepting the fact that government did tap the telephonic conversation because if it did not, there would be no foreign investment.[12]

The political uproar in Egypt was only a call against the abuse of human rights, curtailment of political rights, projection of hereditary succession, manipulation with political institutions like huge rigging in all Assembly elections, and shrinking role of Egypt in regional affairs, where it had changed itself from a frontline state of the Arab world against the imperial power to a close ally of Israel and the United States.[13]

---

[11] Muasher, *The Second Arab Awakening and the Battle for Pluralism*, 32.

[12] Jalal Amin, *Maza Hadasa Lil-Saurah-al-Misriyah* [What Happened to the Egyptian Revolution] (Cairo: Dar AlShorouk, 2012), 80.

[13] Safinaz Mohammed Ahmad, *Madarat* (Yemen: Sheba Centre for Strategic Studies, January–April 2001).

The Arab system and society had become so status quoits that a French magazine wrote in reaction to the present unrest in the Arab world, 'See even Arab can have a revolution'.[14] Late Hussein Kaykal, a political commentator of great repute in Egypt, put it very truly, 'Arab Spring is the outcome of what we have done to ourselves, what the regime has done to us and what Israel has done to us.'[15] It was a wail against securitized nationalism where denial of all freedom was so far the key political philosophy.

Now, I will briefly deal with the, geo-economic, geo-political, geo-social and contextual reasons for the revolt known as the Arab Spring.

Geo-economic Realities of the Arab Spring

The Arab world has been economically stifled for decades as the economic burden of the centralized totalitarian regime may be noticed at all levels. The whole Arab world's gross domestic product (GDP), according to the UNDP, is merely equal to Spain.[16] Arab economy has been characterized by rapid human development and a slow productive growth. Once a Lebanese feudal lord was asked why his constituency did not know how to read and write, he answered, 'What do they need that for, if my family can.'[17] Educational growth has not been translated to equal economic growth, and the overall prosperity of the Arab world did not exceed what one observes in South East Asia. Government wages in the Middle East and North African (MENA) countries are 3.4 times the level of per capita GDP as compared with those (3.0) in Asia. Egypt alone provides more than 6 million public sector jobs, which indicates a more bloated public sector and labour market, leading to triple whammy: low

---

[14] Ziyad Hafiz, 'Sauratu Yanayir Fi Misr: Tasaulatal-Hazir wal-Mustaqbil', *Al-Mustaqbal Al-Arabi*, no. 358 (2011): 101.

[15] *Akhbaralaalam*, 14 November 2011.

[16] Wissam S. Yaffi, *Inevitable Democracy in the Arab World: New Realities in Ancient Land* (London: Palgrave Macmillan, 2012), 4.

[17] Yaffi. *Inevitable Democracy in the Arab World*, 4.

productivity, a drop in wages and unemployment that caused a great chaos and political disorder.[18] Neoliberalism resulted in a massive redistribution of income from the poor and the middle class to the elites, a process that led to the emergence of neo-populist regimes. Egyptian revolution can be characterized as a popular revolt against neo-liberalism, corruption and the authoritarianism.[19]

The policy of privatization that different governments of the Arab world followed was also significantly responsible for this upheaval. In its drive of 2001 economic reform, Egypt alone sold 379 public sector companies between 2004 and 2010, rendering thousands jobless. Electricity and transport services were the main victims of this economic reform.[20] The Egyptian government relinquished the people's constitutional right of guaranteed employment, and being unable to change the constitution, it resorted to various measures to nullify that right.[21] A large number of youths were employed only on contractual basis under the new economic policy without the provision of medical facilities, and the employees of public sectors were forced to join labour unions controlled by the government.[22] In the late 1980s itself, there were a lot of protests in Cairo when the government planned to sell out the Al-Jazeera and Muhammad Mahmud Khali museums to reduce the national budget deficit.[23]

President Mubarak had inherited an economy where the neo-rich had all control over the state agency—army, police, bureaucracy and ministers. This was a class of crony capitalists, which gave rise to a nexus between populism, neo-liberalism and neo-populism and had become a system that promoted a

---

[18] Yaffi. *Inevitable Democracy in the Arab World*, 8.

[19] Dan Tschiragi, Walid Kaziha, and Sean S. McMahon, eds., *Egypt's Tahrir Revolution* (Boulder: Lynne Rienner Publisher, 2013), 47.

[20] Tschiragi, Kaziha, and McMahon, *Egypt's Tahrir Revolution*, 54.

[21] Tschiragi, Kaziha, and McMahon, *Egypt's Tahrir Revolution*, 53–54.

[22] Bahjat Al-Qarni et al., *Al-Rabi-Al-Arabi Fi Misr-Al-Saurahwama Baadaha* [The Arab Spring in Egypt: What Afterwards] (Beirut: Centre for Arab Unity Studies, 2012), 75.

[23] Amin, *Maza Hadasa Lil-Saurah-al-Misriyah*, 48.

close nexus between the capitalist and the political class of the country.[24]

This point is further explained very succinctly by former professor of Cairo University, Jalal Amin, as he says:

> Egyptians possess what they do not possess in reality, and if they possess anything, it is confined only to prosperous and capitalist class. What an ordinary Egyptian listens is that the son of the President is the apparent heir to him, he is going to US; he talks to US President and the President asks Israel not to create problems in the succession of his son.[25]

He further argues that Egyptians were made to accept what they did not want. Mubarak tried to impose his son over millions of Egyptians and people asked in what capacity did he go to the United States and why TV shows were organized for him where top US political commentators, like Faraid Zakaria, interviewed him about the national development.[26]

The situations in Tunisia were not different from what one witnessed in Egypt. Tunisians did not merely revolt against the monopoly of power, but they also rebelled against the political economy of the country, which fetched nothing to the common masses. To quote Jalal Amin again: 'The embrace between oppressive economic policy and dictatorship is very common because this sort of economic policy cannot be pursued without an autocratic model of politics'.[27]

The number of unemployed in Tunisia only grew by double in the last ten years. Tunisia is the example of triple whammy as it has to absorb the over-educated fellows in the already bloated government apparatus. It was the economic deficit suffered by the people at large and the unrest, which was the voice of the liberation of the orphans of the globalization and the corruption-laden economic policy, which had established a sort of kleptocracy.

---

[24] Amin, *Maza Hadasa Lil-Saurah-al-Misriyah*, 31.
[25] Amin, *Maza Hadasa Lil-Saurah-al-Misriyah*, 3220.
[26] For detail, see Amin, *Maza Hadasa Lil-Saurah-al-Misriyah*, 110–113.
[27] Amin, *Maza Hadasa Lil-Saurah-al-Misriyah*, 117.

Geo-political Realities of the Arab Spring

The rebellion was a culmination of existing geo-political realities of the Arab world and a refusal of the obedience to the autocratic and foreign-dictated regime. In the eyes of the rebels, the system had become external, and the role of the indigenous members was not more than an implementing agency. After its independence, Arab sovereignty turned into an alibi for keeping the people down and the self-declared ruler became the real enemies of their own people.[28] Collusion between the agent of external hegemony and perpetuators of internal tyranny sabotaged the purpose of the entire freedom and liberation movement from the colonial masters. The political class had become very indifferent and insensitive to the day-to-day grievances of the common masses. It has been aptly described by Professor Jalal Amin as follows:

> 'When people talk about politics, political class talk about money, people talk about bread, they talk about cake, people talk about the educational crisis, and they think how to make money by leasing out the Alexandria University to the foreign investors.[29]

The national politics in Egypt had itself become a family affair. Mubarak's last years were fully committed to ensure the succession of his son after his departure. He sought to ensure the loyalty of senior commanders for his son, and it was rumoured that he sent an extra allowance to the senior echelon of the army for this purpose.[30]

Arab world's dream of liberation from colonialism turned into another form of struggle against neo-imperialism. Civil society groups initiated an Egyptian movement or change known as *Kifayah* which challenged restriction on freedom of assembly and organized demonstrations against the political high-handedness. The Arab Spring has raised the question about the potentiality of democracy in the Arab world and forced a

---

[28] Bishara, *The Invisible Arab*, 23.
[29] Amin, *Maza Hadasa Lil-Saurah-al-Misriyah*, 79.
[30] Tschiragi, Kaziha, and McMahon, *Egypt's Tahrir Revolution*, 19.

new debate about the compatibility between democracy and Islam and if it is culturally and religiously possible. The very regime the United States has been propping up has encouraged this Islamic terrorism and mode of the Arab Spring. Promotion of democracy in the Middle East was not a matter of national egoism but rather it had become a matter of national well-being, even survival.[31]

The impact of a possible influence of democratization in the Eastern Europe on the government and people of the Arab world cannot be denied. Unfortunately, the United States and Europe failed to promote similar democracy with similar enthusiasm in the Arab world as the United States was busy in its own backyard of Latin America and so was Europe in its own way.

One of the senior fellows at the Council on Foreign Relations, Richard Murphy, saw that US commitment to defend Saudi Arabia from the international threat does not translate into its willingness to intervene to protect the region from domestic challenges.[32] The realization that democracy and the oil interest were not necessarily in conflict had become yet another geo-political reality, and this realization was confirmed by the state-ment of Obama when he said that, 'If America is to be credible, we must acknowledge that our friends in the region have not all reacted to demands for the change consistent with the principles.[33]

Globalization forms another geostrategic and political real-ity of the Arab Spring. It is the homogenization, standardizing market force and technology that make up today's globalized economic system.[34] Globalization has triggered a new wave of democracy in different parts of the world but in the Arab world, there was little change and still a lot needed to be done to address the backlog of deprivation and imbalance. In his book *Jihad versus MacWorld*, Benjamin Barber argues that cul-tural tribalism (as represented by jihad) and globalization (as represented by the MacWorld) are clashing in every region of

---

[31]   Yaffi, *Inevitable Democracy in the Arab World*, 47.
[32]   Yaffi, *Inevitable Democracy in the Arab World*, 59.
[33]   Yaffi, *Inevitable Democracy in the Arab World*, 59.
[34]   Friedman, L. Thomas, *The Lexus and the Olive Tree*: *Understanding Globalization* (London: Picador Press, 2012), 35.

the world. Societies are finding it difficult to cope with all these exogenous influences. He writes, 'The complaint MacWorld represents impatience not just with its consumption-driven market and technocratic imperative, but with its hollowness as a foundation for meaningful moral existence.'[35]

Geo-social Realities of the Arab Spring

The explosion of youths in the region had already strained the education and economic system. It is witnessing a demographic explosion, and population in each nation of the Arab world is increasing and there seems to be no correspondence between the growth and the development of infrastructure. The Arab population is 350 million and is expected to grow to 450 million by 2020.[36] More than 75 percent population of the majority of the gulf nations is urbanized. Saudi Arabia will need to create jobs for more than 5 million over the next twenty years, and thus alarming figures are causing massive unrest in the region.

Arab women have come a long way in the last three decades and have impacted the society at different levels, offering their children all sorts of political education. No religious underpinning has impeded the institutionalization of gender equality.[37] In the Egyptian revolution, diverse mixes of women were seen marching and chanting slogans and running here and there in different corners of the Tahrir Square, and Egyptian women deserve as much credit for the revolution as do the men. There was nothing new in people's coming out on the streets as there has been a series of political movements, strikes, gatherings, civil disobedience in the past and all these helped in evolving the culture of protest and demonstration.[38] This upsurge was an

---

[35] Barber, *Jihad versus McWorld*, 275.

[36] *Arab Human Development Report*, UNDP, Regional Bureau of Arab States, New York (2002), 144.

[37] Yaffi, *Inevitable Democracy in the Arab World*, 27.

[38] Tariq Bashri, 'Ilaqatu-al-Din Bid-Daulah: Halat-al-Misrbadas-Saurah' [State and the Religion in Post-revolutionary Egypt], *Al-Mustaqbal al-Arabi* 407 (2013): 80–100.

outcome of the political deficit faced by the masses at the hands of authoritarian-despotic political and governance systems. No sign of political dissent was acceptable. Most of the elections or referenda that take place in the Arab world usually result in fantastic pre-fixed victories by the incumbent who often gets well over 90 percent of the votes cast. In the case of even more ridiculous referenda, the victory is usually above 97 percent.[39]

Technological Realities of the Arab Spring

The Arab world has been feeling the immense effect of technology. Nowhere has it been more salient than through the proliferation of mass communication in the arena of satellite, TV, mobile technology and the Internet. Regionalization and globalization of TV culture has been nothing short of a revolution. Al-Jazeera became a leader with programmes 'The Opposing Direction' and 'Beyond Borders'.[40] Revolutionized by news from the likes of Al-Jazeera with continuous daily broadcast, discussion and debates, the Arab world today has shown that it was not only ready but also willing to tackle its major issues through open debate.

Satellite television and the Internet have knelled the death toll of censorship. New power of the press was more apparent in Syria after the assassination of Hariri in 2005. In Iraq after the departure of Saddam, the first thing that happened was the introduction of freedom of press. Internet freedom in the Middle East was more moderate than the press freedom. Censorship is a long gone victim of technological progress. Islamic sites have popped up from Indonesia all the way to the United States. Facebook may very well end up being the single most exogenous factor that led to the latest uprising in Tunisia and Egypt more so than any diplomatic corps or military influence. It is reported that around 10 percent of Tunisian had Facebook account when

---

[39] Yaffi, *Inevitable Democracy in the Arab World*, 34.
[40] Yaffi, *Inevitable Democracy in the Arab World*, 34.

the revolution took place.[41] A Tunisian activist living in France expressed his feelings in the following words:

When a father can no longer feed his children, he loses his place... and his dignity.... It is not just a question of money. It is a question of honour. The psychological barrier of fear has fallen. People now know it is possible to go to the street, cry 'Freedom' and say; we do not want a President for a life. The credit goes to the Facebook which broke the silence and the timidity barrier by spreading the words all over the world.[42]

In another interview, Wael Ghonim, the Egyptian Marketing Executive of Google stated that all he did was typed on a key-board. Soon everyone was using it, even that organization that had been around since the 1920s, like the MBH.[43]

Technology and the Internet have been slowly shaping the Arab world politics for a long time, and its use appears to shape the Arab attitude towards a number of political concerns. Overall, it appears that Arabs with Internet access are more concerned with the civil and political rights, moral standards and their personal economic situation. Technology has virtually let the jinn of freedom out of the bottle. Arab masses are becoming more vociferous in demanding political, economic and social liberalization.

Technology can be said to be an enabler and in itself is not the reason behind the revolution. Generational and structural changes in the nature of the political communication represent the most fundamental and significant real effect of the new social media. The Arab world was integrated with shared political space and shared fate. According to the Ministry of Communication of Egypt, the number of Internet users in the country increased from 16.3 million in 2009 to 22.6 million in December 2010.[44]

---

[41] Yaffi, *Inevitable Democracy in the Arab World*, 41.

[42] Yaffi, *Inevitable Democracy in the Arab World*, 41.

[43] Tim Lister and Emily Smith, 'Social Media @the Front Line in Egypt', http://edition.cnn.com/2011/WORLD/africa/01/27/egypt.protests.social.media/index.html (Accessed on 4 April 2013).

[44] Tschiragi, Kaziha, and McMahon, *Egypt's Tahrir Revolution*, 17.

The media culture created a bond among the victims and a unified political landscape, thereby unifying the grievance of the people. Social media helped in internalizing a new kind of pan-Arab identity and protestors developed a pan-Arab outlook.

It unfolded as a single unified narrative of protest with shared heroes, common stakes and deeply felt sense of shared identity. The Arab world became united by shared transnational media and bound by a common identity. Crystallization of a shared narrative across the region is the unique contribution of the new media.

Rich Is Knowing: Global Competitiveness and National Economic Security

Twentieth-century Arab resembles the 16th-century Spain in many ways. Spain's misfortune was due to its unproductivity, as argued by Harvard's David Landes, as it depended more on raw materials coming from colonies, and three centuries later Arab economy would see the same fate. Local Arab innovation and value added are very low, causing the region to be highly uncompetitive as compared to the other regions in the world.[45]

Explaining the present economic peril of the Arab world, one leading Arab expert states the following:

> Rich is education... expertise.... Technology and rich is knowing. We have money, yes, but we are not rich. We are like the child who inherits money...he has it in his hands; he does not know how to use it. If you do not know how to spend money, you are not rich. We import everything. The bricks to make houses, we import. The men who build them, we import'.[46]

The Arab world's biggest commodity is the crude oil. Through the process of creativity, industry and marketing, one manages to turn $5 assets into $50. The concept of innovation, productivity and commerce is completely lacking.). The region's

---

45 Yaffi, *Inevitable Democracy in the Arab World*, 10.
46 Yaffi, *Inevitable Democracy in the Arab World*, 11.

large oil reserves and the Arab countries' influence over the price of oil since 1970 have proved as much a curse as a blessing.[47] Foreign direct investment (FDI) and trade are the two main competitive weaknesses. The Arab world has only 1 percent of the overall world FDI, and this amount is concentrated in merely five countries. In such a grim situation, nepotism rules supreme, and in Tunisia only popular anger built around Bin Ali's greed. He had amassed more than $5 billion, most of which was packed into Europe.[48] His wife was described the Arab world's equivalent of the Philippine's Imelda Marcos and fed fortune to her relatives from the Traboulsi family.[49]

The economies of countries such as Tunisia and Egypt have been devastated by unbridled liberalism and the diktats of the International Monetary Fund (IMF) and the World Bank. Liberalized economy has led to concentration of wealth in few hands and creation of nexus between capitalist and government bureaucrats that deprived millions of their opportunity of livelihood. For example, in Egypt alone, more than 50 percent people live below poverty line or earn only $2 a day.[50] This liberal economy gave rise to a culture of crony capitalism where few fat cats monopolized the state enterprises, depriving a large number of state resources.

Political Islam as a Force in the Past in Egypt

If one really seeks to interpret the nature, dynamics and trajectory of political Islam, he or she needs to examine the history

---

[47] Muasher, *The Second Arab Awakening and the Battle for Pluralism*, 19.

[48] Nabila Ramdani, 'Greed of the Tunisian President's Wife that Drove a Nation on to the Street to Start a Revolution', http://www.dailymail.co.uk/news/article-1347626/Tunisia-riots-Presidents-wife-Leila-drove-nation-streets-start-revolution.html (Accessed on 3 April 2013).

[49] Ramdani, 'Greed of the Tunisian President's Wife'.

[50] Ziyad Hafiz, 'Sauratu Yanayir Fi Misr: Tasaulatal-Hazirwal-Mustaqbil [The January Revolution in Egypt: Present Apprehension and the Future]', *Al-Mustaqbal Al-Arabi*, no. 358 (March 2011): 71.

of Al-Ikhwan al-Muslimeen (MBH) founded in Egypt in 1928 by Hasan Al-Banna. Probably each Islamic movement in the Arab world owes something to the thought and ideas of the MBH in one form or another. No doubt, there are contextual and ideological variations amongst different movements, but the core of the philosophy of political Islam emanates from the ideological undercurrent of the MBH.

The relationship between the MBH and regime touched the lowest ebb during the era of Colonel Nasser in the 1950s as a part of his ideological necessity and political strategy to crush all voices of opposition to achieve the long-cherished dream of socialism—one of the core objectives of pan-Arabism. Enforcing his secular pan-Arab nationalism, in no lesser time, Nasser made it categorical that he had neither desire to introduce an Islamic order nor was ready to tolerate any dissent to his authoritarian rule. According to one political analyst, Osama Ghazali, 'Nasser had skilfully exploited existing regional and global political situation in his favour and was able to marginalize the other centres of power too including the MBH.'[51]

In 1954, a large number of members and sympathisers of the MBH were jailed, and in the ensuing election of the legislative council in 1957, MBH nominations were rejected en masse.[52] Nevertheless, the defeat of the Egypt-led Arab world in 1967 caused a different course of relationship between religion, state and the society. This particular moment was a blessing in disguise for the MBH. Nasser, through his March Declaration of 1968, introduced some major changes in his policy aiming to provide political space for the oppositions.[53] Large numbers of MBH cadres were freed and only 140 members were left in jail in 1970 when Sadat came to power.[54]

---

[51] Hisham Al-Auzi, *Siraaala-Al-Shariah Al-Ikhwanul-Muslimunwa Mubarak, 1984–2007* [Contestation for Legitimacy Between Mubarak and the MBH] (Beirut: Mrkaz-Dirasatyl Wahdatul Wataniyah, 2009), 69.

[52] Al-Auzi, *Siraaala-Al-Shariah Al-Ikhwanul-Muslimunwa Mubarak,* 71.

[53] Al-Auzi, *Siraaala-Al-Shariah Al-Ikhwanul-Muslimunwa Mubarak,* 73.

[54] Sami Sharf, *Abdul Nasser: Kaifa Hakama Misr* [Abdel Nasser: How He Ruled Egypt] (Cairo: Madbuli-al-Saghir, 1996), 23.

To leave the legacy of Nasser behind and to get rid of communists, his successor Anwar Sadat adopted the policy of coexistence with the MBH. Exiled MBH members were allowed to return to the country. President Sadat even suggested the MBH to merge with other existing political blocks of the country. In the first election of 1976 under Sadat, the MBH fought the election under the banner of the Arab Socialist Party and six of its members made to the Egyptian Parliament. Given the growing recognition of the MBH, it refused the constant offer of President Sadat to mutate MBH into a charitable organization.[55]

The most impulsive phase of the relationship between state and the MBH ensued when President Sadat landed in Israeli Knesset, paving the way for signing the Camp David Agreement in 1979. Sadat responded to the rejection of the MBH of his new policy with a large-scale crackdown, and hundreds of MBH members were sent to jail.

Mubarak's era can be said to be an era of open confrontation between the militarized regime and the MBH. The main objective of State's overarching power was to oppress all sorts of Islamic voices. At first, Mubarak had softened his policy towards the MBH as he had set free thousands of Islamists thrown in prison during last days of Sadat. There was a complete distinction between law-abiding opposition and the radical opposition during Mubarak's regime. A two-pronged strategy was also there to deal with the opposition where an obedient opposition was tolerated and the radical Islamists were left for the security forces to be handled.[56] In the election of 1984, the MBH entered into parliament for the first time as an opposition block with alliance of the Wafd Party, which had fifty-eight seats, while the MBH had eight to its credit. One of the erstwhile members of the MBH commented saying that 'We are not worried about the size of our numbers here but what is important for us at this moment is to make our presence realized by both people and the state'.[57]

[55] Al-Auzi, *Siraaala-Al-Shariah Al-Ikhwanul-Muslimunwa Mubarak*, 83.
[56] Tschiragi, Walid, and McMahon, *Egypt's' Tahrir Revolution*, 15.
[57] Al-Auzi, *Siraaala-Al-Shariah Al-Ikhwanul-Muslimunwa Mubarak*, 129.

By the late 1980s, the MBH had emerged as a force that could not be ignored anymore since it had established itself as major political power among student unions and other political entities and syndicates. Their voice was no more confined to seek the recognition for itself but they were determined to play an important role in shaping the contour of the national politics.[58] This phase saw an era of moderation when they cooperated with other political actors to reach a compromise unlike a religious organization with unbending ideological views.[59]

In the election of 1987, the MBH made alliance with the Labour and Ahrar Party and enhanced its performance by gaining thirty-six seats and emerged as the single largest opposition party.[60] In its attempt to counter the extremist voices, state itself adopted the policy of Islamization. It started Islamic daily and weekly like *Lawau-al-Islam* and *Aqeedati* and extended the hours of TV and radio programmes devoted to religious teaching. The beginning of 1990 witnessed a fundamental change in relation between the two, which can be well described as a shift from contestation to confrontation. The victory of Islamists in Algeria and growing popularity of Hamas in Palestine had provided new fervour to the MBH.

The MBH had decided to boycott the election of 1990 due to apathetic attitude of the government, but it participated in the election of 1995 under its own banner. Because of the large-scale rigging and manipulation, only one member of the MBH could succeed, who was later ousted allegedly for his association with an illegal group.[61] The election of 2000 was judicially administered, where members of the MBH also participated as an independent group. The slogan like 'Islam is the only solution' was completely absent and they were able to secure eighteen seats and again became the largest opposition block.

The election of 2005 proved to be a catalyst for the MBH as 88 members won out of a total of 161 members who contested the election. They had been tacitly encouraged by the regime to

[58] Ismail, *Rethinking Islamic Politics*, 33.
[59] Muasher, *The Second Arab Awakening and the Battle for Pluralism*, 49.
[60] Al-Auzi, *Siraaala-Al-Shariah Al-Ikhwanul-Muslimunwa Mubarak*, 168.
[61] Al-Auzi, *Siraaala-Al-Shariah Al-Ikhwanul-Muslimunwa Mubarak*, 239.

campaign as a legal body, which they did so with alacrity. The reason the regime allowed this was to get the American of its back. It was to validate the US claim of a region-wide campaign of democratization in several Arab countries.[62]

To check again the growing popularity of the MBH, a comprehensive constitutional amendment was introduced in 2007, granting sweeping power to security forces and banning all political parties with religious or any particular ideological leaning.[63] The MBH in its eight decades of political existence has been suppressed and their voices dashed, giving rise to profound bitterness. The political space for Islamic forces was shrunken during the successive autocratic regimes in Egypt and no scope was left for the expression of free religious or political voices.

Arab Spring, Political Islam and Its Transformation

It was the 25th of January 2011 when people in large numbers came on the streets of Cairo, their first demand being the invocation of long-imposed emergency in the country and a political reform. It was also an opportunity for the protestors to express their anguish and anger against Mubarak's perceptible plan to hand over the power to his son in the next election. The issue of succession was at the core of the Egyptian political debate since 2002, which was catalyzed by the suspicion that a dynastic succession was in the offing.

In the beginning, President Mubarak was adamant not to heed to the demands of the masses, but as the pressure mounted, he ensured some political reforms and announced that he would not contest the next election. Conceding further, he announced to dissolve the parliament, but it was too late and the protestors were not ready for anything less than his final exit from the presidential palace.

---

[62] Based on personal conversation with Nabil Zaky in Cairo.
[63] Al-Auzi, *Siraaala-Al-Shariah Al-Ikhwanul-Muslimunwa Mubarak*, 272.

President Mubarak was very indecisive at the critical juncture and decided to address the nation on 9 February 2011 and
promised to hand over power to his newly appointed deputy
Mr Suleiman, but did not keep his words, presumably because
of the growing pressure from his ambitious son and his wife.[64]
Meanwhile, the Defence Minister and the Army Chief,
Tantavi, announced in a meeting with his subordinates that they
would not shot a fire and they had all respect for the people's
aspiration. Compared to forces of Libya and Tunisia, Egyptian
forces are more professional and enjoyed a greater autonomy.
It was the army's circumstantial decision to side along with the
masses that could have prevented the succession of Mubarak's
son.[65] The army was the most formidable barrier to the realization
of Gamal Mubarak's ambition of succession and, perhaps, this
was one of the reasons of army siding with the revolutionaries.[66]
One of the prominent journalists of Egypt, late Hussein Hayek,
wrote in a daily column in an Arabic daily (*Almisr-Alyum*), 'The
army is the real arbitrator between the people, the real source
of authority, and the authority in form of President Mubarak
who has lost his legitimacy.'[67] It was the moment when historic
slogans were chanted on the streets of Cairo and Alexandria,
'The people and the army are the one hand.'[68]

On 28 January 2011, US President Obama spoke to Mubarak
on phone seeking political reform in the country, while Mubarak
is reported to have told him back, 'You are a nice man but you
do not know the reality of my country and I do not want dicta-
tion from outside.'[69]

There is a decade-old history of growing animosity between
US administration and the Mubarak regime. Among others,

---

[64] Mustafa Bakri, *Al-Jaish—wal-Ikhwan: Asrar-khalf-al-Sataar* [Army and the MBH:
Secret Behind the Curtain](Cairo: Aldarul-Misrioyah-al-Lubnaniyah, 2012), 13.

[65] Bakri, *Al-Jaish—wal-Ikhwan*, 15.

[66] Tschiragi, Kaziha, and McMahon, *Egypt's Tahrir Revolution*, 19.

[67] Bakri, *Al-Jaish—wal-Ikhwan*, 32.

[68] Hani Shukrullah, 'A People's History of the Egyptian Revolution', *Ahram
Online*, http://english.ahram.org.eg/NewsContentPrint/4/0/81295/Opinion/0/A-
people%E2%80%99s-history-of-the-Egyptian-revolution-.aspx (Accessed on 25
September 2013).

[69] Bakri, *Al-Jaish—wal-Ikhwan*, 53.

refusal of Mubarak to permit the establishment of military airbase in the Red Sea, his refusal to send troops to Iraq after the withdrawal of US forces and denial to put pressure on President Abbas of Palestine at the behest of United States to resume negotiations with Israel were the primary reasons for these growing differences between the two.[70]

The situation on the street was unfolding very rapidly. On 10 February 2011, Army Chief, Mushir Hassan Tantavi, announced in his maiden statement that it was the duty and responsibility of the army to protect the people and respect the aspiration of the masses, and told that the army would not be a barrier in the face of the people's demand. He also ordered to remove all the barriers so that the president could listen to the cry of the people.[71]

On 11 February, Mubarak's deputy, Omar Suleiman, announced in a brief televised statement Mubarak's surrender of his presidential powers to the Supreme Council of Armed Forces (SCAFs).[72] When the demand of the people that 'Mubarak should go' was heeded, they could not help thinking that what they had achieved was a revolution.[73] Mubarak ruled Egypt longer than Nasser (eighteen years) and Sadat (eleven years) put together and had made it clear that he had the plan to rule the country till his death. For Egyptians, it was the only moment when they had experienced national pride; it was a redemptive moment when dignity and humility were reclaimed.[74]

After the departure of Mubarak, the army took over the task of conducting the affairs of the country and promised to hold the election within a fixed timeframe. The army statement says, 'SCAF takes over the responsibility of running the country in this hour of crisis.'[75]

---

[70] Bakri, *Al-Jaish—wal-Ikhwan*, 54.

[71] Bakri, *Al-Jaish—wal-Ikhwan*, 34.

[72] Shukrullah, 'A People's History of the Egyptian Revolution'.

[73] Hugh Roberts, 'The Revolution That Wasn't', *London Review of Book* (12 September 2013), http://www.lrb.co.uk/v35/n17/hugh-roberts/the-revolution-that-wasnt(Accessed on 29 October 2013).

[74] Tschiragi, Kaziha, and McMahon, *Egypt's Tahrir Revolution*, 109.

[75] Bakri, *Al-Jaish—wal-Ikhwan*, 47.

A large number of the political observers and experts started raising their eyebrows over the absence of the Islamists in this hour of upheaval and some unhesitatingly announced it a revolution without the Islamists. There was a general consensus among the people that it was not an Islamic uprising, Islamists were not leading it and Islamic ideology was not colouring it.[76] In the beginning of the revolution, the response of the MBH was the most surprising and complicated too. The official statements of the MBH were quite vague and blurred, as its statement of 26 January 2011 reflects, 'MBH would participate in the revolution in its individual manner and the government should respect the sentiments of the people.'[77]

It was later on 28 January that the streets of Cairo were swamped with the cadres of the MBH which tried to offer a leadership to the uprising. At this juncture, when they were sure of crumbling power of the state and given the pro-protester mood of the army, the MBH first flocked behind the protestors and later led the protestors. On 28 January 2011, its first statement came supporting the revolution. MBH General Guide, Mohammad Badie, called for a movement in the pursuit of peaceful and social political agenda and under no circumstance would it grab power through violence. The MBH also began to debate the greater, albeit indirect, role for the party in the national political life.[78] Erstwhile US Secretary of State, Hillary Clinton, on 30 June, told that there had already been a channel of communications between the US administration and the MBH, and the MBH had been asked to respect the Camp David and to rescue Israel from the terrorist groups.[79]

Given the religiosity of the cultural domain of the Arab street in general, one could not harbour any apprehension that any development in the region would re-carve a political landscape where political Islam would have emerged as an inevitable force to reckon with in a new appearance and in a new form.

---

[76] Tschiragi, Kaziha, and McMahon, *Egypt's Tahrir Revolution*, 110.
[77] Al-Qarni et al., *Al-Rabi-Al-Arabi Fi Misr-Al-Saurahwama Baadaha*, 161.
[78] Bishara, *The Invisible Arab*, 195.
[79] Bakri, *Al-Jaish—wal-Ikhwan*, 60–61.

Islam of awakening emerged as a powerful wave of world-historic change that swept across the Muslim world. Islamic presence was seen strengthened everywhere in the wake of the uprising. The ordinary Muslims, notably in Egypt and Tunisia, framed their mobilization for freedom and justice in an Islamic idiom.[80] Election results in the post-revolutionary countries have re-enforced the prevailing long-term notion that Arab future would be marked by the presence of the Islamists in power in one way or the other.

With the decline of autocratic regimes, the Islamists in Egypt and Tunisia were sure that they were poised to make the gain in any ensuing political and social vacuum, and in a week's time, MBH and Ennahdha in Egypt and Tunisia, respectively, emerged as the biggest recipients of the movement. Religious parties found two voids to fill: One was the abandonment of the social terrain by ruling cliques increasingly interested in lining their own pockets, and the other was the political void created by the suppression of the secular opposition.[81]

After throwing the regime, the religious groups became more visible in the public sphere. Islamists availed of all opportunities of political openness to expand its social base through ideological and organizational mobilization. They were no more confined to symbolic and ritualistic limit. The grassroots networks, organized structures and social subsidiaries of the MBH in Egypt were instrumental in consolidating its position in the post-Arab Spring phase.[82]

One member of the MBH (Syria), Mr Bayamon, put it very rightly in his remarks, 'For every success there is context and that must be respected and the Arab Spring created a situation where no longer it is possible to denounce the Islamists.'[83]

After the departure of Mubarak, the MBH started sending feelers to the army about their involvement and participation in the future national political dialogue. Their earlier demands did

[80] Raymond W. Baker, 'The Paradox of Islam', *Political Science Quarterly* 127, no. 4 (Winter, 2012): 519–66.

[81] Muasher, *The Second Arab Awakening and the Battle for Pluralism*, 34.

[82] Bishara, *The Invisible Arab*, 198.

[83] *Akhbaralaalam*, 25 November 2011.

not accede to political reform, fresh election and release of their prisoners.[84] Later, the Islamists called for complete departure of the remnant of Mubarak too in the form of erstwhile Prime Minister Ahmad Shafeeqe and Vice President Suleiman and wanted an early election and transfer of power to an elected government. This hasty and major departure in their policies was because they were well convinced of the fact that the MBH was the only alternative for Mubarak in the absence of other political forces and they would eventually rule the country if a fair election, as promised by Supreme Council of Armed Force (SCAF), is held. The MBH joined the movement later, most likely because of three reasons: unintended to accord it an Islamic colour, not aware of the exact trajectory of the revolution and sure to yield the real fruit of the political changes. Moreover, it did not participate in the movement because of its past image as an extremist, and avoided the state oppression.[85]

Before the revolution, the religious–political domain of Egypt was occupied chiefly by five key Islamic streams: first represented by the official Islam of Al-Azhar; second was the MBH itself—the biggest political opposition group and most rooted of all; third was the Salafist group; the fourth group was dominated by the Qutb school of philosophy; the last group was the Sufi groups residing in the socio-religious domain of the subaltern groups.[86]

It was a well-known fact to everyone amidst the revolution that the MBH was the only non-qualifier political group after the army and judiciary to take the reign of power in terms of numbers, self-discipline and cultural coherence. The MBH for decades has been at the centre of the Egyptian civil society. Its prominent role in offering the social service to the public coupled with the increasingly declining role of the Egyptian state.

While discussing the transformation of political Islam, I will primarily focus on the MBH and the Salafist movement in Egypt because they represent true transformation in the orientation of political Islam in the wake of the Arab Spring.

---

[84] Bakri, *Al-Jaish—wal-Ikhwan*, 31.
[85] Al-Qarni et al., *Al-Rabi-Al-Arabi Fi Misr-Al-Saurahwama Baadaha*, 176.
[86] Al-Qarni et al., *Al-Rabi-Al-Arabi Fi Misr-Al-Saurahwama Baadaha*, 161.

After the beginning of the political process in the country, there were mainly two players in the political arena: army and the MBH, and the past relationship between the two is well-known. The MBH was trying to constrict every move on the part of the army to show its newly achieved political strength, which was contained for decades, while the army was trying to maintain its legacy of power.

SCAF declared on 11 February 2011 that they could never be a substitute to the legitimacy expressed by the people in order to allay the apprehensions of the political opponents and it also exhorted that they would instead act as an implementing agency alone.[87] Next day, the erstwhile Prime Minister Shafeeqe was asked to form a new government, which was followed by a constitutional declaration dissolving the parliament, nullifying the 1971 constitution of the country.

By this declaration, the SCAF authorized itself to make laws, and a committee was constituted under Tariqe Basher to amend few clauses in the constitution in correspondence with the wishes of the people.[88] The amended constitution along with the choice of constitution-first or election-first was put to referendum to bring 77 percent votes in the favour while 23 percent choose to oppose it. Meanwhile there was a growing demand for a new constitution, but this demand was aborted by the MBH because they were more interested in an early election to exploit the charged political environment of the country. It was very much obvious to all that the MBH would love to have a constitution of their own choice and they could do it only when it would be drafted after the election as they were sure to receive the majority in the parliament. Other political groups knew it and so they were more interested in the constitution-first scheme.

The MBH was in all hurry to take over the country and consequently they were mounting heavy pressure on the army. The army was repeatedly stating that it had no interest in political affairs of the country. The chief of SCAF, Mushir Tantavi, said

---

[87] Bakri, *Al-Jaish—wal-Ikhwan*, 68.
[88] Bakri, *Al-Jaish—wal-Ikhwan*, 70.

in a private conversation that they would go back to their barrack as soon as normalcy and political stability are restored.[89]

It was a time when the generational difference within the MBH appeared in public and dawned a new phase of political and ideological rift inside the MBH. The MBH had announced ahead of the time that it would not participate in the demonstrations, and its members were issued strong warning accordingly. However, this did not stop the revolutionaries, who were also part of the 6 April movement. The young blood did not want the central leadership to enter into any kind of dialogue with the regime as they were now the part of the heart and pulse of the masses.[90] Many young members of the MBH were in the crowds, some spearheading the marches.[91] They accused their elders of surrendering the national interest for political benefits, but to satisfy the youth, MBH leadership did retreat from its past decision of holding further dialogue with the army and particularly with the new vice president of Egypt, Omar Suleiman. Haytham Abu Khalil, one of the prominent leaders, resigned from the MBH because of the difference with the MBH for their secret meeting with Omar Suleiman.[92] So far the Islamists had an ideological contestation with the national elite, but now they were faced with an internal criticism from Salafism and other traits of Islamism.

After the end of the Mubarak regime, the MBH deepened their political activities and announced the formation of its political wing, the 'Freedom and Justice Party (FJP). The FJP was formed under the leadership of its three members: Shura, Mohammad Morsi, Essam Elarian, Mohammad Saed el-Katatny, Secretary General. In August 2011, the FJP had special election to replace these three in order to maintain organizational separation between the political party and the religious propagation.[93] This was the first free and open election in party history.

---

[89] Bakri, *Al-Jaish—wal-Ikhwan*, 79.
[90] Al-Qarni et al., *Al-Rabi-Al-Arabi Fi Misr-Al-Saurahwama Baadaha*, 161.
[91] Tschiragi, Kaziha, and McMahon, *Egypt's Tahrir Revolution*, 113.
[92] *Istaqalatun-Qiyadi-al-Ikhwani*, 31 March 2011, http://www.masrawy.com/news/egypt/politics/2011/march/31/mus_brth.aspx (Accessed on 2 May 2013).
[93] Bishara, *The Invisible Arab*, 208.

The theological approach to politics was opposed by many after the revolution and many opposition groups united to defeat the Islamist. Some were more afraid of Islamist totalitarian takeover than the secular one. The liberals saw the implementation of shariah as a sign of regression and totalitarianism while other Arab nations saw the rise of Islamist political power on the basis of their vision for the governance and commitment to democracy and pluralism. Dr Yahay Jameel, one of the deputy prime ministers in the transitional phase, described the ascendance of Islamists to power as an arrival of dark and regressive forces in the country.[94]

At this point, one of the chief strategists of the MBH, Khairat Al-Shater, emphasized the commitment of the MBH to the civil society and the peaceful alternation of power. He said:

> Our aim is to build a modern and democratic system that builds institutions, respects the rules of law, human rights, minority rights and the independence of the judiciary, and is based on most transparent criteria in modern states, all of which we lack now.[95]

On ideological and political grounds, a number of split took place inside the MBH and the split was more of a pragmatic manifestation within. The split groups formed their own parties, triggering a blame game against each other. One of the prominent leaders, Dr Ibrahim Al Zafarani, formed his own Ennahdha party. He was considered to be one of the most important MBH reformers of the 1970–80s. He announced that his party agenda focussed on the idea of a civil society and the right of the citizens.[96] There were several insiders who had all sort of condemnations for the MBH on the issue of freedom of women and Coptic rights as a minority. Haytham Abu Khalil, other prominent leader of the MBH, resigned and founded a new party 'Al-Riyada' because of the difference with the MBH for their secret meeting with the then vice president of Egypt,

[94] Bakri, *Al-Jaish—wal-Ikhwan*, 83.

[95] Muasher, *The Second Arab Awakening and the Battle for Pluralism*, 53.

[96] Khalil al-Anani, 'The Role of Religion in Public Domain in Egypt after the January 25 Revolution' (Arab Centre for Research and Policy Studies, 2012), 3.

Suleiman.[97] While another member of the MBH and a member of constitutional amendment committee, Sobih Saleh, called for an establishment of an Islamic government as the next objective of the MBH. However, he was forced to retreat and apologize after facing a lot of condemnations.[98]

The real concern for the believer in political Islam was now to highlight the democratic element of Islamic polity. The FJP, which included Coptic Christians too, went out of its way to claim that it seeks a constitution that respects both Muslims and non-Muslims and was committed to pluralistic and democratic Egypt. Prayers for the absent and Sunday Mass for the souls of the martyrs were conducted in Tahrir Square, where Muslims and Copts were seen protecting each other.[99]

There was more telling story about the changing political environment in the country. The MBH Iftar party was graced by members of the Supreme Military Council, something unheard of in the previous decades. The participation of a conservative party like Salafist in the election of Egypt is itself suggestive of this radical transformation within political Islam.

A new culture of intra-Islamic dialogue was noticed after the revolution. As one Islamist states that democracy is a sin, while other claims that democracy is a form of culture of consultation, and it would lead to the convergence between Islamic values and democracy.[100] One member expressed his views that entering into legislature is a sin because it does not work under the law of Quran while the other supported the claim that by entering into parliament, Islamists can raise their Islamic issues.

Similarly, there appeared the issue about the rule of women. A group of members cited the statement of great Islamic Jurist Hanifa who did not see any violation of shariah in the rule of women. This revolution necessitated a culture of dialogue as one member of the MBH remarked that in civil society, there

---

[97] *Istaqalatun-Qiyadi-al-Ikhwani.*

[98] *Al-Masry Al-Youm*, Cairo, 26 May 2011.

[99] 'Protestors Plan Coptic Mass on Martyr's Sunday', *Ahram Online*, 6 February 2011, http://english.ahram.org.eg/News/5046.aspx

[100] Auda, *Baynal-Shariahwa-l-Siyasah*, 77–78.

should be no religion, while other claimed that in civil society there should be elements of both Din and democracy.

At this stage, they learned to work within a certain defined political process. The JFP, in its political manifesto, consistently held the position that the right of women and Coptic Christian would be respected. At the international level, the MBH was not tired of stressing that the Camp David agreement (once the central means of Islamic rhetoric) would be respected. It is not the Islamic rhetoric but the question of democracy and political engagement that were nearer to their heart now. The FJP sent its representative to attend the Coptic festival of Cairo and entered into intense dialogue with the Christian Coptic youth movement and three Christian organizations, and the first political alliance comprising both the MBH and Coptic members came into existence.[101]

Islamists obtained an independent and new public space for the first time. The success of Islamists in Tunisian elections and victory of a large number of FJP members along with other Islamic groups in the Egyptian parliament set the ground for a multiple and different future of political Islam. Political maturity of Islamists in Egypt and other countries are helping them confront the traditional ideology couched in national secular and liberal phases but oppressive and autocratic in nature.

The democratic wave across the Arab world compelled the Islamists to abandon their exclusive and narrow Islamic character of politics and to join the mainstream national polity. The legitimacy and authenticity accorded to the Islamist forces brought modesty in their mode of political engagement. For instance, the Ennahdha leader of Tunisia, Rachid, told to Al-Jazeera in an interview that he was directly opposed to Caliphate and was a supporter of the democracy, and he summarized the vision of democracy in the following words:

> Democracy is when the people rule themselves by themselves through an authority that represents them. They should be able to constantly oversee it and overthrow it when they want. It is

---

[101] Mohammad Hafez, *Al-Ahram* (Weekly), 16 November 2011.

when citizen can enjoy their personal freedom, regardless of their colour, wealth, religion and way of thinking. It is when the state is built on citizenship basics, which means the state does not belong to a certain family, person or party. It belongs to all its citizens.[102]

The post-Arab Spring pushed the Islamist forces on a protective mode and they strode a cautious path. During the heyday of the revolution in Egypt, the MBH did not create its own rhetoric to convey its message. According to one of the official members of the MBH, they had opted not to play a remarkable role in the revolution just to preserve the national and secular identity of the revolt.[103] The compulsion of politics of negotiation and accommodation bought some fundamental changes in the political approach of the Islamists.

A sense of pragmatism prevailed over the Islamists in the aftermath of this upsurge and they were no more adherents of regressive politics, but were acting in a more progressive manner. The MBH political manifesto did not highlight the issue of Palestine, but like all other political denominations of Egypt, it talked of employment, social justice and poverty.[104] The formation of the FJP placed the MBH on equal electoral footing in terms of having a national party platform and specific policies. The FJP, like all other national parties, lost its ideological past and was busy in making and breaking promises.

The most appalling was the ideological dilution and alteration in the century-old thoughts of the Salafist group following the Arab Spring. The Salafists do not follow one leader or belong to one political party. 'Salafi' is a catchall term for individuals who adhere to a strict interpretation of Islam and who seek to return to Islam as it was practised under Prophet Mohammad and the first generation of his followers.[105] No doubt, the new millennium has witnessed a steady rise of the Salafists in Egypt and its impact has been growing for some years. The rise of

---

[102] Bishara, *The Invisible Arab*, 207.
[103] Hafiz, 'Sauratu Yanayir Fi Misr', 101.
[104] 'Munaqashaat', *Al-Mustaqbal Al-Arabi*, no. 358 (March 2011).
[105] Muasher, *The Second Arab Awakening and the Battle for Pluralism*, 46.

the Salafist group in Egypt may be more owed to the growing influence of Gulf and Wahabi ideology of Saudi Arabia than to the impact of Al-Azhar. In Egypt, some scholars, like Hossam Tammam, have distinguished between the Wahabi Salafist and the Egyptian Salafist, where the latter has its ingenious origin. The former does not want any kind of political participation, while the latter is equally politically active as other political entities of the country.

The growing usage of satellite, Internet and constant flow of people from both sides further deepened the impact of Salafism in the country. Moreover, they were encouraged by the authoritarian regime as an alternative to the MBH, because their puritan version of Islam advocates total obedience to the ruler.[106]

Salafists, in the beginning of the revolution, were at the periphery and their first statement, issued on 9 January 2011, mentioned nothing about the participation in the protest.[107] The prolonged silence of the Salafists was also a cause of anxiety for the youths associated with the movement, which gradually led to an ideological division within the movement. After the departure of Mubarak, their only worry was to preserve the religious identity of the state. This outlook of the Salafists vis-à-vis the revolution remained obscure until Mubarak was dethroned. For the first time, in its statement of 2 February 2011, it condemned the violence of the protestors and came up with a road map and a new blueprint for the political future of Egypt. Some of the Salafists were seen along with the protesters on the streets.

However, for the Salafists to launch their own political party and enter the electoral arena was virtually unprecedented. The MBH was bound to see it as a threat to its own electoral prospect. A movement that remained so far a non-entity in political sphere came out as one of the biggest political forces in the country. Earlier, there was no connivance on the ideological and political levels between the MBH and Salafists, but now they joined hands to project a united Islamic front to evolve a new power structure in Egypt.

---

[106] Muasher, *The Second Arab Awakening and the Battle for Pluralism*, 47.

[107] Abdul Ghani Imad, *Islamiyyuna Baina-al Saurahwal-Daulah* (Beirut: Markaz-al-Dirasat-al Wahdah-al-Watniyyah, 2013), 106.

Like the MBH, Salafists too floated a political party, Al-Nour, to contest the election. Al-Nour party's agenda represented a turning point in the political discourse of the country. The party proposed an agenda for political, social and economic reforms and talked of giving highest authority to the shariah. It also proposed a democratic polity through the framework of shariah laws.[108]

Salafists called the politics to be under virtues and prevention of vice.[109] Despite their denials, they were a political party and supported the entire Islamic block in the country with three conditions: faith in shariah, their integrity and efficiency. The FJP has come close to accept some principles of societal pluralism, whereas the Salafists remained adherent to some of the rigid instance earlier represented by the MBH.[110]

The most startling was the emergence of Salafists as a political force in the first democratic parliamentary elections held in Egypt after the revolution. 'Al-Nour' performed quite well, taking second place with 27.8 percent of the votes and 123 seats, compared with the FJP-led alliance with 37.5 percent votes and 235 seats. The victory of the Salafists in the election with the 25 percent of seats elevated the political stature of the Salafists. Commenting on this victory, a professor of an American university, Ashraf Shareef, said: 'The Islamists have gained major political dividends in a very short span of time and they have received all sorts of local, regional and global recognition.'[111] The emergence of the Salafists made it impossible for the MBH to make an alliance with any other political groups without putting its internal unity at stake.

The entry of the Al-Nour in the lower house (dissolved on 14 June 2012 by the SCAF at the recommendation of the

---

[108] Al-Anani, 'The Role of Religion in Public Domain in Egypt after the January 25 Revolution'.

[109] Ali Abdul Al, 'Al-Salafiyah Tahziru Min-al-Masaas', *Islam on Line* (9 February 2011), http://www.onislam.net/arabic/newsanalysis/newsreports/islamic-world/128475-q-q------.html(Accessed on 25 April 2013).

[110] Dietrich Jung, *Islamist Politics after the Spring: What do Salafist Parties Want* (Centre for Mellemos Studier, Syydansk University, 2012).

[111] *Asharq Alawasat*, 21 December 2011, http://www.aawsat.com//details.asp?section=4&article=655306&issueno=12076#.UYdNjaJyDcM (Accessed on 22 January 2012).

Supreme Constitutional Court, SCC) was nothing short of a political miracle for the entire nation. Salafists in the past had always condemned political participation for its non-religiosity. However, the changing political environment forced it to join the fray, and they fared well. For the first time in the history of Egypt, Islamists had captured the National Assembly and were able to have their own speaker. Not only this, they were in direct negotiation with the military regime to transfer the power to elected representatives, which, in no way, was possible before the revolution.

The political instance of Salafists was not stable and keeps on changing, which was reflected in the presidential election of Egypt. Salafists were more of missionary orientation than political, while the army was more of professional orientation than political.[112] Even the Salafists had seen the split on the line of the MBH, and several offshoots of the party had come out manifesting its internal ideological diversities. There were rise of parties like *Al-Asala* (authentic) and *Al-Fadila* (virtues) that emerged from the heart of the philosophy of the Salafist movement.[113] The Salafists witnessed internal ideological religious battles since its inception. Some of the members of Al-Fadila were of extremist nature and called for resistance to the rulers. The members of Al-Asala were committed to their Salafist background. Al-Fadila called for a secular state within an Islamic framework. No party or Islamic blocks were immune from the internal ideological or political division and transformation in the post-Arab Spring phase.

Mushrooming of the parties out of several Islamic blocks became an unprecedented phenomenon following the Arab uprising. Islamic Jihad, a traditional Islamic group, also decided to form a party of its own, 'Safety and Development Party', and this initiative originated from Al-Azhar.[114] Likewise, Al-Gama Al-Islamiyya group formed a political wing of its own, 'Building

---

[112] Bashri, 'Ilaqatu-al-Din Bid-Daulah', 80–100.

[113] *Alyum-al-Sabee*, Cairo, 11 July 2011, http://www.youm7.com/News. asp?NewsID=452334 (Accessed on April 2013).

[114] Al-Anani, 'The Role of Religion in Public Domain in Egypt after the January 25 Revolution'.

and Development Party'. The main slogan of the party was 'Shariah law is the main source of the legislation and a reference to ensure the maintenance of the national identity' and they further called Egypt an Islamic state and asserted that woman and Coptic Christians could not become president.[115] Liberals too did not lag behind in asserting their religiosity, which shows the grasp of Islamists over the political landscape of the country.

Here are the few words about the changing character of the Al-Azhar after the revolution. After the revolution of 1800–05, when the Ulema of Al-Azhar and traders were at the forefront under Pasha, it was for the first time during the Arab Spring that Al-Azhar men were seen very active at all fronts of national politics.

Al-Azhar, which was weakened as a prestigious religious institution of the country under Nasser, received a new lease of life in the backdrop of the Arab Spring. Under Nasser, the authority of Al-Azhar had no choice but to surrender to the dictate of Nasser. The Islamic institute of great repute was nationalized in 1961.[116] This move was described as a reform initiated by the erstwhile Egyptian government.

However, after the Arab Spring, the role of Azhar became prominent and this was taken as an opportunity to be free from the political tutelage as its duty was reduced only to accord the legitimacy to the regime. The revolution of 25 January 2011 gave Al-Azhar an opportunity to reiterate its demands of autonomy, and it was an era of strategizing its future relationship with the state. This was evident when they played a mediatory role in agreement between the government and the National Salvation Front.

Al-Azhar played an important mediatory role at several occasions and sorted out the differences between the army and the MBH leadership. It was at the behest of Al-Azhar that the MBH, for the first time, was invited for talk with the army. Al-Azhar sent Dr Shafei as its representative to the constituent assembly,

---

[115] Al-Anani, 'The Role of Religion in Public Domain in Egypt after the January 25 Revolution'.

[116] Daniel Crecelius, 'Al-Azhar in the Revolution', *The Middle East Journal* 20, no. 1 (1966), 22–40.

which was a major shift in the policy of the prestigious institute, and it emerged as a new political pressure group in the country.

From Opposition to the Power: Back to Square One

The 18-day protest on the streets of Cairo and in different parts of the country was able to throw the shackles of fear and submission, transforming people from century-old subjects to citizens. The removal of the barrier of fear and horror was one of the historic achievements of the uprising across Egypt.

After the departure of Mubarak and settlement of the revolutionary dust on the streets, the election process was the first issue before the nation as promised by the SCAF. No political group or state agency had any apprehension about the victory of the MBH-led FJP in the proposed assembly election. All other political groups were well convinced that the Islamists would be the real harvesters of this prolonged struggle on the streets. People had no choice but to vote for the Islamist block because they were the most organized and ready to take the call. One of the professors of Manufiya universally remarked very pertinently that Islamists had no opposition and they fought the election against themselves alone.[117]

Those fighting against the Islamists were an amalgam of different voices consisting of the Coptic, business-oriented middle class, socialists, leftists, liberals, secularists, Arab nationalists and democrats. These groups had nothing in common except hatred for the Islamist and their primary objective was to prevent the Islamist form coming to the power.[118] Moreover, other parties were nascent and the revolutionaries had no organization of their own. The rest were of old generations

---

[117] Based on conversation with Dr Makkaviin Manufiya University during my visit to Egypt in September–October 2013.

[118] Samuel Tadros, 'Egypt's Election: Why the Islamist Won', *World Affairs* (March–April 2012), http://www.worldaffairsjournal.org/article/egypt%E2%80%99s-elections-why-islamists-won

whose mindsets had been configured merely in the course of thirty years of the opposition.

There were scores of parties that had mushroomed in the span of six months before the election and were ready to enter the fray. These parties were as follows: FJP, Alnour, Wafd, Construction and Development Party, Moderate, Dignity, Reform and Development, Socialist People Alliance Party, Tajammu, Egyptian Social Democratic Party, Free Egypt Party and National Committee for Change.[119] All these parties had existed in the past merely in name and were associated with one or other ideological streams, like Construction and Development Party was the political wing of the Jamaat-al-Islami in Egypt.

The MBH and its political affiliates too were optimistic that they had a free domain to trample any opposition. The first-ever free and fair parliamentary election held in three rounds between 28 November, 2011 and 11 January 2012 witnessed a huge victory for the Islamists, and two major Islamic blocks, FJP and Al-Nour, achieved overwhelming majority in the parliament. The sound victory defeated those predictions and arguments which were seeing the Islamists as scarecrow and were not more than salt in ocean.[120]

The FJP won the largest number of seats under Egypt's complex electoral system and the hardliner Salafist Al-Nour party emerged second. The MBH had its own huge network made up of charitable institutions and thousands of mosques attached to it offering all the social services including health and education. The FJP alone obtained 35 percent of votes and the total seats captured by the Islamists were 70 percent of the parliamentary seats, while the MBH share was alone 40 percent.[121] One can judge the popularity and appeal of the Islamists in the first democratic election in Egypt where the MBH-led alliance won 485 seats with 40 percent of seats for itself.

What was more astounding was the performance of the Al-Nour party, which secured one-fourth of the votes in the new parliament taking second place with 27.8 percent of the votes

---

[119] Bakri, *Al-Jaish—wal-Ikhwan*, 287.
[120] Tadros, 'Egypt's Election'.
[121] Bakri, *Al-Jaish—wal-Ikhwan*, 102.

and 123 seats compared with the FJP-led alliance with 235 seats. Immediately after the victory, the opposition groups which were as divided as never before started blaming the Gulf nations for felicitating the victory of the Islamists, while ignored the fact that it was only Islamic groups which had borne the brunt of the past oppressive regimes during the last six decades. These were the Islamists who had acted some times as an opposition, and sometimes as pressure groups and very often remained in jails as political prisoners.

Like parliamentary election, there were some predictions for the presidential election as well, anticipating that the Islamist-led block would swing down to the third, while the rest would be taken over by the combined NDP mixture of old and new parties and the independents.[122]

The first round of presidential election held in May–June 2012 saw a poor turnout in comparison to parliamentary election. The results were split between Mohammad Morsi—FJP Islamist candidate, Mr Shafeeqe—representative of the old guard, Hmadeen Sabahi—an old Nasserite, Amr Mousa—statesman of the Arab politics and Aboul Fotouh—a renegade of the MBH and a liberal face and great advocate of minority and women rights. It was altogether a different story that the FJP nominee for the post of president was the deputy of Supreme Guide, Khairat al-Shatir. However, his nomination was rejected on the ground that he had been imprisoned during Mubarak regime. Now they fell back on the chairman of the FJP, lacklustre Mohammad Morsi.

The first round of election took place on 23–24 May 2012 and put Morsi ahead of all the candidates. However, this election was a jolt for the Islamists who failed to make a straight victory and forced to face the runoff against none other than old guard face—Mr Shafeeqe. In the first round, Morsi achieved 25 percent of the votes followed by Shafeeqe with 23.7 percent. Both were followed by Sabahi—Nasserites with 21 percent, Fotouh with 20 percent. Fotouh had a rainbow of coalition support from liberals, Islamists and the secularists who appealed to the democrats and liberals on the one hand and the radical and conservative Islamists on the other.

---

[122] Shukrullah, 'A People's History of the Egyptian Revolution'.

The entry of Shafeeqe was a throwback against millions who had fought against the departed regime valiantly not earlier than a year. People were expecting the same result in the presidential election too but the popularity graph of the Islamists had declined increasingly and they had lost almost 7 million of votes just after four months of victory in the parliamentary election. The FJP achieved merely 5 million votes, a group that was able to garner 10 million votes a few months before. The 50 percent drop in less than four months is too staggering to explain.

The last round of presidential election was a litmus test for the Islamists whose popularity had already been waning. The final round gave the much-acclaimed Islamists a thin majority, with merely 50 percent of total votes over his rival, former Prime Minister Shafeeqe. The runoff between Islamist and Mubarak's loyalist was an indication that post-revolutionary political domain in the country did not belong exclusively to the Islamists.

The fact that a high-profile associate of the defunct regime made it to the runoff election indicated that there was something wrong with the Egyptian revolution.[123] There were reports that 95 percent of the Coptic voted for Mr Shafeeqe and also some civil servants chose to vote for their old leader because of the instruction from their present bosses, while the Islamic opposition blamed that it was the state machinery behind his 23.7 percent in the first round and they must have played an instrumental role.

Some had already expressed their caution over the victory of Islamists in Egypt and called Egypt in advance the Islamic republic of Egypt under Qarzavi.[124] One of the political commentators described the development in the following words: 'The people who have paid high price will not ripe the fruit because of its Islamic character.'[125] Tariq Khouli, head of the 6

---

[123] Khashan, 'The Arab Spring and Democratisation in the Middle East', *World Affairs* 16, no. 04 (2012): 132–47.

[124] *Al-QudsAl-Arabi*, London, 25 November 2011.

[125] 'Egypt is not Tunis! Or is it', *'Qantara Dialogue*, 11 November 2011, http://en.qantara.de/content/the-reaction-of-egyptian-politicians-to-the-elections-in-tunisia-egypt-is-not-tunisia-or-is

April movement, said: 'we do not accept either man Mohammad Morsi or Ahmad Shafeeqe as our president.'[126] On a similar note, the president of the Association of Egyptian Judges announced on the eve of the runoff elections between Morsi and Ahmad Shafiq, 'If the group members had known that Islamist would win most of the seats in Parliament after election that ended in January [2012] they would not have supervised the voting and he suggested that they might refuse to observe the runoff.'[127] When the Islamists came to power, there was issue in the air about which model the MBH would adopt—Turkey, Pakistan or Iran—but the MBH claimed that it would have its own model in the country.

When the Islamists were boasting of giving an elected Islamic president to the history of the Arabs for the first time, the military was setting the ground for a prolonged battle with democracy. The military was threatened with the democratic upsurge in the country and moreover they were anxious over the ascendance of Islamists at the helm of the affairs. On the other hand, the Islamists vehemently bent upon showing no respect for the voices of opposition—a backbone of the democracy.

To ascertain its hegemony on the political institutions and to not let the new political institutions emerge, the SCAF came out with a series of decrees amidst the presidential election itself, scuttling the democratic aspirations and banging the newly evolving democratic institutions. On 13 June 2012, the SCAF issued a decree authorizing itself to arrest the civilians and try them in the military court, and in a sudden move, dissolved the parliament elected six months before citing the procedural irregularity in certain constituencies. Immediately after one day before the runoff, the SCAF issued another decree arrogating several presidential powers to the SCAF, like power to appoint the army chief. There was a large-scale condemnation from the Islamist block over these sweeping amendments which reflected that the army was not interested in the smooth transfer of the power. The Islamists showed no sign of confrontation with the military at this critical juncture.

---

[126] Khashan, 'The Arab Spring and Democratization in the Middle East', 132–47.
[127] Khashan, 'The Arab Spring and Democratisation in the Middle East', 132–47.

These three major decrees within a week were sufficient to discern the dynamics and nature of the ensuing relationship between the executive authorities on the one hand and the military on the other. How a battle between the power-stuck army and the power-aspirant Islamists would sabotage the democracy would constitute the next section of this chapter.

What Went Wrong?

The arrival of Morsi ushered in a new battle between a power-aspirant and old power-stuck military which was finding it difficult to abandon the behind-the-door political play in the national affairs they had unfailingly enjoyed for decades without any element of responsibility.

The initial differences had not crept merely between military and the Islamic blocks but earlier than that there was already a feeling of animosity growing between the masses and the MBH and its affiliates. The January protestors who had forced the ouster of Mubarak were content with the revolutionary zeal of the youths and could not have accepted the ownership of the revolution by any particular group, particularly the Islamists who had all intention to do it. The millions on the streets were not calling for the shariah rule and, instead, they were crying for justice, freedom and human dignity. Protestors were of the belief that it was their own revolution and not guided by any single organization or ideology—let alone an Islamic figurehead.

One of the protestors claimed, 'I am not aware of any religious slogans in the street rallies'; on the contrary, at least one chant, sung by the crowd in Cairo's Tahrir Square on 28 January 2011, projects a very different meaning—'our revolution is civil; neither violent, nor religious' (al-ThowratnaMadaniyya, la Sayfiyya, la Diniyya)'.[128]

---

[128] Asef Bayat, 'Egypt and the Post-Islamist Middle East', *Open Democracy*, 8 February 2011, http://www.opendemocracy.net/asef-bayat/egypt-and-post-islamist-middle-east

The Islamists failed to unearth the feeling of collective ownership of the revolution and that was the beginning of fissure between the masses' hopes and the political aspirations of the Islamists. The revolutionaries and the protestors felt deceived when different groups of religious persuasions tried to own the achievement exclusively for themselves and were diffident to share it with the millions who had scarified enough to achieve the dream.

The FJP committed a bundle of blunders and had become a baggage of disillusion for the masses who had woven a dream around a new democratically elected Islamic government. The revolutionary impulses of the streets sank down immediately after the victory of the FJP. It made a series of high claims and failed to keep those. The most obscured reason for debacle that ensued was the mistakes on the part of the Islamists of not keeping the promises they had made to the people.

The FJP had announced that it would not contest for the post of the president and had suggested that it would enter the fray for not more than one-third of the total National Assembly seats in the parliamentary election. The self-imposed limit of running a third of the seats was the first to go out of the window and they ran for every single seat. They also fought the election for the post of president and the subsequent volte-face came under heavy attack from their rivals and adversaries. It was God-sent substance for the rival groups to mobilize the masses against them who were now subjects-turned-new citizenry of the country.

The reason that led to change their mind (to contest Presidential election) might have been guided by the fear of being outflanked by other emergent Islamic groups, such as the 'Al-Nour party' and 'Construction and Development party'. Moreover, it was the reflection of their anxiety when a prominent member and a liberal face of the MBH, Abdul Moneim Aboul Fotouh, broke the rank and decided to contest the post of the president as an independent candidate.

What scared and antagonized the people most and exposed the autocratic face of Morsi's rule in Egypt was the announcement of 21 November 2012 by Morsi of a new constitutional declaration according all immunities to himself and his decision from judicial overview. The decree prevented the SCC from dissolving the constituent assembly or the upper house of the national assembly. Through the same decree, he removed the Attorney General of the country, which was in complete contrast to the constitutional convention in the country.[129] There were aggression in the constitutional court; the SCC premise was blocked for more than a month by the cadres of the MBH, which had never happened in the past. This was very damaging to the repute of judiciary and the constitutional authority of the country was taken to a bad beginning.

The MBH had a plan to appoint 600 fresh graduate judges who were the members of the MBH. The execution of the plan would have changed the structure of the judiciary. The MBH had the plan of appointing 3,600 new faces sympathetic to the MBH out of 35,000 in the police academy. Apart from ruling the nation, the MBH wanted to change the structure of the power there.[130] This led to a huge resentment in the corridor of judiciary, and the intelligentsias of the nation felt threatened by this new evolving autocracy in the country. This was an attack on autonomy and the independence of the judiciary, which had ably managed its freedom at the height of autocracy in the previous decades.

Perhaps Morsi's short tenure of one year was ill fated to face all sorts of crises and Morsi was an ill-advised man to fail at every step. After a historic presidential election, an Islamic president was asked by SCC to come for the oath taking ceremony in the absence of the National Assembly that stood dissolved. It triggered a new crisis when the president was himself being asked by SCC to come to his office for being administered the oath of the office. Constitutionally, the ceremony could not have taken place in the assembly when the assembly was nonexistent. SCC was adamant that the president should go there, and, in turn, the presidential office sent its own feeler that SCC should come to the parliament for oath, but it was refused

---

[129] Bakri, *Al-Jaish—wal-Ikhwan*, 411.

[130] Based on conversation with a Cairo University Professor, Mustafa Alavi, in Cairo University during my visit to Egypt in September–October 2013.

by SCC. The president had no option but to take the oath in the SCC building, which was the first major defeat for an elected president. It was a defeat of Morsi's words to his cadres that he would take oath in the parliament alone as he did not approve the 14 June dissolution of the parliament by the SCC.[131] Issues like this led to the deepening of crisis between different state institutions in Egypt.

Perhaps Morsi failed to understand how incessantly his government was losing the legitimacy and popularity among the masses. His policy of exclusion cost him dearly when he opted for an open altercation with the army after breaking the rank with his own allies and later with other state institutions: the media and judiciary. When the country was facing a deep economic crisis, completely stripped of cash for public spending, and anxiety was growing on the part of people, the government was least bothered about it despite constant pressure from the army. The country's defence minister had very vividly remarked, 'In case of further danger or when a country is in the danger of facing a civil war, army cannot be a mute spectator.'[132]

There was a constant campaign and war of words with the army by the MBH cadres and its leadership. Army was constantly subjected to humiliation on TV channels and in print media by the leaders and responsible officials. In February 2012, the first meeting between parliamentarians and SCAF took place where the SCAF had expressed its anguish at the way media was being used against the army in the country, and the defence minister had clarified that they do not want power.[133]

The MBH was trying to *Ikhwanize* the army itself. Morsi always wanted army to come along with the MBH and crush all those protestors airing their grievances against his rule but it had repeatedly explained that it would not involve in the political battle and this non-compliance of the army further created rift between two institutions complicating the crisis.[134] The same defence minister, Tantavi, who was once addressed as

---

[131] Bakri, *Al-Jaish—wal-Ikhwan*, 289.

[132] Bakri, *Al-Jaish—wal-Ikhwan*, 412.

[133] Bakri, *Al-Jaish—wal-Ikhwan*, 106.

[134] Bakri, *Al-Jaish—wal-Ikhwan*, 414.

the Prince of the Faithful, had become a hatred figure amongst the Islamist group.[135]

The MBH was intent upon not only using the army for its own political usage but was also making all sorts of mockery and fun of the most prestigious institution of the country. One prominent member of the MBH wrote poetry in a national magazine in honour of a girl who was to be felicitated in the office of the FJP. The poetry was not merely a mockery of the national army but was very critical of its historical role in Egypt, a stanza of which reads as follows: 'In peace they are brave, in crisis they are frightened; what a value army does has when it is led by a rat.'[136] These lines were directed against the army, which was never tired of boasting itself as defender of a nation from one of the biggest power on the earth: Israel. The military came with an immediate reply: 'MBH are used to venture in the dark and hideouts and their history is full of blood and killing of the innocents. Army always defends the soil of the nation at the time of war and peace.'[137]

The new defence minister of the country, Mr El-Sisi, warned the opponents in the following words: 'We would take action against any one on the basis of army rule and we know how a shrill campaign has been launched to malign the image of the army and create the instability in the country.'[138]

The MBH also adopted a policy of creating a split between different echelons of the army itself and was playing against one another. The MBH leadership was constantly putting pressure on the army to accommodate the members of the MBH in the army, which was conventionally banned. Commenting on the situation in the last days of Morsi, one Christian Science Journal commented that 'when army tells us of a collapsing state, it is a matter of great concern'.[139] The MBH was of the view that army was a real stumbling block in the way of implementation of the Islamic agenda and its ideology. The order of 12 August

---

[135] Shukrullah, 'A People's History of the Egyptian Revolution'.
[136] Bakri, *Al-Jaish—wal-Ikhwan*, 424.
[137] Bakri, *Al-Jaish—wal-Ikhwan*, 425.
[138] Bakri, *Al-Jaish—wal-Ikhwan*, 417.
[139] Bakri, *Al-Jaish—wal-Ikhwan*, 419.

2012 to remove Tantavi along with Sami Anna was enough to antagonize the army top echelons further. It was for the first time in the history of Egypt when an elected government or head of a civilian government had altered the critical decision made by the head of the military establishment.

In one year of Morsi's rule, the country went into further deep crisis, foreign currency reserve was depleting and there was a dearth of fund to cover the public spending. There was an intense pressure from the IMF to do away with the subsidies to put the economy in order, tourism was collapsing because of the prevailing instability in the country and local economy was in a shabby shape because of the fragile political situations. Security and economy are closely related to each other and cannot prosper unless one supports the other. The people's living conditions significantly deteriorated. Crises of gas, bread, electricity, incredible price hikes, rising unemployment instead of job creation and deterioration in public services were all features of pre-30 June. FDI was at halt, trade with the EU had slipped to minus and growing budget deficit had sounded a warning bell for the economic disaster. The army was not ready to sacrifice its long-term economic interest in the form of perks and other several preferential treatments.

At this hour of deep economic crisis, the MBH was more concerned with its ideological foundation and their debate was revolving around the shariah and the female circumcision. In economic policy, since their arrival to power, it had been dominated more by days of Mubarak. The policy of the MBH was to seize rather than reform. They ignored the fact that the issue of bread, freedom and justice could not be overcome by ideological slogans and the Islamic ideology had nothing to tell about the existing grave political and economic conditions.[140] One shopkeeper told a journalist, 'He supported the revolution that toppled Hosni Mubarak.... But political change did not put any extra meat on his table.'[141]

---

[140] Based on conversation with Nabil Zaky during my visit to Egypt in September–October 2013.

[141] Borzou Daragahi, 'Revolutionary Ideals Fade as Egypt Decides', *Financial Times*, 6 June 2012, http://www.ft.com/intl/cms/s/0/810b6f92-aff2-11e1-b737-00144feabdc0.

To quote further Professor Mustafa of Cairo university:

> MBH was completely an inexperienced entity and there was no fresh thinking on their part and were more adhered unnecessarily to the ideology of Banna and Qutb. They failed to read the pulse of the masses. They did not listen to others, did not believe in partnership and felt that they were competent enough. Morsi made no effort to learn, did not listen to his advisors, showed reckless attitude, lacked political flavour, relied on Guide of MBH rather than on his own rational mind, he lacked sensibility of the politics issues.[142]

The sound victory for the FJP in the first democratic election gave a new turn to the persisting crisis between the government and the parliament. Immediately after the parliamentary election, the FJP started displaying its urge for power. They exerted all pressure on the SCAF seeking the removal of the erstwhile SCAF-appointed Prime Minister Kamal Gasnzouri. This was the same MBH that had welcomed him after he had become the prime minister. On 23 January 2012, the first parliamentary meeting took place and again they were demanding for an interim president but Tantavi's statement in parliament clarified that SCAF would hand over power to the president-elect on 30 June.[143] How a revolution can be transformed into a system, what is the mechanism and what sorts of tussles one faces in this process of transformation can be witnessed in case of Egypt.

The newly elected Islamic government was always marred with one crisis or another and it was difficult for it to measure its quantum or gravity. Immediately after the parliamentary election, the 100-member constituent assembly was formed and the committee was naturally dominated by the Islamists given their huge victory in the previous election. The preponderance of the Islamic groups created a fear among the civil society, and they demanded re-election of the body to make it more inclusive. There were complaints that it did not represent

---

html#axzz2RqoT4NDF (Accessed on 29 April 2012).

[142] Based on conversation with him during my visit to Egypt in September–October 2013.

[143] Bakri, *Al-Jaish—wal-Ikhwan*, 103.

the Coptic community and others. This created another crisis for the ruling party, which was adamant that it was an elected body, while the opposition was of the views that the constitution could not be based on the majority–minority verdict and was not ready to accept the majority–minority formula. They wanted a consensual constitution expressing the will of all and one which should not be a spokesperson or mouthpiece of a single ideology.

Morsi's government was not receptive to the idea of re-election and out of anger he once told, 'What does it mean for 30 million voters who voted for Parliament and do you want us to leave the country.'[144]

FJP also wanted to add a transitional clause in the constitution stripping the SCC of its power to dissolve the assembly that was enough to decipher the future political plank of the Islamic government. This stance of the Islamic group was enough to create an environment of animosity among the people, particularly when they had heard Morsi claiming not long ago that,

> [P]eople are the source of authority and its will is above all. It is they who throne and dethrone and you are the men of authority and it is for you to grant and refuse the permission to rule. I will resort to the people if someone tries to usurp the authority.[145]

According to an Ahram poll conducted among different sections of the civil society, 82.3 percent wanted another constituent assembly.[146] Others were demanding a fresh constitutional declaration under clause 60 of the SCAF to expand the assembly and to make it more inclusive. There was also a deep difference about the proportion of insiders and outsiders in the assembly. The SCAF chief was a vehement advocate of the constitution-first and had told his confidant that SCAF would love to see an inclusive constitution, for present and future and for all Egyptians.[147]

---

[144] Bakri, *Al-Jaish—wal-Ikhwan*, 130.
[145] Bakri, *Al-Jaish—wal-Ikhwan*, 292.
[146] http://en.wikipedia.org/wiki/Constituent_Assembly_of_Egypt
[147] Bakri, *Al-Jaish—wal-Ikhwan*, 145.

Moreover, the MBH was trying to delay the process for constitution in the presence of SCAF at the helm of the affairs while the SCAF again and again stated that there would be no election in the absence of the constitution.[148] Amidst an intense phase of debate and discussion about the validity and legitimacy of the constituent assembly, the Administrative Judiciary Court found the method of election of the assembly illegal in the light of clause 60 of constitutional declaration. An agreement to form a more balanced assembly was reached on 7 June 2012. Accordingly, thirty-nine seats would be filled by members of parliament, six by judges, nine by law experts, thirteen seats by unions and twenty-one by public figures. Five seats would be filled by the Al-Azhar University and four by the Coptic Orthodox Church and one each by a member of the armed forces, the police and the justice ministry.

There was no dearth of issues in the post-revolutionary Egypt to pollute the political environment and to weaken the yet-to-be-born democracy in the new Egypt. The biggest challenge for the Islamic government was to specify the identity of the newly born democratic nation. There were intense demands from other radical Islamic groups like Salafists to render an Islamic orientation to the constitution and demanded shariah to be the primary source of legislation, while others adhered to make shariah merely a principal source of legislation.[149]

Morsi's government did not only commit blunders but they also refused to acknowledge that the nation was on the brink of collapse. The protests and the demonstrations never stopped since the January revolution. The people did not take to the streets because of media incitement or deals with rediscovered godfathers of former regimes, but because they were already on the streets with what Morsi's presidency described as its 'challenges'. In this span of one year, there were more than 5,000 demonstrations and 7,700 social protests around different parts of Egypt.[150]

---

[148] Bakri, *Al-Jaish—wal-Ikhwan*, 154.

[149] Bakri, *Al-Jaish—wal-Ikhwan*, 138.

[150] Wael Gamal, 'Who Really Decides in Revolutionary Egypt', *Ahram Online*, 11 July 2013, http://english.ahram.org.eg/NewsContent/4/0/76234/Opinion/

The mood of denial was the beginning of hijacking of the political space and sign of political assertiveness and dominance by the MBH. The MBH showed all kinds of hast and urgency to capture the power which was well demonstrated during the assembly election when they raised the slogan of 'election-first' and 'constitution later'. No revolutionary in recent history has made so many foes like the Islamist in MBH did in short span of one year after coming to power. They not only antagonised the immediate or real enemies, but they also annoyed those passionate democrats who could have been swayed merely by allaying their fears and apprehensions about their ideological undercurrent. They were fond of creating enemy and later facing failures to deal with them.[151]

The *Ikhwanization* of a highly intricate administrative apparatus has been cited alternatively as an evidence of greed of power, a redistribution of spoils. The MBH failed to dismantle the autocratic structure of the state. They also used the octopus like bureaucracy for their own benefit. They subdued the judiciary and replaced Mubarak's men with their own men and made all attempt to disenfranchise the Coptic minority and crushed those who were opposed to the rule by Islam and were atheists.[152] To quote one professor here, 'MBH promoted its own people and gave out of way promotion and sabotage was the part of MBH politics and President Morsi had created own personal cadres for his safety.'[153]

The MBH government was more guided by their guidance bureau than immediate demands of the time with the chants of 'Command Oh Badie, you command and we obey'.[154] 'The MBH was mutating itself into the very caricature of itself as painted by its bitterest enemies.' The MBH did not understand that people had now transformed themselves from subjects to self-entitled,

---

Who-really-decides-in-revolutionary-Egypt.aspx

[151] Shukrullah, 'A People's History of Egyptian Revolution'.

[152] Based on conversation with a Cairo University Professor during my visit to Egypt in September–October 2013.

[153] Based on my interview with Professor Mckawi in Cairo.

[154] Hani Shukrullah, 'The Decline and Fall of Muslim Brotherhood', *Ahram Online*, 6 December 2012, http://english.ahram.org.eg/News/59933.aspx

self-empowering, self-emancipating citizens of highly diverse and most profoundly pluralistic nations.

The posts of dozens of deputy ministers, governors of twenty-two governorates, advisors and other heads of different political units, local governments and departments at district and village levels had been grabbed by them. The people, who had voted for them, had a better chance of receiving the favour in the form of tender, low-level jobs and contracts in the government departments.

The MBH had started the politics of dividing the society in the name of religion. In the very first referendum on the constitutional amendment, they had sought votes in the name of Islam and it was the beginning of the ideological and political polarization of the country.[155] They failed to learn from Mubarak's template, ignored popular outrage and were ruling with a single dictum 'what God has ordained' not by transforming previous state into one governed by righteousness.[156]

The president trampled the very constitution that he swore to uphold by immunizing his decision against judiciary review. This did not bode well in terms of his glorious democratic promises he had made to the people. The Supreme Juridical Council—the country's highest body of Judges—called the decree an unprecedented assault on the people.[157] Moderate Islamists and the former presidential candidate Fotouh also condemned the decree. People chanted for an end to the rule not of Morsi but of the supreme guide of the MBH, Mr Badie.[158]

Sometimes Islamist transcended the boundary of disrespect to the rule of law more grievously than the previous regime. Morsi refused to accept the dissolution of the parliament, while the era of Mubarak had suffered the dissolution of the parliaments twice in 1984 and in 1987 and even he was obliged to accept it.[159] It seemed that the MBH would take where Mubarak had left.

---

[155] Amin, *Maza Hadasa Lil-Saurah-al-Misriyah*, 299.

[156] Shukrullah, 'A People's History of the Egyptian Revolution'.

[157] Yasmine El Rashidi, 'Egypt: Whose Constitution'? *New York Review of Books* (January 2013), http://www.nybooks.com/blogs/nyrblog/2013/jan/03/egypt-whose-constitution/

[158] Rashidi, 'Egypt: Whose Constitution'?

[159] Shukrullah, 'A People's History of the Egyptian Revolution'.

It was MBH's new tactic of hide-and-seek with the SCAF, exerting all sort of pressure, exercising political manoeuvring, entering into constant fight with the army and threatening instability in the country. The MBH showed no sign of political vision, no political blueprint and showed no respect for the institutions of the country.

Sometime the MBH and its affiliate's cadres were accused of hobnobbing with the SCAF to protect its own interest at the time of SCAF rule. The Islamic groups were found absent whenever there were protests or demonstrations against them during one and a half year of its rule. On 27 May, 'Day of rage', when there was sit-in at Tahrir Square demanding the ouster of Shafeeqe, the MBH was found to be absent and the slogan reads, 'Here is the Tahrir and where is the MBH'.[160]

The Islamic government failed to take any measure commanding or winning the trust of the masses or demonstrating that the Islamic government would be different from its predecessors. Not a single piece of authoritarian legislation was repealed, no authoritarian structure was touched by legislative reforms and no move was in evidence to fight the inequality. The government was not about promotion of democracy, social justice or freedom and they had no comprehensive plan about economic and political reforms but they focused on means to acquire more and more power. Their major thrust was implementation of Islamic ideology and making ideological rhetoric, which was far away from the reality.

No attempts were made to reform the police—a major demand of the people, no effort to bring retribution to the killers and the torturers—another demand of the people. MBH members had a political bias towards other political entities and traditional political class and their treatments towards them was very much discriminatory. Morsi was seen hobnobbing with Mubarak's era oligarchs. He would take a fugitive like Rashid in business delegation to Turkey and Qatar who was absconding from UAE fearing the arrest in Egypt during Mubarak's era. When he visited China, he went along with a 60-member delegation and all were members of Mubarak's cliché.

---

[160] Shukrullah, 'A People's History of the Egyptian Revolution'.

Immediately after coming to power, the FJP leadership started ignoring its political ally, Al-Nour party, which had played an instrumental role in facilitating the victory of the FJP. It was the combined victory of both that had frightened the masses. With their combined victory, people had an apprehension that the Islamist would impose a new religious state in Egypt. The entry of the Salafists in the Egyptian Parliament had not been welcomed by the Western media, and in one of its editorial, *The New York Times* wrote that it was an anarchical beginning in the politics of Egypt.[161]

A new battle had begun between the two in new Islamic political space and both were trying to capture the political space for oneself alone. The entry of the Salafists had created a wedge between the ideologies of two. This rift was well noticed when one of the Salafists, while taking oath in the parliament, supplemented to his oath that he would not abide by any law which was in violation of the shariah.[162] They had already begun a scathing attack on the Ulema of Al-Azhar in defence of their ideology. It was the poor administration of Morsi's government and, moreover, their marginalization and subordination by the FJP-led government which further led to their isolation.

Al-Nour always endorsed the legitimacy of the Morsi government but was against discarding the voices of opposition as un-Islamic voices. They always opposed the policy of branding the political battle as a clash between infidel and the Muslims.[163] Gradually, the difference between the FJP and the Salafists deepened when the Salafists accepted the demand for an early election and formation of a technocrat government, while Morsi and his government adhered to the principle of full four-year term. The growing danger of political chaos in the country and the inflexible political instance of the MBH aggravated the situation within the Islamic camp leading to open split between the Salafists and the MBH.

---

[161] *Ashorooq Daily*, Cairo, 25 January 2012.
[162] *Ashorooq Daily*.
[163] Ahmad Zaghlool, 'Hizbun-Nourwa Tadaayat 3 Ulyo', *Al-Demoqaratiyah*, no. 52 (2013): 132–36.

The contestations among the political blocks or state agencies were not merely confined to the internal ideological, economic or political domain but there were international issues that had instigated the masses against the Islamists. The new foreign policy of the government caused a major point of departure between the army and the new government. The tunnel across Gaza and Sinai was a long contentious issue for the army, which wanted its demolition because of the primacy of security. However, the president, who was still nostalgic about his ummah dream, was against it. The tunnels were creating security problems in Sinai and had become a fertile ground for militant activities.[164]

There were reports that Morsi during his visit to Sudan in April 2013 had promised to return a triangular region (natural reservoir Halayeb and Shalteen) to Sudan. The official website of the MBH showed it as a part of the Sudanese territory and that was enough for the military to dig the government and to take the relations to the lowest ebb between two power centers.[165] One of the members of the MBH is said to have told that'[t]his donation would not affect the Egypt because it was a move to create a larger and unbroken ummah. Muslims should not fight for a tract of land here and there and national boundary is the creation of the colonial power'.[166]

This issue raised the question of territorial integration and the national sovereignty and also challenged the power of the army. The army immediately hit back and told that the region was not for the romance between Morsi and Sudan. Similarly, the growing intimacy of Egypt with Iran and Turkey was not taken in good sprit within the military camp. Army was not comfortable with Iran because Iran was an axis of evil near the United States and army had never learnt to antagonize the United States. The policy of over-involvement of Islamic government in Syria had no convergence with the conventional foreign policy of Egypt. It had always maintained that there should be no ethnic, sectarian

---

[164] Bakri, *Al-Jaish—wal-Ikhwan*, 417.

[165] Bakri, *Al-Jaish—wal-Ikhwan*, 428.

[166] Bakri, *Al-Jaish—wal-Ikhwan*, 430.

or racial division of the region while Morsi had started sending open signals to the Sunnis in Syria that the Egyptian Islamic government was with them.[167]

A Power-stuck Army

The Egyptian revolution was a product of the struggle of several sociopolitical determinants which challenged Mubarak's status quo. Nevertheless, the army believed that the principal elements of the status quo be maintained. This hard-core objective of the army to adhere to status quo during the SCAF period was the main source of mistrust and suspicion between the political groups and the army in the evolving political architecture of the country.

The army that enjoyed all the economic leverage for decades could not have imagined being subservient to a civilian government. It was trying to act above the state and had no interest in easing the control over the state after the parliamentary and the presidential elections of 2012. The army was in no mood to see any shift in the balance of power after the ascendance of a civilian government. They were not ready to sacrifice the privilege for the sake of the civilian government. The military wanted the supremacy of its institutions over all elected bodies, and it was well demonstrated when Defence Minister El-Sisi himself came on the state TV dissolving the parliament, ousting the president and suspending the constitution.

The arrival of a civilian government at the helm of the affairs was a big jolt for the army, which had so far acted as a supreme state institution compared to all other institutions, including elected bodies as well as the executive and judiciary. The army never showed any inclination of heeding the advice of the government. There was a constant threat emanating from the barrack. The army tried to preserve as much as possible

---

[167] Based on conversation with Mohammad Anis Salem during my visit to Egypt in September–October 2013.

the old autocratic system and its perks and privileges. They were not ready to sacrifice the constitutional prerogative that legitimized army's interventions in the politics. They wanted an intact economic empire, legal immunity from prosecution and constitutional provision to protect itself from the reach of civilian laws. They were more interested in a veto power on high policies like issue of national security and relations with Israel. No doubt, there was a gap between historic religious discourse and the reality of politics, but the problems further aggravated in the absence of cooperation from institutions like the army and the police.[168]

Civilian control of the armed force, military and police oversight by a civilian government, and call for budget transparency of the army were quite novel experiences for them, which they refused to accept. SCAF took no time in dissolving the parliament despite the fact that 30 million voted for assembly and that dissolution had vested all legislative powers with the SCAF just a day before when the new president was to join office in July 2012. The army wanted a weak parliament with weak power, subservient to the army.

Military intelligence and military police were granted powers to arrest the civilians on charges as minor as traffic disruption and insulting the army (the president and the interior minister were assumed to be civilians).[169] While the national economy was in a mess, the government could not resort to move against the military's civilian assets by revising the provision of preferential treatment to them. The army had always enjoyed preferential custom and exchange rate, tax exemption, land ownership and confiscation rights. No doubt, SCAF took some democratic decision because of the mass pressure but they could not have taken or adhered to it for a long time.

---

[168] Hiba Rauf Izzat, 'Ma-Baad-al-Islamiyah: Nazratun-Naqdiyah', *Al-Demoqeratiya*, no. 52 (October 2013): 112–15.

[169] Omar Ashour, 'Ballets versus Bullet: The Crisis of Civil-Military Relations in Egypt', *Report* (Al-Jazeera Centre for Studies, 2013), http://www.brookings.edu/research/articles/2013/09/03-civil-military-relations-egypt-ashour (Accessed on 20 October 2013).

If the Islamic parties failed to sense the pulse of the street and were devoid of any pragmatism, the army too was not ready to read the writing on the walls. A new crack appeared between the government and the army over the issue of the formation of the National Defence Council (NDC). It was decided that the NDC would have a majority of military commanders and the military would have an edge over the civilians on the issue of security and foreign policy. There was a prolonged scuffle inside the NDC over the number of representatives from both sides, and one day a military representative yelled in the constituent assembly over El-Beltagy, an FJP leader and said, 'If you put one of yours, I will put one of mine.'[170] Moreover, former defence minister Tantavi had told one of his confidants that he would not go down in history as one who handed over Egypt to the MBH.[171]

Downfall of Morsi

At last, Morsi would drink from the same cup two and a half year later which Mubarak had drunk from. There had been a military coup at every major step in the two years of Egyptian revolutionary history—against Tantavi, against SCAF and, at last, against the MBH itself.[172] It was a revolutionary coercion than simply a coup. The army intervention was the endgame of the monumental uprising when 17 million people from all socio-political streams gathered to depose an Islamic government.[173] Millions of people once again rose into rebellion against the government of Morsi and it was for the first time that history brought down an Islamic government through popular uprising. It was a death knell of the so-called Islamic revivalism that was

---

[170] Ashour, 'Ballets versus Bullet'.
[171] Shukrullah, 'A People's History of the Egyptian Revolution'.
[172] Based on personal conversation with Nabil Zaky in Cairo.
[173] Asef Bayat, 'Midwife for a Pregnant Egypt Woman', *Ahram Online*, http://english.ahram.org.eg/NewsContentP/4/76162/Opinion/Midwife-for-a-pregnant-Egypt.aspx (Accessed on 11 November 2013).

sounded. The uproar against the Islamic government was not confined to only the urban zone, but it was well spread far and wide to the rural areas as well demolishing the proposition that revolution in general was an urban phenomenon.

No event could have been more astounding than the deposing of the first democratically elected president in the modern history of Egypt. The removal of Morsi was also a watershed in the three-year history of the Arab Spring that swept across the Arab world. It was perhaps another revolution in the post-revolution Egypt when on 3 July 2013, Egyptian Defence Minister and Army Commander Abdel Fattah El-Sisi, in a national televised address, declared the removal of President Morsi, suspended the constitution, dissolved the parliament, appointed Adley Mansour as an interim president and placed a civilian government in place. Three Islamic channels were shut down and arrest warrants were issued against at least 300 MBH cadres with a call to dissolve the MBH. The military takeover was welcomed by Saudi Arabia, UAE and Syria while Turkey criticized the move of the army. Saudi King praised the army for managing 'to save Egypt at this critical point from a dark tunnel'.[174]

It all began when a group called 'Tamarrod' (rebellion, mutiny) spearheaded a shrill campaign against the rule of Morsi in the month of June 2013. Tamarrod was a new group that consisted of the veterans of a previous movement 'Egyptians Movement for Change' of 2004, which had acquired a new name in April 2013. Members of Tamarrod were once members of the Kifayah movement, dominated by the secularists, socialists, Nasserites, liberals, moderate Islamists and the communists. The group started a petition campaign nationwide in June and announced to have obtained 22 million signatures for the removal of Morsi. Earlier they had set the target of 15 million just to exceed the numbers who had voted for Morsi (13.23 million). One of the Tamarrod members quoted by *Observer* on 6 July said that:

---

[174] Talmiz Ahmad, *The Islamist challenge in West Asia: Doctrinal and Political Competition after the Arab Spring* (New Delhi: IDSA/Pentagon Press, 2013), 120.

Sisi and the army took their cue from the people. They had many previous chances to do what they did but they did not take them. But once the millions of people came on the streets exhorting the army to intervene, they took their order from us.[175]

In response to huge mass uprising and anger on the street against the Morsi government, the pro-Islamist groups formed a countergroup, 'National Alliance in Support of Legitimacy', and began a sit-in on the podium of a mosque in 'Rabaa al-Adaviya and Nahda'. They began their protest on 28 June 2013 and this was the beginning of the ensuing clash between the military and the government. In this fraught environment, head of the Army General Command issued a 48-hour ultimatum, calling on the government to bow to the will of the people.[176]

Security forces moved in to break the six-week sit-in in Rabaa al-Adawiya and Nahda Square across the capital by pro-Morsi cadres. In this clash, more than hundreds were killed, but growing resentment against the MBH fuelled the support for military crackdown against the Islamists. A nation which rose in rebellion against the army was chanting for the army at Tahrir Square after the removal of President Morsi. One of the students said in Cairo, 'I am with the army and the Police against the MBH'.[177]

There were some who had disassociated themselves from what the army had done against the Islamists after deposing Morsi from the power. According to Mr Majeed, a close and insider to the MBH,

MBH tried to normalize the situation and called several times the opposition parties to have a dialogue and diffuse the tension. But they were vehemently bent upon removing the government and create a situation where the MBH would be forced to be ousted. The kind of treatment meted out to the Islamists at the behest of the army was even worse than what one had seen in China during the Tiananmen Square.[178]

---

[175] Roberts, 'The Revolution That Wasn't'.
[176] Ahmad, *The Islamist challenge in West Asia*, 119–20.
[177] Ian Balck and Patrick Kingsley, 'Egypt: Resentment towards Brotherhood Fuels Crackdown', *Guardian*, 16 August 2013.
[178] Based on conversation with him during my visit to Egypt in September–October 2013.

Commenting on the post-Morsi scenario in the country, Mr Hazem Kandil, an Egyptian political sociologist at Cambridge says, 'Some support the army while being suspicious of where things are heading. Some are even calling Sisi to take power.'[179]

According to a political theorist of Egypt, 'One year of MBH rule has proved their lack of vision for the state embodied in an integrated project to achieve justice, dignity, humanity and moreover a balance between political institutions and the sovereignty.'[180] While another member of the MBH owes this upheaval to the constitutional declaration of 22 November by Morsi, which heralded the beginning of a long period of political upheaval that climaxed with anti-Morsi nation-wide demonstration. The call for realism or pragmatism should have been heeded by Morsi and his clique.[181]

Abdel Fattah El-Sisi also announced a fresh road map stipulating a future political plan in which he promised to draft a constitution, hold parliamentary election and, finally, the nation would go for electing the new president. While making this announcement, Sisi was flanked by representatives of Egyptian Church, Al-Azhar, Al-Nour party and the much-acclaimed civilian leader, El-Baradie.

What was more ironical was the embrace of the Salafists, a radical group, by the army and the growing distance between the MBH and the Salafists. The decision of Salafists to go along with the military and National Salvation Front was perhaps taken not to let the Islamic space be captured by some other infringe groups.[182]

It was a situation back to square one where the dream of people for a new democratic Egypt had been shattered. Military intervention was fraught with danger and was likely to reverberate throughout the region. The transition would be quite

---

[179] Balck and Kingsley, 'Egypt: Resentment towards Brotherhood Fuels Crackdown'.

[180] Izzat, 'Ma-Baad-al-Islamiyah', 112–15.

[181] Dina Ezzat, 'What Chance Reconciliation', *Ahram Weekly*, 9 October 2013, http://weekly.ahram.org.eg/News/4385/17/What-chance-reconciliation-.aspx

[182] Kama Habib, 'Al-Islamiyyunwal-Anf Baad 30 Unuu', *Al-Demoqeratiya*, no. 52 (October 2013): 116–19.

complicated from autocracy to democracy. The mass uprising and constant protests on the streets of different cities had lost all meaning and relevance and people were again forced to be ruled by the same military that had ruled them for almost six decades in the past. This all came just two and half years after millions had swamped the Tahrir Square (iconic symbol of protest and dignity across the Arab world) to oust the army-back rule of Mubarak for thirty years.

The removal of Morsi again brought the military at the centre-stage of the political affairs. Military owed it to the missteps, ill-governance and overambitious policies of the Islamic-oriented government after Morsi had come to office.

The army blamed the Islamist for this mishap and claimed that it was a move to correct the 25 January revolution, to restore the fundamental logic of 11 February 2011 and achieve the real objective of the mass revolution. The cheerleader of 3 July presented what transacted as the renewal of January and February. Morsi's downfall was much the result of resistance by the key state institutions—the military, security and the judiciary from which he had lost support gradually.[183] Army Commander himself told in an interview with the Egyptian daily *Al-Masry Al-Youm* that he had advised Mr Morsi to be more inclusive and had asked him to resolve the outstanding issues with the opposition group—the church, Al-Azhar, media and the judiciary.[184]

It was the distrust, non-cooperation, stubbornness, blame game, inter-party conflict, political ambition, ideology-driven polities that had reigned in the free political domain of the country in the last two years. Gradually, relations were getting strained among different state institutions during Morsi's rule. No faction or group was prepared for reconciliation and the army had warned more than once that in face of looming danger over the national security and anarchical situation in the country, it could not afford to be a mute spectator. Moreover, it was the growing hostility between the military and ruling party

---

[183] Based on conversation with Dr Makkaviin Manufiya University during my visit to Egypt in September–October 2013.
[184] *Almisr-al-Yum*, Cairo, 11 October 2013.

that led to the political disaster. The army was well cognisance of the fact that the unfolding situation was an alarming one for the stability of the country and it might lead to a civil war.

Domestic and Regional Implications

The removal of Morsi raised great uncertainties not only about Egyptian political future, but one group of the observers adhered to the view that it would also lead to the vicious cycle of violence in the country similar to what one had been witnessed during the era of Nasser almost half a century ago. Brotherhood was of the view that it was an elected and legitimate government removed at the behest of Gulf Cooperation Council (GCC) nations and the national army. It could also repeat the Algerian experience of 1990 that culminated in the establishment of an autocratic rule.[185] The violence in Egypt and constant confrontations suggested that it could be in for a prolonged period of confrontation between the MBH activists and security forces.

The 'National Alliance to Support of Legitimacy' called for reinstating Morsi's regime as he is the embodiment of new electoral democracy in Egypt. Pro-Islamist groups are vehemently demanded the restoration of the constitution and the parliament because people had voted for it and it enjoys the legitimacy. Different cities and the peripheries of Egypt have witnessed constant protests and demonstrations condemning the army rule in the country. They also mounted pressure for international intervention.

There is another group of analysts that expect the MBH to handle the situation with care if it desires to remain in the political arena of the country and also urged to go for deep-introspection and be prepared in a better way to participate in the governance. This event witnessed an ideological and generational battle inside the MBH where one could eschew violence while other radicals might call to resort to the politics

---

[185] Ahmad, *The Islamist challenge in West Asia*, 123.

of violence. One also sees the present development as an opportunity for the MBH to earn the sympathy of the masses after they have been removed which would boost them further for more aggressive posturing. One does not know how long army rule will last and how the other Islamist partners of the army like Al-Nour would behave in near future or how the regional power is going to deal with the army or if they would come under pressure to eliminate the MBH in Egypt.

The recent scenario might be a catalyst for the emergence of a third force as well which would neither be committed to Islamic project of the MBH nor adhere to the autocratic policy of the old guard, but would work for the political pluralism.[186] The fight of the third force for pluralism would preferably force both the secularist and the Islamist to join a new political fray in the country. The third force would begin a battle for new political ideas that were absent in the country: the battle for cultural and political pluralism.

The implication of the ouster of a democratically elected government would not be felt at domestic front alone. As mentioned earlier, Saudi and the UAE supported the ouster of the MBH with a long-term strategic impact in the region. Abdul Bari Atwan, former editor of Al Quds Al-Arabi, pointed out that GCC nations had every reason to feel insecure in the face of the MBH because it is now a global organization and has considerable influence among the youths of the GCC whom it had mentored.[187]

New Egypt would not be that warm towards Iran and to the Sunnis of Syria after what it witnessed in the short span of one year of Morsi's rule in the country. One observer has put in the following words: 'Egypt–Iran ties during Morsi's role blunted the hostility with which Mubarak's Egypt had viewed Iran'.[188]

Morsi's removal dealt a blow to the politics of Turkey and its desire to be imitated as a role model in the new Arab world and be a significant player after Iran in the new Arab order.

---

[186] Muasher, *The Second Arab Awakening and the Battle for Pluralism*, 37.
[187] Ahmad, *The Islamist Challenge in West Asia*, 108.
[188] Ahmad, *The Islamist Challenge in West Asia*, 112.

Now the future will tell what lies ahead for the Islamists in Egypt and in the region as a whole. The removal of Morsi has offered a staple diet for an intellectual discourse and tangible substance for blame game to different ideological groups. The study of post-Islamism in Egypt, of course, requires a deep introspection that does not fall under the purview of the present study. Moreover, the fluidity and uncertainty of the day-to-day developments puts its own limitation and constraints on advocating or preaching the eventuality of the matter. But, of course, while concluding the book, I will try to offer a snapshot of the likely scenarios in the backdrop of emerging political developments in the country.

Tunisia

It was the Jasmine Revolution of Tunisia that brought not only a political change but also a major shift in the Islamic ideology of Ennahdha movement—the mainstay of political Islam in the country. In the past, President Ben-Ali's regime of Tunisia had oppressed all sorts of opposition voices, and political opposition was almost non-existent. Like Mubarak of Egypt, he too had put behind bars all those who seemed to be a threat to his rule. Rachid Ghannouchi, head of the Ennahdha—the victorious political party of Tunisia—was his victim who had suffered a long exile.

Rachid Ghannouchi's party, formerly known as Islamic Tendency Movement (MTI), had a powerful voice in Tunisian politics for a long time, though it was an illegal party under the rule of Ben-Ali. In the election of 1981, President Bourguiba allowed no space for MTI to act as a legal political party. Members of MTI were put behind bars on one pretext or another. Under Ben-Ali, MTI tried to appease the government by changing its name to Ennahdha in 1989 in order to become a legal entity in accordance with the rules that prohibited any religious denomination to the party.

Their bid was rejected again as President Ben-Ali realized that Ennahdha had been gaining ascendant support throughout

Tunisia. Under immense pressure from the government and escalating tensions, Ghannouchi left Tunisia in 1990 to lead the movement from abroad, first from Algiers, and later from the UK. Ensuing period saw an ideological and political contestation between Islamic groups and the ruling party, Rally for Constitutional Democracy (RCD).

After the Jasmine Revolution, the transition in Tunisia was relatively peaceful and it was possible because of open military support to the protestors. Tunisian military leader, General Rachid Anmmar, proclaimed, 'The army will protect the revolution and our revolution is a young revolution.'[189]

Amidst the unfolding crisis, Ben Ali dissolved the parliament but after his fleeing the country, Tunisian Constitutional Court—the highest legal authority on the constitution—ruled that the speaker of the house, Fouad Mebazaa, would be the interim president of the country. President Fouad Mebazaa asked Mohammad Ghannouchi, one who had already served as prime minister for the last twelve years, to form a coalition government. But people were not ready to accept any symbol of the past regime.

The Jasmine Revolution changed the fate of Ennahdha movement and they emerged as an irresistible and impeccable force in the new political sphere. In the post Jasmine Revolution election of 23 October 2011, Tunisian first elections in twenty-three years, Ennahdha secured 89 seats out of the 217-member constituent assembly and formed coalition with both liberal and the secularists.[190] Forty-nine women were elected to the new parliament and forty-three of them came from the rank of Ennahdha.[191] It was its popularity and part of household imagination that brought Ennahdha to the forefront of political success in the country. Unlike the MBH in Egypt, Ennahdha quickly demonstrated its willingness to work with the secular party. Ghannouchi's writings as well as party's programme

---

[189] Bishara, *The Invisible Arab*, 117.
[190] *Asharq Alawasat*, London, 21 December 2011, http://www.aawsat.com//leader.asp?section=3&article=655348&issueno=12076#.UYdPFaJyDcM
[191] Muasher, *The Second Arab Awakening and the Battle for Pluralism*, 58.

published in September 2001 indicated a greater commitment to political pluralism than the MBH.[192]

While Ennahdha was aware of the questions surrounding their ability to govern Tunisia, Rachid Ghannouchi has worked tirelessly promoting a positive image of the party. In trying to reassure the people who had no confidence in the democratic credential of Ennahdha, Ghannouchi said,

> [W]e are serious about our projects in establishing democracy and assuring development…the people who do not trust us, it's normal, because for 22 years they have been subject to propaganda from Ben-Ali which has discredited us, and made people fearful of us.[193]

Since Ennahdha won the majority of the votes and had formed the coalition with liberals and secularists, a new scope of liberal interpretation of Islam emerged. An ideological division within Islam such as Salafist and moderate voices also gave space to intra-Islamic debate within the country on the line of Egypt.

To allay the fear of the opposition, Rachid Ghannouchiin an interview with an Arabic Daily *Asharq Al-Awsat* said,

> His party had chosen the politics instead of an ideology and his party never wanted to impose the ideology of one party. If we had opted for an ideological politics, we would have sought an alliance with some independent blocks. The role of state is not to impose a particular model for the masses but state is meant to offer security, justice and services. Man should be left free to choose his own life as Quran says there is no compulsion in religion.[194]

---

[192] Muasher, *The Second Arab Awakening and the Battle for Pluralism*, 96.

[193] M. Lynch, 'Rashid Ghannushi: The FP interview, *Foreign Policy Magazine*, 5 December 2011, http://lynch.foreignpolicy.com/posts/2011/12/05/ghannouchis_advice

[194] *Asharq Alawasat*, London, 21 March 2013, http://www.aawsat.com/details.asp?section=4&article=721651&issueno=12532#.UU_7gxdyDcM (Accessed on 25 March 2013).

Ennahdha promised that they would not harm tourism through a ban on alcohol or force women to wear the veil. Ennahdha assured to respect personal rights and continue to let the wearing of the veil be determined by the woman. Its political statement reiterated that they would respect women's rights and will remain a progressive moderate party, with a socio-economic model that would appear Scandinavian.

However, since the elections, Ghannouchi continued to articulate a moderate stance, suggesting that they inherit a similar model of Turkey. The Party also stated that their priorities were achieving stability, conditions for a dignified life and the building of democratic institutions. In addition to this, Ghannouchi also stated that he did not want his party to be referred to as Islamist because it usually suggests theocracy in Western eyes. Instead, he would prefer his party be an Islamic party.

To enforce his points further, he added,

> We should fight those monsters who make the enemy of Islam believe that Islam is an autocratic system and usurp the right of others. While the truth is that it is the source of all legitimacy and sovereignty for the people and even sovereignty of God comes through the people alone.[195]

To allay the fears of international community about the rising power of Islamists in Tunisia, he rejected any attempt to convert the Tunisian revolution into the Iranian model.[196]

In another interview with a Jordanian scholar, he stated that he had full faith in the rotation of power and, according to him, if Communist party were to win the election in Tunisia, his party would abide by the result. He also challenged one way of reading of Quran, 'there is no compulsion in religion', and

---

[195] Taufeeq al-Madeeni, 'Rabeeus-Saurat-al-Demoqaratiyyahal-Arabiyah', *Al-Mustaqbal Al-Arabi*, no. 386 (March 2011).

[196] Marwan Bukhari and Ahmad Fuad Rahmat, 'Case for Post-Islamic Revolution', *Harakah Daily*, 6 January 2012, http://en.harakahdaily.net/index.php/articles/depth/4143-a-post-islamic-revolution.html#.UYcy5aJyDcM (Accessed on January 2012).

stated that if Muslims were to convert out of the religion, he or she would be judged by the God not by the man.[197]

He argued that there is complete synthesis between Islam and democracy and claimed that failure of Islamic system in Sudan and other places was due to the same autocracy that oligarchy Islamists had fought against and the autocrats were just after making money and promoting nepotism.[198]

In Tunisia, Islamists political discourse was opposed to imposition of majority views unlike Egypt and it was stated very vividly by Rachid, 'Tunisian constitution should be consensus-based and should not be left to the majority'.[199]

In order to rescue the tolerant, liberal and inclusive image of Islam, Rachid told Mr Bishara in an interview that Al-Qaeda was 'finished', thanks to the revolution in Tunisia.[200] He termed Al-Qaeda leader, Zawahiri, a catastrophe for Islam and said, 'thank God' Al-Qaeda has no influence in Tunisia, and Tunisian Salafists were not the part of Al-Qaeda and they are of Tunisian origin.[201]

Rachid constantly espoused the egalitarian views of Islam with an emphasis on social and economic justice. In another interview he said, 'The Ennahda movement accepts the principle of political diversity, alteration in power and the rule of majority under a democratic constitution. He interpreted the rule of God as ordained in the will of the people.'[202]

To enforce his democratic credential, he summarized his vision of democracy in the following words:

Democracy is when the people rule themselves by themselves through an authority that represents them, they should be able to constantly oversee it and overthrow it when they want. It is only then when citizens can enjoy their personal freedom, regardless of their colour, wealth, religion and way of thinking. It is when the state is built on citizenship basics, which means

---

[197] Muasher, *The Second Arab Awakening and the Battle for Pluralism*, 56.
[198] *Asharq Alawasat*, London, 16 November 2011.
[199] Muasher, *The Second Arab Awakening and the Battle for Pluralism*, 57.
[200] Bishara, *The Invisible Arab*, 202.
[201] *Al-Quds Al-Arabi*, London, 15 June 2012.
[202] Bishara, *The Invisible Arab*, 207.

the state does not belong to a certain family, person or party. It belongs to all its citizens.[203]

Its stance on minority was also well articulated and it was always trying to catch with the pace of the modern time to highlight its plural and inclusive character in the society. One member of the political bureau of Ennahdha, Nuruddin, pointed out that his party was committed to build a democratic institution based on the respect for law and right of women and independence of Judiciary irrespective of citizen's sex, religion or ideology.[204]

Ennahdha showed all respect to all the political and state institutions of the country and they had a complete vision and blueprint for the governance. Speaking on the subject of the system of government, Mr Rachid told an Arabic daily, *Assabah*, that the parliamentary system of government was the best political systems in the world. The Parliamentary system is the root of democracy as it transfers the power from people to the assembly. Those who think they will enjoy the permanent majority are on the wrong side and we cannot keep out system according to our own interest and wishes.[205] In the same interview, he said that there was no ideal system in this world either in presidential or parliamentary form. It speaks in volume about the major ideological shift the Islamic leadership has adopted in Tunisia.

The changes in tone and posture of political Islam can be gauged from the statement of another prominent member of Ennahdha Mr Ali Larayedh when he stated in an interview with the *Counterpunch*:

> We have suffered abuse; we know what the violation of human right means. We have lived in fifty different countries. And we have learned about democracy and women's right. So we should be judged by the long way we have come. See how we live, us

---

[203] Bishara, *The Invisible Arab*, 207.

[204] *Asharq Alawasat*, London, 26 October 2011, http://www.aawsat.com//leader.asp?section=3&article=646928&issueno=12020#.UYdFbqJyDcM

[205] *Akhbar Assabah*, Morocco, 13 March 2013, http://www.akhbarassabah.com/# (Accessed on 13 March 2013).

and our families: My wife works, my daughters study, one of them does not put the veil.[206]

The situation has reached to a point where Islamists across the board are pretending to be more secular while the liberals are posing to be more Islamist, and invoking of Islam has become the parlance of hypocrites. A secular Tunisian leftist commented sarcastically on the paradox of interest and values, thus:

> Ben Ali's son in law, Sakhr el-Materi [hardly religious], bought a large estate and named every road on the property after one of the Prophet's 99 names. He founded Zeitouna Islamic and opened radio station with the same name broadcasting religious programme only....Rachid took refuge in the UK, a secular state — Ben Ali in Saudi Arabia — facts are better than theories.[207]

With the ascendance of the Islamists to the centre of power, there are sign of contestation between the pragmatism of governance and preservation of ideology. This contestation seems to be unfolding in different directions and paving the way for a liberal and multi-layered democracy. Recently, there was difference between Rachid and Prime Minister Hamadi Al-Jbali about the formation of a new technocratic government. Defending his stance, Rachid told the media persons that he was least fearful of his party and his top priority is the country. Parliament did not approve the technocratic government of Hamadi Al-Jbali and after the resignation of the prime minister, Ali Larayedh became new prime minister who had once said that constitution must draw on the Arab and Muslim religious sources.

When Hamma Hammami of *Parti Communiste Ouvrier de Tunisie* (PCOT) was asked about the religion, he replied it was a tricky question while another member said, Tunisians are Muslims and this does not pose a problem to the future of the country. We defend individual freedom, freedom of faith, freedom of expression. The party is not against religion and not

---

[206] Serge Halimi, 'Tunisia: Democracy Year One', *Counterpunch* (7–9 October 2011), http://www.counterpunch.org/2011/10/07/tunisia-democracy-year-one/ (Accessed on 28 March 2013).

[207] Halimi, 'Tunisia: Democracy Year One'.

against mosques.[208] One of the lawyers who suffered under Ali expresses his apprehension over the rise of the Islamist whose one banner reads, 'No voice can be raised above the voice of Muslim people.'[209]

The emergence of new Salafists has triggered a new debate within the ideology of Islam itself in Tunisia like the one in Egypt. They showed their harsh Islamic posture against the liberal social fabric of the country. Very recently, they have come out against nightclubs and they were involved in the act of vandalism and attacked one TV station for airing an anti-Islamic film.

Ennahdha distinguished itself from other Islamic movements by the degree to which it insisted on the need for constant renewal within Islam: by its willingness to work within the political context rather than adherence to his personal religious belief.

Its leadership was astute enough to comprehend their future plan in the national politics of Tunisia and maintained all ideological and the political distance with the radical groups like the Salafists. Commenting on the political plank of the Salafists in the country, one of the prominent clergy of Tunisia, Sheikh Farid Al-Baji, Grand Mufti and Director General of Hadith Academy of Tunisia suggested that Ennahdha should avoid any association or proximity with the Salafists because they believe in terrorism and it would tarnish the image of Ennahdha because they are thirsty for the blood of the enemy. He was of the firm belief that Tunisian voters would never say yes to the Salafists. Salafists are political terrorists and they do not read the modern history. Earlier alliance with the Salafists was a blunder on the part of Ennahdha and Farid Al-Baji also advocated that Bourguiba and the Salafist are the two side of the same extremism.[210]

Ennahdha has to work against hard secular groups in the coalition and this coalition itself is forcing a transformation in the Islamic rhetoric and ideology of Ennahdha. There are internal rifts among the coalition in the government as well. The

---

[208] Halimi, 'Tunisia: Democracy Year One'.
[209] Halimi, 'Tunisia: Democracy Year One'.
[210] Based on my conversation with him during my visit to Tunisia in October 2013.

President of Congress for People's Republic Moncef Marzouki points out, 'What complicates the situation further is the growing feeling that our Ennahdha brothers are working to control the administrative and political apparatus of the state.' This coalition culture of politics is a positive trend in an evolving democracy, which would leave no space for a dominant ideology to control the political discourse of the nation.

Rachid has expressed his opposition to violence and he announced that he would not go for any kind of political confrontation with his allies. He showed his optimism that army would not intervene in the political affairs of the country.[211] He also underlined that national dialogue is the most important requisite for today, pointing out that there was no substitute to the preliminary or founding committee, which is the legitimate voice of the people and real representative of the masses.

The same Islamists in Tunisia who had been, for decades, in no mood to accept anything short of the Quran as a constitution are now transforming themselves and now talking in terms of Western liberal constitution. They are talking of accommodating different voices and opinions in the evolution of the constitution. Speaking on the subject, Mr Rachid said, 'that constitution formation takes time as it is cooked on cold fire and constitution is destined to take long period of time and it is the basis of our political, social and economic life'.[212]

Sheikh Farid Al-Baji said in an interview:

> Islam was not opposed to the democracy. Tunisia always believes in the objective of Islamic jurisprudence and it believes first in the interest of the countrymen and Tunisian political Islam is not a new phenomenon and democracy is for all social groups. In new Tunisia, Iranian model is not possible and the Shariah cannot be the source of legislations. Tunisia is already an Islamic state because Islam is a state religion and language is Arabic and there is nothing new for Ennehda to add in the islamicacy of Tunisia.[213]

---

[211] 'Tunisia at the Cross Road: An interview with Sheikh Rachid al-Ghannouchi', *Al-Quds Al-Arabi*, London, 11 February 2013, http://81.144.208.20:9090/pdf/2013/02/02-11/All.pdf (Accessed on 25 March 2013).

[212] *Al-Quds Al-Arabi.*

[213] Based on my conversation with him during my visit to Tunisia in October 2013.

Not only the leader of Ennahdha is convincing the international community about its secular and tolerant pluralistic credentials but global leaders are equally concerned about the ensuing political situation in the Arab counties. French Minister of Foreign Affairs expressed confidence that Tunisia Ennahdha would not attempt to impose shariah on society.[214] One woman said, 'If Arab and Muslim democracy does not work here, it will work nowhere.'[215]

The coalition politics has put the Islamists in the direction of multi-polar democracy. Rachid declared that politics was not the world of prohibition but it is the world of interest.[216]

The country is grappling with a host of political and social questions after the October 2011 election. The division of power among different political institutions, place of religion in the state, state's role in the economy, form of government and the question of Arab–Muslim democracy are some of the pressing issues which the constituent assembly would need to introspect and pay serious attentions to. Ennahdha itself faces a series of internal challenges from the hardliners, and its chief, who had decided to retire, was prevailed upon to stay to prevent the conflict within the party

There is an obvious division between the political trajectory of Tunisia and Egypt. The situation in Tunisia is completely different from Egypt in terms of history and culture. In Tunisia, the army has apolitical approach with no material and economic stake in the state unlike Egypt where army was a state within the state. Unlike the exclusive politics of the MBH that ultimately led to its exit, Nahda always believed in dialogue and inclusive politics.

According to Sheikh Farid Al-Baji, Ennahdha did not focus much on the issues of shariah because 95 percent of the Tunisian laws are already deduced from the shariah. Moreover, Ennahdha preferred and worked for the success of the revolution. It did

---

[214] Khashan, 'The Arab Spring and Democratisation in the Middle East', 132–47.

[215] Halimi, 'Tunisia: Democracy Year One'.

[216] *Asharq Alawasat*, London, 21 March 2013, http://www.aawsat.com/details. asp?section=4&article=721651&issueno=12532#.UU_7gxdyDcM (Accessed on 25 March 2013).

not go for victory; neither had it opted to impose the majority verdict that might have caused the anarchy. When you try to get everything, a day will come when you might have to lose everything and this philosophy was well followed by Ennahdha; so they, from day one, shared power even with the communists and loyalists of the previous regime.[217]

National Dialogue in Tunisia

On the second anniversary of the revolution, the mood in Tunisia was sombre and there was all-pervasive dissatisfaction with the slow pace of economic change. This dissatisfaction found a widespread and robust expression following the assassination of the two opposition leaders of Tunisia, Comrade Chokri Belaid and Mohamed Brahmi, within five months of putting the evolving national democracy in danger. Reacting to their murder, Rachid said, 'It is common for a country which is witnessing the revolution of this magnitude and it is a handiwork of anti-revolutionary forces.'[218] He also added that the interest of anti-revolutionary forces of Tunisia converge with the Arab and non-Arab together.

Two successive assassinations of the opposition leaders created new crisis in the Tunisian coalition government. There had been a mounting pressure on the Islamic-led government to step down after their assassination. This act created a sense of insecurity and unease in the country, which was surging towards a workable democracy after the victory of the Islamists in the election. A new crisis developed when most of the members of the constituent assembly belonging to the opposition parties boycotted the proceeding business and threatened to interrupt it in future too if the present government did not resign.

---

[217] Based on my conversation with him during my visit to Tunisia in October 2013.

[218] *Asharq Alawasat*, London, 11 February 2013, http://www.aawsat.com/leader.asp?section=3&article=716732&issueno=12494#.UX4yaqJyDcM (Accessed on 25 March).

A much-awaited dialogue between the so-called troika government with an Islamist majority and the opposition mediated by General Federation of Tunisian Workers (GFTW) with three other civil society organizations began in October 2013 without making any headway. There was an air of mistrust between the ruling party and the opposition over the road-map plan, which stipulated the resignation of the present prime minister. Opposition demanded an immediate resignation of the government and its replacement by a technocrat, independent and non-political government. Opposition accused the present Islamic government of having collusion with the terrorist groups creating instability in the country. The road map also demanded that a new constitution should be in place after the beginning of a new dialogue, which seemed impossible.

A French Daily commenting on the complicated national political scenario noted: 'The national dialogue does not have an easy mission. How political parties can come to an agreement within three weeks to a month over problems they have not been able to overcome for two years'.[219]

The failure of the dialogue did not bode well for the democratic future of the country which seemed to be going through a very peaceful transition until recently but the announcement of the suspension of the dialogue led to further swirling of the crisis. After floundering for three months in political disorder, Tunisia failed to rescue the national dialogue.

Mr Houcine Abbasi, head of the Tunisian General Labor Union (UGTT) federation mediating the crisis said, 'We have decided to suspend the national dialogue until there are favorable grounds for talks to succeed'.[220]

The ruling Islamists and the opposition opened hard-won talks on 25 October 2013 again to form a government of independents, shape the much-delayed constitution and prepare for elections as part of a roadmap. Tunisia also faced serious

---

[219] Kamel Abdallah, 'Tunisian Dialogue Kicks Off', *Ahram Weekly*, 29 October 2013, http://weekly.ahram.org.eg/News/4505/19/Tunisian-dialogue-kicks-off.aspx

[220] Lassad Ben Ahmad, 'Dialogue Dashed', *Ahram Weekly*, 5 November 2013, http://weekly.ahram.org.eg/News/4574/19/Dialogue-dashed.aspx

security threats in the form of an unprecedented outbreak of terrorist attacks that had already claimed several lives.

There were a set of differences between the present government and the opposition that were hindering the progress in the dialogue. Few of the prominent differences between the two are as follows: appointment of new election board; issue of a mini constitution for the transitional phase; representation of the civil society members in the constituent assembly; formation of new technocrat government and tussle between the adaptation of the consensus model of the majority–minority verdict in the constituent assembly.[221]

After the suspension of the talk, one of the executive members of the Ennahdha Al-Ajmi-al-Warimi said, 'Ennehda is a democratic institution and believes in the politics of consensus and accord. The country of Tunisia is for everyone and there is no place for majority–minority conflict and autocracy.'[222] He also added in the same interview that his party was well aware of the political realities of the country and would work for a model which pleases every one.[223]

Despite some deep and some superficial political fault lines between the Islamic blocks and the communist- and socialist-led opposition, the political situation in Tunisia would not go the way one witnessed in the case of Egypt and other parts of the Arab world after the uprising. The real discourse in Tunisia would be dominated by the economic issues and political stability instead of the shariah or Islamic governance. The shape of political discourse would be more driven by pragmatic and contextual policies of the new Arab world.

Commenting on the primary political issues in the future, Mr Al-Baji told that Tunisia need not ponder over the laws and religion as the laws of the land are very liberal and very lenient. Even the Europeans after colonization could not bring much change to the laws because they found it well advanced and accommodative in tone and content. Even Bourguiba, in

---

[221] *Maghrab Daily*, Tunis, 10 October 2013.

[222] *Maghrab Daily*.

[223] *Maghrab Daily*.

the long span of his three decades of the rule, could not change much of the laws because these were very comprehensive and could bring only ten modifications out of 4,000 personal laws.[224]

It is not only in Egypt and Tunisia where Islamists have made a headway, but other parts of the region have also witnessed the rise of Islam as a political force, and the Islamic ideology of the MBH has swept across the region, which can be seen as a reaction to half a century suppression by autocratic and the so-called secular regimes. Islamist forces have captured the centre stage in all parts of the Arab world. One Arab scholar Khattar Abu Dayyab claims that similar results would be witnessed in other parts of the Arab world.[225] The MBH in different countries are known differently like in Kuwait, it is known as Constitutional Movement, in Jordan it carries the name of Islamic Action Front, in Palestine it is called Hamas, the Yemeni branch carries the name of Reform Movement and in Algeria it is Peace Movement.[226]

The Islamists have fared well in the election of Morocco and Kuwait. The Islamic Justice and Development Party took the biggest share of vote in Morocco and has formed the coalition government for the first time in history.[227] Like all other Islamist blocks around the Arab world, the Islamic Justice and Development party too is trying to allay the fears of the international community. Abdul-Ilahi Bin Kiran, the leader of the party said that 'There is no need to be fearful of this Islamic victory and our relation with the west will be intact'.[228]

In a recently concluded election in Kuwait, Islamists had secured more than 60 percent seats in the national parliament. There are speculations that in case elections take place in near future in Yemen, Yamani Congregation for Reform—an Islamic block—will emerge victorious. Dozens of new parties have sprung up in Libya and a mildly Islamist strain runs through

---

[224] Based on my conversation with him during my visit to Tunisia in October 2013.
[225] *Akhbaralaalam*, 27 October 2011.
[226] Al-Auzi, *Siraaala-Al-Shariah Al-Ikhwanul-Muslimunwa Mubarak*, 52–53.
[227] Khashan, 'The Arab Spring and Democratisation in the Middle East', 132–47.
[228] *Asharq Alawasat*, London, 27 November 2012, http://www.aawsat.com//details. asp?section=4&article=651761&issueno=12052#.UYdKN6JyDcM

almost all the parties. Mr Jaleel, head of the National Transitional Council of Libya, has already started sounding Islamic as he has banned interest-based economy and allowed polygamy.

Islamist movements, especially those inspired by the ideology and philosophy of the MBH, are surging ahead as a result of the uprising. Even in Jordan where the MBH maintains a low profile and always exhibits loyalty to the monarchy, they demanded for the downfall of the king. One of the protestors commented about King Abdullah in the following words, 'He is coward; you saw what happened to Mubarak, Qaddafi and Bin Ali.' They cried 'No to Abdullah and no to Hussein.'[229] Recently, they boycotted the national election after the king limited the share of national electoral list to 17 in a 140-seat assembly. This trend is likely to continue until the process of political transition completes a full circle. In Syria, Islamists joined the opposite coalition of Ghalyoun along with liberal, leftist and the secularists despite the differences in theological and political approach amongst them.

Constitution, Shariah and the Constitution

The role of constitution cannot be undermined in any country striving to transit towards a democracy. Constitution is a very vital document according to which country carries out its day-to-day affairs. A constitution is a contract between the people and the state. The primary function of a constitution is to lay out the basic structure of the government according to which people are to be governed and different sections of the society are to be treated.

In the post-revolutionary phase, the most important issue for the countries of the Arab world which had witnessed the revolution was laying down a democratic constitution, which would guide them towards a functioning democracy. This was

---

[229] Katie Paul, 'In Jordan's Tafilah: Demands Escalates for King's Downfall', *Al-Monitor*, 16 November 2012, http://www.al-monitor.com/pulse/originals/2012/al-monitor/jordan-king-talifah.html (Accessed on 30 April 2013).

more important for countries such as Egypt and Tunisia that had suffered for decades under a series of autocratic regime. The constitution was a litmus test for both the Islamists and the liberals and it was to decide the future of national politics in Egypt.

Without going into much details and the background to the referendum and the issue of the election, I will come to the centrality of the constitution question and the raging debate about it among different political factions in Egypt.

Immediately after the sign of peace was experienced on the streets of Egypt, SCAF decided to form a committee to look into the constitution of 1971 and suggest the amendments. The committee was headed by Tariq Bashri, a man with Islamic learning. His appointment was seen as an act of covert understanding between the MBH and the army. A majority of the members wanted the same constitution barring few amendments but some wanted its nullification with the views that constitution must also go with the regime.

One major divisive point between the Islamists and the liberals was the election, whereas the MBH and its affiliates were adamant on prioritizing election over constitution and the liberals were obstinate about prioritizing constitution over election.[230]

Both groups had their own reasons and apprehensions. Islamists were frightened that in case of constitution-first, liberals would have every scope for manipulating the identity, while in case of election-first, the liberals were fearful that Islamists would sweep the election and would form the constitution accordingly. One of the Salafist members, Yassir Burhani, declared that his main battle is to defeat the constitution-first campaign.[231]

But SCAF went by the majority's views, and despite all resistance and opposition from different quarters, the army put the document for the referendum on 19 March 2011 and majority of the people voted for election-first; it was the first major victory for the Islamists who were able to pass the test of democracy. One should not judge the popularity of the MBH by the victory it achieved in the constitutional referendum of 19 March 2011, where 77.2 percent voted in favour of referendum.

---

[230] Al-Qarni et al., *Al-Rabi-Al-Arabi Fi Misr-Al-Saurahwama Baadaha*, 84 and 152.
[231] Arab Centre for Policy and Research Studies.

Now the next battle was the formation of the first post-revolutionary constitution of Egypt and that was to take place after the election to both the houses of parliament. The Islamists were able to capture both the houses of Parliament and an Islamist, Mr Morsi, was the first elected president of Egypt after defeating the old loyalist of Mubarak, Ahmad Shafiq.

There was an unceasing debate on the role of shariah in Egypt after the revolution. The debate was mainly about if the shariah would be one of the sources of legislation or it would be the only source of laws. The existential question was the place of the Islamic shariah in the national document and who would be the defining authority of the shariah. In the newly amended constitution, there were repeated references to Arabization and the Muslim world which, according to some, showed how Islamists were preoccupied with the concept of ummah and the caliphate and less interested in the affairs of Egypt.[232]

A major point of divergence between the liberals and religious parties was Article 2, which envisaged that shariah should be the main source of legislation. Salafists launched a national campaign to retain it and held a number of conferences in different parts of the country, sending stern warnings to those who harbour any plan to amend this provision.

Sheikh Ahmed al-Tayeb, the Grand Imam of Al-Azhar Mosque, emphasizing Al-Azhar's position, rejected any changes or amendments to Article 2 of the present constitution, which talked about the role of shariah in drawing the laws of the country. He stressed the need to preserve the current content of the article in order to preserve the nation's identity. He maintained that the principles of shariah should be the main source of legislation, noting that 'this is our responsibility before God and the nation'.[233] He explained that Article 2 of the constitution instructs the Egyptian legislators to refer to sharia law while crafting the laws in Egypt.

---

[232] Rashidi, 'Egypt: Whose Constitution'?

[233] Ahmad al-Buhayri, 'Al-Azhar Insists Keeping Shariah Law in the Constitution', *Al-Monitor*, http://www.al-monitor.com/pulse/politics/2012/07/al-azhars-sheikh-we-insist-on-pr.html (Accessed on 25 April 2013).

He also reiterated that Islam is the official religion of the state, Arabic is its official language and the principles of sharia law are the main source of legislation. This came in opposition to certain liberal groups in Egypt which would have liked to see the term 'the principles' removed from the article. The Coptic, on the other hand, demanded that Article 2 be put for discussion and deliberation before the nation. Many called for seeking inspiration from the 1923 constitution, which considered all the Egyptians equal in civil and political rights.

Another contentious issue was the use of the term 'principle' or 'provision' regarding Islamic shariah. Dr Shafei, representative of Al-Azhar to the constituent assembly, said that in this case, the word 'principles' refers to the origins and foundations of Islamic law, and remarked that the current content of Article 2 is more appropriate and powerful for the Egyptian constitution than the two other alternate terms: provisions and shariah.[234] He further pointed out there was not much difference between principles of shariah and purpose. Principle and purpose are two means to understand the ethical basis of shariah and they are not shariah in itself.

The first constituent assembly witnessed an intense debate over each clause of the constitution which contained 236 articles. The head of the constituent assembly, Hossam Al-Ghiryani, is alleged to have pushed the members to finish the debate on the entire clauses at the earliest. Constitution retained the old provision that Islam will be the principle of legislation but added one more clause envisaging the Ulema of the Al-Azhar is to be approached from time to time in order to seek the advises on the issue of the Islamic shariah and define the principles.[235]

This particular clause is revealing about the changing role of Al-Azhar in a new political entity. One major impact that had been observed after the revolution was a sense of autonomy achieved by Azhar, which was historically autonomous until it was politicized by Nasser five decades ago.

---

[234] 'Al-Azhar Insists Keeping Shariah Law in the Constitution'.
[235] *Al-Quds Al-Arabi*, London, 21 December 2012.

Like the referendum on the constitutional change, parliamentary election and the presidential election, FJP was able to win the constitutional referendum held on 15 and 22 December 2012—the day SCC was to rule over the constituent assembly. It is altogether a different story that only 33 percent of the registered voters participated in the referendum where pro-Constitution groups received 64 percent votes. A regional variation was also noticed in the choice of the people.

People in the Alexandria and Cairo voted against the referendum, while people in Port Said, Sinai of North and South (a pro-MBH zone) voted in favour of the MBH version of the constitution.[236]

In the first round, it got only 57 percent votes, and reacting to this, one member of the Left group, Mr Yusuf, said that there was no such thing called constitution imposed on the basis of 50 percent votes.[237] However, MBH members claimed that a constitution was a must for a successful democratic transition and people should be ruled in the light of Islam because majority are Muslims.

One of the veterans of Egyptian Journalism, Mohammad H. Haykal, said that the first round of referendum on the constitution already showed the division in the country and the ensuing election would further divide the country, and that Egypt was heading towards a culture of Nazism.[238]

Reacting to the result of the first round of election on 15 December 2012, Mohamed El Baradei called for uniting against the dictatorship of the MBH. He also called to vote 'No' in the second phase because his party wanted an element of shariah and 'No' should be for the sake of Islamic shariah in the country.[239]

The MBH claimed that division is a common phenomenon in politics and they did not want to take away the right of the others but they wanted implementation of the majority voices. One of the members of the MBH said that political division did not mean

---

[236] *Al-Quds Al-Arabi*, London, 18 December 2012.
[237] *Al-Quds Al-Arabi*, London, 21 December 2012.
[238] *Al-Quds-Al-Arabi*.
[239] *Al-Quds-Al-Arabi*.

the outbreak of world war.[240] Doctor Hussein of the MBH told that his party did not want to have a secular state like Turkey nor a religious state like Iran. In an interview with Today's Zaman, he said that they support a civilian state ruled by people.[241]

Similar controversies were witnessed in Tunisia after the revolution. Article 1 of the present constitution in Tunisia — which says, 'Tunisia is a free, independent and sovereign nation, its religion is Islam, language is Arabic and is a republican government' — triggered much controversy. Religion being Islam could be mandated as making the Quran a main source of legislation. Tunisian political landscape witnessed the same battle like Egypt on the provision of the constitution.

The inclusion of shariah contained in Article 1 of the draft constitution sharpened the difference between Ennahdha and the Salafists who wanted shariah to be the only source of legislation. After a long bargain, Ennahdha won the battle over Article 1 and was able to amend it to the 'the main source of legislation'. There was internal division within the Ennahdha group itself because very few were in favour of inclusion of shariah in Article 1.

However, the leader of Ennahdha endeavoured hard to convince the liberals that each and every right of every section would be protected in the new constitution. One of the liberals of the Tunisian politics, Mr Hammami, argues that the Islamists began the debate to set a trap for the secularists but they themselves fell into the trap; '[W]hy do they want to stress that Tunisia is Muslim, what for — to enforce shariah law, to challenge equal rights for women.'[242]

The process of constitution-making in Tunisia seems to be much serious and prolonged in comparison to its counterpart in Egypt. In one of the preliminary meeting, Professor Ben Achour addressed the members and criticized Article 148, which states that 'Islam is the religion of the state', in following words:

---

[240] *Al-Quds Al-Arabi.*

[241] Sayfa Bulunamadi, 'Egypt's MB against Idea of Having Secular or Religious State', *Today's Zaman*, 16 September 2012,http://www.todayszaman.com/news Detail_getNewsById.action?newsId=292465 (Accessed on 2 May 2013).

[242] Halimi, 'Tunisia: Democracy Year One'.

'Those words can be interpreted in various ways, which can go as far as considering Islam to be the only source of legislation, with all that entails and Islam may be interpreted according to Wahabism.'[243] He also cautioned that totalitarianism may grow under the guise of religious theocracy. Another member similarly blasted Article 148 saying that it would be a blow to Tunisian civil society because civil society has no religion of its own.[244]

The case of Tunisia is very different from the case of Egypt in political, cultural, ethnic and religious terms. Identity of the Tunisian people is deeply imbued with Arab Muslim values and further enriched by successive civilization. The constituent assembly in Tunisia acted with the consent of expert groups and other prominent members of civil society. Civil society members have been able to force some changes in the second draft of the constitution like provision of criminalization of attacks on sacred. The clause of criminalization of normalization of relation with Zionism and the Zionist state has been dropped.[245] Role of Islamic Higher Council in Tunisia, like Al-Azhar, was a major contentious point in the present constitution inviting battle. The members of Ennahdha were ardently in favour of according power to the council in matter of religious affairs. But the commission on constitutional Bodies at the Tunisian National Constituent Assembly voted against the draft law on enshrining the Higher Islamic Council into the constitution.

Conclusion

We have seen how the reign of authoritarianism and popular impotence has been broken by the event of the Arab Spring that

---

[243] 'Tunisia's Latest Draft Constitution under Review', *Al-Monitor*, http://www.al-monitor.com/pulse/politics/2013/01/tunisia-constitution-political-islam.html

[244] 'Tunisia's Latest Draft Constitution under Review'.

[245] 'Letter to National Constituent Assembly on the Draft Constitution', *Human Right Watch*, http://www.hrw.org/news/2013/01/22/letter-tunisian-national-constituent-assembly-draft-constitution

gave a new trajectory to the national political discourse making the Islamists a dominant voice.

In particular, the rise of the MBH and Ennahdha in Egypt and Tunisia, respectively, has been phenomenal, but it has witnessed many social and political constraints affecting its ideological underpinnings of the last few decades. Ennahdha was forced into a policy of pragmatism that was visible in its politics of alliance with the liberal and secularist forces of the country. The evolving democratic institution might impose certain changes on the rhetoric of other religious parties too and drive them to keep religion out of the business. Arab Spring ushered in a new era where the Arabs might be forced not to restrict their politics to any religion-centric political culture.

What model of Islam will be integrated in the revolution-invested countries—Saudi or Turkey or Iran—is not obvious. Turkish prime minister's visit to Egypt and Tunisia immediately after the revolution had created an apprehension amongst the Arabs who saw it as an endeavour for re-Ottomanization of the land and some expressed anger when he suggested embracing of secularism by the new Arab.

The series of revolution witnessed in the Arab world have created a virtual image of pan-Islamism and a shadow representation of ummah, which the Islamist groups have been cherishing for centuries. The Arab Spring has brought a unity among people of all ideological persuasions and turned the table against extremist groups such as Taliban and Al-Qaeda. Tunisian Islamic leader, Rachid Ghannouchi has very rightly pointed out in an interview in 2011 that Al-Qaeda was finished, thanks to the revolution.[246]

It is time for the Islamic leadership to allay the apprehensions of the masses vis-à-vis political Islam, as one woman said that the MBH would work with the feeling of revenge while another added that Egypt would be on the path of progress if it remained united and powerful enough to fight the fascism of the MBH.[247]

---

[246] Bishara, *The Invisible Arab*, 202.
[247] *Al-Quds Al-Arabi.*

Some of the Islamist blocks like Salafists have not committed themselves unequivocally to the democratic principle and it was not clear what they would do if or when they take or share power. The next few years seem to be difficult for those nations that have gone through the revolution. One needs to counter the looming force of reactionary and religious politics. The Arab Spring in Tunisia and Egypt gave way to a heated summer in Libya, Syria and Yemen. Religion will have an important role in determining the democratic transition in the countries. The future will witness a fragmentation and the more regions move towards democracy, there will be more shift in the rhetoric of new and old Islamic parties.

The FJP need not be overenthusiastic about the election verdict the nation has witnessed earlier because there have been instances in the past in Egypt where the high mandate could not help the party to implement its agenda. The Wafd party, after the revolution of 1919, had captured more than 90 percent seats in the national assembly election of 1923, but the government lasted merely ten months.[248] In three decades of its existence until 1952, the Wafd party was destined to capture the power six times out of ten elections held but the total duration of its rule did not exceed seven years. It shows that centres of power are not merely represented in the majority votes or in the strength of political parties, but true political power is represented in the popularity among the masses and the state apparatus.

Ideological division and Islamic–secular polarization will divert the energy towards something else. This ideological contestation and political battle might exhaust the entire national project and which in turn might hamper the peaceful transition to democracy. Ideological battle may transform into a class struggle, as liberals and the secularists form a class of elites, causing a prolonged struggle and sabotaging the birth of a true democracy. The constant demand on the part of the liberals for the exclusion of the Islamists from the public sphere would create a situation full of conflict and a vicious circle of violence.

---

[248] Bashri, 'Ilaqatu-al-Din Bid-Daulah', 80–100.

Elections in Tunisia and Egypt have made it clear that changes have not sunk deep enough and they seems not to have spread wide enough yet. Much of the fears of Arab democrats and Islamists calling for democracy were grounded in their negative association with the slogan of the West: agenda of promotion of democracy. At present, Arab public seems to have little in common beyond the immediate objective of overthrowing despotic rulers. Social forces are either nascent or remnant of regime brutality. Pluralism is still a vague concept and diverse political agendas invite more discord than cooperation.[249]

There are general perceptions that democracy is the cure for every solution, which is not true. What is important is real political transformation involving freedom and justice. There should be a combination of social justice and free economy, as well as a link between security and freedom and bond between nations and the globe. The real challenge is to dismantle the remnant of the Nasserite regime in Egypt and of the combined socialist–communist forces in Tunisia. It is time for the Arab world to learn to respect the justice and rights of others; they should also advance a culture of debate and discussion, which is the true ethos of any democracy.[250]

---

[249] Khashan, 'The Arab Spring and Democratization in the Middle East', 132–47.
[250] Auda, *Baynal-Shariahwa-l-Siyasah*, 58.

5

Arab Spring: Changing Landscape and Implications for India

The term 'Civilizational Link' is perhaps the most sacred expression in the Indian foreign policy lexicon, invoked very often to describe India's relationship with the Arab world, individual as well as collective nations of the region.

The lineage of these traditional and historic ties can be traced back to its close association with all the monolithic religions cropped up on the soil of the Arab. Indians have a long history of their association with the Jewish community of the region as the Jews had long back established a series of trading ports in the western parts of the country. Islam, too, had paved its way into the land of the Indian subcontinent not long after its origin in the Arabian Peninsula. The largest number of Baha'i people are found in different parts of western India, while the fact remains that Iran was their birthplace. Similarly, the Zoroastrians constitute the fourth largest population in India after they came in hordes and settled down here in the wake of rapid Islamization of Iran.

India's relationship with the Arab-Islamic world is rooted in the history and has been enriched over the centuries by an intense and prolonged phase of exchange of ideas and people from both the sides. This old cultural link assigns a unique status to the Indian relationship with the Arab world.

These closeness and proximity in cultural and civilizational terms between the two regions are well reflected at present when one witnesses the level of trade between the two regions and the presence of large number of Indian expatriate workers in different countries of West Asia. India from its own cultural and geostrategic prism sees the Arab world in three parts: Gulf, Maghreb and West Asia; India evades the practice of making usage of the Eurocentric term 'Middle East' to describe the region, but it addresses broadly the whole region as West Asia.[1]

In modern time, and particularly after the arrival of British colonial masters in India, our connection with the West Asian region acquired a new geostrategic dimension to this traditional civilizational link. The British policy towards the Arab world was determined, pursued and administered from the Bombay port, as it was the closest town to the West Asia in geographical terms. The constant perusal of geostrategic policies towards the region added a new fillip to the multidimensional association between the two.

Historically, the Arab world has been an area of considerable significance to India. Besides the historical linkages and economic interactions, the region has occupied an important place in India's commercial relations with the West. During the past two decades, the region has figured prominently in not only India's economic growth but also its great power aspirations.

India's ties with the Arab world spurred with a new zeal after the oil boom of 1973 when a large number of Indian workers landed in the region in search of jobs, and today one will find large numbers of Indians placed in different economic sectors of the Arab world. Since the oil boom in the early 1970s, the Gulf region became a major destination for large-scale migration of Indians. Unlike other migration, this one was spurred by the economic considerations whereby scores of unskilled, semi-skilled and skilled as well as professional Indians sought employment in the oil-rich countries of the Gulf. While the actual number remains contested, it is generally accepted that at least six million Indian nationals are currently working in the Gulf countries, including over one and a half million in Saudi Arabia

---

[1] Rajendra Abhyankar, 'Protest and Possibilities: West Asia and India' (research paper no. 8, Mumbai Gateway House, Indian Council on Global Relations, March 2013), http://www.gatewayhouse.in/wp-content/uploads/2013/04/West-Asia-Online.pdf. (Accessed on 25 June 2014).

alone. In the UAE, they constitute the largest single group, vastly outnumbering the Emiratis.

India has a high economic and commercial stake in the region as it receives the huge amount of remittance annually from the GCC countries. The World Bank estimates that non-resident Indians remitted around US$64 billion to India during 2011–12 and a significant proportion of this came from the diasporas in the Gulf countries.[2]

There are around six million workers in the Gulf nations who are the backbone of the remittance part of Indian economy. The Indian remittances accounted for 49 percent of the total remittances sent from the Gulf nations in 2012 alone. The Gulf nations also accounted for 47 percent of the total remittances to India globally in 2012.[3] This figure of remittance is an obvious indication of the well-woven economic relationship between the two, which assumes additional significance when India topped the list of remittance received in 2012 with US$69 billion.[4]

The level of the economic relations between the two sides can be determined by the fact that 50 percent of the oil India consumes comes from the Arab world and Indian nationals form the largest expatriate community in the Arab world. GCC countries alone constitute India's largest socio-economic partner anywhere in the world. Trade (both oil and non-oil), remittance, investments and expenditure by Gulf citizens visiting India and so on totalled up to US$200 billion or more in 2011–12.[5] This total volume in terms of value is much more than the values of India's financial ties with any other groupings in the world like the EU, ASEAN and North America.[6]

---

[2] Adith Charlie, 'Decoding India's Response to Arab Spring'. *The Journal of Turkish Weekly* http://www.turkishweekly.net/op-ed/3071/decoding-india-s-response-to-the-arab-spring.html (Accessed on 5 July 2013).

[3] IANS, 'Half of Remittance from Gulf Nations went to India', *Madhyamam*, http://www.madhyamam.com/en/node/11905 (Accessed on 4 July 2013).

[4] 'India tops Global Remittences List', *The Hindu*, 20 April 2013.

[5] Ranjit Gupta, 'Arab Spring and West Asia: Challenges for India' (lecture, Madras University, 8 January 2013).

[6] Talmiz Ahmad, 'The Arab Spring and Its Implications for India', *Strategic Analysis* 37, no. 1 (New Delhi): 119–27.

Saudi Arabia meets nearly one-fourth of India's energy needs and is home to one of India's largest expatriate communities.[7] The value of two-way trade with Saudi Arabia alone in 2010–11 topped US$25 billion, rising an incredible seven times in five years making Saudi Arabia India's fourth largest trading partner in the world.[8] Sociocultural exchanges resulting from centuries-old ties strengthened over the years due to large number of Indian hajj pilgrims to the holy shrine add another dimension to this relationship. Even before the Arab Spring was witnessed on the shore of the region, Saudi Arabia had reached out to India to upgrade and expand the confines of its economic activities, and, as a result, only between 2006 and 2010 a low profile relation was transformed into strategic partnership with Riyadh Declaration signed in 2011. The Riyadh Declaration commits both the sides to the significant expansion of their defence, security, and economic and cultural ties.[9]

In fact, defence and security cooperation in addition to the economic and commercial ties have added another boosting dimension to the core feature of India's relations with the GCC. The extradition of two alleged Indian terrorists from Saudi Arabia last year suggests the deep-rooted nature of the growing security cooperation and concern in both the countries. Over time, a series of issues, such as growing global trade, energy security and political concern vis-à-vis Pakistan, have made the Arab world vital for India.[10] Moreover, the presence of extra actors and players in the region, namely the United States, China and Pakistan, has strategized the relation between the two.[11] Traditional Arab support for Pakistan, especially during conflict with India, did not influence the attitude of the latter. Cognizant of the Arab support for its fellow Islamic country,

---

[7] Rumel Dahiya, ed., *Developments in the Gulf Region: Prospects and Challenges for India a Next Two Decades* (New Delhi: IDSA, 2014), 23.

[8] Gupta, 'Arab Spring and West Asia: Challenges for India'.

[9] Ahmad, 'The Arab Spring and Its Implications for India'.

[10] 'Debate: India and Turmoil in the Arab World', *India Foreign Affairs Journal* 6, no. 2 (April–June 2011): 111–51. http://www.associationdiplomats.org/publications/ifaj/Vol6/6.2/DEBATE.pdf (Accessed on 23 August, 2014).

[11] Dahiya, ed., *Developments in the Gulf Region*, 23.

India never insisted on reciprocity when dealing with Arab and Islamic countries.[12]

India's growing economic strength and its willingness to strengthen ties with the Gulf nations have converged well with its Look East Policy. The core elements of India's policy vis-à-vis the Arab constitute its support to Palestinian cause, cooperation with secular and democratic regimes in the region, security and stability in the Gulf and enhancement of bilateral economic relations, safeguarding its energy interest. Traditionally, India has carved out its own autonomous trajectory of relationship with the Arab world without being dictated or swayed by any other global power or existing regional dynamics. However, in the last two decades some occurrence of global significance such as rise of terrorism, piracy and money laundering have imposed new imperative for the national foreign policy vis-à-vis the region.

India's association with the Arab world cannot be confined to the economic periphery only, but both sides have shown their political engagement equally for last several decades. The political ties between India and the Arab world deepened after the independence of India when both expressed its full solidarity with other aspiring for liberation from the yoke of the colonial powers. India has always followed the two-pronged policy towards the Arab world—extending all support to political movement of the region and later displaying close engagement with the secular and democratic regimes there.[13]

India enjoys traditional political ties with the most important Arab-African nations of the region like Egypt. The political association between Egypt and India goes back to pre-independence days when both were pursuing the ideal goal of freedom and liberation. In the post-independence years, the relationship between India and Egypt was driven by ideological congruence—both had shared history of anti-colonial struggle and were committed

---

[12] P.R. Kumaraswamy, ed., *Persian Gulf, 2013: India's Relations with the Region* (New Delhi: SAGE, 2014), 7.

[13] P.R. Kumaraswamy, *Reading Silence: Indian and the Arab Spring* (The Hebrew University of Jerusalem: The Leonardo Davis Institute for International Relations), http://www.dmag.co.il/pub/huji/ReadingtheSilence/view_book.html (Accessed on 25 June 2012).

to principles of the Non-Aligned Movement (NAM). The creation of NAM in 1961 under respective leadership of President Gamal Abdel Nasser and Prime Minister Jawaharlal Nehru is still considered a landmark of Indian foreign policy success. It was through NAM that India sought to pursue its economic and political interests in the Arab world, and this forum brought few other nations of the region close to the heart of erstwhile Indian leadership. Over the decades, both have worked to improve South–South relations. In 2007, an India-specific industrial corridor was implemented along the Suez Canal development area for collaboration with the Egyptian companies to capture the European and African markets. Indo-Egyptian trade is worth nearly US$3 billion and there are substantial investments in the oil and gas sectors, automobiles and the IT sector, which are suffering from the lockouts due to the current protest.

It was the traditional strength of political ties and deep-rooted economic interest of India that deterred it for decades from entering into any diplomatic tie with the state of Israel and instead, India never hesitated in calling Israel an aggressor. India had extended all support to Egypt in the war of 1956 and Indian Prime Minister Nehru even threatened to withdraw from the Commonwealth of Nations. In the Arab–Israel war of 1967, India expressed its full solidarity with the Arab world. In 1977, New Delhi described the visit of President Anwar el-Sadat to Jerusalem as a 'brave' move and considered the peace treaty between Egypt and Israel a primary step on the path of a just settlement of the West Asian problem. India has always stood by the cause of Palestinians and always demanded the establishment of an independent Palestinian state. India's pro-Arab stance, its close relation with the Palestinian leadership and its decision not to establish its diplomatic ties with Israel for a long time have earned a good repute for India there. India's open support for Syria on the question of Golan Heights has added further credentials to Indian policy of solidarity with the Palestinians. India was also among the first few countries to recognize Palestinian Liberation Organisation (PLO) along with China and the Arab league.[14]

---

[14] Kumaraswamy, *Reading Silence.*

India sought to maintain good relationship with the Ba'athist regimes of Iraq and Syria after the demise of Nasser's secularist regime and resultant rise of the Islamic forces there. India's relationship with Saddam of Iraq was so warm and cherished that India refused to call Iraqi attack on Kuwait in 1990 an aggressive one.[15] Similarly, Turkish invasion of Cyprus and Iranian occupation of three islands of the UAE have remained non-existent issues for India.[16]

Core Features Determining India's Responses to the Arab Spring

Like many other nations of the world, India, too, was completely baffled and astounded over the sudden upsurge of the mass movement in the Arab world against the incumbent regimes. The Indian establishment and the intelligentsia by any stretch of imagination had no clue of looming revolution in the horizon. Unlike other major powers of the world, India's initial response was much delayed and much guarded and later it was the manifestation of its indifferent attitudes towards the happenings. It might also be the refection what Professor Kumaraswamy observes that the 'Middle East has never received adequate importance in India's foreign policy agenda'.[17] However, when the situation reached to the point of no return, India was forced to react but it was primarily guided by its core domestic political and the economic interests.

It has never been the core of India's foreign policy to promote democracy, and India was ready to accept the choice of its own people and to determine their future through the means they prefer. India has always succeeded in striding a balanced path without opposing or supporting any one and the adherence to this principle was well reflected during the eight-year-long Iran–Iraq war. Since Independence, India has consistently

---

[15] Kumaraswamy, *Reading Silence.*

[16] Kumaraswamy, *Reading Silence.*

[17] Kumaraswamy, ed., *Persian Gulf, 2013*, 35.

adopted the policy of Middle Path on several divisive issues of the Arab world. It has adhered very religiously to the policy of maintaining equidistance in intra-regional conflict and never allowed its economic interest to be damaged by siding along with one faction against other on the contentious political issues.

Addressing the 16th NAM conference on 30 August 2012 in Tehran, Indian Prime Minister Manmohan Singh stated:

> 'The progress, prosperity, well being, political stability and plurality of the Asia to our West have always been of equal historical and civilizational significance for us. A West Asian region that can realise its full development potential, live in peace and harmony and join the comity of the democratic and plural societies will contribute enormously to human progress and peace in the 21st century'.[18]

Apart from this long-term traditional foreign policy principles and preambles, as mentioned earlier, there were a number of issues and core interests that shaped and guided Indian responses and reactions to the event called the Arab Spring. The high level of trade with the region and its reliance on the energy sources constituted the guiding principle of Indian reactions.

While dealing with the complex situation of the magnitude of the Arab Spring, India had to navigate between its desire to cherish the democratic urge of the masses and protect its deep-noosed economic and strategic interest. The foremost effort of Indian policy was not to be looked as an interventionist and, meanwhile, not to let its interest be hampered.

Elucidating the approach of India to the development in the Arab world, veteran strategic thinker C. Raja Mohan says, 'India will have to approach the Middle East on the basis of its own internal dynamics rather than a preconceived idea of preferences'.[19]

---

[18] Abhyankar, 'Protest and Possibilities: West Asia and India'.
[19] Abhyankar, 'Protest and Possibilities: West Asia and India'.

While assessing the Indian response to the developments in the Arab world, one can identify five essential components which were instrumental in shaping its policy vis-à-vis the region since the eruption of the crisis: protection of national interests, safety and welfare of overseas citizens, maintaining equilibrium at home, re-enforcing principles of state sovereignty and non-intervention, and inclination towards preserving the status quo.[20]

When the Middle East's share of the global recoverable reserves is itself declining and is already below 16 percent, the locus for oil demand is shifting to the United States, Canada, Brazil, Russia, Central Asia and other countries.[21] The United States is ending its dependence on oil imports from the Middle East as the new sources of fossil energy have appeared such as shale gas, and new gas fields are being discovered. The old assumptions regarding the West's dependence on the steady flow of cheap oil from West Asia and the politics that devolved upon it are becoming redundant. This is a good omen for the West but India cannot afford to abandon or ignore the development in the Arab world because of its oil dependence. India's growing energy requirement is met by the oil-rich countries of the Arab world. Currently, the Gulf region, including Iran, alone supplies about 60 percent of India's total import of oil and natural gas.

Economic liberalization has spurred a new energy requirement for the Indian markets and even the inroads of new source of energy in the form of shale gas and biogas; wind energy has not diluted the significance of the gas and energy for growing industrial markets of India. India's demand for oil stood at 3.34 mbd in 2010, 3.46 mbd in 2011 and 3.58 mbd in 2012. Corresponding domestic production during the same period stood at 0.86, 0.9 and 0.92 mbd, respectively.[22]

In 2008–09, 92 percent of India's import from Saudi Arabia was only energy-centred and it reflects the magnitude of Indian

[20] Charlie, 'Decoding India's Response to Arab Spring'.

[21] Bhadrak Kumar, 'Arab Spring through Indian Eyes', *Russian and Indian Report*, http://indrus.in/articles/2012/08/29/arab_spring_through_indian_eyes_17265.html (Accessed on 5 July 2013).

[22] Kumaraswamy, *Reading Silence*.

reliance on the energy resources of West Asia. This was true of Kuwait (96 percent during 2006–07), Qatar (88 percent during 2009–10), Egypt (89 percent during 2006–07) and Yemen (99 percent during 2009–10). Only the UAE has more diversified trade with India, where energy imports constitute less than 50 percent of India's imports.[23]

Saudi Arabia and Iran remain the biggest providers of oil and hydrocarbon to India. Iran remains a gateway for India to access the Caspian Sea and, moreover, India needs Iran for its petroleum reserve. On the recent turmoil in the Arab world, Indian Prime Minister Manmohan Singh told the group of editors on 29 June 2011 that this was an area of acute concern and he recalled that there are six million Indians working there and India imports two-thirds of its oil from there.[24]

Moreover, energy supplies are the major component of India's trade with the Gulf countries. With the notable exception of the UAE, oil and gas imports constitute over 80 percent of India's imports from these countries. Energy products constitute a substantial portion of India's exports to the outside world, accounting for about a sixth. The share of West Asia in India's total foreign trade had gone up to 30 percent by 2009–10 and Saudi Arabia and UAE had remained top ten trading partners with India for a long time. UAE alone in 2011 was India's largest trading partner overtaking China.[25]

Indian National Security Advisor, Mr Shivshankar Menon, summed up the implications of the Arab Spring on India's energy security as follows:

> Now the Middle East accounts for less than 16 percent of global recoverable reserves. New shale oil and new gas fields are coming into production in the next few years. This reduces the West's dependence on the West Asian oil supply. Obviously, in geopolitical terms, the West is comfortably placed to be on the 'right side of history'.[26]

---

[23] Kumaraswamy, *Reading Silence.*
[24] 'Debate: India and Turmoil in the Arab World', 111–51.
[25] Kumaraswamy, *Reading Silence.*
[26] Kumar, 'Arab Spring through Indian Eyes'.

Thus, any major upheaval in the Arab world would completely disrupt the flow of energy and oil from the Gulf. This would not only mean supply disruptions but also massive price escalations, and both would have cascading effects upon the already sluggish Indian economy.

The region has continued to see India as someone dependent on its oil and never expected India to be a major political player in its internal turmoil. India's stance on the development has been criticized on several grounds such as indifference of India to the rise of political Islam, to the regional instability, vague stance in the United Nations Security Council (UNSC) and for drawing no blueprint to deal with the new Arab world.[27]

According to Professor Kumaraswamy, 'Though India not being the part of the drama but cannot remain disinterested because of its oil interest and whatever happens in the Middle East will have far reaching implications for India'.[28] He further argues that the remittance that India receives through its expatriate workers in the form of foreign exchanges was another detrimental factor in shaping and guiding Indian policy towards the Arab Spring. India receives US$50 billion as remittance and any disturbance in the region would hamper the flow of this huge foreign exchange, having a direct impact on India economy.[29]

In the beginning of political upsurge, India's main concern was the continuity of its project work, investment and collaboration in the region. India has huge investments in Egypt, Libya, Jordan, Syria, Saudi Arabia and GCC. In Egypt only, India has the investment of over US$2.5 billion.[30]

India's economic concern in dealing with the new Arab world was followed by its worry for its trapped workers and employees in the Arab Spring-infested countries. The security and safety of its people were the major source of concern for

---

[27] Abhyankar, 'Protest and Possibilities: West Asia and India'.

[28] 'Debate: India and Turmoil in the Arab World', 111–51.

[29] Kumaraswamy, *Reading the Silence.*

[30] 'Indian Investment in Egypt exceeds $2.5 billion', *Ahram Online*, 20 November–14 July 2012, http://english.ahram.org.eg/NewsContent/3/12/58688/ Business/Economy/Indian-investment-in-Egypt-exceeds–billion-Ambass.aspx (Accessed on 14 July 2013).

the government and similar was the case during the Gulf Wars I and II and Lebanese War of 2006. The total number of Indian workers varies from four to six million and there is no exact report in this regard. In March 2011, answering a question in the Rajya Sabha, the government put the number of Indians in the region at nearly five million only.[31]

The 2010–11 *Annual Report* of India's Ministry of External Affairs, which is otherwise silent on the Arab Spring, does provide an idea of the Indian expatriate population presence in some of these troubled places. According to its estimates, there are 0.4 million Indians in Bahrain, 0.573 million in Oman, 0.5 million in Qatar and 1.75 million in Saudi Arabia. Even though there are some discrepancies in the figures, these are suggestive of the prospect of the magnitude of the potential problems for India if things go terribly wrong there.[32]

The presence of a large number of Muslim communities and, moreover, existence of overwhelming number of Shiite sects in different parts of India played a very decisive role in making its policy statement on the sectarian violence in Syria. India strode a very cautious path while dealing with the situations in Syria where political battle from the very inception has acquired a sectarian colour. In Syria, the regime is dominated by the minority Shiite Alawite sect, while the majority of the citizens are of Sunni origin, which also happens to be the dominant Muslim sect in India.

Any vocal policy statement in favour or in opposition to the violence in the country might have its long-term bearing on India where relationship is already very delicate between the two sects. Few cities of India such as Kashmir, Lucknow and Chennai are already bearing the brunt of the Syrian sectarian turmoil. Thousands of Indian Shiites visit Syria and other places such as Iraq for pilgrimage purposes, and open association with any of the political entities would hamper this exercise

---

[31] 'Recent uprisings in Arab countries', *Rajya Sabha, Parliament Q&A*, Q.822 *MEA*, http://meaindia.nic.in/mystart.php?id=220117334 (Accessed on 22 August 2011).
[32] Kumaraswamy, *Reading Silence*.

and unnecessarily create disharmony and mistrust between the minority and the state.

The growing ambition of India to acquire permanent membership in UNSC was another catalyst in shaping the Indian stance on the developments in the Arab world. India moved very cautiously posing its great power, non-interventionist stature and behaving in a very responsible manner. This attitude of India is well reflected in the statement of India's permanent representative to the UN, Hardeep Suri, when he said, 'India entered the UN after 19 year and [has] no intention of leaving', when its term come to an end in December 2012.[33]

It was the urge of India to achieve the permanent seat in UNSC that made India make all its statements and opinions through the global forum as long as it was holding the membership of UNSC. India, however, being the largest practising democracy of the world, had no other option but to support the democratic wave across the region.

There are some strategists and political analysts who have vehemently criticized India for overlooking the rise of Islamists to the cradle of power. They opine that India should not lose the sight of the reality of the rise of the Islamists to the power and should be well guarded and protected and extra cautious while dealing with the new political realities of the region.

The rise of the Islamists to the apex of power might strengthen the global Muslim powers against India, particularly in Organisation of Islamic Cooperation (OIC). India can be subjected to much harsher stance on Kashmir, which has already exhibited its interventionist posture and issued several démarche to India. In the future, India cannot afford to overlook this possibility, and moreover the rise of the Islamists to its neighbours has already done great damage to the national interest of India.

Mr Kanwal Sibal, former foreign secretary of India and well-known political commentator, writes:

---

[33] 'India may enter UNSC by 2012 end, says Indian Envoy to UN, Hardeep Puri', *India Today*, 23 September 2011, http://indiatoday.intoday.in/story/india-may-enter-unsc-by-2012-end-hardeep-puri/1/152474.html (Accessed on 14 July 2013).

India cannot be comfortable with the replacement of authoritarian secular-minded regime in West Asia by Islamist regime backed by highly conservative authoritarian Gulf monarchies. The impact of this will be felt closer to our borders where Pakistan is already lurching towards greater radicalism and the Taliban are likely to be accommodated in Afghanistan. India's relation with the GCC will continue in the field of energy, oil and manpower because of the mutuality of the interest.[34]

While another strategic thinker of our time, Professor C. Raja Mohan, holds the view that New Delhi, with a relentless focus on India's interest, must find a way to contribute to the emergence of stable regional balance of power over the long term.[35]

India's Policy Position: Variant and Diverse Reactions to the Turmoil in the Arab World

Keeping its spirit of foreign policy, India took its own time in responding to the development in the region. It was primarily because of the presence of a large number of Indians there, but gradually the Indian government started airing some well-guarded views and opinions and extended support to the democratic waves in the region.

The constant flow of oil and gas remains the major concern of India, as the increasing demand of energy in the Indian market is being met by imports largely from the Middle East, which accounts for two-thirds of India's oil trade.[36] India is the world's fourth largest importer of oil and so the slightest

---

[34] Kanwal Sibal, 'Do Not Take Side on Syria', *Mail Online India*, 13 March 2012, http://www.dailymail.co.uk/indiahome/indianews/article-2114185/KANWAL-SIBAL-Dont-sides-Syria.html (Accessed on 14 July 2013).

[35] C. Raj Mohan, 'Revisiting Damascus', *Indian Express*, 24 July 2012, http://www.indianexpress.com/news/revisiting-damascus/978428/4 (Accessed on 14 July 2013).

[36] Charlie, 'Decoding India's Response to Arab Spring'.

upward movement in crude prices could have upset the centre's fiscal calculations. In the last two years, India saw its average cost of importing crude rise by US$27 per barrel, bloating the oil import bill to US$140 billion from US$100 billion. Oil import costs have gone up by more than three times from US$48 billion in 2006–07. Moreover, the centre subsidizes the commercial use of gasoline, diesel, liquid petroleum gas and kerosene. A 2011 Goldman Sachs study linked a US$10 rise in global oil prices to a 0.2 percentage points decline in India's economic growth.[37]

Speaking at a meeting organized by a think tank last year, India's National Security Advisor Mr Shiv Shankar Menon, stated:

> The Western developed economies can now afford the chaos that the so-called Arab Spring is bringing to the Middle East. They can actively encourage regime change in the area. The main victims of uncertainty in supply will be emerging economies like China and India who are still to diversify their sources of supply into long-term flexible contracts with others outside the region.[38]

It was traditional status quoits policy of India that was well reflected in present Indian stance to the Arab world uprising. What Mr Menon stops short of mentioning is that India has several reasons to back the status quo. India has strong ties with states in the West Asia despite many of them being autocratic regimes. India is reluctant to preach about political and structural changes even to its immediate neighbourhood. Professor P.R. Kumaraswamy, an expert on the Middle East who is also associated with The Leonardo Davis Institute for International Relations, alludes to this in *Reading the Silence: India and the Arab Spring* in the following words:

> India's preferred option has been to allow different societies to determine their individual destinies and democracy promotion as such has never been India' Foreign Policy agenda.[39]

---

[37] Charlie, 'Decoding India's Response to Arab Spring'.
[38] Charlie, 'Decoding India's Response to Arab Spring'.
[39] Kumaraswamy, *Reading Silence*.

India's official response to the Arab Spring exposes clear and basic traits of maintaining a well-guarded silence. India remained extremely cautious in responding to the evolving developments, especially those accompanied by the violence and turbulence. In addition, the prerogative of making official policy statements was confined to the prime minister, foreign minister or diplomatic representatives of the government; other functionaries of the government refrained from airing their views, at least in public.

India's silence or handoff attitude on one of the biggest episodes of the modern Arab world had been subjected to scathing attack from across the academia and strategic community. Mr Satish Chandra and Mr Sushant Sareen castigated the lack of response saying:

> At a time when there is great tumult in the entire Arab world, India's continuing silence on the developments in a region of critical strategic and political importance is not just inexplicable but also deafening. Whether this is borne out of abundant caution or a natural proclivity for fence sitting until the situation crystallizes, or even the result of an increasing tendency in Indian diplomacy to wait for a cue from the Western world [read USA], is not quite clear. Being a merely mouthed fence sitter is not an option for a country aspiring to play a major role on the world stage. India will have to identify with the popular aspirations of the peoples, but without burning its bridges with the rulers and establishments of these countries.[40]

Lamenting the overall approach of India towards the political development, Professor Kumaraswamy says, the 'Best way to describe India's response would be "silence is the gold" and this is what aptly sums up the India's response to the tumults in the Arab world'.[41]

No Indian official report on Indian foreign policy mentions the overthrowing of the two presidents and referring of Gaddafi

---

[40] Satish Chandra and Sushant Sareen, 'India's Deafening Silence on the Tumult in the Arab World' (New Delhi: Vivekananda International Foundation, 27 February 2011), http://www.vifindia.org/article/2011/february/25/Indias-Deafening-Silence-On-The-Tumult-In-The-Arab-World (Accessed on 25 January 2012).

[41] Kumaraswamy, *Reading Silence.*

in International Criminal Court, which others have described as a deafening silence.[42]

In the beginning of the Arab revolt, India displayed some level of reactive behaviour when India's foreign minister expressing India's willingness to be very positive said:

India does not believe in interfering in the affairs of another country. We will take the cue at an appropriate time depending on how they want India to help. India will be willing to be of some assistance to them. But let the situation arise.[43]

India's view on the uprising evolved on the selective basis, and it has not adopted a uniform policy towards the Arab uprising. India condemned the violence on both sides but failed to take any firm stance when countries like Tunisia, Egypt and Libya were engulfed in the political crisis, and so it failed to win the friend anywhere with the new regime of the above-mentioned nations.

India opted for a policy of complete refrain while responding to the developments. On 30 January 2010, India reiterated its close and friendly relationship with Egypt and hoped for an early and peaceful resolution of the situation without further violence and loss of lives. It took almost a week for India to make any statement on the development, and first Indian reaction on the protest of the Tahrir Square came only on 29 January 2011. On 3 February 2012, India issued an advisory to its people after some journalists had been beaten there. On the same day, India suggested President Mubarak subtly to step down and in an interview with a national TV news channel 'Headlines Today', Indian foreign minister said: 'People of Egypt were clear in their thinking and action and those who are ruling Egypt must see the writings on the wall'.[44]

---

[42] Chandra and Sareen, 'India's Deafening Silence on the Tumult in the Arab World'.

[43] Sandeep Dixit, 'India Can Help Build democracy in Arab World', *The Hindu*, 27 February 2011, http://www.thehindu.com/news/national/article1493338.ece (Accessed on 21 July 2012).

[44] 'India for Mubarak Stepping Down', *The Hindu*, 3 February 2001, http://www.thehindu.com/news/national/india-for-mubarak-stepping-down/article1150641.ece (Accessed on 6 July 2013).

He also said that 'it will be in the larger interest of the bilateral relationship that power is taken over by same, rationalist and pluralistic leadership which will be to the benefit of Egypt and our bilateral relationship'.[45]

After the departure of Mubarak on 11 February 2011, a number of high-level Egyptian delegations visited India and the primary objective of most of the visits was not to hamper the trade, investment and fast growing mutual economic interest. Despite some growing concerns and anxiety over Islamists' rise to power in the form of Freedom and Justice Party (FJP), a political wing of MBH, India welcomed their victory in the first-ever democratic election. The reason for this hasty positive gesture towards new political entity could be read in the growing animosity that had crept of late between Indian establishment and former Egyptian President Mubarak.

India had chosen President Mubarak for the prestigious Jawaharlal Nehru Award for International Understanding. President Mubarak, one of the traditional allies of India in the Afro-Arab world, took not less than fourteen years to accept and receive it while he paid official visits to China every year in that span of fourteen years. This unfriendliness on the part of Egyptian regime was reflective of Egyptian envy over growing Indian economy, recognition of India as a major global power and, moreover, rising Indian clout in regional arena in the last two decades.[46]

As mentioned earlier, India's response remained country-specific, and India dealt with the particular country keeping its economic and political interest at its top priority. For instance Libya, with whom India had a flourishing trade in the past in the oil sector and there are almost 28,000 Indians employed in different economic sectors of Libya. India voiced its concern and objection along with China and Russia when West sponsored UNSC Resolution 1973 (2011) imposing a no-fly zone over Libya. It was reflective of India's adherence to its principles of opposition to the use of force when other means had not been exhausted so far.

---

[45] 'India for Mubarak Stepping Down'.
[46] Abhyankar, 'Protest and Possibilities: West Asia and India'.

In Libya, India adopted recourse to procedural gambit instead of objecting directly, as India's permanent member spoke about the resolution in the following words:

The report of that Envoy and that of others had not been received. As a result, the resolution of today was based on very little clear information, including lack of certainty who was going to enforce the measures.[47]

These vocal Indian reactions came under scathing global criticism, and some of the nations pointed out to India that it would have to share global security burdens if it wished to be seriously considered for a permanent membership in the UNSC. However, its principal stand of not interfering in the internal affairs of the country was coupled with ensuring the safety of about 28,000 Indians working on various projects in Libya.[48]

India faced a great dilemma at the critical juncture and it was not easy for India to condemn the Libyan regime because of the security concern of its citizens. India has applied the similar policy to all the turmoil-infested nations of the region. The immediate concern was to facilitate the return of Indians residing in Egypt and Libya. Their numbers were relatively smaller and through special flights and ships, India brought home 750 from Egypt and 18,000 from Libya. Conscious of the possible ramifications and precedence, the government claimed that it was merely 'facilitating' the return of those wishing to leave the troubled countries. 'Home Coming' was the name given to such an operation for Indians stranded in Libya.

Commenting on India's callous approach to the regional developments, Nihal Singh, a veteran journalist, writes with disappointment about India's inability to leverage its membership in UNSA to stop the intervention in the Arab world in the throes of political upheaval and days India should move beyond its timidity in the international arena.[49]

---

[47] Abhyankar, 'Protest and Possibilities: West Asia and India'.
[48] 'Debate: India and Turmoil in the Arab World'.
[49] Abhyankar, 'Protest and Possibilities: West Asia and India'.

But later, India had to change its traditional stance given the growing cases of brutality on the part of Libyan regime. India voted with other big powers to put sanction on Colonel Gaddafi's regime. This act drew India closer to the decision-making process along with other nations in the region. India recognized the Libyan National Transitional Council (NTC) in November 2011 in a meet of 'Friend of Libya' in Istanbul, Paris and London and donated US$1 million in addition to another US$1 million for life-saving drugs in 2012.[50]

India once again preached the mantra of respect of sovereignty in case of Libya. India did not hesitate in expressing its unrest with the notion of 'Responsibility to Protect' (R2P) which was applied in Libya. India continues to be in dilemma on the Westphalian system of sovereignty and territorial integrity, under which internal affairs are the exclusive purview of the state.

R2P empowers the international community to prevent large-scale human rights violation in a state through coercive means if the state has been unable or unwilling to do so itself. It supports external intervention to prevent or halt four types of atrocities, namely genocide, war crimes, crimes against humanity and ethnic cleansing.

India has been critical of the selective implementation of R2P. According to its permanent representative to the UN, Mr Hardeep Singh Puri, R2P is 'being selectively used to promote national interest rather than protect civilians'. While R2P was invoked by major Western economies in support of an intervention in Libya and Syria, there was a disconcerting silence to apply the same principle when state security forces crushed rebellions in Bahrain and Yemen.

India feared that the R2P doctrine could be exploited for meddling in its internal affairs. There have been a number of armed conflicts and freedom movements in the northeast of

---

[50] Samir Zaptia, 'India's ambassador meets Libyan Minister of International Cooperation', *Libya Herald*, 25 December 2011, http://www.libyaherald. com/2012/12/25/indias-ambassador-meets-libyan-minister-of-international-coopera-tion/ (Accessed on 20 July 2013).

India for many years. India has been refusing international intervention in the row with Pakistan over its control of the 'disputed territory' of Jammu and Kashmir. India does not want to take cues from the international community on how to solve its bilateral conflicts and internal disagreements. Moreover, the Indian government has a questionable human rights record in Jammu and Kashmir. The security establishment has been accused of systemic human rights abuses that range from mass killings, forced disappearances, torture, rape and sexual abuse to political repression and suppression of freedom of speech.

India's fixation with the Westphalian system is perfectly analyzed by Professor Kumaraswamy in his work on the Arab Spring:

> Indian silence on issues such as democratisation, human rights, and governance brought into the open by the Arab Spring should be viewed within the context of its domestic situation; its fear of encouraging similar interventionist policy by the world body. Like many other Third World countries and vulnerable countries, New Delhi takes refuge in sovereignty and non-interference.[51]

This point of Professor Kumaraswamy is further strengthened when one intends to introspect the statement of former Foreign Minister of India, S.M. Krishna.

> Depending on how the situation develops, India will certainly try to position itself to be of advantage to forces of democracy so dear to India's heart. India does not believe in interfering in the affairs of another country. We will take the cue at an appropriate time depending on how they want India to help. India will be willing to be of some assistance to them. But let the situation arise.[52]

---

[51] Kumaraswamy, *Reading Silence*.
[52] Richard Fontaine and Daniel Twining, 'India's Arab Spring Opportunity', *The Diplomat* (24 August 2011), http://thediplomat.com/2011/08/24/india%E2%80%99s-arab-spring-opportunity/ (Accessed on 5 July 2013).

India has always adhered to its policy of not distinguishing between the people and the regime, and for India choosing and rejecting their leaders are the prerogatives of the respective citizens alone. India has proved its adherence to its principle by hosting the first democratically elected Islamist President of Egypt, Mohammad Morsi, in 2013 despite some unrest and anxiety on the part of members of strategic community. It has been a part of Indian policy to maintain a balance between national interest, political idealism and global values.

India facilitated the exit of Indians from Egypt, helped the evacuation of its nationals from Libya and advised its nationals in Yemen to leave the country given the fragile state of affairs there. India remained very cautious in its official pronouncements and always took calculated steps for the safety of its citizens and other interests.[53]

India was equally worried about the security of its citizens in Bahrain, Libya and Yemen, which dictated and subjugated the country's positions there. Bahrain, Libya and Yemen together were home to more than 0.4 million Indians. The immediacy of the Indian government's response was directly determined by the number of non-resident Indians in an affected country. This was more evident in the case of Tunisia, where Indians do not live in significant numbers. Therefore, the turmoil in Tunisia did not generate much reaction from the government of India.

While dealing with a new Arab world, the situation in the Gulf region posed the biggest diplomatic and strategic challenge for India as the situation was far more complicated and complex there. During the Iraqi invasion of Kuwait in 1990, India had organized the largest aerial evacuation in its history when it had brought back home 0.14 million Indians. With the sole exception of Qatar, the Arab Spring had spread and could be felt in all Arab countries along with the Gulf. Hence, the fate of about five million Indian expatriate workers living in the oil-rich Arab countries of the Gulf was at stake. Repeating the operation of same magnitude would have incurred great economic difficulties and would have been unimaginable too.

---

[53] 'Debate: India and Turmoil in the Arab World', 111–51.

Bahrain had emerged as the frontline state of cold war between Saudi Arabia and Iran in the wake of the Arab revolt. Two contrary approaches adopted by the Gulf regimes towards Syria and Bahrain on almost similar scenarios have exposed geopolitics in the region. Moreover the divergent approach adopted by the Gulf rulers has the support of few major Western powers which is likely to provide a new trajectory to the politics process of the future. India's worry centred mainly on the safety of 35,000 expatriates there. Because the expatriate community has remained its priority, India provided two sets of assurances to its community. At one level, it sought to ensure their security by engaging with the respective regimes of the day. Accompanied by some community figures, the Indian ambassador in Manama met Bahraini officials and expressed their concerns over the growing violence in the country.

On its part, the crown prince met leaders of the Indian community and reassured them of his government's commitment to provide them individual and economic security. Despite the violence, more than 14,000 labourers were given emigration check required (ECR) during 2011 for employment in Bahrain, indicating that both sides were keen on maintaining a resemblance of normalcy at least on the migration front. Such a visible display of assurance was less apparent in Yemen largely due to spate of violence in and around the capital town of Yemen.

At a secondary level, the Indian government assured assistance to those willing to leave the troubled countries. The stance of advisory to leave the country was more apparent in Yemen but less visible in Bahrain because of different security situations. According to Ministry of Overseas Indian Affairs (MOIA), about 850 Indians were provided assistance to leave Yemen during 2011. Hence, despite the widespread violence in Bahrain, there was no travel advisory, while a similar policy was adopted in the case of Yemen. The employees in Bahrain and Yemen were less likely to return home because they were mostly from the unskilled group and had fled the country out of the abject poverty. This was evident when the official helpline set up by the Ministry of External Affairs 'did not receive a single' call in 48 hours in Yemen and Bahrain.

The non-issuance of travel advisory vis-à-vis Bahrain and delayed moves over Yemen can be attributed to three inter-linked reasons. Both countries have significant number of Indian people; there were about 0.4 million in Bahrain and 0.1 million in Yemen. In comparison, for example, there were only 3,600 in Egypt and 18,000 in Libya when India organized the evacuation of its nationals. The mere size of the population inhibited India from issuing any travel advisory. Second, any large-scale emigration would have ruined the economies of these countries, something Bahrain or Yemen were not prepared to accept.

Thus, India sought to reassure its nationals of the respective government's assured protection to the Indian communities. Moreover, alternatively, it was prepared to assist their evacuation should they opt for it. At the same time, because of political and economic fallouts, India had refrained from advising, let alone organizing, any large-scale evacuation from Bahrain or Yemen. The absence of travel advisory to Saudi Arabia or other countries of the Gulf implied that the government did not see the protests in these countries as serious threats to the Indian lives and properties in these countries.

Moreover, India echoed its friendly gesture towards Bahrain because of its alliance with Saudi regime and with whom India too had sought its close association in response to the deportation of Abu Jindal under extradition treaty. Moreover, Saudi Arabia was the prospect for compensating the Iranian import deficit of oil in the wake of its inability to export oil to India because of the ongoing sanction against Iran.

In Syria, Indian's first travel advisory did not come until January 2012, nearly ten months after the outbreak of protests against President Assad. India's initial behaviour in the case of Syria could be explained in terms of its oil interest in the Gulf countries whose monarchs want Syrian President Bashar Assad to go. Considering its significantly high stakes in that country, India for some time maintained silence when President Assad's government was subjected to a large-scale condemnation.

In the beginning, India was reluctant to criticize Assad's regime because of the former's relentless support to the issue of Kashmir and substantial level of Indian investment in different projects there. However, in the UNSC resolution of July 2012, India changed its stance and decided to vote along with the United States and other Gulf countries. The sudden shift in its stance alienated Iran further and reminded of its bitter memory of India's votes against Iran at the International Atomic Energy Agency (IAEA), which had drawn a lot of criticism from different strategic communities in India.

Expressing its concern over the India's voting against Syria in the UNSC along with the Western powers against the wishes of rest of the BRICS (Brazil, Russia, India, China and South Africa), Prem Shankar Jha, a well-known Indian political commentator, wrote:

> Will India again vote with the West? Before it does so, it would do well to remember that it has its national building project incomplete. So whatever conventions it allows or help the West establish on the Right to Protect or Intervene may well come back to haunt it in the years that lie ahead. New Delhi needs to bear it in mid that there are striking parallels between what Damascus is facing today and what Delhi faced in Kashmir in the 1990s.[54]

Mr Jha further argued that India has a unique moral position in the world today:

> [I]t's a working democracy; it threatens no country and it is almost completely free from sectarian conflict. A vote by it against the military intervention in Syria will carry a dispro-portionate weight. It could give the West a face-saving way of pulling back from sectarian war.[55]

Commenting on India's diverse and sundry role in the UNSC over the issue of Syria, one of the renowned Arab political columnists and scholar of the Arab world, Fouad Ajami, in his new book, *The Syrian Rebellion*, observed:

---

[54] Prem Shankar Jha, 'India Must Think Before It Acts on Syria', *The Hindu*, 7 August 2012, http://www.thehindu.com/opinion/lead/india-must-think-before-it-acts-on-syria/article3735156.ece (Accessed on 15 August 2012).

[55] Jha, 'India must Think Before it Acts on Syria'.

The sordid vote at the Security Council over Syria was an indictment of three emerging powers that abstained on so simple a proposition—India, Brazil and South Africa. If these powers were making a bid for more permanent role on the Security Council, their moral abdication was a proof that they were not ready to shoulder the burden of maintaining a descent international order. The shame for India, the world's largest democracy, was all its own.[56]

India's position can be explained in the light of its concern about the cut back in the oil supply from the Gulf nations. In the case of Syria, India did not opt for procedural gambit, but it was more confined to the policy of perusal of united voices against the violence in Syria.

Expressing its worry on the human right violation in Syria, India at the 19th session of Human Rights Council said that it supports all efforts to resolve the Syrian crisis through an inclusive Syrian-led process and a similar feeling was expressed by Indian Prime Minister when he said:

As the world's largest democracy, India supports popular aspirations for a democratic and pluralistic order. Nevertheless, such transformations cannot be prompted by external intervention, which exacerbate the suffering of ordinary citizens. The deteriorating situation in Syria is a matter of particular concern.... We should urge all parties to recommit themselves to resolving the crisis peacefully through a Syrian-led inclusive political process that can meet the legitimate aspirations of all Syrian citizens.[57]

Given the Libyan experience, India judiciously abstained from voting in the IAEA, which decided to report Syria to the UNSC over its alleged covert nuclear programme. Russia and China also blocked a proposed Security Council resolution condemning the Syrian government, which could have paved the way for more sanctions and interventions.

With regard to other countries of the Gulf, the Indian trajectory was somewhat different. Despite reports of disturbance and

---

[56] Fouad Ajami, *The Syrian Rebellion* (New York: Hoover Institution Press, Stanford University, 2012), 140–41.

[57] Charlie, 'Decoding India's Response to Arab Spring'.

unrest in some parts of Saudi Arabia, Indian leaders and officials refrained from making any statement, even indirectly, about the safety and welfare of its nationals. The same holds true for India's response to minor protests in other parts of the Gulf region.

While dealing with the case of Bahrain and Syria, India proved once again that it did not subscribe to the narrative that reforms should be limited due to sectarian tensions. While it is not an evangelist of democracy, India supported clamour for regime change and self-rule, if that is what the population wants. However, India did not prescribe or approve of external involvement as the means to achieve this change. For ideological and domestically sensitive reasons, India condemned all forms of outside interventions in the affairs of another state.

This was more palpable in the events of Bahrain and Syria where the battle for democratic transformation transformed into a sectarian strife. While most of Indian Muslims follow Sunni Islam, there is also considerable Shiite Muslim population and, hence, sectarian aspects of the Arab Spring and Saudi–Iran political tensions could have their repercussions within India as well. India thus had this factor while responding to the situations in Syria, Iran and Bahrain.

Furthermore, India could not afford to antagonize rulers of the Gulf where almost six million Indians work by extending support to the Assad regime.[58] India has been the third-largest investor in Syria.

All the authoritarian and sectarian Sheikhdoms in the Persian Gulf producing oil happen to be Sunnis. The growing Indian economy needs their oil. Since they want the non-Sunni Assad to go, India had to concede. There is a bigger picture and that is the calculation that supporting the Americans in the United Nations would eventually strengthen India's claim for the permanent membership in the Security Council. After all, that was what the US President Obama had suggested during his visit to India in 2010.

---

[58] Prakash Nanda, 'Arab Spring: Is India Being Blackmailed', *Indian Defence Review*, 3 August 2012, http://www.indiandefencereview.com/spotlights/arab-spring-is-india-being-blackmailed/ (Accessed on 5 July 2013).

While opposed to regime changes through external intervention, India maintained that it supported the aspirations of the people in these countries to shape their future themselves. Reminding the international community of the core principle of Indian foreign policy, Prime Minister Manmohan Singh had said while addressing the United Nations General Assembly in September 2012: 'Societies cannot be reordered from outside through military force. People in all countries have the right to choose their own destiny and decide their own future'.[59]

One cannot deny the fact that India had always preferred the middle path and its stance on the Arab Spring is largely persuaded and guided by this core principle in addition to its concern for economic and energy security. The high stakes in the region goaded India in a direction that neither appeased nor impeded the designs of Arab states.

This explains why Dr Singh's government refrained from voting on a UNSC Chapter 7 Resolution that sought to enforce a no-fly zone over Libya. In 2012, India once again abstained from a Saudi-drafted resolution imposing sanctions on Syria and calling President Bashar Assad to step down.

New Arab World and Implications for India

In today's globalized world, an incident in one part of the world has its direct and immediate implications in another part of the world. One country or a region cannot evade the resonance of the turmoil taking place in a far-flung region. The same holds true of India in the case of the Arab Spring. India being the contagious neighbour of the West Asian nations would directly bear the brunt of any development in the region.

The powerful forces unleashed by the Arab Spring upturned the existing political order, created a new political alliance and

---

[59] 'India must help Arab World', *Hindustan Times*, 3 December 2011, http://www.hindustantimes.com/India-news/NewDelhi/India-must-help-Arab-world/Article1-777209.aspx (Accessed on 6 July 2013).

pushed the region for much deeper sectarian polarization. In such a situation, it would be difficult for India to preserve its traditional policy of non-involvement in the regional imbroglio.

New Arab world and its evolving geopolitics will be highly influenced by the outcome of Arab Spring laden with an acrimonious Shiite–Sunni (read Saudi Arabia and Iran) divide, and one will observe the response personified as the rise of Sunni world in contrast to what one had seen the consolidation of the Shiite crescent in the past. A sectarian, geostrategic and cold war is unfolding between Saudi Arabia and Iran—a Shiite revolutionary power of the region with a mission to subvert the status quo. The Saudi–Iran rivalry is a very old one but two developments—Iranian nuclear ambition and the Arab Spring—sharpened the antagonism, and this growing bitterness would push Saudi Arabia further close to Pakistan and would be a major source of unrest for India.[60]

This redesigned and redrawn strategic map of the Arab world would force its direct bearing on the external response of the Indian government. India will have to opt for a balanced approach while dealing with two regional hegemonies: Saudi Arabia—an economic power—and Iran—a military power.

The sectarian violence in Syria and Bahrain would shape a new alliance among Syria, Iran and Hezbollah and put them in one strategic club. With Saudi Arabia, UAE, Turkey, Jordan and other small belligerent forces in another camp would pose a different strategic challenge for India. India cannot remain oblivious to the fact of the rise of Turkey, Egypt and few GCC countries in the new Arab world. This is a new ordering in the region and it needs a close strategic scrutiny on the part of India.

New emerging political alliances and involvement of major global powers like Russia, China and United States to support and oppose the respective alliances and camps might force India to revisit its traditional policy of neutrality. To create a harmonious relationship bilaterally despite differing world views would be the biggest challenge for India such as dealing

---

[60] Shashank Joshi, 'New Delhi's Balancing Act in West Asia', *The Hindu*, 13 April 2012, http://www.thehindu.com/opinion/op-ed/new-delhis-balancing-acts-in-west-asia/article3308145.ece (Accessed on 12 July 2013).

with the Islamist government in Egypt and Tunisia and new evolving political formation in Libya and Yemen.[61]

In such an environment of interwoven regional political rivalries, it would be the biggest challenge for India to maintain a bilateral relationship, and avoiding to be the part of security and strategic issues of the Gulf would be an uphill task for India. Sectarianism between Iran and Saudi Arabia, and explicit support of Turkey to Syria, would put the curtain on India's bilateral relationship with these nations. India will have a tough time in making a choice between Iran and Saudi Arabia where India needs Saudi oil to compensate for the oil of Iran and cannot abandon its traditional ally Iran for the sake of Turkey or Saudi Arabia. Iran is still important because it seeks 8–10 percent of its oil import from Iran and, moreover, because of growing significance of Chabahar Port project in the regional trade.

The growing proximity of Saudi Arabia to Pakistan is more alarming. It emanates from the fact that during GCC operation in Bahrain, where according to one report more than 10,000 retired and serving army persons of Pakistan were in Saudi Arabia and monitoring the operation in Bahrain.

The growing level of intimacy between two Sunni powers may be a source of concern among the strategic community, but the growing energy requirements of India would make India put these considerations at the backburner and push India to forge closer alliance with Saudi Arabia. India's recently evolved new framework for security with the Gulf nations would be affected, particularly given the rise of terrorism in the region and its long-term implications for India. Under the new security framework, India achieved a major success in securing the extradition of Abu Jindal and other terror suspects from Saudi Arabia wanted in numerous cases of terror plots. Deportation of Aftab Ansari, wanted in Calcutta blast case, from the UAE was a successful story for India.

Political Islam will receive a new lease of life and new fillip in the wake of this political tremor. One cannot deny the fact that political Islam as an ideology has found an amicable and conducive environment to prosper in several countries such

---

[61] Abhayankar, 'Protest and Possibilities: West Asia and India'.

as Tunisia and Egypt along with Libya and Yemen. Egypt was ruled by the Islamists for a short stint of one year, and Tunisian government is dominated by the Islamic block. Morocco has an Islamic prime minister after Islamists secured the majority of the seats in a hurriedly called election. Although in Libya they have been defeated by moderate pro-Business alliance, National Force Alliance, this defeat did not guarantee that Islamic jinn had been put in the bottle. One cannot undermine the presence and popularity of the Islamists, and in future they can exploit any unruly situations in their own favour.

India cannot shy away from expressing its apprehension over growing Islamization of the Arab politics because India has borne the real brunt of religious radicalism in its neighbour. India remains the biggest victim of religious fundamentalism in South Asia, and the Indian unrest and anxiety over the ascendance of the Islamic forces in the Arab world cannot be overlooked because it would not only have its implication at the domestic level but very soon find its echo in its foreign policy too.

These emerging political realities have already started displaying their effects on foreign policy front. President Morsi of Egypt had already indicated that his government would not be guided by the foreign policy preamble of the past vis-à-vis Iran and would like to improve its relation with it. The growing proximity of two radical powers cannot be discounted or overlooked as no nation can afford to evade its after-effect.

Egypt has already shown its centrality in the regional political architecture by playing a very substantial role in bringing the warring factions of Palestine together, and new Islamic government was very instrumental in the ceasefire between Israel and Palestine in the crisis of 2012. These new developments in the Arab world would not bring an inside change alone but these would have their impacts on other nations of the region too. New Islamic government might seek preferably to examine the intricacies of the foreign policy and desire to redefine it in correspondence with the evolving scenario in the region.

The unpredictability and fluidity of the situations would be another major defying moment for India, and it cannot adopt the policy of one-size-fits-all given the variant nature of political developments, our economic interest and the historical constrain of our past. In unfolding the drama, it would be in the interest of India to stride a cautious path and refrain from siding with any of its traditional or new ideological entity. It would not be in India's interest to pick one side over the other in ongoing regional contention because of its substantial stake in the region in various forms and shapes. Moreover, it would also not be in the interest of India to remain aloof from what is occurring to the advantage of other players who are ready to exploit the situation for their narrow gain and benefits which would heavily cost the regional security and stability.[62]

Non-intervention in the internal affairs of any country has been the sacrosanct principle of India's foreign policy, and it has never joined the chorus of any regional group to intervene or meddle in the internal affairs of a country.[63] But the changing circumstances and growing sectarian violence, leading to the death of more than 4 million people in Syria alone, may pose India the bigger moralist challenge and deter it from the 'policy of passivity'. India cannot afford to remain silent and rather would have to preach and propagate its global message of peace and democracy.

There are some who view this Arab Spring as a blessing in disguise for India. They are of the view that it is an opportunity for India to display its full political, economic and strategic stature and strength and make its global ambition felt in the international arena. Mr Rumel Dahiya of Institute for Defence Studies and Analysis is of the view that there will be major changes in politics and governance across the region and India should be prepared to do business with existing or incoming regimes and assist them in ways that help restore peace and stability in the region, which is of vital importance to it.[64]

Echoing the similar views, Ms Sameena Hameed, assistant professor at Jamia Millia Islamia (JMI) reflects:

---

[62] Talmiz Ahmad, 'The Arab Spring and Its Implications for India', 119–27.
[63] Gupta, 'Arab Spring and West Asia: Challenges for India'.
[64] 'Debate: India and Turmoil in the Arab World', 111–51.

In the Post-Arab spring, India's trajectory in the Arab world will not suffer any reverses due to its current positions but may lose the potential momentum, as these nations will look for reliable partners for their reconstruction and political consolidation, when other powers may readily move in. A middle path is consistent with India's interest and image than a mild one.[65]

Other positive aspects of the Arab Spring have been highlighted in terms of the commonality of interest of the other regions of Latin America and principal countries of Asia and Africa. Their primary concern, similar to India, is to assure the persistent flow of oil. It is here that BRICS countries with the help of other influential nations in the region such as Japan, Turkey, Indonesia, Malaysia and Republic of Korea could come forward to help in the evolution of the post-Arab Spring Arab world with their technological, political, military and cultural assets. India along with these countries can act like a torchbearer for newly emerging democracy in the Arab world.[66]

Conclusion

It was merely high level of economic, political and energy stakes in the region that subjugated and shaped the India's response to the Arab Spring. India has once again proved that it would never embrace the policy of 'democracy promotion' or intervention in the internal affairs of a sovereign country.

India's stance in the case of Syria and Libya conveyed an explicit message to the global community that India could not compromise its growing global stature as it was fully critical of R2P principle for its selective application. The calculated and interest-driven policy removed the apprehension of many that Indian aspiration for great power would be consensus-driven and not to be achieved through some imposition what the present global order has been witnessing.

---

[65] 'Debate: India and Turmoil in the Arab World'.

[66] Ahmad, 'The Arab Spring and Its Implications for India', 119–27.

One cannot deny the fact that India's initial unvocal and indecisive response had surprised many, particularly the regional powers that had imagined that India's ambition of 21st century supremacy would be reflected in its emboldened policy. But India did not transcend the confines of legal and moral boundaries of existing international laws and moreover did not compromise over its sacrosanct element of traditional foreign policy principles.

In the span of three years of the revolutionary phase, India proved that it would not transcend the moralist principle, but now it is high time for India to rush immediately to cement new ties with the new emerging political landscape for the sake of its economic security and political stability.

New Delhi did not have just a moral stake but also a national interest in building a steady and stable tie with the new region. Egypt, Tunisia, Libya, Yemen, Syria and the Gulf states need to establish the institutions of good governance ranging from strong political parties to independent judiciaries. New Delhi's advice and assistance would be welcomed in these countries given its long expertise in engagement with the democratic institutions. Although India does not favour the import or export of democracy, but, if asked, it should share its experiences and be ready to help in the development of democratic institution as it did in Afghanistan in the past.

India being the largest democracy in the world can offer its help in the transitional democratic phase. India's credential as the biggest practising electoral democracy is known worldwide, as it conducts the election for more than hundreds of millions of people regularly that accords additional strength in the field of democracy. The MBH of Egypt had approached India seeking its assistance in holding the first democratic election. A high-level Egyptian delegation of election commission visited India prior to the election. Even the former US Secretary of State, Ms Hillary Clinton, had raised the issue of India extending its know-how in holding the elections in Egypt.[67] India offered to help in the conduct of elections in Egypt and is prepared to help other

---

[67] Fontaine and Twining. 'India's Arab Spring Opportunity'.

countries too. It would also be willing to contribute financially— both bilaterally and multilaterally—and would engage with all governments in the region irrespective of their nature.

One of the well-known political commentators associated with International Institute for Strategic Studies, Mr Emile Hokayem, has urged India to play a role beyond 'trade'.[68] India has always had excellent relations with all the regimes—based on the basic principle of dealing with the regime in power and not commenting on internal systems. India needs to have direct access to the region in order to garner support for its permanent membership in the UNSC, and one major objective of India in the Arab world should be to mobilize the OIC leadership in favour of India.

The role of India becomes more important when Pakistan is marred with a series of political and institutional problems for the last two decades because of the growing sectarian and religious violence there.

India has extra leverage over other nations in approaching the new Arab world as these nations host more than six million Indian workers. It will help India in making them better allies and stabilize the region for great strategic importance to India. India needs to play its card tactfully because of the growing Sunni–Shiite divide between Saudi Arabia and Iran as it requires close intimacy with both the nations for its economic and strategic reason, respectively.

One thing that has emerged out very evidently in the post-Arab Spring era is that the restoration of status quo ante would no more be possible. Regime may survive and may depart but there will be major changes in politics and governance across the region. India should be prepared to do business with existing or incoming regimes and assist them in ways that will help restore peace and stability in the region, which is of vital importance to it.

---

[68] 'The Manama Dialogue'. The 7th IISS Regional Security Summit (Kingdom of Bahrain: IISS, December 2010), http://www.iiss.org/~/media/Silos/Manama/2010/The-Manama-Dialogue-2010/The%20Manama%20Dialogue%202010.pdf (Accessed on 24 July 2013).

People across the developing world have not forgotten India's role in spearheading their cause in various international forums, and once again a time has come when India takes a middle path with proactive engagement with all the stakeholders through Track One and Track Two diplomacy. Adoption of a please-all or mild trajectory that Indian foreign policy is known for would not yield optimum benefits for India in this case because it is all together a different case.

India may lose the potential moment by displaying any sign of indifference or handoff attitude as new nations will look for reliable partners for the reconstruction and political consolidation. India cannot afford to repeat the mistake what it had committed in case of Central Asian nations when it had got seceded from the erstwhile Union of Soviet Socialist Republics (USSR) and had burnt all its bridge, and it has awakened now after a long slumber.

India should shape its politics in coming years in resonance with the sentiments of these nations and its people who have already suffered the US decades-old intervention and subsequent political anarchy and violence. But India should also take cognizance of the fact that it cannot sacrifice or hurt its own strategic interest with US Professor Anwar Alam who advises that India should avoid a close identification with Israel in the new emerging political entity and according to him, 'Goodwill India enjoys in the region would be lost if India "continues to ally itself too closely with United States and Israel"'.[69]

In recognition of its global role and being the biggest democracy in the world, India can play a unique role in supporting the democratic movement there. It will be in the interest of India if it can be drawn into the decision-making process of the region, and it would accord a different stature to India's standing in the evolving global order.

---

[69] P.R. Kumaraswamy. *Reading Silence.*

Conclusion

Political Islamic discourse has always been an indissoluble constituent of the Islamic thoughts throughout the history. There seems to be no rupture among the different phases of Islamic writings when it comes to underline the significance of politics in Islam.

Sometimes the narrative on political Islam is defined invariably as a part of Islamic shariah and sometimes as a part of *Fiqh* (Islamic jurisprudence). In the classical and medieval eras, the political Islamic discourse drew heavily on the Holy Book and the Sunnah of the Prophet, followed by the writings of classical Islamic jurists and commentaries of eminent Islamic thinkers.

During the colonial and post-colonial periods, the discourse was more dominated by an alternative Islamic model against the Western political subjugation and the cultural dominance of the major part of the Arab world—an Islamic order that is cleansed of all innovations, deviations and influences that have crept into it over the years.[1] This was an era when Islam was posited as a comprehensive phenomenon in itself and it was taken as a political blueprint for the *ummah*. The ideological writings always invoked the cultural, political, religious and judicial past of the Muslims, and it invariably represented itself as a cultural model before the onslaught of Western modernity. The colonial period witnessed the rise of political Islam as a cry in the crisis and stood as a dialectical model to the Western one.

The primary objective of the political discourse in Islam has been the creation of an Islamic state and it saw in it the real transformation of the meaning, progress and objective of *ummah*. The immediate objective of the Islamic ideological discourse between

---

[1] Talmiz Ahamad, *The Islamist Challenges in West Asia: The Doctrinal and Political Competition after the Arab Spring* (New Delhi: IDSA, 2013), 1.

both the Shiites and Sunnis was the creation of an Islam-driven system and a political translation of the Islamic spirit.

The Islamic discourse of MBH did not mature until it attained the objective of the creation of an Islamic state. On the other hand, for the Shiites, the objective was the establishment of the wilayat-i-faqih (the rule of the jurist) as witnessed in Iran after the Islamic revolution. For the Salafists, political Islam is a combination of efforts to create a prophetic model of society and the state. One can also see an overlap between the idea of a *ummah* and the Islamic state, and very often the debates have failed to determine the exact primacy between the two.

Islamic political debate has always harboured a utopia of creating a state for itself but largely remained devoid of evolving a mechanism to achieve a civic state in modern sense, promote the citizenry, establish a state institution, and separate and distribute the power which is the mainstay of Western liberal democratic state. Instead, its ideologues have deliberated more upon the issues like Islamic identity, protection of the Islamic heritage, execution of the shariah, creation of the *ummah* and the Islamic vanguard and preaching the belief in divine sovereignty. Modern ideologues have failed to engage with the existing state because it was an illegal, temporary and usurped state as per the Shiite doctrine.

There has been no single universal model of political Islam that could be applied across the globe irrespective of its different cultural, political and civilizational persuasions. There are different models emanating from different geographical, cultural and political confines, like Taliban and Jihadist, who give jihad and violence precedence over the political engagement to bring the rule of the Almighty. There are Turkish models that seem to be more pragmatic in their engagement with the issue of state, freedom, citizenship, economic development and international relation. There are reformed versions of MBH that have developed over the years and emerged as advocates of citizenship, democracy, politics of consultation, multi-party system and the political participation, which are the signs of the dominant political culture at present. There is an Iranian model that craves for the rule of jurist enjoying all powers in order to extend their rule beyond the region in an endeavour to foster the support for its spiritual leaders.

The dominant political Islamic discourse in the Arab world had not matured to comprehend a new vision of a civilian state in its lexicon. It perhaps failed to understand or absorb the core and generic of state in the true modern Western sense. Its ideological rhetoric, which is marred by the traditional thoughts rather than rationality, could not absolve itself of age-old debate of the primacy and subordination between the tradition and the rationality. This may be owed to the involvement or engagement of the generation of the Islamic ideologues with the classical Islamic epistemological reservoir with an emphasis on Quranic injunctions as a regulatory body of the state without resorting to its rational interpretations or explanations.

It fails to bring the Islamic injunctions out of its contextual incarceration, leading to the irrational rationality behind the plea of application of the Islamic teachings in all times to come. Not only this, it remains ambivalent to the changes taking place in the modern world and is oblivious of the political complexities and nuances involved in today's global order. When the modern-day political discourse is more concerned with the human rights and citizenry, the Islamic ideological rhetoric is completely devoid of pressing issues like national community, political community and the civil society whose protection is the primary objective of any state. It is more concerned to protect the religion, life, honour, wealth and mind, which have been the part of classical Political Islamic discourse since ages.

The Islamic discourse has also displayed the sign of selectivity in its unilateral choice of the Islamic heritage despite the insistence of some like Banna and others who resorted to other ideas and thoughts as well while formulating a political blueprint. Modern-day Islamists ignore the accommodative, reconciliatory and conformationist teachings of thinkers like Tahtawi, Afghani and Abduh, who tried to create a harmony between Islam and modernity. This was witnessed in the 18th century when a series of Arab delegations travelled to Europe and learnt the modern art of politics. It was under this impact that the Ottoman had established the first parliament on the Western model and that happened in almost every Arab country. Even Banna, despite his difference with the formation of political parties, had labelled the constitutional representative government as the best one.

Today's Islamists failed to grasp modern realities and adhered to the old classical underpinning of Islam. This adherence to the classical underpinning led to the shrinking of the space of shariah in its application to resolve the day-to-day crisis and went to the extent of even losing its relevance. They made the shariah such a conditional and regulatory mechanism that it failed to offer any solution for the day-to-day crisis. These ideological deviations among different generational thinkers reflect the exiting rupture between the streams of their ideas and these differences fail to create an exemplary model of an Islamic state.

The existence of the secularists, liberals and socialists on the one hand and the Islamists on the other in the political domain of the Arab world created a fissure what we have been witnessing in Egypt and other nations in the wake of the Arab Spring.

The secularists have always been receptive to the political and liberal ideas of the West and were against the imitation of Islamic tradition with the blind eyes, conservative minds and without interrogating its context and circumstances. The creation of the MBH was the reflection of these liberal ideas, but over the years, when the second generation took over its leadership in the form of Qutb and other like-minded people, it turned into a radical political group discarding all that were emanating from other than Islamic traditions. This was the departure from the civilian nature of the Islamic discourse to the fundamentalist discourse advocating a narrow meaning of Jihad.

This new dominant stream within the MBH gave rise to the novel idea that the shariah and not the *ummah* is the component of the Islamic project and the real Islamic state meant for the Islamization of the society. State is for the application of the Islamic laws and, moreover, state would not be a state unless it implements the religion of Islam in its comprehensive manner regardless of whether citizens are Muslims or non-Muslims. Shariah became a source of authority and it is the duty of the state to preach religion and the shariah, and the state is an organ to implement the true Islamic laws.

These radical thoughts were being rooted in the Arab world when the politics of Arab nationalism was trying to sabotage the Islamic project. Arab nationalists resorted to the revolutionary ideologies to counter the Islamists and that delayed the process and progress of real political debate based on the political ethics. The confrontation between these two forces deprived the common masses of human freedom and political rights, and no place was left for dignity and equality.

The project of pan-Arabism failed to create a national political identity where the state failed to create a civic state. The political disaster of the Arab project was exploited by the Islamists who captured the political space within the Arab world. The failure of the Arabism paved the way for the rise of the rhetoric ideology of Islam, and the political domain of Arab nationalists was crushed and trampled by the Islamists. The efforts of the autocrat to scuttle the opposition voices and prevent it from emerging as a political opposition led to fill the vacuum by the Islamists alone instead of the liberals, secularists and socialists as well. The rise of these conservationist forces may also be owed to the autocratic policies carried by the so-called liberals, secularists and socialists. This conservative phenomenon of Islam created another Islamic project to mobilize people in the name of the failure of the other Arab projects.

Here came the Arab Spring which offered a new breath of life to the suppressed and thwarted voice of political Islam for decades in different parts of the region. The Arab Spring provided an opportunity to the Islamists to translate its age-old ideological rhetoric into reality, which had been never experimented or tested in the past with one or two exceptions. Thus far, they had talked of Islamic political idealism in terms of authority and power but were deprived of an opportunity to transform it into a practical and existing reality.

The Arab Spring came along with an open space to translate the rhetoric of decades which remained confined to the ideal writing of the ideologues, jurists and legal experts. For instance, Ennahdha in Tunisia, after the uprising, turned its discourse more towards pragmatism and realism going far away from its traditional slogan. There was no more chanting of 'Islam is a solution' or 'Islamic state'. Islamic project was no more the part of their political manifesto, and they were more concerned with other serious issues like economic advancement, political rights, freedom and establishment of a civic state. This uprising offered an opportunity to accommodate the Western political thoughts too in its exclusive political lexicon in order to expand the scope of classically engraved model of the state that has been ignored by their theorist.

However, there are others, like Salafists, who still adhere to the old classical sloganeering: the questions of the state identity and the application of the shariah. The Salafist agenda was swamped with the same issues before the revolution too and they are still harbouring the old classical view of Islam. This cultural stagnation has created a split with other Islamic groups who are calling for a new *Fiqh* of necessity as opposed to the *Fiqh* of objectives.

After the Arab Spring, there have been growing trends of politicization among different Islamic groups, and a culture of political engagements has emerged which is endeavouring to negotiate with the new realities. This has been coupled with the proliferation of political parties, and even the Islamic groups are not lagging behind. Several new Islamic groups have emerged with different names, such as Jamaat-e-Islami, which named its political arm 'Construction and Development Party' that is an unprecedented and novel experience. The series of revolutions witnessed in the Arab world has created a virtual image of pan-Islamism and shadow representation of *ummah*, which the Islamist groups have been craving for decades. It has brought a unity among people of all ideological persuasions. It has also turned the table against extremist groups, such as Taliban and Al-Qaeda. Tunisian Islamic leader, Rached Ghannouchi, very rightly pointed out that in the autumn of 2011, Al-Qaeda was finished, thanks to the revolution.[2]

Sharef Saleh, in his book *Arab Spring in the Light of Philosophy of History*, very rightly claims that the Arab Spring from its

---

[2] Marwan Bishara, *The Invisible Arab: The Promise and the Peril of Arab Revolution* (New York: Nation Book, 2012), 202.

philosophical point of view represents a progressive movement in general course of movement of the history. Introducing the Hegelian philosophy, he challenges the doom and gloom theory of the Arab Spring and argues that negativism manifested by sacrifices of the people of Egypt and Tunisia is a precondition to achieve the positive and that is the birth of a genuine democracy. It is the Hegelian dialectic, an idea challenged by a counter idea subsequently to produce a new idea.[3] He also cautions that the battle needs to be won first intellectually and later on politically and precedent of intellectual victory will enlighten the Arab masses at large. The democracy being talked about in the Arab world in the post-Arab Spring phase is stripped of true and real sprit of democracy and it is a hollow sloganeering.

We have seen how the reign of authoritarianism has been broken by the event of the Arab Spring that has given a new trajectory to the national political discourse where Islamists have emerged as the dominant voice. The rise of MBH and Ennahdha to the centre of power—a first instance in modern history when Islamist parties came to power through the democratic process—has been phenomenal. Both had difficult time in the government because they are devoid of past experience of governance. It is also true that one year was a very short period to judge one's performance, particularly when one had no experience of governance in the past and especially when they were subjected to a deep scrutiny and were faced with a plethora of economic and political demands of the people.

The downfall of Morsi was too early to predict as it has exhausted all the post-MBH predictions on the ground, and one needs to re-introspect what went wrong and what lies ahead for a country and for the region as a whole. History punished the Egyptian revolution for naivety—for being insufficiently prepared to carry the vision of the freedom. The Egyptian revolution, particularly in all its three stages—Supreme Council of the Armed Forces (SCAF), MBH and military—carried its own baggage of illusions, weakness, distortion and a set of unique

---

[3] Sharef Saleh, *Arab Spring in the Light of the History of Philosophy* (Beirut: Dar Al Sharqi, 2012), 67.

challenges. First, Tahrir saw the inauguration of Osama Sharif, inauguration of Morsi and the same place saw the coming together of the people, police and the army where people were holding the portrait of El-Sisi. The first revolution was against Mubarak, second, was against SCAF when on 12 August 2012 SCAF was thrown out by Morsi and the last one was seen to be against the Islamists themselves. Morsi's ouster will have far-reaching implications for political Islam in the region passing through a highly volatile phase. Now, it is an open-ended question before the Islamists who can ask themselves whether the democracy had any place in the Arab world. The revolution that had introduced an element of democracy in the Arab politics would be thwarted once again in this counter-revolution and would reinforce the argument of the radicals who always invariably profess that change cannot come through democracy and violence is the only true path.

The ouster of Morsi was a well-manifested fact of the short-sightedness of the Islamic rule which showed no interest in reconciliation or in broadening its support base or exhibiting any seriousness to promote democracy. Morsi could not reinvent himself; he could not be the Mandela his people wanted.[4] He could not divest himself of the most stringent aspects of his own heritage, the vision, belief system and agenda of MBH, whose heritage did not include breadth of vision and liberal mindsets.

In comparison of MBH, Ennahdha has fared marginally well; the country is more homogenous than Egypt and in better shape economically. Moreover, Ennahdha avoided the doctrinal approach in crucial areas when it came to the real and pure politics which Morsi could not overlook. When the government and the political approach of MBH were more driven by the traditional belief system and detest for the current political outlook, the mode and approach of Ennahdha was more guided and shaped by practicality and pragmatism. What one Tunisian clergy, Al-Baji, has pointed out is that while MBH opted for victory, Ennahdha endeavoured for the success of the revolution.[5] The success of Ennahdha can also be attributed to

---

[4] Ahamad, *The Islamist Challenges in West Asia*, 126.
[5] Based on my conversation with him during my visit to Tunisia in October 2013.

politics of accommodation across the spectrum rather than of exclusion, which was the hallmark of MBH after they arrived into the cradle of power. MBH failed to reach a formula to run the country, and the downfall of Morsi shows the internal weakness of MBH. While Tunisia opted for a politics that carried the views of every one, particularly when the democracy was in a very immature stage. The Islamist ideologues in Tunisia knew well that any confrontation at this stage with the other stream of national politics would be disastrous for the future of the democracy. There must be a political solution to accommodate these voices and they should not be allowed to remain outside of the political structure.[6]

The leadership of Ennahdha was astute enough to comprehend their future plan in the national politics of Tunisia and maintained all ideological and political distance with the radical groups like the Salafist. On the other hand, Morsi's plan of governance was completely devoid of such far-sightedness and was oblivious of the fact that they were to confront new people, new aspirations and new challenges emanating from a different set of circumstances. Unlike MBH, Ennahdha leadership prioritized its plan and worked accordingly. They acted first to fulfil the objectives of its own people and help cherish the revolutionary dream of the masses where MBH left behind the objective of the revolution—dignity, freedom, bread, unity—and devoted more energy in the implementation of the out-dated agendas which were dear to them alone. The Arab political life is too diverse to allow one single political grouping or the party to dominate the entire system, even with the MBH and Ennahdha being considered the best-organized political groups in Egypt and Tunisia, respectively.[7]

The installation of democracy will not happen as quickly as many Arabs are imagining or thinking. In the absence of autonomy to other branches of the government, the existence of a divided society would make the transition difficult. In case of

---

[6] Kama Habib, 'Al-Islamiyyun wal-Anf Baad 30 Unuu', *Al-Demoqeratiya*, no. 52 (October 2013): 116–19.

[7] Ahmad H. al-Rahim, 'Whither Political Islam and the Arab Spring?' *Institute for Advance Studies in Culture: The Hedgehog Review* 13, no. 3 (Fall 2011).

Egypt, where Army is still all powerful with multi-billion stakes in the establishment and corporate enterprises, the entrenchment and diffusion of democratic seeds would be a real, challenging and difficult task. However, one reality has emerged that democracy would only be a political plank for all political persuasions what Oliver Roy had rightly pointed out after the Arab Spring, that is, Islamism and democracy have become interdependent and neither can survive in absence of the other.[8] Some have written the obituary of the Islamists after the exit of Morsi, but this is not a true anticipation because the religion of Islam constitutes the core of the identity and political Islamic discourse is likely to dominate the future political campaign.

However, Islamists need to respond to a series of questions in the revolutionary era: the role of shariah, its relation with the extremist groups, place of woman in politics, relation with the people of other community, questions of human rights and minority rights and Islamic activism should or should not be part of social organization. What model of Islam will be integrated in the revolution-invested country—Saudi Arabia, where democratic election is still as contrary to Islamic tradition, or Turkey, which has taken up the Islamic project of democracy and where shariah is taken as strive to lessen the corruption and promote freedom or the Iranian model which was not hesitant to claim the Arab Spring was an extension the Islamic Revolution—is not obvious. The time has come when the Arabs might think that they should not restrict themselves only to religion-centric political culture, and the scope of the religions needs to be widened and broadened further.

It is the time for the Islamic leadership to allay the apprehensions of the masses vis-à-vis political Islam, as one Arab woman noted that MBH would work with the feeling of revenge while another woman added that Egypt would be on the path of progress if it remains united and powerful enough to fight the fascism of MBH.[9] Some of the Islamist blocks like Salafists have not committed themselves unequivocally to the democratic principle, and it is not clear what they would do if or

---

[8] Ahamad, *The Islamist Challenges in West Asia,* 128.
[9] *Al-Quds Al-Arabi,* 21 December 2012.

when they take power. The next few years seem to be difficult for those nations that have gone through the revolution. One needs to counter the looming force of reactionary and religious politics. The Arab Spring in Tunisia and Egypt gave way to a heated summer in Libya, Syria and Yemen. Religion will have an important role in determining the democratic transition in these countries.

The future of Egypt democracy is in danger when the elected government is removed by the military and the takeover has proved that the Arab spring failed to fulfil the aspirations of the masses. It might lead to a military dictatorship for a longer period of time, military dominion of the politics, civil war or a mix of all. There would be an escalation in the region with the passage of time, having disastrous impact on the region and the globe. The removal of Morsi was a step back in civil–military relations and more worrying is its regional outcome, and one needs to watch how it will impact the rest of the Arab world. It will also send a message that only army guarantees the political rights and not the constitution or the democratic institution.

MBH must be a part of any political process in the future and stability would not come only through providing security to the people but when there is inclusive politics and each political block would have its space. There must be participation from all walks of life in the evolving democracy in the region. Political reconciliation and inclusion are very important. A proper and long-lasting deal must be clinched with the Islamic forces of the country. Political memory is very short and every government should be aware that the same resurgent group who came out to oust Islamism can come out again to oust them. Popularity and trust do not last long.

The Islamic cadres are well mobilized to be cohesive in their opposition to the regime, while the army would try to prove their commitment to their road map. The culture of resistance on the part of the Islamic cadres would not pave the way for democracy. The ongoing trial of Morsi has deepened the polarization within Egyptian society. This polarization serves Islamists because it helps them to tell common masses that they are being targeted and the army seeks it as an excuse to tell the nation that they are defending the people. In this binary struggle, the biggest victim is the objective of the January revolution: democracy, social justice and freedom. The struggle is no longer over economic and political rights but over power and the state. Both sides are avoiding to answer the questions about the political and economic rights since democracy has dawned. MBH is claiming to represent Islamic ideology and exhibiting all love and concern to religious identity. The very query on the part of the Islamists about the choice between MBH and non-MBH deprives one of their democratic choices about political and economic rights.

After the overthrow of Morsi in July 2013, the army is asking the same question that whether the people support the army or the MBH. The central theme at present should be how to protect and translate the slogans of the 25 January Revolution into politics that could bring better future for Egypt and Egyptians. Morsi will be remembered in history less as a first democratically elected government in the post-Revolution Egypt than as a failed leader who fell short of translating the objective of the revolution in the programmes and failed to achieve anything from the revolution. His policy demonstrated that his party had a long way to go before it was ready for the government despite being the world's largest and best organized Islamic party.

Now the army sees the present as an opportunity to shape the Egypt of its own choice, and it would love to remain free of the control of any civilian government in the near future. The army can see the risk of the radicalization of Islamism across the region and they might argue that an Islamist attempt to work within a democracy would be doomed to failure. The sense of disenfranchisement is reinforced once again, and one can see the repression in the past in Egypt, Turkey and Algeria, where they had been targeted. The military intervention is a watershed that is fraught with danger and likely to reverberate throughout the region. The transition will be quite complicated from autocracy to democracy.

The regime of Morsi inherited a set of problems but failed to understand its complexities like the military dynamic in the state structure, bureaucratic red-tapism and its entanglement in day-to-day state policies, role of the police forces, administrative barrier and the embedded root of secularist and the liberal agency what the media has called the deep state. Moreover, the new Islamic government failed to foster the support from other state agencies and was constantly subjected to non-cooperation from other state institutions.[10]

The new ruling party failed to comprehend that the security and economy were closely related to each other and could not prosper unless one assured the other. The division and deep polarization of the society among the Islamists, moderates and secularists are obvious in the case of Egypt.

Since the election was held just after ten months of the revolution and people's votes were the votes of protest and votes to do away not just with the regime alone but also with the system itself. It was also a failure on the part of the Islamists to consider that anti-Mubarak votes belonged to the Islamists and they were the natural inheritor of the power in Egypt. The Islamists takeover cannot be attributed to its ideological appeal alone but it was also because of the absence of other voices in the last sixty years. The response of Islamists to social upheaval was one of the key reasons for their success.[11]

The FJP was overenthusiastic about election verdict it received, but it forgot that Egypt had witnessed it earlier too. There have been instances in the past in Egypt where a high mandate could not help the party to implement its agenda. The Wafd Party's government, which after the revolution of 1919 had captured more than 90 percent seats in the national assembly election of 1923, lasted merely ten months.[12] In three decades of its existence until 1952, the Wafd Party was destined to capture the power six times out of ten elections held, but the total duration of its rule did not exceed seven years. It shows that centres of power are not merely represented in the majority votes or in the strength of political parties but true political power is represented in state apparatus.

---

[10] Hiba Rauf Izzat, 'Ma-Baad-al-Islamiyah: Nazratun-Naqdiyah'., *Al-Demoqeratiya*, no. 52 (October 2013): 112–15.

[11] Noah Feldman, *The Fall and Rise of Islam* (Princeton: Princeton University Press, 2008), 3.

[12] Tariq Bashri, 'Ilaqatu-al-Din Bid-Daulah: halat-al-Misr badas-Saurah' [State and the Religion in Post-revolutionary Egypt], *Al-Mustaqbal al-Arabi* 407 (2013): 80–100.

There is a need for pragmatism rather than ideology to deal with the new emerging realities and perhaps this was the reason which forced youths to come out of the ideological burden and form their own pragmatic group. The commitment to pluralism is a prerequisite for political and economic renewal of the Arab world and it must be demanded of every one, Islamists and secularists alike. Instead of marginalizing the Islamists and fearing them, all countries need to ensure that no group can monopolize the truth, rule indefinitely and deny the right of others. Pluralism cannot survive unless all parties concede that only state can carry the arms, in line with the Weber's monopoly of the legitimate use of physical forces theory.[13]

Both the secularists and Islamists need to work harder for the democracy and to advance accountability. It is a time when the politics should replicate the ideology and the Islamists should come out of their ideological cover, guide their political behaviours in the light of modern realities, go for assimilation instead of politics of isolation and exclusion, and should be subservient to the politics of absorption. Now new groups of youths have emerged to bring the ideology out of politics, opting to think independent of the religion and calling for a discourse with a primacy to the civilian issues. There are numerous instances in the history where ideology gets defeated by politics and the same might be seen in the Arab world in the near future. There are also evidences of ideological rhetoric of opposition turns into political pragmatism in the power. Ideological rhetoric is replaced by practicalities in the practice and power makes one forget the politics of ideology and principles.

Now the Islamists will have to break the fort of the religion that they have erected around themselves. Most of the Islamists see democracy still as a means of the governance but forget to concede it as a part of political culture. Democracy is a foundation to learn the means of the governance, its philosophical engagement is must and one cannot pick the one element of democracy and abandon the others.

---

[13] Marwan Muasher, *The Second Arab Awakening and the Battle for Pluralism* (London: Yale University Press, 2014), 167.

Democracy cannot root and sustain itself unless it is derived from the civilizational and cultural core of given geographical landscape. It is not a task of politics to make people religious or fix their religious orientation; instead, it should aim to cater to the interest of the community. Politics is about the programme and social and economic projects to seek the legitimacy from the masses. It is for the religion alone to transform the religious consciousness of the masses. Politics will not remain politics if it moves out to achieve some other objectives.

State is a pragmatic institution and through it people want their needs to be fulfilled. The state is an institution based on the accord and not a thought or set of beliefs. It cannot be a preaching institute because it would not help resolve the poverty and other issues of present time. Democracy cannot be achieved without putting faith in the value of man. Political Islam has wasted a lot of time in the politicization of the religion and that is how they reached to the zenith of the power but they failed to present a model state for the Muslim community itself, let alone the whole political community. Political Islam ignores the preliminary side of the political engagement with the people who are the real motive behind the formation of the state.

Islamists too along with other political players must develop serious economic programme and should stop wasting energy in declaring each other backward and irrelevant, and if one thinks that Islamists are gone, they are wrong. They cannot be stopped away from participating in the democracy, and historically pushing the Islamists out of political process has historically resulted in a cycle of violence and retaliation—a process that ultimately radicalized the Islamists. The Islamic groups may once again take shelter in the politics of violence and if not the core group, there may emerge other factionalism within which they might challenge the central leadership and take the arms. MBH of Egypt may abet other radical groups like Salafist Jihadist when they are on retreat but at the same time they make some cohesion with the liberals to counter the ideologies of the Salafists who are hobnobbing with the army after the exit of MBH. MBH enjoys all influences over the Salafist jihadist and it is evident from the fact that the number of attacks in Sinai had lessened after the arrival of Morsi to the power.

Morsi too had claimed that if he had come to power, the attacks in the peninsula would be stopped.

Arab world is the mosaic of ethnic and religious communities and while the Arab prides itself on its diversity, its politics and culture do not meet the rhetoric. What they need to respect are the rights of all minorities and no ethnic community or sect should be treated like a second-class citizens. Inclusion is, therefore, a core component not only of political pluralism but also of social, geographical and political cohesion. There is a general perception that democracy is the cure for every solution but that is not true. What is important is real political transformation involving freedom and justice; there should be a combination of social justice and free economy and there should also be links between security and freedom and between nation and the globe. It is the time for Arab to learn to respect the justice and rights of others, and they should evolve a culture of debates and discussions which is the true ethos of democracy.[14]

Masses chose to bring the Islamists to the power in the name of democracy and to establish a civil state, and accordingly the Islamists should respond to it and come up with a project of modernity to bring them out of their material backwardness. People should be brought out of intellectual and scientific ghettoism to earn the political legitimacy and popular acceptance and to prepare a blueprint away from idealism of Islam in a world so complicated itself. No thought in this world should be statist or frozen but it should move and transform with the changing time. What is required is to shrink the gap between the historic religious discourse and the reality of the modern politics. It is not the change that needed to be paced, rather the pace that needed to be changed.[15] The situation is crystallized at different levels after the Arab Spring, and one needs to see how the nature of politics changes in the region.

Similarly, the culture of freedom is completely absent from the land of the Arab world. In the post-revolutionary era, Arab

---

[14] Jasser Auda, *Baynal-Shariah wa-l-Siyasah: Aselah Ma badas-Sauraat*, 58.

[15] Yafi Wissam, 'Pacing Change or Changing Pace', *Al-Jazeera*, 21 March 2011. http://newrealitiesinanoldworld.blogspot.in/2011/03/op-ed-pacing-change-or-changing-pace.html

masses should strive to advance the project for freedom and the question of freedom must be prioritized over the application of Islam in civil and political life.[16] Men should enjoy all sort of freedom to accept or reject the Islamic project of different Islamic groups active in the region. Islam has different meanings and different interpretations for different sets of people, and it is the primacy of freedom which would provide all space to accept or reject one particular interpretation and this absence of freedom leads to ascendancy of extremist ideas.

Likewise, there should be a campaign for the rule of law in practice and culture and it should be preceded by a legal reform. Sovereignty or rule of law is an indissoluble part of Islamic legal system and the principle of Islamic shariah itself commands that law should be equal for all whether he is strong or weak, ruler or ruled, young or old.[17]

There can be splits among different Islamic groups who had been the part of alliance in past given the isolation of the MBH and its exclusion from the national political process or reconciliation. The ideological gap and the difference might diminish because of the growing frustration among these groups and all may choose or resort to the politics of violence. The Salafists might emerge as the most powerful political force and it may be owed to two reasons: Army in Egypt would like to go along with Salafists with intent to convey the feelings that army was not anti-Islamic per se but were opposed to the exclusive ideology of MBH. Other, the Salafists would like to dominate and fill the vacuum left by the MBH and would not allow the other liberals or secularists to take over that space. One may also observe a noticeable transformation in the political stance of the Salafists having learnt a bitter lesson from the confrontation between the military and the MBH.

Ideological division and Islamic–secular polarization will divert the energy towards something else. This ideological contestation and political battle will exhaust the entire national project. This would hamper the peaceful transition to the democracy and create narrow interest groups in the country.

---

[16] Auda, *Baynal-Shariah wa-l-Siyasah*, 59.
[17] Auda, *Baynal-Shariah wa-l-Siyasah*, 61.

The ideological battle may be transformed into a class struggle as liberals and secularist are taken to be from an elite and rich class and it will be a prolonged struggle. The constant demand on the part of the liberals for the exclusion of the Islamists from the political sphere would create a situation full of conflict. The liberals being more open and receptive to political changes should show all sorts of tolerance.

Elections in Tunisia and Egypt have made it clear that changes have not sunk deep enough and they do no seem to be spread wide enough yet. The old force remains intact but this would not last long. Much of the fear of Arab democrats and Islamists calling for democracy was grounded in its negative association with the liberal democracy of the West-like agenda of promotion of democracy. At present, Arab public seems to have little in common beyond the immediate objective of overthrowing despotic rulers. Social forces are either nascent or remnants of regime's brutality. Pluralism is still a vague concept and diverse political agendas invite more discord than cooperation.[18]

The issue of democratization within the Islamic project will be the biggest challenge in the ensuing days. The political Islamic movement should not be oblivious of the fact that a true political movement should be ready to fill the vacuum left by the predecessors. The Islamists should make all efforts to allay all apprehension the liberals and secularists are harbouring after their arrival to the helm of the affairs.

The basic hurdle to the transition of the Arab societies lies with emancipating the Arab culture and political thoughts as prerequisite for fostering individualism. Political liberation without social and economic liberation is a recipe for anarchy and prolonged instability. Arabs everywhere are developing a test for freedom and personal expression. The freedom of expression is primarily a building block of democracy, but it is counterproductive without the recognition of others and existence of an inclusive political community. This is the time for creativity about the future where investment and sustainability,

---

[18] Khashan Hilal, 'The Arab Spring and Democratization in the Middle East', *World Affairs* 16, no. 4 (2012): 132–47.

not consumerism and militarism, are the bedrock of the Arab development.

Arab society needs to make a political community based on the rule of laws and consensus on fundamental rule of exchange. A prerequisite for ushering in this daunting process involves advancing an independent critical thinking in order to equip entrants into politics with negotiation skills that accommodates the others and recognises the merits of others. Arab needs to learn to disagree respectfully.

As far as India is concerned, it needs a multi-pronged and long-term strategy to deal with the new Arab world. I have noted in the previous section how India was also completely baffled and astounded over the sudden upsurge of the mass movement in the Arab world against the incumbent regimes. India dealt with the complex situations in accordance with its huge economic interest involved in the region. Moreover India never wants to be seen as an interventionist power and at the same time not letting its multiple interest be hampered. There were a few prominent factors, which guided and reflected the Indian response to the Arab Spring, namely the protection of national interests, safety and welfare of overseas citizens, maintaining equilibrium at home, re-enforcing principles of state sovereignty and non-intervention, and inclination towards preserving the status quo. India also adopted a multi-pronged policy on the international forum and there were lack of consistency too which was reflected in cases of Libya and Syria.

One of the biggest challenges for India is to prevent itself from falling into the orbit of Iran and Saudi Arabia — two hegemonic rivals in the region, and both an insoluble source of energy for India. Moreover, India's growing energy requirement is met by the oil-rich countries of the Arab world. Currently, the Gulf region, including Iran, alone supplies about 60 percent of India's total import of oil and natural gas. India's economic concern in dealing with the new Arab world was followed by its worry for its trapped workers and employees in the Arab Spring-infested countries. The security and safety of its people were the major source of concern for the government and similar was the case during the Gulf Wars I and II and Lebanese war of 2006. The total number of Indian workers varies from four to six million and there is no exact report in this regard. The safety of Indians overseas prompted the Indian government to take an immediate measure to evacuate them from the conflict zone. Moreover, India is highly conscious of the large-scale presence of the Shiite sect in the country before making any policy statement given the sectarian character of the violence in countries such as Syria, Iraq and Lebanon and involvement of two Sunni–Shiite rivals in the region: Saudi Arabia and Iran.

Apart from this traditional stance of passivity and indifferent attitude and act-merely-on-temporary basis, there was no clear or ideal response from India's side which was subjected to large-scale condemnation and some described the Indian policy, 'the silence is the gold'. This 'fence sitting attitude' on the part of India was criticized more when India saw itself as a great power, and international community also wants India to share the responsibility if it desires to be accepted as a global power. In the 21st century, India cannot afford to be adhered to its cold war era policy of equidistance. This is an era of evolving multilateral world system where world has been divided into multiple blocks and what is required now is an assertive policy but without sacrificing national and regional interest. Here, one is not exhorting to abandon the core ideals of foreign policy, but adherence does not necessarily mean stagnation and status quo when world is changing every moment and what happens in the confines of the nation becomes global in a fraction of a second.

It is time for India to not only activate its foreign policy but also determine the priority in the world politics, and it should divest itself of over-involvement in other regions to pay adequate attention. The dwindling political engagement must be corrected and must take cognisance of the growing significance of the region, not only for the sake of oil but also for growing proximity of the region and enhancing danger of global extremism and terrorism, and the region happens to be the hub of them. Growing cooperation to combat terrorism between India and few Gulf nations is a good sign but more needs to be done in this regard. India needs to stride a conscious path while dealing with the Arab–Persian war. Moreover, India needs to monitor the emerging fault lines in the region after the Arab Spring. The Arab Spring is a major source of instability in the whole region, which might affect the sectarian coherence here as well. India should try hard to prevent this cleavage in its own country because the presence of large number of Shiite might lead to this fragmentation.

Epilogue: Islamic State of Iraq and Syria

Amidst the array of narrative and counter-narrative about the origin, evolution and prospective multi-layered implications of the Arab uprising, a new phenomenon emerged in the Arab world, which not only changed the contours of discourse about Arab politics but also changed the entire trajectory of political developments in the region. This phenomenon is known across the world as the Islamic State of Iraq and Syria (ISIS).

The new jihadism has not ushered in a new era of extremist and radical Islamic polity only but has impacted the political and geostrategic dynamics of the region and opened a new chapter in the strategic polity of the Arab world. It has introduced a new set of politics, created an additional faultiness and engendered new alliances in the region, which has, again, made West Asia a hostage to the politics of regional and global power when one had begun to assume that the Arab uprising would not only get rid of prolonged and lingering autocracy but also be a free and autonomous entity in the global politics.

Much has been written and is still being explicated to narrate the story of its origin and evolution. Some have attributed its evolution and emergence on the political horizon to the exclusive and exploitative sectarian politics in Iraq in the wake of the demise of Saddam's regime, subsequent assertion and intervention of Iran in the region, and execution of divisive policy in so-called liberated Iraq at the behest of the United States. What has been more startling and alarming about the ISIS is the pace at which it acquired a global phenomenon, and very soon it was the possessor of huge territories in both Iraq and Syria. One of the special operation commanders of the United

States stated: 'We have not defeated the idea and even we do not understand the idea'.[1]

The world came to know about the ferocity and the real objectives of ISIS when they declared, at the beginning of January 2014, in Fallujah in Iraq, an Islamic state, and its statement said: 'We declare Fallujah an Islamic state and we are here to defend you from the army of Maliki (erstwhile Prime Minister of Iraq) and Iranian Safavid'.[2] They did not stop there only, and very soon on 29 June 2014, on the first day of the holy month of Ramadan, ISIS declared itself as a caliphate, with Abu Bakr al-Baghdadi as Caliph Ibrahim, calling all Muslims around the world to immediately express loyalty to the caliphate.[3]

The document, 'The Promise of Allah', which carries the declaration of the establishment of caliphate, says:

> There only remained one matter, a *Wajib-e-Kifayah* (collective obligation) that the Umma sins by abandoning. It is a forgotten obligation. The Umma has not tasted honor since they lost in 1924 when Kamal Ataturk abolished the Caliphate. It is a dream that lives in the depths of every Muslim believer. It is a hope that flutters in the heart of a monotheist. It is the caliphate. It is the Caliphate—the abandoned obligation of the era.[4]

It was the time when they controlled the territories worth the size of 423 miles in Iraq and Syria.[5] This bold move on the part of

---

[1] Graeme Mood, 'What Does ISIS Really Want'. *The Atlantic*, March 2015, http://www.theatlantic.com/magazine/archive/2015/03/what-isis-really-wants/384980/ (Accessed on 22 December 2015).

[2] Yasir Ghazi and Tim Arango, 'Iraq Fighter, Qaeda Allies Declare Fallujah an Islamic State'. *New York Times*, 3 January 2014. http://www.nytimes.com/2014/01/04/world/middleeast/fighting-in-falluja-and-ramadi.html?_r=1 (Accessed on 5 January 2015).

[3] Pieter van Ostaeyen, 'The Islamic States restores the Caliphate'. *Pietervanostaeyen*, https://pietervanostaeyen.wordpress.com/2014/06/29/the-islamic-state-restores-the-caliphate/ (Accessed on 24 August 2014).

[4] Abu Muhammad al-Adnani Al-Shami, 'This Is the Promise of Allah', Alhayat Media Centre, 19 June 2014, https://ia902505.us.archive.org/28/items/poa_25984/EN.pdf (Accessed on 12 August 2015).

[5] Charles Lister, 'Profiling the Islamic State' (analysis paper, Brooking Doha Centre, November 2014), http://www.brookings.edu/research/reports2/2014/12/profiling-islamic-state-lister (Accessed on 10 January 2016).

so-far-unknown entity had come when they had captured within twenty-four hours large swaths of territories in the northern town of Mosul in Iraq after ousting the US-trained Iraqi army on 9–10 June 2014. They not only captured the town but also issued a charter for the city, outlining new laws for the land. The regulations imposed on the cities were the same that were already imposed in the town of Raqqa in Syria. The ISIS was able to fill that vacuum through a set of administrative laws, including humanitarian, economic and educational services to the people in the absence of state welfare policies there.[6]

Very soon, the ISIS became a territorial entity and when its chief made his first public appearance on 4 July 2014, it had full control, from the al-Bab of Aleppo in Syria to Suleiman Bek of Saladin province of Iraq to Raqqa in Syria as its proclaimed capital.[7] What is more surprising is that only before the capture of Mosul, the total net value of ISIS's wealth was around US$875 million and it was assessed to be earning around US$2 million of revenue by selling or smuggling the oil of Iraq.[8]

Year of Its Evolution

Like Al-Qaeda and other radical Islamist movements, the ISIS has its origins in the troubled West Asia and its neighbourhood but under different time and space. Their growth and expansion also followed the similar (not-so-similar) trajectories. ISIS has objectives more or less similar to those of its predecessors to pursue the policy and strategies to guide their foot soldiers to establish their credentials, legitimize their causes, expand their reach and strengthen their bases by mobilizing recruitments and

---

[6] Lister, 'Profiling the Islamic State'.
[7] Lister, 'Profiling the Islamic State'.
[8] Luay Al Khatteeb, 'UN Strikes Back at ISIL's Black Money'. *The Huffington Post.* http://www.huffingtonpost.com/entry/the-un-strikes-back-at-isil_b_5702240.html?section=india (Accessed on 24 August 2014).

creating ideologues and sympathizers. In *Dabiq*,[9] the IS instigates the sentiments of Muslims in the Arab world.

> The time has come for those generations that were drowning in oceans of disgrace, being nursed on the milk of humiliation, and being ruled by the vilest of all people, after their long slumber in the darkness of neglect—the time has come for them to rise.[10]

One of its other statements claims,

> The time has come for the Umma of Muhammad (PBUH)) to wake up from its sleep, remove the garments of dishonor, and shake off the dust of humiliation and disgrace, for the era of lamenting and moaning has gone, and the dawn of honor has emerged anew.[11]

For the last fifteen years, Al-Qaeda affiliates had been gaining ground in the region and more effectively in those nations that have become vulnerable, such as Syria, Lebanon, Iraq and other bordering states, particularly after the Arab uprising, which left many states disunited with collapsed state institutions. The ISIS has been frequently heard proclaiming they are 'Lasting and Expanding'. If the deep consolidation of ISIS can be attributed to power vacuum in the region in the wake of the Arab uprising and particularly the rise of sectarian political divide and its execution, then the real origin may be dated back to the persisting politics of last days of the second millennium when its father figure, Abu Musab al-Zarqawi, was released from the jail of Jordan after serving the term for possession of weapons and being the member of Bay'at al-Imam (House of Leader).

Zarqawi, after his release, moved to Afghanistan and wanted to revive his contact with the jihadists, and by the time the US forces launched its campaign in Iraq in 2003, the Zarqawi group

---

[9] *Dabiq* is the English magazine of ISIS, which is named after a place in Syria where the ISIS is said to have begun its mission in Syria.

[10] 'The Return of Khalifah'. *Dabiq*, 1, no. I (1435 Ramadan: June 2014), 8.

[11] Jessica Stern and J.M. Berger, 'Islamic States'. *The Guardian*, 9 March 2015 http://www.theguardian.com/world/2015/mar/09/how-isis-attracts-foreign-fighters-the-state-of-terror-book (Accessed on 5 December 2015).

had consolidated itself in the vicinity of Mosul and that was the beginning of the real consolidation of Zarqawi's jihadist agenda in the Arab world. The year 2003–04 witnessed an intense phase of suicidal attacks and suicidal car bombings in and around the prominent official and global official buildings like UN offices in Iraq's cities, including the attacks against the Shiite shrine, and a revered Shiite clergy, Mohammad Baqir al-Hakim, the spiritual leader of the Supreme Council for the Islamic Revolution in Iraq, was also killed in a bomb attack.[12]

Zarqawi's entire theological underpinning was based on anti-Shiite rhetoric whom he considered a heretic and inside enemy of Islam, and he very often invoked medieval jurists to target the Shiite; he referred to Shiite: 'They are the enemy. Fight them. Beware of them, By God, they lie'.[13] This was the time when the influence of Al-Qaeda was waning in Iraq and its cadres were deserting in mass and paying allegiance to the leadership of Zarqawi. After an intense phase of negotiation for eight months, Zarqawi paid allegiance to Osama and Al-Qaeda.[14] From then onwards, the JTWT was known as Al-Qaeda in Iraq (AQI). But the difference between the two persisted because of the sectarian focus in the ideological and operational milieu of Zarqawi, who always maintained that Shiites are equally responsible for the predicament and vulnerability of the Muslim world, unlike his master in Al-Qaeda in Pakistan and Afghanistan who, of course, had some animosity towards the Shiite but nothing to the magnitude and enormity of Zarqawi. Zarqawi wanted an immediate result for his strategy and imminent fruit in the form of fulfilment of Islamic objectives, but Al-Qaeda leadership was more for an evolutionary change and patient strategy to defeat the Western powers. However, nothing stopped Zarqawi from accomplishing his self-woven thread of dream of establishing an Islamic state and he would compromise for nothing less than an Islamic state.

---

[12] Lister, 'Profiling the Islamic State'.

[13] *Zarqawi Letter*, US Department of State Archive, 4 February 2004, English translation of letter from Zarqawi was received by United States government in Iraq. http://2001-2009.state.gov/p/nea/rls/31694.htm

[14] AlJamma Hussan Hussain Ali Ahl Islam, 'How to Face the War of Technology', *Maskar Al-Battar*, no. 21: 20014 https://ia600407.us.archive.org/6/items/AL-BATAR-Leaflet/021.pdf

There was no decline in the pre-eminence of AQI on either the ideological or the pragmatic levels, and its expansion was intertwined with forging a major alliance with other dominant resurgent Islamic groups. These new alliances made AQI more powerful and visible in the ongoing resurgence against the US forces and other Shiite militias which were conceived to be a heretic in the eyes of AQI's ideological teaching. The AQI was so entrenched in the resurgence of Iraq that even the death of Zarqawi in June 2006 could not bring any sign of its waning influence. The new leader of AQI within four months paid allegiance to the Islamic State of Iraq (ISI) leader, Abu Bakr al-Baghdadi.

The rapid rise of ISI and its consolidation in the political dynamics of Iraqi transitional phase brought altogether a sea change in the Iraq–US strategy to counter the sectarian and military influence of ISI. A new Sunni tribal council (Sahwa) was formed in the areas of ISI dominance in Anbar Province to combat the Sunni-centric ideology and military strength of ISI force. This *Sahwa* (awakening) had the full support of the US forces and local police. Sahwa militia with the knowledge of local geographical terrains proved a catalyst in weakening the ISI. The involvement of Sahwa against the ISI turned the entire insurgency into a full-fledged sectarian battle in Iraq, which was demonstrated in a major car bomb attack by the suicide bombers of the ISI against a Yazidi village in northern Iraq, killing more than 800 people in August 2007.[15]

However, the gradual withdrawal of the US forces from Iraq and the subsequent political upheaval in the Arab world, causing a major power vacuum in different countries, brought another upsurge among the members of ISI as Sahwa was on the retreat. ISI kept on expanding its bases in the country and, moreover, the exclusive policy of the erstwhile regime in Iraq led by Nouri al-Maliki also helped in widening its appeal among the Sunni majority. Meanwhile, ISI's frequent attacks in Iraq had rendered the erstwhile regime completely vulnerable. For

---

[15] 'Yazidis in Iraq: A Tough Time'. *The Economist*, 13 November 2013, http://www.economist.com/blogs/pomegranate/2013/11/yazidis-iraq (Accessed on 20 December 2015).

instance, on 15 August 2011 alone, it conducted twenty-two coordinated bombings in the city of Baghdad and twelve other locations.[16]

Now ISI had attained a level of the full-fledged state where it had established a full intelligence, bureaucratic and judicial system, distributing much higher salaries to its cadres than what the Iraqi government employees were receiving. It was their intelligence service that helped to locate and identify the place of imprisonment of the Sunni populace who were later made free.

What turned the fate of ISI was the outbreak of the Arab uprising, paving the way for its further expansion into Syria. Syrian fighters had close ties with Iraq, and according to reports around 80–90 percent fighters were flocking from Syria alone during the height of the insurgency in Iraq.

The current civil war in Syria was fully exploited by the ISI, and it helped to make inroads into the battlefield very soon and established itself as a major force in the politics of the country. Baghdadi sent his men under the stewardship of Jowlani to open a new affiliate of ISI in Syria, which later emerged on the global scene in January 2012 as Jubhat al-Nusra (Victory Front). Very soon, because of some political and ideological differences, the Victory Front and ISI became arch-enemies of each other, and the leadership of the front denied having any sort of association with the ISI.

Having seen the ease and comfort at which the Victory Front captured the territories in parts of Syria, Baghdadi also turned towards Syria and announced that Victory Front was a part of ISI, but it was denied by the independent leadership of Jowlani. This contestation and confrontation between the two became a ground for the further estrangement between the two, later enhancing the sphere of ISI into Syria, which later became the ISIS. Now, Syria became the hub of ISIS activities, where it was confronted by the regime of Assad, moderate forces of opposition and militias of Victory Front.

---

[16] *Reuters*, 'Fact Box: Security Developments in Iraq'. 15 August 2011, http://www. trust.org/item/?map=factbox-security-developments-in-iraq-august-15/ (Accessed on 20 August 2014).

Meanwhile, Al-Qaeda also announced to abandon the ISIS. It was on 29 June 2014 when the ISIS announced the caliphate with Abu Bakr al-Baghdadi as the head of the caliphate, and the town of Raqqa in Syria became its capital. The ISIS issued a series of video cassettes explicating the aims and objectives of the ISIS, calling to end the Sykes–Picot agreement and breaking the false Arab borders. One of the videos was about the creation of caliphate.

This body claimed the territories between Aleppo town of Syria and a large swath of territories in the eastern part of Iraq. It became very difficult for an already crumbling regime to check the march of ISIS, which kept on grabbing more and more territories. There are reports of thousands of people joining the ISIS in its fight against the regime in Syria, and even thousands of blue-eyed youths from Western countries joined it. According to one report, ISIS and other terrorist organizations have been joined by around 25,000 youth from more than 100 nations in the recent past.[17] ISIS has emerged as a terrifying entity in recent past, which is not only involved in killing and cleansing but is also bent on destroying the antiques of the past. The destruction of the Arch of Triumph in the city of Palmyra is a living example which was condemned worldwide.

The Director-General of UNESCO stated that the destruction shows how terrified the extremists are to history and culture because understanding the past undermines and delegitimize the pretext they use to justify their crimes.[18]

Even the coalition forces led by the United Sates have failed to check the expansion of ISIS, as President Obama himself has been reported saying that ISIS is a long-term phenomenon.[19]

[17] 'Extremist Terrified of History, UNESCO Chief says, Deploring Destruction of Arch of Triumph in Palmyra', United Nations: Meeting Coverage and Press Release, 24 September 2014. http://www.un.org/press/en/2014/sc11580.doc.htm

[18] http://www.un.org/apps/news/story.asp?NewsID=52170#.VhW8-24bHIV

[19] Christopher R. Hill, '*Minal Mutasabbib Fi Azamatil-Lajeeen*' [The Reason for the Refugee Crisis], *Al-Jazeerah*, 23 September 2015, http://www.aljazeera.net/knowledge-gate/opinions/2015/9/29/%D9%85%D9%86-%D8%A7%D9%84%D9%85%D8%AA%D8%B3%D8%A8%D8%A8-%D9%81%D9%8A-%D8%A3%D8%B2%D9%85%D8%A9-%D8%A7%D9%84%D9%84%D8%A7%D8%AC%D8%A6%D9%8A%D9%86 (Accessed on 5 January 2016).

Today, around 60 percent of territories in Syria are under the control of ISIS and one does not know what is in the offing in the country because it does not acknowledge any opposition groups in Syria and they stand for eliminating anyone they deem to be heretic. The latest involvement of Russia in air strikes has further complicated the already entangled crisis.

Ideology and Strategy of ISIS

When it comes to defining the ideology and strategy of the ISIS, it is completely different from other contemporary or previous Islamist organizations. The US State Department Deputy Secretary for Iran and Iraq stated that it is worse than Al-Qaeda and it is no longer a terrorist organization. It is a full-blown army.[20] Its primary ideology is drawn from the basic assumption that religion should be the instrumental part of governing the state and the society, and there must be no difference between the region and the state. What it argues further is that no decree of religion can be executed without the assistance of the state. What differentiates the ISIS is the method, approach, strategy and the necessary condition to establish its own version of an Islamic state. The ISIS glorifies jihad and calls upon Muslims to become martyrs and victorious. It writes in one issue of *Dabiq*: 'The sun of jihad has risen. The glad tidings of good are shining. Triumph looms on the horizon. The signs of victory have appeared'.[21]

ISIS has shown a strong commitment to restore the golden age of the prophetic era of the Muslims by 're-establishing' or 'reviving' the caliphate.[22] In *Dabiq*, the ISIS writes, '[T]he goal of establishing the Caliphate has always been one that occupied

[20] Kristina Wong, 'ISIS is now "full-blown army" official Warns'. *The Hills*, 23 July 2014. http://thehill.com/policy/defense/213117-us-officials-warn-isis-worse-than-al-qaeda (Accessed on 23 December 2014).

[21] Stern and Berger, 'Islamic States'.

[22] The AQ also believes in re-establishing Caliphate but first it emphasizes correcting the basics of the Muslims, while the IS talks of the 'revival', the practice of

the hearts and minds of the mujahidin since the revival of jihad this century'. Similarly, in an English magazine, *Resurgence*,[23] Zawahiri also proclaims the establishment of a caliphate and Islamic state. He says:

> The Islamic State will be established—by the help and will of Allah—at the hands of the free, sincere and honorable Mujahedeen. It will be established with their sacrifices, generosity, consent and collective choice.[24]

One of the core objectives of the missionary zeal of both has been to implement the shariah of their own literal interpretation, rebutting the Western political system and removing its influence from all spheres of Muslims' life, including culture, education, lifestyle and cleaning society by whipping up anti-US/West sentiments, The ISIS condemned and attacked the local allies of the West as apostate, calling the Muslims to wage a war against them. The ISIS resorts to violence as a means to achieve its goals and has proved more brutal and inhumane than the other contemporary groups.

One can determine its approach to the establishment of the Islamic state and the caliphate by their immediacy of establishing the state in complete variance with all the previous Islamist teachings that called for the gradual Islamization of the society first entwined with a pragmatic approach to the final execution of the Islamic design.

Their stern belief in the medieval theology is well reflected in the appointment of the caliphate in the form of Abu Bakr al-Baghdadi. He was appointed to the post because of his Quresh lineage (lineage of the Prophet) in concurrence with some of the puritanical medieval theology that envisages that head of the caliphate should be preferably from the lineage of the Quresh, like the Prophet. The ISIS focused more on the prophetic lineage

---

Caliphate, mentioned in the first Issue of English magazine *Dabiq*, 'The Return of Khalifah', Issue I, Ramadan 1435.

[23] *Resurgence* is the second English propaganda magazine of Al Qaida.

[24] Shykh Abu Dujan Al Pasha, 'Land of Prophet Waits You', *Resurgence*, Issue 1(Fall 2014), 38.

of Baghdadi than on any other norm while naming him the caliphate. They drew allegiance from the prophetic leadership and, moreover, they had an equal belief in controlling the territories very much in concurrence with the establishment of an Islamic state in the city of Medina by the Prophet.

Their rejection of any innovation or addition to the pure teaching of Islam is very much similar to the Salafist ideology, and zero tolerance for any other creed within Islam is well documented in the mass killing of those Muslims who in their eyes are nothing less than apostate and their doctrine allows to declare them heretics and eliminate them.[25] The philosophy of monotheism is very sacred in the teaching of ISIS, and they very often invoke this concept to propagate the ideas. Not an iota of disrespect to monotheism is acceptable within the camp of the ISIS. The strict form of the implementation of *hudud* (fixed Islamic punishment for serious crimes) is central to the edicts of ISIS's governance model. They have imposed in their sphere of political influence five-time prayer, banned alcohol, gambling and music, and imposed the Hijab.

One of the medieval theological edicts, *Dhimmi*, is also reported to have been in practice in the towns like Mosul and Raqqa controlled by the force of the ISIS. This practice has placed non-Muslims under the protection of the Muslim rulers as long as they pay Jizyah (tax imposed only on non-Muslims), an example drawn from the prophetic times in the city of Medina. Non-Muslims in these towns are prohibited from exhibiting any sign of their faith or carrying arms and making additional places of worship. People belonging to the Shiite and Christian groups are reported to have fled the place of living after their properties were confiscated under the laws of Jizyah and second-class citizenship status.[26] It was their faith in monotheism and hatred

---

[25] Shane Drennan, 'Constructing Takfir: From Abdullah Azzam to Djamel Zitouni'. Combating Terrorism Centre, 15 June 2008 https://www.ctc.usma.edu/posts/constructing-takfir-from-abdullah-azzam-to-djamel-zitouni (Accessed on 31 December 2015).

[26] Cathy Otten, 'Last Remaining Christians Flee Iraq's Mosul'. *Aljazeera*, 22 July 2014. http://www.aljazeera.com/news/middleeast/2014/07/last-remaining-christians-flee-iraq-mosul-201472118235739663.html (Accessed on 29 July 2014).

for heretic practices that made them justify the killing of Yazidis in large numbers in parts of Iraq. They not only justified the killing but also legalized the Yazidi women as their concubines.

Most of the religious edicts of the ISIS are the invocation of a medieval jurist who has exhorted for the supremacy of the Muslims through the imposition of the power across the territories. Their ideological proposition seems to centre on the theological obligation rather than on political compulsion, and within their ideological rubric there is no place for pretence and Islam in totality needs to practice where theology has overshadowed the core principles of the Quran. In a nutshell, their objective is to create a puritanical Sunni Islamic state where no other creed or sect confession would be allowed to exist.

Despite being touted as a next generation of jihadism in the Arab world, there are some stark differences between the ISIS and other present and previous Islamist movements. Unlike Al-Qaeda, which first tried to habituate and correct the common Muslims to lead a life based on the fundamentals of Islam and gradual purification of human souls and Islamization of the society through all possible means, including violence and extremism, ISIS wasted no time and very soon established the caliphate and declared Abu Bakr al-Baghdadi the caliph, the 'leader for entire Muslims of the world'. It boasted the revival of the caliphate after a gap of ninety years, which was abolished by Mustafa Kemal Ataturk in 1924.

The ISIS is the first entity among all the Islamist movements to occupy a large swath of land in Iraq and Syria, equal to the size of England or Jordan with around seven–eight million inhabitants. Looking at the expanding role of the ISIS, it appears that the organization has tried to emerge as a parallel 'quasi-radical' state by establishing provinces and its capitals, judicial courts, police stations, vigilance, media and foreign affairs departments in both Iraq and Syria. With its ideology and modern means of communication, the ISIS aims to reach the global Muslims and win their hearts and minds.

The ISIS also differs in their policies towards expansion, recruitment and the tools they adopt to propagate their ideologies and messages. The AQI had not been as ferocious as the ISIS even during its heyday. The former tried to expand its network by establishing pockets of influence in the WANA region and tried first to regroup the Mujahideen who fought in Afghanistan against Soviet Russia. Although the ISIS and other radical movements in Islam have similar views on some of the principles of Islam, the ISIS has proved more fanatical and hardliner than the later. For instance, both the groups are opposed to *shirk* (including other with the 'Oneness' of Allah) and declare that visiting any shrines and tombs is tantamount to committing *shirk*, which is a 'major sin' never to be forgiven by God. However, in practice, the AQI has hardly taken any firm action of destroying any shrines or tombs, whereas, since the beginning, the ISIS has continuously been destroying shrines, tombs and *Hussainiyahs* (congregation hall for Shiite commemoration), wherever it could.

What has surprised many about the ISIS is its strategy of mobilizing youth from across the continent. It possesses a huge compile of ammunitions, sophisticated weapons, tankers, armoured vehicles, rocket launchers, anti-tank guided missiles, field artilleries and numerous air defence systems, high-tech information equipment and other high-standard weapons, which one could perhaps have never imagined in the recent past that such small group would hold a small army of themselves. They have professional, organized and ideologically motivated groups who can sustain for a longer period of time. The recruits are from across the countries, and they are required to receive a vigorous training before joining the war on the battlefield. New members are trained to handle new weapons and to mobilize the youth on social media, and currently most of the recruitments are done through the social media.

Newcomers are trained in a way that they become both the religious preacher and warrior on the ground, to combat both the Muslim heretic groups and opponents on the field like the forces of the regime and other coalition forces. Their most immediate strategy is to spark the sectarian tensions to consolidate it because the regions where they are most active (Iraq and Syria) are ruled by Shiite regimes, while the Sunnis are in the majority. This tactical sectarian and majority–minority card would benefit them in mobilizing the majority Sunni against the minority Shiite rule. They have not employed their strategy against ideological opponent alone, but they are equally hostile to the Sunni groups who do not adhere to their puritanical ideology or fight their independent battle in Syria or Iraq.

Their strategy of generating huge revenue to sustain the prolonged war is also a naval idea, and this has put the ISIS on a different trajectory from all the pit predecessors who never employed a strategy to have a constant source of revenue. To fulfil their economic needs, they have captured a series of oil fields in the towns of Syria and most prominently in Iraq. They are reported to have been smuggling a huge amount of oil from the Iraqi oil fields. According to some media reports, Turkey is also buying oil from the ISIS-controlled refinery on a much cheaper price than the global oil market. An opposition member in Turkish parliament, writing in *Insurgentelligence*, accuses Turkey along with North Atlantic Treaty Organisation (NATO) of harbouring ISIS[27] and estimates the quantity of ISIS oil sales in Turkey at about US$800 million — that was over a year ago. At present, ISIS is able to acquire the deleverage necessary to have local dominance and its units control local affairs in the controlled territories. According to one of the British ISIS fighters, 'Our average day here is now normally much of the same manning checkpoints, going on patrolling in the areas, settling disputes between locals and the tribes and lot of meeting with village elders and local leaders'.[28]

The ISIS has various short-term and long-term goals to advance in the region. After having controlled a large swath of territories in Iraq and Syria and establishing its own reign, they are moving both westward and eastward and their presence is spreading to the region of South Asia and the European territories. One of its leaders claimed, 'we are getting strong every day in Sham and Iraq but it will not end there—of course, one day we will defeat all the *Taghut* (Oppressor) regime and bring back

---

[27] Nafees Ahmad, 'NATO is Harboring the Islamic Sates'. *Insurgentelligence*, 19 November 2015 https://medium.com/insurge-intelligence/europe-is-harbouring-the-islamic-state-s-backers-d24db3a24a40#.sw61sfknv (Accessed on 20 December 2015).

[28] Lister, 'Profiling the Islamic State'.

Islam to the whole region including the Jerusalem'.[29] Moreover, the growing sectarian strife in the region has eased their task of inflaming the battle in a different nation of the region. The absence of a state institution and a power vacuum in the wake of the Arab uprising is likely to strengthen it more in the near future. The more the discontent would be in the region, the more amicable environment the ISIS would get to prosper. The circumstances seem to be rife for its expansion, given the volatile situation in the region and, moreover, the sectarian identity they are inflaming in the region to reap the benefit of the deepening division in the Arab world.

In the last two years, the spread and consolidation of ISIS has changed the entire strategy of the global powers to reign in the ISIS. A catalyst moment came when the United States started air strikes in Syria with an apparent objective of eliminating the ISIS, a proposition that many never took at face value. It had become a long wait for Russia to confront the United States only diplomatically, and in October 2015, Russia also launched its own air strikes to eliminate the same global enemy: the ISIS.

The current war seems to be an unending one because it is not against territorial and national entity but non-state actors without any blueprint. The shooting down of the Russian plane in the Sinai region of Egypt and the subsequent attack in Paris in 2015 apparently by the ISIS have not only changed the entire image of the ISIS but also altered the nature of preceding discourse and strategy about the ISIS.

International terrorism in the form of the ISIS has pushed Russia and the West to work together but so far nothing substantial has been achieved against the ISIS despite constant bombardment against the known and unknown ISIS bases and their hideouts in Syria and Iraq. The rise of the ISIS has created several new alliances in the region, brought old political and ideological foes together, added a new chapter to the ongoing discourse on political Islam and has created new power vacuum in West Asia; moreover, one does not know how long this issue of the ISIS will linger on, how many new strategic avenues it

---

[29] Lister, 'Profiling the Islamic State'.

would open in the region and how many new disclosures on political Islam it would usher into.

Islamism Is No More a Ruling Ideology for Tunisia

We have seen how the vertical and horizontal spread of the ISIS across the globe has changed the trajectory of entire discourse on Islamism and divested it of the conventional understanding of the subject. On the other hand, what is happening today with regard to 'political Islam' in Tunisia is a complete departure from the past, and it is heading towards something that may be termed as 'civic Islamism' which is likely to deprive it of either Islam or politics. It is something that is undoing of MBH in Egypt and emulating of Justice and Development Party (AKP) in Turkey. Some are now also claiming that Ennahdha never had any ties with the MBH, and today its relationship with other Islamist politics and its own changing political identity seem to be natural outcomes of the existing situation in the country and in the region.

No doubt, the Ennahdha in Tunisia has maintained its distinctive ideological and political traits both amidst and following the uprising showing pragmatic elements in its day-to-day political behaviours. It entered into political alliance with the secular and far left forces of the country leading a troika government and, unlike MBH of Egypt, it was not swayed by the urge for the political power. In 2014, it stepped aside and allowed neutral interim government to take over the final drafting of the constitution and since January 2016, it holds a majority but does not stake claim for power. The last five years of its political journey and its engagement with other political forces offered some allusion about its political pragmatism inching towards a politics defined by civility and sensibility. One has seen how it played defensive in various transitional and coalition governments in the last five years and it took five years to gauge the national political pulses. One of the most fascinating debates in the history of Ennahdha took place in May 2016 when representatives of the first and second generations assembled to provide a new orientation to the party.

However, what surprised many in Tunisia and contemporaries of Ennahdha in other parts of the Arab world was its announcement of disengaging religion from the politics in the 10th congress of Ennahdha held in May 2016 in the capital town of Tunis. It was an explicit sign of Ennahdha evolving from defending identity to ensuring the democratic transition, and today it moves on to focus on the political issue of economic development, unemployment and corruption. This move represents a rebranding by Ennahdha and formalization of a long-brewing trend within the party.

The congress did not only redefine political ideology of Ennahdha but it also abandoned most of its ideological vision that was upheld from more than three decades. It has shown high level of professionalism and pragmatism and is trying to maintain its relations with the elements of deep state which must have come to them after the debacle in Egypt.

For the first time, it talked about distinguishing between the missionary work (religion) and full-fledged politics in day-to-day life of Ennahdha. By defending a new identity that separates the religion from politics, Ennahdha has turned an important corner on the way to a full-fledged civil political party. The party has passed this amendment to its ideological core with a majority of 800 plus votes to prove that several months of internal debates have come to full fruition for the reformist within the party. An effort has also been made to broaden the base of the decision-making body, and the executive body of the party has been further empowered. This was unthinkable before the Arab Spring of 2011 and, no doubt, it has produced a factionalism that is a part of evolving democratic culture and leads towards a check-and-balance exercise.

The congress talked of broadening its membership to include more and more youth and women, removing the earlier clause of 'morality', a prerequisite for becoming its member. It will not allow its members in parliament to hold leadership position in civil society (like social and charitable organizations) unlike in the past. Preachers will have to abandon their elective position in the national politics. Now the party has evolved from an opposition ideological movement to become a full-fledged national political party that requires swapping its baggage-ridden Islamist label. The first phase of Ennahdha was characterized by fear-driven competition between secularists and the Islamists, and the party feared that the counter-revolutionary forces in the style of Egypt's coup could reverse democratic gains and send the Islamists back to the prison or in exile.

The new narrative with Ennahdha has recast Islamism as a kind of situation-contingent liberation theology. According to one of its members, Islamism is not an ideology for ruling but it is a language of opposition. Many in Ennahdha now believe that Islamism is ill adapted to a context in which liberation has been achieved and in which religious parties must govern pragmatically.

Perhaps the party had adopted this novel approach to distinguish itself from other streams of political Islam in Egypt and Syria, which are in direct confrontation with the regimes. Moreover, the ISIS and Boko Haram have given a bad name to the existing Islamic political discourse and all are being clubbed together. This also seems to be an effort to redefine itself in opposition to other radical forces in addition to the ISIS. It is also a message to the detractors of the ISIS who have been advocating that all Islamists once come to power will impose dictatorship. The 10th congress of Ennahdha formally announced itself to be Muslim Democrats, like the Christian Democrats of Germany, seemingly inching closer to AKP of Turkey, which has of late shown a sign of entering into full-fledged national politics. This major shift in its political programme and ideological outline must have not come from top-bottom imposition but it must have been an outcome of internal democratic evolution coupled with intense debates and deliberations.

The congress has tripled the number of clauses in the existing constitution, which is reflective of it diversifying its focus on other national issues. Its policy priorities have shifted from defending the Arab-Islamic identity to addressing the material concerns of average Tunisians. Now the party does not seem to be hesitant in allying with others to broaden electoral base in order to show the sign of commonality. It was evident when the president of the country, Beji Caid Essebsi, was invited to be the keynote speaker at the inauguration of the 10th congress. It is the Nidaa Tounes party of the same president, which was established in 2012, that opposed Ennahdha alone. He had lambasted the party in the past as backward and supportive of terrorists and criminals, but in the 10th congress he endorsed the Ennahdha as a party moving in the right direction. He also stated that Ennahdha has become a civil party and Islam does not contradict democracy. These are the signs of movement towards adoption of a consensual and reconciliation approach in the future national politics. Ennahdha has chosen the safe path. Political movements themselves are living creatures, and sometimes fear and sensitive are not bad things, but these should drive a political movement with such a long history and sacrifice to make panicked and hasty decisions.

Glossary of Arabic Terms

Aayah
(pl. *'aayaat*): Quranic verse.

'Alim
(pl. *'Ulema*): Scholar, especially in religious matters.

Ansar: People at Medina who had extended all help to the Prophet and his companions.

Aqqidah: Belief, creed.

Bay'ah: Ceremony of investiture where fealty is pledged to the new leader.

Faqiih (pl. *fuqahaa'*): Muslim jurist.

Fatwah: An opinion articulated by an *'alim* on Islamic law.

Fiqh: Islamic jurisprudence.

Fitrah: Innate nature.

Hadith: A saying from, or anecdotes about, the Prophet Muhammad.

Hakimiyya: Sovereignty; a recent neologism, used extensively first by Sayyid Qutb.

Harakah: Action, movement.

Hijrah: Flight of Prophet Muhammad from Mecca to Medina on 24 September 622.

Hukm: In the Quran, it usually has the meaning of 'judge'; it has acquired the meaning of 'rule' in the eyes of modern Islamists.

Ibaadat: Act of worship that relate humans directly to God, in contrast to *mu'aamalaat* (explain further).

Ijma':	'Consensus' of the *'Ulema*; *'ijmaam'* is generally recognized as one of the bases of Islamic jurisprudence (*fiqh*).
'Ilm:	Learning, knowledge, science.
Imam:	Leader in *salaat* prayers; in *Shii'ah* Islam, the divinely ordained leader of the whole Muslim *ummah*.
Insaan:	Human being.
Insaaniyyah:	Humanism.
Iraadah:	Will.
Isnaad:	Chain of authority through which the authenticity of a *Hadith* is validated.
Istihsaan:	Use of discretionary opinion in cases where strict use of analogy (*qiyaas*) leads to undesirable results.
Jaabiriyyah:	Extreme predestination.
Jaahilii:	That which is related or pertains to *Jahiliyyah*.
Jahiliyyah:	Period before the advent of Islam; used by Mawdudi and then Qutb and other Islamists to denote a state of non-Islamic rule.
Jihad:	Striving to overcome challenges and obstacles; the term has come to be equated with warfare against unbelievers.
Karamaat:	Miracles.
Khalifa:	Vicegerent, custodian, deputy; the term is also used to describe successor to Muhammad's leadership of the *ummah*.
Khilafat:	Technically 'succession', but Qutb uses it with the meaning of vicegerency.
Khutbah:	Sermon given by the *imam* in the Friday prayer (*salaat*).
Kaafir (pl. *Kuffaar*):	Unbeliever.

Manhaj: Method, programme.

Maslaha: Interest, welfare.

Mu'aamalaat: Social relations, actions that engage human beings only; see in contrast *'ibaadaat*, which refers to relations between man and God.

Muftii: Religious scholar who has the authority to issue fatwa.

Musnad: Corpus of *Hadith* compiled by Ahmad ibn Hanbal (780–855).

Naamuus: Laws divinely ordained.

Nass: Explicit Quranic text.

Nizaam: Order, system.

Qaanuun: Law.

Qiyas: Analogy; analogical thinking.

Rabbaaniyyah: Divinely ordained.

Sahiih: Well supported in the chain of *isnaad*.

Salaat: Prayer.

Shahaadah: Testimony, especially that 'There is no God but Allah and the Prophet Muhammad is his messenger'.

Shar' or *shariah*:   The divinely ordained law that God has devised for human life.

Shii'ah: The second major sect in Islam; the other being the majoritarian *Sunni* sect.

Shirk: Association to the single sovereignty of God, that is, considering or treating entity other than God as a divinity.

Shura: Consultation between the ruler and his community.

Siirah: The Prophet's model of conduct.

Sunnah: The example of the Prophet.

Sunni: The major sect in Islam; the other major sect being the *Shii'ah*.

Taaghuut:	The oppressor, the usurper of God's sovereignty.
Tafssir:	The interpretation and explication of Quranic text.
Takfiir:	Declaring someone as unbeliever.
Talfiiq:	The invocation of opinions from various schools in Islamic orthodoxy, rather than the traditional exclusive acceptance of opinions from one school.
Taqliid:	Imitation.
Tasawwur:	Conception; Qutb often uses the term to mean 'paradigm' or 'world view'.
Tawhid:	The assertion of God's unity.
Ta'wiil:	The esoteric interpretation of the Quranic text.
Thawra:	Revolution.
Tulaqaa':	Meccan who did not join the ranks of the Prophet until after the surrender of Mecca.
Ubuudiyyah:	Submission in servitude to God.
'Ulema (sing. *'Alim*):	Official scholars in *fiqh* and *tafsiir*.
Uluuhiyyah:	The quality of being divine.
Ummah:	The entire Muslim community.
Ustaadh:	Professor.
Waaqi'iyyah:	Realism.
Wijdaan:	Existence.
Zakaat:	The compulsory proportion of wealth a Muslim must pay the poor.

Bibliography

Primary Sources/Arabic

Abu Zahra, Muhammad. *Ibn Taymiyyah: Hayatahu, Asrahu, Araahu was Fiquhu.* Beirut: Darul Fikr al-Arabi, n.d.

Ahmad, Al-Mousalli. *Jadliyat-al-Shura wa-al-Dimmuqeratiyyah: Al-Al-Qarni, Bahjat Al-Rabi-Al-Arabi Fi Misr-Al-Saurah wama Baadaha.* Beirut: Centre for Arab Unity Studies, 2012.

Ahmad, Mohammad Sharif. *Tajdid al-Mauqif al-Islami* [Renewal of Islamic Attitude]. Washington, DC: International Institute of Islamic Thought, 2004.

Al-Afghani, Sayyid Jamal al-Din. *Al-Urwa al-Wuthqa.* Cairo: Dar-al-Arab, 1957.

Al-Aqqad, Abbas M. *Abqariyyat Umar.* Beirut: Dar al-Kitab al-Arabi, n.d.

Al-Harkat al-Islamiyah wad-demoqaratiyyah. Beirut: Center for Arab Unity Studies, 2001.

Al-Mawardi, Abul Hassan Ali Bin Mohammad Bin Habib al-Basri. *Al-Ahkam al-Sultaniyyah-wa-al-Wilayatud-Diniyyah.* Beirut: Darul-Kitab-al Arabi, 1991.

Al-Sawani, Yusuf Mohammad Jumma. *Libya: Al-Saurah a-Tahaddiyatu-Bana-al-Daulah.* Beirut: Markaz-al-Dirasat-al Wahdah-al-Watniyyah, 2013.

Amin, Jala. *Maza Hadasa Lis-Saurah-al-Misriyah.* Cairo: Dar Al Shorouk, 2012.

Annadvi, Abul Hassan Muzakkarat. *Saih fi-shsharqil-Arabi.* Beirut: Muassasatur-Risalah, 1975.

Aqueel, Abdullah. *Min Aalamil-harkatil-Waddawt-Islamiyah-al Muasirah.* Kuwait: Maktabul-Manar-al Islamiyyah, 2001.

Ashmavi, Ali. *Al-TAreekh-al-Sirri-Lil-Ikhwan-al-Muslimeen.* Cairo: Mrkz-Ibn-Khaldoon, 2006.

Auda, Jasser. *Baynal-Shariah wa-l-Siyasah: Aselah Ma badas-Sauraat* [Between Islamic Law and Politics: What Is the Post-revolution Phase]. Beirut: Arab Network for Research and Publishing, 2012.

Azzam, Yusuf. *Ashshaheed Sayyed Qutb: Hayatahu wa Madrasatahu wa Asarahu.* Beirut: Darul Qalam, 1980.

Bakri, Mustafa. *Al-Jaish-wal-Ikhwan: Asrar Khalfal-al-Sataar.* Cairo: Darul-Misr-al-Labnaniyah, 2013.

Balqazir, Abdullah. *Ad-Daulah fil-Fikril Islami al-muasir.* Beirut: Center for Arab Unity Studies, 2002.

Banna, Hasan. *Majmuatu-Rasail-i-al-Imam-al-Shahid Hssan-al-Banna.* Beirut: Muassatu-Azzabi Littabah-wattauzi, n.d.

Biyanat-Al-Zikra-al-Tasees Liharkah-Annahzah-Al-Islamiyyah. Tunis: Nahza Publication, 2012.

Dimmuqeratiyyah wa Huququl Insaan Fil-Fikril-Islami. Beirut: Markazi-Dirasat-Al-Wahadatul-Arabiyyah, 2007.

Ghannuchi, Rashid. *Al-Harakaat-al-Islamiyyah wa-masalatu-Taghyeer.* Tunis: Darul Mujtahis Lin-Nashr wal-Tauzee, 2011.

———. *Muqarabat: Fil-Al aniyah wal-Mujtamaa-al-Madani.* Tunis: Darul Mujtahis Lin-Nashr wal-Tauzee, 2011.

Gharayba, M. Rahil. *Al-huquq-wal-hurriyat-al-siyasah fish-shariya-al-Islamiyah.* Washington, DC: International Institute of Islamic Thoughts, 2001.

Hassan, Ali Ibrahim. *Attarikh-al-Isla-al-Aam.* Cairo: Maktaba Annahzah al Misriyyah, n.d.

Hassan, Hassan Ibrahim. *Tarikh-e- Islam,* Part 4. Cairo: Maktaba Annahzah al Misriyyah, 1967.

Hussaini, Ishaq Mussa. *Al-Ikhwan-ul-Muslimun Kubra-al-Harkat-al-Islamiyah-al-Hadisah.* Beirut: Daru-Beirut Littabaah Wan-Nashr, 1955.

Imad, Abdul Ghani. *Islamiyyuna Baina-al Saurah wal-Daulah.* Beirut: Markaz-al-Dirasat-al Wahdah-al-Watniyyah, 2013.

Khabbas, Abdullah Auz. *Sayyed Qutb: Al-Adib al-Naqid.* Jordan: Maktab-al-Manar, 1983.

Khalidi, Salah Abdul Fattah. *Sayyed Qutb: Min-al-milaad-ilal-Istishhad.* Syria: Daral-Qalam, 1991.

Khan, Najeeb. *Kunto raeesan Li-Misr.* Cairo: Almaktab-Al-Misri-al-Hadith, 2003.

Laoust, Henry. *Nazariyyat Sheikh-al-Islam Ibn Taymiyyah fi-assiyasah wal Ijtama.* Translated by Abdul Azim Ali (Cairo: Dar-al-Manar, 1979).

Mahmood, Abdul Halim. *Al-Ikhwanul-Muslimun: Ahdas Sanat at-tarikh,* Part One. Alexandria: Darud-Dawah, n.d.

———. *Al-Ikhwanul-Muslimun: Ahdas Sanat at-tarikh.* Part Two. Alexandria: Darud-Dawah, n.d.

Mohammad Shauqi. *Tahrik-i-Ikhwanul-Mulsimin: Mazi aur Haal.* Translated by Rizwan Ali Nadvi. Karachi: Majilisi-Nashriyatu-Islam, 1999.

Qutb, Sayyed. *Ma'rakat al-Islaam wa al-ra'smaaliyyah.* Beirut: Dar Al Shorouk, 1951.

———. *Diraasaat Islaamiyyah* [Studies in Islam]. Beirut: Dar Al Shorouk, 1953.

———. *Haadaa al-diin.* Beirut: Dar Al Shorouk, 1960.

———. *Al-Islaam wa mushkilaat al-hadhara.* Cairo: Daru-Ihyail-Kutub-Al-Arabiyya, 1962.

———. *Al-Atyaf al-Arbaah.* Beirut: 1967.

———. *Al-'adaala al-ijtimaa'iyyah Fil-Islam.* Beirut: Dar Al Shorouk, 1967.

———. *Nahu Mujtama Islami.* Jordan: Maktab-al-Aqsa, 1969.

———. *Naqdu Kitabi Mustaqbilu-s-a Saquafh-fil Misr.* Jeddah: Darus-Saudiyah Lin-Nashr-Wattauzi, 1969.

———. *Ma'rakatuna ma'a al-yahuud.* Jeddah: Addar-a-ssaudi-Linnashr-w-attauzee, 1970.

Qutb, Sayyed. *Al-Jihad Fi-Sabililllah*. Riyadh: Al-Ittihadul-Islami Lil-Munazzamt-attulabiyah, 1970.

——. *Fiqh-al-Dawah*. Edited and Translated by Ahmad Hassan in the light of Exegesis of Quran. Beirut: Ashshirkatu-al-Muttahidah Littauzee, 1970.

——. *Al-mustaqbal lihaadaa al-diin*. Beirut: Dar Al Shorouk, 1978.

——. *Ma'aalim fii al-tariiq*. Beirut: Dar Al Shorouk, n.d.

——. *Tafsiri-Suratu-sh-Shura*. Beirut: Darul Arabiya Littabaah Wan-Nashr Wattauzi, n.d.

Sayyed, Abdul Kari Qasim. *Al-Ikhwanul-Muslimun wal-Harkatul Islmaiyyah fil Yaman*. Cairo: Maktaba Madbuli, 1995.

Schalabi, Ahmad. *Attarikh-al-Islami wal Hazarah-aliSlamiyyah*, Part 2. Cairo: Maktaba Annahzah al Misriyyah, 1969.

——. *Attarikh-al-Islami wal Hazarah-aliSlamiyyah*, Part 4. Cairo: Maktaba Annahzah al Misriyyah, 1969.

——. *Attarikh-al-Islami wal Hazarah-aliSlamiyyah*, Part 1. Cairo: Maktaba Annahzah al Misriyyah, 1970.

——. *Attarikh-al-Islami wal Hazarah-aliSlamiyyah*, Part 5. Cairo: Maktaba Annahzah al Misriyyah, 1972.

Shauqi, Al-Azam Mohammad. *Tahrik-i-Ikhwanul-Mulsimin: Mazi aur Haal*. Translated by Rizwan Ali Nadvi. Karachi: Majilisi-Nashriyatu-Islam, 1999.

Sultan, Bayumi. *Al-Ikhwanul-Muslimun wal-Jamat-al-Islamiyah fil-Hayat al-siysah-al-Misriyah 1928–48* (Cairo: Maktaba Zahbah, 1978).

Tarifee, M. Amin. *Tashkil-al-Waaa-al-Arab-al-Jadeed: Lima La Baada-al-Rabi-al-Arabi*. Tunisi: Matbaatul-Wafa, 2013.

Taymiyyah, Ibn. *Al-Hisbah Fil-Islam*. Cairo: Al-Matbaatus-Salfiyyah, 1378.

——. *Al-Khilafah wal-Mulk*. Jordan: Maktab-al-Manar, 1988.

Yunis, Bin Kamala. *Al-Islamiyun-wal-Almaniyun Fi Tunis: Minas-Sojoon-wal- Iztihaad Ilaa Tahaddi Hukmul Bilad*. Tunis: Barq, 2012.

Zaki, Mohammad Shauqi. *Al-Ikhwanul-al-Muslimun wal-Mujtma-almIsari* (Cairo: Maktaba Zahbah, 1992).

Zauq, Jabir. *Mazabihul Ikhwan fi-Sujuni-Misr*. Cairo: Darul Itisam, 1978.

Urdu Sources

Falahi, Ubaidullah Fahad, and Umri M. Salahuddeen. *Sayyed Qutb Shaheed: Hayat wa Khidmat*. Lahore: Manshurat, Ahad Press, 1999.

Maher, Maulana Ghulam Rasul. *Mukhtasar Tarikh-e-Islam*. Karachi: Sheikh Ghulam Ali & Sons, Pvt. Ltd, 1985.

Mohammad, Hamidullah. *Khutbat-i-Bahalwalpur*. New Delhi: Islamic Book Foundation, 2000.

Shah, Akbar Najibabadi. *Tarikh-i-Zawal-e-Ummat*. Delhi: Islamic Book Centre, 2000.

Shhaaz, Rashid. *Idraak-e-Zawaale Ummat*. New Delhi: Milli Publication, 2005.

Zahid, Chaudhri. *Musalmanon Ki Siyasi Tarikh* (Part 2). Edited and compiled by Hassan Jaffar Zaidi. Lahore: Idareh Mutaal-e- Tarikh, 2003.

Zaki, Mohammad Shauqi. *Tahrik-i-Ikhwanul-Mulsimin: Mazi aur Haal*. Translated by Rizwan Ali Nadvi. Karachi: Majlisi-Nashriyatu-al-Islam, 1999.

English Sources

Abrahamian, Ervand. *Khomeinism*. London: University of California Press, 1993.

Abu Rabi, Ibrahim M. *Contemporary Arab Thoughts*. London: Pluto Press, 2004.

——. *Intellectual Origin of Islamic Resurgence in the Arab World*. Albany: State University of New York Press, 1996.

Ahmad, Talmiz. *The Islamic Challenges in West Asia: Doctrinal and Political Competitions after the Arab Spring* (New Delhi: IDSA, 2013).

Ahmed, M. Basheer, Syed A. Ahsani Syed, and Dilnawaz A. Siddiqui, eds. *Muslim Contribution to World Civilization*. Washington, DC: International Institute of Islamic Thoughts, 2005.

Ajami, Fouad. *The Syrian Rebellion*. Washington, DC: Hoover Institution Press, Stanford University, 2012.

Al-Alwani, Taha Jabir. *Issues in Contemporary Islamic Thought*. Washington, DC: International Institute of Islamic Thoughts, 2005.

Al-Azme, Aziz. *Islams and Modernities*. London: Verso, 1993.

Al-Barghouti, Tamin. *The Umma and the Dawala: The Nation State and the Arab Middle East*. London: Pluto Press, 2004.

Al-Faruqi, Ismail Raji. *Al Tawahid: Its Implication for Life and Thoughts*. Washington, DC: International Institute of Islamic Thoughts, 2000.

Al-Raysuni, Ahmad. *Imam al-Shatibi's Theory of Higher Objectives and Intents of Islamic Laws*. Washington, DC: International Institute of Islamic Thoughts, 2005.

Al-Werfalli, Mabroka. *Political Alienation in Libya: Assessing Citizens Political Attitude and Behavior*. London: ITHCA Press, 2011.

Ali, Ameer. *The Spirit of Islam*. Delhi: Low Price Publication, 2002.

Ansari, Muhammad Abdul-Haq, ed. and trans. *Ibn Taymiyah Expounds on Islam: Selected Writing of Shaykh al-Islam Taqi ad-Din Ibn Taymiyyah on Islamic Faith, Life and Society*. Kingdom of Saudi Arabia: Imam Muhammad Ibn Saud University, 2000.

Armstrong, Karen. *A History of God*. London: Vintage Press, 1993.

——. *Muhammad: The Prophet for Our Time*. London: Harper Press, 2006.

Arnold, Thomas W. *The Caliphate*. Delhi: Adam Publisher and Distributors, 1994.

Askari, Hasan. *Society and State in Islam: An Introduction*. New Delhi: Islam and Modern Age Society, 1978.

Ayubi, Nazih N. *Political Islam: Religion and Politics in the Arab World*. Routledge: London, 1991.

Beaulieu, Peter D. *Beyond Secularism and Jihad: A Triangular Inquiry into Mosque, the Manager and Modernity*. Maryland: University Press of America, 2012.

Benjamin, Barber. *Jihad vs. McWorld*. (New York: Ballantine Books, 1996.

Bishara, Marwan. *The Invisible Arab: The Promise and the Peril of Arab Revolution*. New York: Nation Book, 2012.

Black, Antony. *The History of Islamic Political Thoughts: From the Prophet to the Present*. Karachi: OUP, 2004.

Bluntschli, Johann K. *The Theory of State*. New York: Book for Libraries Press, 1961.

Brown, L. Carl. *Religion and State: Muslim Approach to Politics*. New York: Columbia University Press, 2000.

Bullock, Katherine. *Rethinking Muslim Women and the Veil*. Washington, DC: International Institute of Islamic Thoughts, 2003.

Burgat, Francois. *Islamism in the Shadow of Al-Qaeda*. Translated by Patrick Hutchinson. (Austin: University of Texas Press, 2008.

Butterworth, Charles E., and I. William Zartman. *Between the State and Islam*. Cambridge: Cambridge University Press, 2001.

Carl, W. Ernst. *Following Mohammad: Rethinking Islam in Contemporary World*. New Delhi: Yoda Press, 2005.

Cook, Michael. *Commanding Right and Forbidding Wrongs in Islamic Thought*. London: Cambridge University Press, 2000.

Crone, Patricia. *Medieval Islamic Political Thought*. Edinburgh: Edinburgh University Press, 2004.

Dahiya, Rumel. *Developments in the Gulf Region: Prospects and Challenges for India in the Next Two Decades*. New Delhi: IDSA, 2014.

Davidson, Lawrence. *Islamic Fundamentalism*. London: Greenwood Press, 1998.

Durkheim, E. *On Morality and Society (Heritage of Sociology Series)*. Chicago: University of Chicago Press, 1973.

Eisnensadt, S.N. *Fundamentalism, Sectarianism, Revolution: The Jacobean Dimension of Modernity*. Cambridge: Cambridge University Press, 1999.

Esposito, John L. *Islam: The Straight Path*. New York: OUP, 1998.

Fahmy, Ninette S. *The Politics of Egypt: State–Society Relationship*. London: Routledge, 2002.

Fatah, Tarek. *Chasing a Mirage: The Tragic Illusion of an Islamic State*. Ontario: John Wiley and Sons Canada Ltd, 2008.

Fisher, Sidney Nettleton. *The Middle East: A History*. London: Routledge and Kegan Paul, 1969.

Friedman, Thomas L. *The Lexus and the Olive Tree: Understanding Globalization*. London: Picador Press, 2012.

Fuller, Graham E. *The Future of Political Islam*. New York: Palgrave Macmillan, 2003.

Geertz, C. *Islam Observed: Religious Developments in Morocco and Indonesia*. Chicago: A Phoenix Book University of Chicago, 1971.

Haddad, Y., John Voll, and John Esposito. *The Contemporary Islamic Revival*. Connecticut: Greenwood Press, 1991.

Halliday, Fred. *Islam and Myth of Confrontation*. London: I.B. Tauris, 1999.

Hamid, Eltigani Abdelgadir. *The Quran and Politics*. Washington, DC: International Institute of Islamic Thoughts, 2004.

Hamid, Enayat. *Modern Islamic Political Thought*. London: I.B. Tauris, 2005.

Hitti, Philip K. *Makers of Arab History*. New York: Harper and Row, 1971.

———. *The Arab: A Short History*. Washington, DC: Regency Publishing, 1996.

Hodgson, M. *The Venture of Islam*. 3 vols. Chicago: University of Chicago Press, 1971.

Humphreys, R. Stephen. *Islamic History: A Framework for Inquiry*. Karachi: OUP, 1991.

Ikram, M. Chaghatai, ed., annotator and trans. *Jamal Al-Din Al-Afghani: An Apostle of Islamic Resurgence*. Lahore: Sang-e-Meel Publication, 2005.

Iqbal, Mohammad. *The Reconstruction of Religious Thoughts in Islam*. New Delhi: Kitab Mahal, 1990.

———. *New Dimension*. Edited, annotated and translated by M. Chaghatai Ikram. Lahore: Sang-e-Meel Publication, 2003.

Iqtidar, Humeira. *Secularizing Islamist: Jamat-e-Islami and Jamaat-ud-dawa in Urban Pakistan*. London: University of Chicago Press, 2011.

Ismail, Salwa. *Rethinking Islamic Politics: Culture, the State and Islam*. London: I.B. Tauris, 2003.

Khalil, Mohammad Hassan. *Islam and Fate of Others: The Salvation Question*. New York: Oxford University Press, 2012.

Khan, Qamruddin. *The Political Thought of Ibn Taymiyah*. Islamabad: Islamic Research Institute, 1983.

Khosrokhavar, Farhad. *The Arab Revolution That Shook the World*. London: Paradigm Publisher, 2012.

Keddie, Nikki. *An Islamic Response to Imperialism: Political and Religious Writings of Sayyid Jamal ad-Din al-Afghani*. Berkeley: California Press, 1964.

———. *Sayyid Jamal ad-Din al-Afghani: A Political Biography*. Berkeley: California Press, 1972.

Kumaraswamy, P.R. *Reading Silence: India and the Arab Spring*. The Hebrew University of Jerusalem: The Leonardo Davis Institute for International Relations, 2012. http://www.dmag.co.il/pub/huji/ReadingtheSilence/view_book.html (Accessed on 21 September 2016).

———. *Persian Gulf 2013: India 'Relations with the Region'*. New Delhi: SAGE Publications, 2014.

Lewis, Bernard. *The Political Language of Islam*. London: Oxford University Press, 2002.

———. *The Crisis of Islam*. New York: Modern Library, 2003.

Linjakumpu, Aini, ed. *Globalization and State in the Middle East*. Akerlundinkatu: Temper Peace Research Institute, 2003.

Lynch, Marc. *The Arab Uprising: The Unfinished Revolutions of the New Middle East*. New York: Public Affairs, 2012.

Mahfouz, Naguib. *Midaq Alley*. Cairo: The American University in Cairo Press, 1992.

Makari, Victor E. *Ibn Taymiyyah's Ethics: The Social Factors*. California: Scholar Press, 1983.

Mandeville, Peter. *Transnational Muslim Politics*. London: Routledge, 2001.

Martin, R. *Approaches to Islam in Religious Studies*. Tucson: University of Arizona Press, 1985.

Martin, Vanessa. *Creating an Islamic State: Khomeini and the Making of a New Iran*. London: I.B. Tauris, 2000.

Mernissi, Fatima. *Islam and Democracy: Fear of Modern World*. New York: Addison Wesley Publishing Company, 1994.

Miller, Roland E. *Muslim Friends: Their Faith and Feeling*. Hyderabad: Orient Longman, 2000.

Mohammad, Arkoun. *Rethinking Islam: Common Question and Uncommon Answer*. Builder: Westview Press, 1994.

Moosa, Ebrahim. *Ghazali and Poetics of Imagination*. Karachi: OUP, 2005.

Morty, Martin E., and R. Scott Appleby, eds. *Religious Ethnicity and Self-identity: Nations in Turmoil*. London: Salzburg Seminar, 2001.

Moussalli, S. Ahmad. *The Islamic Quest for Democracy, Pluralism and Human Right*. Florida: University Press of Florida, 2003.

Muashir, Marwan. *The Second Arab Awakening and the Battle for Pluralism*. London: Yale University Press, 2014.

Nabavi, Negin, ed. *Iran: From Theocracy to the Green Movement*. New York: Palgrave McMillan, 2012.

Nadvi, Abul Hasan Ali. *Western Civilization—Islam and Muslims*. Translated by Mohammad Asif Kidwai. Lucknow: Academy of Islamic Research and Publication, 1979.

Narton, Anne. *On the Muslim Questions*. New Jersey: Princeton University Press, 2013.

Nasr, Vali Raza. *Mawdudi and Making of Islamic Revival*. London: OUP, 1996.

Piscatori, James, ed. *Islamic Fundamentalists and the Gulf Crisis*. Chicago: The American Academy of Arts and Sciences, 1991.

Qasim, Muhammad Zaman. *Modern Islamic Thoughts in a Radical Age: Religious Authority and the Internal Criticism*. New Delhi: Cambridge University Press, 2012.

Qutb, Sayyed. *Milestone*. New Delhi: Ishaat-e-Islam Trust, 2000.

Rahman, Ali. *Pioneer of Islamic Revival*. London: Zed Book Limited, 1994.

Ramadan, Tariq. *Islam and the Arab Awakening*. New York: OUP, 2012.

Roy, Oliver. *Globalize Islam: The Search for New Ummah*. New Delhi: Rupa, 2005.

Sadiki, Larbi, Heiko Wimmen, and Layla Al-Zubaidi, eds. *Democratic Transition in the Middle East: Unmaking Power*. New York: Routledge, 2013.

Safran, N. *Egypt in Search of Political Community: An Analysis of the Intellectual and Political Evolution of Egypt, 1804–1952*. Boston: Harvard University Press, 1981.

Said, Edward W. *Orientalism*. Delhi: Penguin, 1995.

Saleh, Hashem. *Arab Spring in Light of the History of Philosophy*. Beirut: Dar Al Saqi, 2012.

Salt, Jeremy. *The Unmaking of the Middle East: A History of Western Disorder in Arab Lands*. London: University of California Press, 2008.

Seth, Sanjay, ed. *Postcolonial Theory and International Relations: A Critical Introduction.* New York: Routledge, 2013.

Shushtery, A.M.A. *Outline of Islamic Culture.* Bangalore: Bangalore Printing & Publishing Company, 1954.

Smith, Huston. *The Religion of Man.* New York: Harper and Row, 1958.

Smith, Wilfred Cantwell. *Islam in Modern History.* Princeton, NJ: Princeton University Press, 1957.

———. *Islam in Modern History.* New York: Mentor Book, 1959.

———. *An Understanding Islam: Selected Studies.* New York: Mouton Publishers, 1981.

Sorman, Guy. *The Children of Rifaa: In Search of Moderate Islam.* New Delhi: Penguin, 2004.

Taymiyah, Ibn. *Concept of Worship in Islam.* Translated by Muhammad Abdul-Haq Ansari. Kingdom of Saudi Arabia: Imam Muhammad Ibn Saud University, 2001.

Tibi, Bassam. *Arab Nationalism: A Critical Enquiry.* Translated and edited by Marion Farouk Sluglett and Peter Sluglett. Frankfurt: Macmillan Press, 1990.

———. *Arab Nationalism between Islam and the Nation-State.* London: Macmillan Press Limited, 1997.

———. *The Challenges of Fundamentalism: Political Islam and New World Disorder.* London: University of California Press, 1998 (updated edition 2002).

Tschirgi, Dan, ed. *Egypt's Tahrir Revolution.* London: Lynne Rienner Publisher, 2013.

Umari, Akran Diya. *Medina Society at the Time of Prophet.* Translated by Huda Kattab. Virginia: International Institute of Islamic Thoughts, 1995.

Walker, Benjamin. *Foundation of Islam: The Making of World Faith.* Delhi: Rupa, 2002.

Walt, W. Montgomery. *Muhammad at Medina.* London: Oxford Clarendon Press, 1956.

Yared, S.N. *Secularism and the Arab World.* London: Saqi Books, 2002.

Journal Articles/Arabic

Al-Auzi, Hisham. 'Al-Nizam-al-Misri Wal-Ikhwan: Siraa-al-Shariat-al-Baqa'. *Almustaqbil-al-Arabi*, no. 353 (July 2008): 85–102.

Al-Hammar, Mohammad. 'Alsunniyaat Li-Ihya-al-Kifaah Fi Fahmil-Islam wal-Hiyatt: Kaifa Yartqil al-Muslimun Min-Tauril-JOmood Ilaa Tauril-Harkah'. *Almustaqbil-al-Arabi*, no. 373 (March 2010): 93–107.

Al-Jaludi, Alyaan Abdul Fattah. 'Tatawwar Mafhum-al-Sultah Wa Ilaqatuha Bil-Khilafah'. *Al-Islamiyah-al-Marifah*, no. 51 (2008): 175–208.

Al-Kilani, Abdullah Ibrahim. 'Al-Ruyah-al-Islamiyah Lil Alam Wa Asruha Fi Tahdee-al-Siyash al-Kharijiyah'. *Al-Islamiyah-al-Marifah*, no. 45 (2006): 25–64.

Al-Najjar, Baqar Suleiman. 'Al-Mujtam-al-Watani Fil-Watan-al-Arabi: Waqi Yahtaju Ila-al-Islah'. *Almustaqbil-al-Arabi*, no. 338 (April 2007): 60–71.

Ali, Maryam Ayat Ahmad. 'Al-Wastiyah Wa-al-Salam-al-Fikri'. *Al-Kalimah*, no. 54 (Spring 2008): 87–100.

Attar, Ahmad Abdul Ghafur. 'Sayyed Qutb yakhtalifu maa Abdun Nasir'. *Kalimatul Haqe*, no. 2 (May 1967): 37.

Bamyut, Khalid. 'Al-Muwatanah Fil-Fikr-alSiyasi-al-Islami'. *Al-Kalimah*, no. 54 (Winter 2007): 141–53.

Bilqiz, Abdul Ilah. 'Mnan-Nahza Ilal-Hadash'. *Almustaqbil-al-Arabi*, no. 365 (January 2009): 56–62.

Fathi-Al-Afifi. 'Al-Siyuqaratiyah-al-Almaniyah Fi-al-Dawalah-al-Khalijiyah-al-Muasarah: Dirasat Fi-al-Tarikhiyah-al-Hadasiyah'. *Almustaqbil-al-Arabi*, no. 350 (April 2008): 137–54.

Habib, Kama. 'Al-Islamiyyun wal-Anf Baad 30 Unuu'. *Al-Demoqeratiya*, no. 52 (October 2013): 116–119.

Hassan, Ammar Ali. 'Al-Khusisiyah al-Saqafiyah Fil-Khitab al-Fikri-al-Islami-alMuaasir'. *Almustaqbil-al-Arabi*, no. 340 (January 2007): 24–42.

Ishaaq, Saali Khalifah. 'Tatawarul-al-Ilaqah Baina-al-Din Was-Siyasah Fi Uroba: Al-Ahzab al-Demoqaratiyahal-Masihiyyah: Italiya Wa-al-Maniya Namuzajan'. *Almustaqbil-al-Arabi*, no. 373 (October 2009): 26–50.

Izzat, Hiba Raduf. 'Ma-Baad-al-Islamiyah: Nazratun-Naqdiyah'. *Al-Demoqeratiya*, no. 52 (October 2013).

Labeez, Salim. 'Alhawiyah: Alislam, Al-Uroobah, Al-Tunusah'. *Almustaqbil-al-Arabi*, no. 361 (March 2009): 67–75.

Muazzam, Yusuf. 'Raidul-Fikr-al-Islami'. *Aman*, no. 9 (1979): 26.

Mukhlis-al-Siyaadi. 'Al-Harkah-al-Islamiyah-al-Muasarah: Raddi Fel Am-Istijabe Li-Tahddu'. *Almustaqbil-al-Arabi*, no. 369 (November 2009): 7–27.

Musaddiq-al-Jaleedi. 'Baina-alManiyah-al-Muminah Wal-Imaan-al-Almani: MUnaqishah Liutruha-alDin Fi-aldimoqaratiyah'. *Almustaqbil-al-Arabi*, no. 366 (August 2009): 33–46.

Qutb, Sayyed. 'Al-Miratu Laghzun Basitun'. *Usbu*, no. 45 (October 1934): 7.

——. 'Nafsat...Ammahu'. *Ar-Risalah*, no. 381 (1940): 1602.

——. 'Addalu Baramijikum-Au-Insahabu-qabla Fawati-l-Awan'. *Ar-Risalah* 2, No. 627 (1945): 1309.

——. 'Hazihi Hiya Faransa'. *Ar-Risalah*, no. 624 (1945): 632.

——. 'Ilal-Iskandriyyah'. *Ar-Risalah*, no. 681 (1946): 796.

——. 'Lughatul Abid'. *Ar-Risalah*, no. 709 (1948): 134.

——. 'Al-Kutlatul-Islamiyyah fil-mIzanuddawali'. *Ar-Risalah* 2, no. 949 (September 1949): 1022.

——. 'Hamaim fi New York'. *Al-Kitab* 2, Part 10 (December 1949): 666.

——. 'America allati raitu fi mizanil qayyam al-insaniyyah'. *Ar-Risalah*, no. 957 (1951): 1245–47; no. 959: 1301–06.

——. 'Turkiya as-Saghirah'. *Ar-Risalah* 2, no. 955 (October 1951): 1189–91.

——. 'Hazihil ahzab Ghair Qabilatun -lil-Baqa'. *Rauz Yusuf*, no. 1268 (September 1952): 10.

Qutb, Sayyed. 'Nahnu al-Shab Nuridu'. *Al-Risalah* 2, no. 1005 (October 1952): 1105.

———. 'Qaziyatun Wahidatun Wa Ummatun Wahidatun'. *Al-Ikhwanul Muslimun*, no. 8 (1954): 3.

Sati, Abdul Ilaah. 'Almilkiyah al-Muarazah-al-Islamiyah: Aaliyat-al-Idmaaj Wal-Iqsa Fil-NIzam-al-Siyasi-al-Maghribi'. *Almustaqbil-al-Arabi*, no. 370 (December 2012): 99–119.

Journal Articles/English

Abu Rabi, Ibrahim. 'Sayyed Qutb: From Religious Realism to Radical Social Criticisms'. *Islamic Quarterly* 28, no. 1 (1984): 104–26.

Abu Rabi, Ibrahim. 'Discourse, Power and Ideology in Modern Islamic Revivalist Thoughts: The Case of Sayyed Qutb'. *Islamic Culture* 65, nos. 2–3 (April–July 1991): 84–102.

Adelowo, E. Dada. 'The Concept of Tauhid in Islam: Theological Review'. *Islamic Quarterly* 35, no. 1 (1991): 23–35.

Al-Rahim, Ahmad H. 'Whither Political Islam and the Arab Spring'. *Hedgehog Review* 3, no. 3 (Fall 2011). http://iasc-culture.org/THR/THR_article_2011_Fall_al-Rahim.php (Accessed on 21 September 2016).

Alinejad, Mohmoud. 'Coming to Terms with Modernity: Iranian Intellectual and the Emerging Public Sphere'. *Islam and Christian Muslim Relation* 13, no. 1 (January 2002): 25–48.

Andrew, Flibbert. 'The Consequences of Forced Sate Failure in Iraq'. *Political Studies Quarterly* 128, no. 1 (2013): 69–95.

Aslam, Adnan. 'The Concept of Ahl-Dhimmi and Religious Pluralism'. *Islamic Culture* 47, no. 1 (2003).

Baker, Raymond W. 'The Paradox of Islamic Future'. *Political Science Quarterly* 27, no. 4 (Winter 2012): 518–66.

Berggren, D. Jason. 'More than the Ummah: Religious and National Identity in the Muslim World'. *American Journal of Islamic Socials Science* 24, no. 2 (Spring 2007): 71–93.

Beri, Benedetta, and Yoel Guzansky. 'Is the New Middle East Stuck in Its Sectarian Past? The Unspoken Dimension of Arab Spring'. *Orbis* 57, no. 1 (Winter 2013): 135–51.

Brohi, A.K. 'Idea of Islamic Order'. *Islamic Quarterly* 27, no. 1 (1983): 1–11.

Cleary, Matthew, and Rebecca Glazier. 'Contemporary Islamism: Trajectory of a Master Frame'. *American Journal of Islamic Socials Science* 24, no. 2 (2007): 1–21.

Dajani, Munther S. 'Analyzing the Obvious: Is It the Culture of Civil Unrest or the Culture of Uncivil Rest That Needs to be Revisited in the Arab World'. *Palestine–Israel Journal* 18, no. 1 (2012): 5–9.

El-Sherif, Ashraf Nabih. 'Institutional and Ideological Reconstruction of Justice and Development Party (PJD): The Question of Democratic Islamism in Morocco'. *Middle East Journal* 66, no. 4 (August 2012): 660–82.

Elharathi, Milad. 'Understanding Political Culture in the Arab Mediterranean Revolts: Challenges and Prospects for the European Union'. *World Affairs* 6, no. 4 (December 2012): 124–47.

Emily, Regan Wills. 'Democratic Paradoxes: Women's Rights and Democratization in Kuwait'. *Middle East Journal* 6, no. 2 (2013): 173–84.

Esposito, John L. 'Moderate Muslims: A Mainstream Modernist, Islamist, Conservative and Traditionalist'. *American Journal of Social Science* 24, no. 2 (Spring 2007): 11–20.

Fahad, Obaidullah. 'Some Notes on Western Democracy and Islamic Shura: Introductory Outline'. *Islamic Quarterly* 45, no. 1 (2001): 19–37.

Faks, Mahmud A. 'The Islamic State System: A Paradigm for Democracy'. *Islamic Quarterly* 28, no. 1 (1984): 5–23.

Farooqi, Jamil. 'Bases of Social Life in Islam'. *The Islamic Quarterly* (Hyderabad) 46, no. 3 (2002): 259–75.

Gibb, H.A.R. 'Al-Mawardi Theory of the Khilafah'. *Islamic Culture* 11 (1987): 291–302.

Goddard, Hugh. 'Islam and Democracy'. *The Political Quarterly* 73, no. 1 (January–March 2002): 3–9.

Hamid, Mavani. 'Khomeini's Concept of Governance of the Jurisconmsult (*Wilayat al-Faqih*) Revisited: The Aftermath of Iran's 2009 Presidential Election'. *Middle East Journal* 6, no. 2 (2013): 208–28.

Jan, Abid Ullah. 'Moderate Islam: A Product of American Extremism'. *American Journal of Social Science* 24, no. 2 (Spring 2007): 29–38.

Jeremy, Black. 'Western Encounter with the Islam'. *The China Journal* (Winter 2004): 19–28. http://deathandreligion.plamienok.sk/files/37-The%20 Western%20Encounter%20with%20Islam.pdf

Khan, M.A. Muqtedar. 'Islamic Democracy and Modern Muslims: The Straight Path Runs through Middle'. *American Journal of Social Science* 22, no. 3 (Summer 2005): 39–50.

Khan, Sadruddin Agha. 'Islam and the West'. *Islamic Quarterly* 29, no. 2 (1985): 65–74.

Khatab, Sayyed. 'Citizenship Right of Non-Muslims in the Islamic State of Hakimiyya Espoused by Sayyed Qutb'. *Islam and Christian Muslim Relation* 13, no. 2 (April 2002): 163–87.

Klein, Menachem. 'Is the Arab Spring Israel's Winter?' *Palestine–Israel Journal* 18, no. 1 (2012): 27–33.

Lebel, Leslie S. 'The EU, the Muslim Brotherhood and the Organization of Islamic Conference'. *Orbis* 57, no. 1 (Winter 2013): 101–18.

Mahmud, A. Faksh. 'The Islamic State System: Paradigm for Change'. *Islamic Quarterly* 18, no. 1: 5–24.

Matthiesen, Toby. 'A "Saudi Spring?"': The Shia Protest Movement in the Eastern Province 2011–2012'. *Middle East Journal* 66, no. 4 (August 2012): 628–59.

Mohammad, Aishah. 'A Critique of Jamal-Al-Din-Al- Afghani's Reformist Ideas and Its Importance in the Development of Islamic Thoughts in 20th Century'. *Islamic Quarterly* 45, no. 1 (2001): 49–66.

Motin, A. Rashid. 'Pure and Practical Ideology: The Thoughts of Mawlana Mawdudi'. *Islamic Quarterly* 28, no. 1 (1984): 217–40.

Mumtaz Ali, Muhammad. 'Liberal Islam: An Analysis'. *American Journal of Islamic Socials Science* 24, no. 2 (2007): 44–70.

Muqtedar Khan, M.A. 'Radical Islam, Liberal Islam'. *Current History* 102, no. 668 (December 2003): 417–22.

Olayivola, Abdur Rahman O. 'Democracy in Islam'. *Islamic Culture* 65, nos. 2–3 (April–July 1991): 63–83.

Ouis, Pernila. 'Islamization as a Strategy for Reconciliations between Modernity and Traditions: Examples from Contemporary Gulf States'. *Islam and Christian Muslim Relation* 3, no. 3 (July 2002): 315–32.

Podeh, Elie. 'Farewell to an Age of Tyranny? Egypt as a Model of Arab Revolution'. *Palestine–Israel Journal* 18, no. 1 (2012): 10–18.

Rahman, Fazlur. 'Some Aspects of Iqbal's Political Thought'. *Studies in Islam* (New Delhi) 5, nos. 2–3 (April–July 1968): 161–66.

Robinson, Francis. 'Islamic Reform and Maternities in South Asia'. *Modern Asian Studies* 43, no. 2 (2008): 259–81.

Samuel Tadros. 'Egypt's Election: Why the Islamist Won'. *World Affairs* (March–April 2012). http://www.worldaffairsjournal.org/article/ egypt%E2%80%99s-elections-why-islamists-won (Accessed on 12 March 2013).

Sefaettin, Seevercan. 'Prophethood and Politics'. *Islamic Quarterly* 41, no. 1: 39–47.

———. 'Prophethood and Politics'. *Islamic Quarterly* 45, no. 1 (2001): 40–47.

Seferta, Yusuf H.R. 'The Concept of Religious Authority According to Mohammad Abduh and Rashid Rida'. *Islamic Quarterly* 26, no. 1: 159–64.

Sikand, Yogindr S. 'Islamic Mission and Inter-religious Dialogue in Minority Context: The Jama'at-i-Islami of India'. *Islam and Christian Muslim Relation* 13, no. 1 (January 2002): 49–64.

Sivan, E. 'Sunni Radicalism in the Middle East and the Iranian Revolution'. *International Journal of Middle Eastern Studies* 21, no. 1 (February 1989): 1–30.

Stev, Hess. 'From the Arab Spring to the Chinese Winter: The Institutional Sources of Authoritarian Vulnerability and Resilience in Egypt, Tunisia and China'. *International Political Science Reviews* 34, no. 3 (2013): 255–71.

Takim, Liyakat. 'Revivalism or Reformation: The Reinterpretation of Islamic Law in Modern Time'. *American Journal of Social Science* 25, no. 3 (Summer 2008): 61–81.

Umar, Muhammad Sadi. 'The Role of European Imperialism in Muslim Countries'. *Islamic Quarterly* 32, no. 2 (1988): 77–99.

Watson, I. Bruce. 'Islam and Modern World Order'. *Islamic Quarterly* 46, no. 1.

Monthly Magazine

Ahmad, Aijaz. 'Autumn of Patriarchy'. *Frontline*, September 2011, 48.
Cafiero, Giorgio. 'Saudi Arabia, Qatar and the Arab Spring'. *Ahram Weekly*, 18–24 October 2012.
Ezzat, Dina. 'Egypt: The President, the Army and the Police'. *Ahram Weekly*, 27 December 2012.
———. 'Trial of Strength'. *Ahram Weekly*, 25 November 2013.
Ibrahim, Ezzat. 'Against Morsi, all United'. *Ahram Weekly*, 10 October 2013.
Maged, Amany. 'Existential Choice'. *Ahram Weekly*, 10 October 2013.

Newspapers

'Egypt: Revolution Revisited'. *Aljazeera*, 16 September 2013.
Jha, Prem Shankar. 'India Must Think before It Acts on Syria'. *The Hindu*, 7 August 2012.

Theses and Research Papers

Dada, Abdessamad Ait. 'Political Islam and Moroccan Arab Spring'. Research paper, Netherlands Institute Morocco, 2012.
Heydemann, Steven. 'Syria's Uprising: Sectarianism, Regionalization and State of Order in Levant'. Working paper, HIVOS and FRIDE, 2013.
Najeeb A. Jan. 'The Met Colonial State: The Pakistan, The Deoband 'Ulema and the Biopolitics of Islam'. PhD dissertation, Michigan University, 2010.

Lecture Papers

Chomsky, Noam. 'Prospects for Peace in the Middle East'. Lecture delivered at the first Annual Marys Mikhael Lecture. Ohio: The University of Toledo, 4 March 2001.
Niblock, Tim. 'Shift to the East/Gulf Response to a Transformed Global Order and a Divisive Regional Environment'. Keynote address delivered in a conference on Arab Spring. New Delhi: JMI, 20 January 2013.

Index

About the Author

Fazzur Rahman Siddiqui is a research fellow at the Indian Council of World Affairs (ICWA), New Delhi. He received his PhD from the School of International Studies, Jawaharlal Nehru University, New Delhi, where his dissertation was focused on Islamic Political Movements in West Asia and South Asia. His research expertise includes Islamic undercurrents in West Asian Politics and dynamics of development and modernization in the Arab World. His knowledge of the West Asian region is grounded in linguistic and Islamic perspectives, with particular attention to the historical evolution of the region. He is proficient in Arabic, Urdu and Persian in addition to being fluent in English and Hindi. He is the author of *The Concept of Islamic State: From the Time of Caliphate to Twentieth Century: Pre-Ikhwan and Post Ikhwan Phase*, published in Lebanon. He has presented papers in national and international conferences in India and abroad and contributed chapters in edited books. Before joining the ICWA, he was associated with the Ford Foundation.